In *Leviathan* Hobbes mounted a famous, or notorious, argument for the creation and maintenance of an absolute sovereign as the means to secure peace. He postulated a "state of nature" in which people would find themselves unable to cooperate or keep contracts without government, but argued that these people would be able to keep a social contract among themselves creating a ruler, and that it was in their self-interest to create only a ruler with absolute power.

Both problematic and influential, this justification for the state is the subject of the present book. Professor Hampton presents a new and comprehensive analysis of Hobbes's argument that draws on recent developments in game and decision theory to establish whether the argument does, or can be made to, succeed. She generalizes her findings to exhibit the structure of any social contract argument, showing its strategy for justifying the state and for explaining the state's structure. Lucidly written throughout, this book will interest students of Hobbes's theory, and of the social contract tradition in political thought.

HOBBES AND THE SOCIAL CONTRACT TRADITION

Hobbes
and the
Social Contract Tradition

JEAN HAMPTON

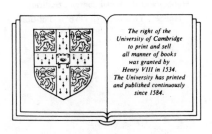

The right of the
University of Cambridge
to print and sell
all manner of books
was granted by
Henry VIII in 1534.
The University has printed
and published continuously
since 1584.

Cambridge University Press

CAMBRIDGE

LONDON   NEW YORK   NEW ROCHELLE
MELBOURNE   SYDNEY

Published by the Press Syndicate of the University of Cambridge
The Pitt Building, Trumpington Street, Cambridge CB2 1RP
32 East 57th Street, New York, NY 10022, USA
10 Stamford Road, Oakleigh, Melbourne 3166, Australia

First published 1986

Printed in the United States of America

Library of Congress Cataloging in Publication Data

Hampton, Jean.
Hobbes and the social contract tradition.
Bibliography: p.
Includes index.
1. Hobbes, Thomas, 1588–1679 — Contributions in
political philosophy 2. Social contract. 3. Political
science — History. 4. Political science — Philosophy.
I. Title.
JC153.H66H36 1986 320.1′092′4 86–2622

British Library Cataloguing in Publication Data

Hampton, Jean
Hobbes and the social contract tradition.
1. Hobbes, Thomas, 1588–1679–Political
science 2. Political science
I. Title
320′.01 JC153.H6

ISBN 0 521 26184 8

TO RICHARD

Contents

CONTENTS

Acknowledgments

This book has been long in the writing, and I have many people to thank for their help along the way.

I am indebted to those people who aided me when I began the project of understanding Hobbes's argument in my doctoral dissertation; in particular, to John Rawls, whose own modern contractarian theory initially sparked my interest in traditional social contract arguments, and to Israel Scheffler, Quentin Skinner, and Richard Tuck.

There have been numerous philosophical conversations with colleagues since then that have helped me to develop my interpretation further. For their help in such conversations I want to thank David Gauthier, Thomas Hill, Gregory Kavka, Warren Quinn, Christopher Morris, Don Hubin, Robert Gerstein, and Stephen Munzer. I am also grateful to the students in my Hobbes seminar at the University of Pittsburgh in the winter of 1984 and to the students in my seminars on contractarian thinking at UCLA in 1982 and 1984. This book has become clearer as a result of their lively questions and challenges.

Any work in philosophy, particularly one in the history of philosophy, builds on the work of others. I am happy to acknowledge two important debts: first, to David Gauthier's *The Logic of Leviathan,* and second, to J. W. N. Watkins's *Hobbes's System of Ideas.* I have disagreed with both, yet learned much from both.

Cambridge University's Rare Book Room and UCLA's William Clark Library provided valuable resources for historical research into the seventeenth century. And I wish to thank UCLA for providing grant support that enabled me to spend time away from teaching and to obtain research assistance. An earlier version of Chapter 2 was read at the Hobbes Tercentenary Congress at Boulder, Colorado, in August 1979, and portions of Chapters 2 and 3 were read at the Conference on the History of Ethics at the University of California, Irvine, in January 1984 (later published as "Hobbes's State of War" in *Topoi,* Winter 1985). The comments I received from the participants in both conferences were very helpful. I also want to thank the Philosophy Department at the University of Pittsburgh, whose invitation to me to visit during the winter of 1984 gave me a stimulating environment in which to work.

I have been very fortunate to have had excellent help in preparing the manuscript for publication: Thanks go to Linda Bidasio and Diane Wells for their word-processing skills and to Betty Wilson and Kristin Carnohan for all sorts of clerical help. Thanks also go to my research assistants Steven Reynolds and Julie Heath Elliott for patient and careful work.

Finally, I must acknowledge a deep indebtedness to two members of my family:

Acknowledgments

first, to my husband, Richard Healey, who has been not only a faithful and invaluable philosophical interlocutor during the writing of this book but also my best friend; second, to Andrew Hampton-Healey, who provided the final impetus I needed to finish it.

Jean Hampton
University of California, Los Angeles

A Note on Texts and References

I have used the author/date system of referencing for all works except those of Hobbes. In order to make the references to Hobbes's work complete, readily understandable, and inconspicuous, I have adopted the following conventions when citing Hobbes:

1. *Leviathan:* Because there is no standard edition of this work, I have referred to the pagination in the original 1651 edition, also given in the Macpherson and Oxford (1952) editions of the book. However, in order to help readers who use other editions to find the passages cited, I have also included the chapter number and the number of the paragraph in the chapter in which the passage occurs. As long as the reader is using an edition of *Leviathan* that has not altered the original paragraph construction of the 1651 edition, this system should make possible easy location of all references. Hence, citations to *Leviathan* will take the following form: *(Lev,* chapter number, number of paragraph in chapter, page number of 1651 edition). All quotations from *Leviathan* use the 1651 text in Macpherson's edition.

2. *De Cive (Philosophical Rudiments Concerning Government and Society):* Here I have used the edition in Volume ii of *The English Works of Thomas Hobbes,* edited by W. Molesworth. Citations are as follows: *(DC, EW* ii, chapter number, section number, page number).

3. *Elements of Law:* Frederick Tönnies's edition has been used (Cambridge University Press, 1928), and references take the following form: *(EL,* part number, chapter number, section number, page number).

4. *De Homine:* I have used Bernard Gert's translation in his *Man and Citizen* (Atlantic Highlands, N.J.: Humanities Press, 1968), and references are as follows: *(DH,* chapter number, section number, page number).

5. *De Corpore:* I have used the edition in Volume i of the *English Works;* references take the following form: *(De Corp, EW* i, part number, chapter number, section number, page number).

6. References to all other works by Hobbes cited in the text will be to the editions of those works in Molesworth's *The English Works of Thomas Hobbes* and will take the following form: (name of work, *EW,* volume number, page number).

7. References to passages found in epistle dedicatories or prefaces will contain the abbreviation "ep. ded." or "pref."

References to Locke's *Two Treatises of Government* will always be to Peter Laslett's edition (Cambridge University Press, 1963, and Mentor, 1965). When referring to

A NOTE ON TEXTS AND REFERENCES

Book II of this work, I shall be using its common title *The Second Treatise*. Citations from Book II will be as follows: *(2T,* section number, page number in Laslett edition).

All quotations from the works of Hobbes, Locke, and other seventeenth- and eighteenth-century political theorists will preserve the original spelling, punctuation, and sentence structure.

Introduction

It is not to revive the corpse of past erudition that I have any desire, but rather to make more vivid the life of today, and to help us envisage its problems with a more accurate perspective. Otherwise my task would be as ungrateful as it is difficult . . . We [must] see our own day as from a watch tower. We are trying to know more closely the road we have been travelling.

J. N. Figgis, *Studies of Political Thought From Gerson to Grotius 1414–1625*

It would be difficult to find a time in history more tumultuous than the period of the English Revolution and Puritan protectorate from approximately 1640 to 1660. In the midst of the tumult, many people offered prescriptions for curing the nation's disorders and achieving its long-lasting health. Hobbes's argument for the institution of an absolute sovereign in his masterpiece *Leviathan* is the most famous and celebrated of those prescriptions, and in this book I will be undertaking an extensive examination of Hobbes's political theory based primarily on his statement of it in *Leviathan* and supported by many of his political and philosophical writings.

However, my concerns go beyond mere analysis of the Hobbesian political position. In recent years, philosophers and historians have displayed considerable interest in social contract theories. But there has been confusion and controversy over the structure and justificational force of social contract arguments, as well as a good deal of perplexity over the nature of the argument used by Hobbes to establish the institution of the sovereign. In this book I want to tackle both problems at once, hoping to shed light on the general structure of all social contract arguments by analyzing and explaining Hobbes's contractarian argument.

Hobbes's argument is well suited for this philosophical purpose, not only because it is probably the finest of the traditional social contract arguments but also because Hobbes worked hard to make its architecture clear in order to persuade his readers of his political conclusions. In all of his political writings he maintains that it was *bad reasoning* that had plunged England and other European political societies into chaos during the seventeenth century, so that the only effective cure for this disorder was to give members of these societies a sound, rational argument for the correct political structure of a state as rigorous as any of Euclid's geometric proofs: "Geometry therefore is demonstrable, for the lines and figures from which we reason are drawn and described by ourselves; and civil philosophy is demonstrable, because we make the commonwealth ourselves." ("Six Lessons to the Professors of the Mathematics," *EW* vii, ep. ded., 184; see also *DC, EW* ii, pref., xiii–xiv) Hence I will be taking Hobbes's geometric analogy seriously, isolating the major premises and examining the inferences of his argument. And if I find that a step is inadequately justified by Hobbes, I will try to justify it by other means. I hope to accomplish more than a description or explication of Hobbes's political philosophy; I am attempting a rethinking of his position. Rather than being merely a commentator or critic, I will attempt to be Hobbes's interlocutor. Only if one tries, in this way, to get the best possible statement of Hobbes's argument for absolute sovereignty will one be able to understand where and why that argument fails, and an understanding of that failure will help us to understand what structure a social contract argument must have if it is to succeed.

My commitment to presenting *Leviathan* as a book that attempts to put forward a unified "geometric" argument places me squarely within the traditional "systematic" camp of Hobbes interpreters, whose approach has been recently attacked by a group of "antisystematic" interpreters emphasizing natural law in their reconstructions of Hobbes's position. Led by A. E. Taylor and Howard Warrender, these critics argue that one cannot get Hobbes's political conclusions to follow from his natural philosophy or his human psychology, and that the political argument in *Leviathan* should be reconstructed to show that the justification for absolute sovereignty must rest on the foundation of natural law developed in medieval Christian philosophy. This attack on the systematic approach has generated interesting debates about how the pieces of Hobbes's argument go together, and it has focused attention on a perennially difficult problem for the systematic interpreters — the role of Hobbes's laws of nature in his argument.

However, this book is an attempt to present a single argument for absolute sovereignty resting on Hobbesian premises about the nature of human beings, their psychology, and their "moral" relationships, each step of which is either explicit in *Leviathan* or consistent with the positions Hobbes takes on psychology, ethics, and natural philosophy. The only way to put to rest the worry that there is no coherent "geometric deduction" for absolute sovereignty in *Leviathan* is to present one. That is what I propose to do.

I will not, however, contend that Hobbes's geometric deduction succeeds. On the contrary, it is invalid, and I will be concerned to determine both where and why it fails. Warrender and others are not, therefore, wrong to suspect that Hobbes's conclusion does not follow from his materialist premises, but they are wrong to deny that Hobbes's primary intention in *Leviathan* was to derive that conclusion from those premises. Moreover, I shall contend that at every vulnerable point in his argument Hobbes wavers, putting forward views to shore up his shaky argument that are importantly at odds with the political conclusion he wants to justify. The passages in which these views are expressed are favorites of the antitraditionalist school, and when I bring these discordant ideas together in Chapter 8, I will show that they form the seeds of a Lockean-style social contract argument. Indeed, if Locke needed a source book of ideas for his own political theory, he needed to look no farther than *Leviathan*. So the antitraditionalist interpreters' claim that there are Lockean views in *Leviathan* is right, but I shall argue that they are wrong to see these ideas as constitutive of the main and "official" Hobbesian argument.

Giving such a rational reconstruction of Hobbes's argument does not preclude taking a historical approach to his work; on the contrary, the historical background is a highly useful supplement to the philosophical analysis of his argument. Placing Hobbes's argument in historical context reveals and clarifies many of the assumptions and theoretical underpinnings of that argument and makes explicit what problems his theory of the state was designed to solve. Indeed, this historical discussion is useful in bringing to light the reasons any philosopher would have for espousing an "alienation" social contract theory. Nonetheless, my commitment to history does not imply slavish adherence to Hobbes's statement of his own argument. I am not loath to use contemporary philosophical and mathematical tools (such as the tools of game theory) to reconstruct his argument. Hobbes meant his work to be appreciated as a philosophical argument for absolute sovereignty, not as an exhibit in a museum of seventeenth-century political beliefs. Hence, the use of any tools of logic or any modern conceptual distinctions that will help to advance, clarify, or improve Hobbes's argument for his political theory is fully in accordance with his purposes and true to the spirit of his work.

Of course, in one sense, most of us in the twentieth century are already confident that the argument fails in some way, for we believe that there is no successful argument for a polity as distasteful to us as absolute sovereignty. An investigation of Hobbes's argument and an appreciation of its failure can help us to explain our rejection of this type of government and thus make more sophisticated our own political beliefs. However, the principal reason for studying Hobbes's work is that doing so will improve our understanding of social contract theories generally. For example, we can learn from an analysis of Hobbes's political theory that it is an example of one *kind* of social contract argument that began to develop as early as the twelfth century, when a debate arose among Roman law theorists concerning a passage in Justinian's *Digest* known as the *lex regia:*

What pleases the prince has the force of law, because by the *lex regia,* which was made concerning his authority, the people confers to him and upon him all its own authority and power. [Morrall 1971, 46; from the *Digest* of Justinian, I, 4, I]

The commentators on the *Digest* were prepared to accept this statement as good evidence that the ruler's power was derived from the people, but they could not agree on how that transfer of power had occurred. When the people "conferred" their power on the ruler, did they surrender their power to him? Or did they merely lend him that power, reserving the right to take it from him if they saw fit? This was more than just an academic dispute about the interpretation of a text; at issue was the fundamental relationship between the ruler and the ruled, and theorists who gave different answers to this question advocated very different polities. If power was merely loaned to the ruler, rebellion against him could be condoned if he violated the conditions attached to that loan. But if the people's grant of power was a surrender, there were no such conditions, and the people could never be justified in taking back that power via revolution.

As English society in the seventeenth century warred over the issue of the nation's political structure, Hobbes put forward the finest statement ever of the position that the ruler is instituted when the people surrender their power to him — what I call an "alienation" social contract theory. Later in the same century, Locke became the most famous spokesman for the position that the ruler's power is only loaned to him — what I call the "agency" social contract theory. My analysis of Hobbes's argument is designed to clarify the structure and strategy of all alienation arguments and to illuminate, by contrast, the different features of an agency social contract argument.

However, one of the most important ways in which a study of Hobbes's social contract theory illuminates other theories in this tradition is by making clear how any social contract argument works as a justification of the state. The belief that such arguments are without justificational force has been widespread since the seventeenth century. David Hume assumed that proponents of this argument used the social contract as a historical explanation of the state's creation, and he brilliantly ridiculed any historical claims these theories might have had (Hume 1965; 1978, III, ii, viii). Defenders of the argument countered that social contracts were only "hypothetical," but more recent philosophers have wondered how a merely hypothetical contract can justify anything. As Dworkin says, "A hypothetical contract is not simply a pale form of an actual contract; it is no contract at all." (1976, 17–18) One of the tasks of this book is to explain the sense in which an agreement instituting a ruler is supposed to be hypothetical and yet justificational and, in particular, how it introduces the notion of consent into the argument for the state's legitimacy. However, using Hobbes's theory, I will make this explanation in a way that will strike many readers as iconoclastic: I will argue that *there is no literal contract* in any successful social contract theory! Only when the nature of the agreements in these arguments is correctly understood can their justificatory and explanatory structure be appreciated. And although I will be explicitly concerned in this book to use this analysis to clarify the strategies of traditional contractarian arguments, such as those put forward by Hobbes, Locke, and Kant, I will at least suggest how this study is relevant to an understanding of the strategies of modern contractarian arguments designed to justify certain conceptions of justice or morality put forward by such contemporary political theorists as John Rawls. I will also argue that this study can educate us about the intellectual roots of the modern state and in this respect lead us to appreciate more fully the theoretical foundations of twentieth-century political philosophy.

Therefore, I hope that by the end of the book the reader will endorse the sentiments of Figgis cited at the outset of this Introduction (1916, 3–4), agreeing that this study of history has enabled us to ascend a watchtower, from which to gain perspective on contemporary political philosophy.

CHAPTER I

"Of Man": The Foundation of Hobbes's Political Argument

> He that is to govern a whole nation, must read in himself, not this or that
> particular man, but Man-kind.
>
> Hobbes, *Leviathan*

1.1 THE PREMISSES OF HOBBES'S ARGUMENT

Every political philosopher is influenced by the economic, social, and political events
of the time, and Hobbes's work was particularly responsive to the political turmoil of
his day. He was born in 1588, just before Philip II of Spain sent the Armada to attack
England during Spain's war with The Netherlands. During his childhood, a civil war
raged within France between Protestant Huguenots and the Catholic crown. The
Thirty Years' War ravaged Europe during all of his early adult years, from 1618 to
1648. And England itself was plunged into civil war and disorder from 1642 to
1649. Cromwell waged war against Ireland, Scotland, and Holland during his protec-
torship, and two other wars between England and The Netherlands erupted in 1665
and 1672. During the 1670s, Holland was also engaged in a war against France,
along with Austria, Spain, and the German principalities. And in 1679, the year of
Hobbes's death, political turmoil in England was increasing as, once again, opponents
of a Stuart king prepared to overthrow him.

Given this kind of violent political turmoil, it is not suprising that a philosopher
should come to hold a view of human beings as creatures who will, if unchecked,
inevitably behave violently toward one another. And Hobbes uses this conception of
human beings to argue that we are creatures who can live in peace only if we subject
ourselves to an absolute sovereign. The first presentation of Hobbes's argument for
absolute sovereignty was in the *Elements of Law,* which circulated in manuscript form
in 1640, arousing enough ire among Parliament members and sympathizers to force
Hobbes to flee to Paris. The second presentation was made in *De Cive,* published in
Latin in 1642, the second (1646) edition of which was translated and published in
English under the title *Philosophical Rudiments Concerning Government and Society* in
1651. However, Hobbes's final and most sophisticated presentation of the argument
was in *Leviathan,* published in English in 1651 and translated (with some changes)
into Latin by Hobbes himself and published (in Amsterdam) in 1668. It is the
presentation of Hobbes's argument in *Leviathan* on which we will concentrate.

In this chapter, I want to discuss certain critical premises of the Hobbesian argument. Because Hobbes's political and philosophical beliefs were designed to form a unified, integrated system, I would have liked to have included a complete discussion of how Hobbes's fundamental metaphysical and epistemological beliefs ground his political conclusions. But such a project would have forced me to write another book in addition to this one, and there are already good discussions of the connections among Hobbes's metaphysical, epistemological, and political positions.[1] Hence, in this chapter, I intend to do something more limited: I will analyze and discuss certain philosophical beliefs about the nature of human beings and the "moral laws" obligating them that act as premises in Hobbes's argument for absolute sovereignty.

Curtailing the discussion in this way is something that Hobbes himself would accept. While he insisted that the human being is both a "natural body" and a part of the "Body Politic" (DH, ep. ded., 35; De Corp, EW i, I, 6, 6, 72; Lev, intro., 4, 2), he nonetheless believed that natural and political philosophy

> do not so adhere to one another, but that they may be severed. For the causes of the motions of the mind are known, not only by ratiocination [science], but also by the *experience* of every man that takes the pains to observe those motions within himself. [De Corp, EW i, I, 6, 6, 73; emphasis added]

So without getting too deeply involved in the principles of natural philosophy, which Hobbes, as a materialist, believes explain all human behavior, I want to discuss aspects of Hobbes's conception of the person that are supposed to be *empirically confirmed* and that underlie premises in his argument for absolute sovereignty.

Some readers will think that by using the phrase "conception of the person" I am referring to Hobbes's psychology of human beings. This is not so. The psychological analyses of human behavior given by Hobbes in his writings already presuppose a certain view of what a person is — one might call it a "metaphysical" view. It is what Martin Hollis (1977) has called a "model of man." Moreover, his conception of the person involves a certain meta-ethical position (best expressed in *Leviathan* and *De Homine*) that we must understand if we are to appreciate both the structure of his argument and the prescriptive conclusions he reaches.

1.2 HOBBES'S RADICAL INDIVIDUALISM

In his article "The Social Contract as Ideology," David Gauthier (1977) argues that Hobbes is a "radical contractarian" who holds

> that individual human beings not only can, but must, be understood apart from society. The fundamental characteristics of men are not products of their social existence . . . man is social because he is human, not human because he is social. In particular, self-consciousness and language must be taken as conditions, not products, of society. [1977, 138]

Gauthier is right to find in Hobbes's theory a very strong brand of individualism, one that regards individual human beings as conceptually prior not only to political society but also to *all* social interactions. In fact, his method of argument both relies on and reveals his view that human beings are individuals first and social creatures

---

1   See, for example, J. W. N. Watkins (1965a), and M. M. Goldsmith (1966).

second. J. W. N. Watkins argues (1965a, 52–65; 1965b, 242–8; see also Randall 1940; 1961) that in his social contract argument Hobbes is implicitly making a certain kind of use of the "resolutive-compositive" method expounded by the Paduan scientists of his day. Harvey, Galileo, and other exponents of this method taught that the best way to understand a system, process, or event is to resolve it into its components, analyze these components, and then recompose them via a theory that explains their interrelationships and interactions. Hobbes's admiration for Harvey and Galileo is well known. And his acceptance of their method is evident in all three of his political writings. In *De Cive,* he writes:

Concerning my method, I thought it not sufficient to use a plain and evident style in what I have to deliver, except I took my beginning from the very matter of civil government, and thence proceeded to its generation and form, and the first beginning of justice. For everything is best understood by its constitutive causes. For as in a watch, or some such small engine, the matter, figure, and motion of the wheels cannot well be known, except it be taken insunder and viewed in parts; so to make a more curious search into the rights of states and duties of subjects, it is necessary, I say, not to take them insunder, but yet that they be so considered as if they were dissolved; that is, that we rightly understand what the quality of human nature is, in what matters it is, in what not, fit to make up a civil government, and how men must be agreed amongst themselves that intend to grow up into a well-grounded state. [*DC, EW* ii, pref., xiv]

Likewise, in *Leviathan,* Hobbes sets out to describe the nature of the state, the "artificial man," and does so first by considering "the *Matter* thereof, and the *Artificer*; both [of] which is *Man*" (*Lev,* intro., 2, 2). He concludes by seeing how these parts coalesce and unify themselves through the actions of agreement and authorization.[2]

However, when looking for "constitutive causes," Hobbes expects to find parts that are, in effect, "wholes" themselves. Just as he believes that dissection of a watch, or even of a human body, produces components that are separately defined but interacting parts of a unified mechanism ["For what is the *Heart,* but a *Spring;* and the *Nerves,* but so many *Strings;* and the *Joynts,* but so many *Wheeles,* giving motion to the whole Body . . . ?" (*Lev,* intro., 1, 1)], so, too, does he think that dissection of the state results in the discovery of separately defined human individuals who, after instituting the sovereign, are interacting parts of this "artificial man." This is why he thinks it makes sense to speak of a presocietal "state of nature" in which men are "even now sprung out of the earth, and suddenly, like mushrooms, come to full maturity, without all kind of engagement to each other." (*DC, EW* ii, 8, 1, 109) In his view, when we theoretically sunder society and put men into this natural state, human individuals are not destroyed when they are stripped of their social connections; rather, they are best revealed by that sundering. Although he admits that people certainly develop interests and ideas as a result of living in a society and cooperating with one another,[3] he contends that people's basic features and defining characteristics arise "from nature, that is, from their first birth, as they are merely sensible creatures, they have this disposition. . . ." (*DC, EW* ii, pref., xvi) And he believes that human beings have natural desires and motivations that, if unchecked, will lead them into extreme and continual conflict with one another.

2 In *De Corpore* there is a fairly extensive discussion of how philosophy follows a method that is both resolutive and compositive in nature; see Part I, Chapter 6, "Of Method."

3 For example, see *Leviathan* (13, 9, 62) on the advantages of culture and industry obtained in civil society and lost in a state of war.

It is important to note that Hobbes's use of the resolutive-compositive method does not generate this individualist position. Aristotle also accepts a resolutive-compositive method of analysis in political matters (1941a, 1252a, 20–30), but for him the constituents of the state are not isolated asocial individuals, but individuals in certain fundamental social relationships with others; namely, master and slave, husband and wife, father and children. (See the *Politics*, 1253b, 4–6.) Moreover, Aristotle argues that society is conceptually prior to the individual person, a position that Hobbes is directly contradicting in his own political writings. So, although it might be easy from our post-Hobbesian perspective to see the resolutive-compositive method as presupposing radical individualism, in fact it only *reveals* rather than creates Hobbes's view of human beings and their connections to one another in society.

In order to understand the exact nature of Hobbesian individualism, I want to explore the way in which this method shows how human beings are parts of a larger social whole; this, in turn, requires us to classify certain properties that any part of a larger whole might have. This classification is not an attempt to exhaust the types of properties that one can isolate in any system of parts, but for our purposes the following three kinds of properties are most important:

1. *Intrinsic properties.* These are properties an object has not in virtue of being a part of a larger whole but simply in virtue of being that object. For example, an airplane wing has the property of being made of metal; this is an intrinsic property, because the wing will have it whether or not it is affixed to the body of the plane. Likewise, an intrinsic property of a human being is having a heart; it is a feature we have in virtue of being such a creature.

2. *Functional properties.* These are properties that an object has in virtue of being part of a whole; specifically, they are properties that relate to or derive from the object's performance of certain roles basic to the purpose or nature of the whole itself. For example, in the human body, the stomach has the functional property of digesting proteins. And in a car, the transmission has the functional property of transmitting power from the engine to the drive shaft. Moreover, being a professor or a janitor or a pilot is an example of a functional property, insofar as it arises out of a person's performance of a role in the social group of which the person is a member.

3. *Interactive properties.* Not all objects that are parts of wholes have these properties, because they are properties that an object *develops over time* as it interacts with other parts of a whole, and not all such objects are able to change so that these new properties can be created. Moreover, these properties result from interaction between some or all of the parts of the whole and either the intrinsic properties of the object or its previously developed interactive properties. We see the development of an interactive property when the teeth of two cogs in a watch, as they come together, wear each other down. Each cog's property "being worn down" is interactive, because each develops as a result of the cogs' interaction. We might also say that a dog's ability to do tricks is an interactive property of the dog, because it is the result of the animal's association with human beings. Finally, we attrib-

ute interactive properties to human beings when they have interacted with other human beings or with other features of their natural environment. Examples of this sort of property in human beings include the following: having a taste for certain foods, such as ice cream or curry; certain sorts of physical abilities, such as the ability to ski; speaking a certain language, such as English or Hindi.

Using this terminology, we can now be clearer about what Hobbes is assuming when he characterizes his "state of nature." For Hobbes, not only our reflexes and animal abilities but also our basic human characteristics, capacities, and desires are *intrinsic* properties. He is not denying that we have functional or interactive properties; one's occupation in the community or one's ability to speak a particular language are clearly examples of such properties. Rather, he is maintaining that these properties are not fundamental to our nature as persons and that we possess intrinsically all motivations and abilities that are characteristically human.

There is overwhelming evidence in all of Hobbes's writings that he is an ardent supporter of this "radically individualist" perspective on human beings. I have already quoted the passage in *De Cive* explaining that in his argument he treats human beings as if they were "even now sprung out of the earth, and suddenly, like mushrooms, come to full maturity, without all kind of engagement to each other." (*DC, EW* ii, 8, 1, 109) Of course, none of us arrives at adulthood so quickly and so asocially. But Hobbes maintains that the social interaction necessary for our physical survival in our childhood years does not in any way play a role in forming us *as human beings.* Indeed, he argues that if we enter into cooperative interactions with other people, it is only because we perceive these interactions to be in our interest in some way: "We do not therefore by nature seek society for its own sake, but that we may receive some honour or profit from it; these we desire primarily, that secondarily." (*DC, EW* ii, 1, 2, 3) That is, we desire society only insofar as it has *instrumental value* for us, which means that our individuality grounds our sociality, not the reverse.

Watkins (1965a, 101ff.) and Michael Oakeshott (1947, liv) have also discussed Hobbes's "privacy thesis," which is importantly connected with the radical individualism I am attributing to him. Hobbes's privacy thesis is the view that our thoughts, beliefs, and emotions are "cut off" from others and confined to the "cell walls" of our person. Throughout *Leviathan*, Hobbes's discussion of human beings assumes that minds never meet, that ideas are never really shared among human beings, and that each of us is always and finally isolated from every other individual. Such a thesis is a natural part of a philosophical perspective that regards human beings as social because they are human, rather than the reverse. It also fits nicely with Hobbes's materialist metaphysics. By saying that "conceptions or apparitions are nothing really, but motion in some internal substance of the head" (*EL*, I, vii, 1, 28; see also *Lev*, 1), Hobbes imprisons those conceptions and apparitions within the person in whom those bodily motions are occurring.

Even our ability to speak a natural language, something that, more than anything else, appears to be evidence for understanding human beings as inherently social creatures, is regarded by Hobbes as an ability in no way dependent for its creation or development on social interaction of any kind. In Chapter 4 of *Leviathan*, Hobbes's account of human speech makes the individual the source of language, and he regards language as of instrumental value only: Words are needed only as "marks" to help us remember our thoughts (*Lev*, 4, 3, 12–13) or as "signes" to help us communicate with other human beings in order to better pursue the satisfaction of our desires (*Lev*, 4, 3, 31). Thus, Hobbes makes language a remarkably private and individual affair.

Many of Hobbes's critics in the seventeenth century disliked his radical individualism intensely. Ralph Cudworth maintained, in the spirit of Aristotle, that

a man cannot apprehend himself as a being standing by itself, cut off, separated, and disjointed from all other beings . . . but looks upon himself as a member lovingly united to the whole system of all intellectual beings. [cited by Passmore 1951, 72; and Watkins 1965a, 101]

And Hobbes's critics were particularly fond of attacking his individualist analysis of the family. In *Leviathan,* Chapter 20, and in *De Cive,* Chapter 9, Hobbes maintains, true to his radical individualism, that family bonds are not natural to individuals but only artificially forged and coerced contracts between an inferior (e.g., the child, the wife) and a superior (e.g., the parent, the husband), the latter providing protection for the former in exchange for obedience. Bishop Bramhall made it clear that he regarded this view as plainly crazy:

[Hobbes] might as well tell us in plain termes, that all the obligation which a child hath to his parent, is because he did not take him by the heeles and knock out his braines against the walls, so soon as he was born. [1658, 534; see also Lawson 1657, 48; and Filmer 1652, 6]

Bramhall and other critics went on to insist that there are *natural* ties of affection binding one person to another that are constitutive of our humanity and that generate commonly shared ethical principles that all rulers must heed. Nonetheless, other thinkers in the seventeenth century found this individualist perspective attractive. As I shall discuss later, the fact that even some of Hobbes's critics attempted to deduce universal moral laws from individual self-interest shows how enticing people in that age found the idea that moral and political theories must start with a view of the "raw" individual, stripped of any social connections.

However, Hobbes's radical individualism is not attractive or compelling to many twentieth-century thinkers, who, in this post-Hegelian, post-Marxist century, believe that fundamental human abilities, such as the capacity to reason mathematically, to learn a language, and to act morally, develop only because each of us interacts with other human beings, and who think that our identities as persons depend on roles we play and have played in family, school, city, and nation-state. Indeed, some Hobbesian critics have argued that this view of human beings is itself a product of the historical period in which Hobbes's thought developed. For example, C. B. Macpherson has argued (1977, chap. II, esp. 23 and 61; 1968) that the behavior that Hobbes attributes to human beings is not "natural" at all but is in fact the behavior of men and women in a "bourgeois market society" (1968, 38). Macpherson even tries to make into an *explicit* premiss in Hobbes's argument the idea that people in the "state of nature" seem in fact to be bourgeois men and women. He argues that in order to comprehend "Hobbes's argument from the physiological to the social motion of man, a social assumption is needed besides the physiological postulates" (1968, 46), for otherwise we will not understand why Hobbes believed that an absolute sovereign was necessary for peace.

But to "fix" Hobbes's argument in this way is to seriously misunderstand the conceptual foundations of his argument. We must distinguish between our appraisal of Hobbes's conception of the person and that conception itself. Although we may reject Hobbes's individualism and seek to understand it as a product of his time, we must attribute to him the individualist view that, as many historians have noted, was so attractive to philosophers in that early capitalist period. And we must recognize that it was important for Hobbes that an initial premiss of his argument be that human beings are not in any fundamental way products of their social environment. Indeed, even from Macpherson's standpoint, it would have been unusual for a person in Hobbes's time and place to hold any other view. Therefore, although I will discuss the social context of Hobbes's thought throughout this book because I eschew his radical individualism, I will not attribute to him nor insert into his argument what he would have considered to be false assumptions about our sociality. And, contrary to what Macpherson says, it will never be necessary to make use of such assumptions in order to see why Hobbes thought that absolute sovereignty was the sole legitimate form of government.

Indeed, I will conclude this book by arguing that the entire social contract argument presupposes at least a moderate indivdualism.[4] And the extent to which we modern political philosophers should want to use this method of argument to justify our political conclusions depends on whether or not we can embrace the individualism inherent in this method.

1.3 HOBBES'S MATERIALIST PSYCHOLOGY

THE MATERIALIST METAPHYSICS

Hobbes's espousal of such a radical individualism is connected with his unabashed acceptance of a materialist picture of man. This materialist position was obviously connected with the new "natural philosophy" of his day, and Harvey's physiological theories were major influences on Hobbes's philosophy of mind and his views on human psychology and physiology.[5] It is a position that many Western philosophers have found attractive since the seventeenth century, and its twentieth-century descendant is generally called physicalism.

The first fundamental component of Hobbes's materialism is almost too obvious to state:

1. There is only one world, which various languages and styles of explanation characterize differently.

Languages with different domains do not establish independent worlds, as some twentieth-century philosophers (for example, Goodman) would have it; for Hobbes, there is only one world, although more than one way of describing it. Second, Hobbes believes that the language of physics, which contains in its domain fundamental objects recognized by this science, can give us a *complete* description of the events of the universe:

2. There is no change in the world without a physical change.

4 See Chapter 9, Section 9.2.
5 See Watkins (1965a, chap. 3) for a discussion of this influence.

Third, he endorses a belief that Quine (1977, 187) says follows from article 2:

3. The materialist language has [or will have] in its domain all and only those fundamental objects that exist.

This means that only the materialist language can explain events by referring to the ultimate existent objects in the universe. It also means that the only existent objects are physical — any object that exists either is one of the ultimate physical particles or is a compound of those ultimate particles. Hobbes's belief in this precept explains his adamant opposition to Cartesian views of the self.[6]

Perhaps even more important, Hobbes believes that an explanation of an event in materialist language must have a certain form:

4. A materialist explanation of an event will always be in terms of the operation of the fundamental physical objects in accordance with laws [which for Hobbes are deterministic].

The importance of article 4 is that it tells us how explanations of the actions of objects that are compounds of the fundamental physical objects will proceed. Hobbes's use of the resolutive-compositive method of his day essentially amounts to a commitment to what is generally called a "mechanistic" explanation of natural phenomena.[7] The nature of a compound is explained by resolving it into its component parts, and then recomposing it by detailing the operation of these components according to natural laws, so that it is treated as a mechanism, that is, as a system of physical parts interrelated and operating according to physical laws.

In all of his writings Hobbes shows himself firmly committed to this materialist view (and 'commitment' is the appropriate word here, because neither in Hobbes's day nor now have these four precepts been proved to be true). But he also embraces a fifth precept that twentieth-century physicalists are much more reluctant to embrace:

5. It is possible to reduce both ethical and psychological language to talk of matter, motion, and the laws of nature.

Indeed, it is an assumption of his "geometric" approach to philosophy that even as the state can be resolved into its component parts to reveal individual human beings as its constituents, these human beings can be resolved into parts to reveal fundamental material particles as their constituents. And in *De Corpore*, Hobbes insists that the explanation of human behavior is to be found in the study of physics:

After *physics* we must come to *moral philosophy*, in which we are to consider the motion of the mind, namely, *appetite, aversion, love, benevolence, hope, fear, anger, emulation, envy*, etc.; what causes they have, and of what they be causes. And the reason why these are to be considered after *physics* is, that they have their causes in sense and imagination, which are the subject of *physical* contemplation. [*De Corp, EW* i, I, 6, 6, 72–3]

Moreover, he insists that recomposing these material parts of a human being into a whole human organism involves making reference to the (deterministic) natural laws of motion that these ultimate particles always obey, one of which is Galileo's law of inertia. (See *De Corp, EW* i, I, 6, 6, 72–3, and II, 9, 7, 124–5.)

6 See Hobbes's "Objections to Descartes's *Meditations*" (1976, 60–78), particularly objection II.
7 This is Daniel Dennett's word for it (1982, 150–73).

In Hobbes's view, analyzing the complicated physical structure of a human being helps us to understand not only how the parts of the human "engine" work but also what fundamental desires and motivations each human being possesses *intrinsically,* in virtue of the way one's body functions. And these intrinsic motivations are important presuppositions in Hobbes's moral and political conclusions. As we have already noted, Hobbes believed that *Leviathan* could have been a book that would first have reduced human beings to organisms with a certain physiological structure, then defined certain desires or aversions that human beings have intrinsically in virtue of how their bodies function, and, finally, used these desires to explain how these human beings could be successfully recomposed into a society. In fact, Hobbes was not able to pull off this full-scale reductionist project (and from the tone of his discussion in Chapter 6 of *Leviathan,* he appeared to believe not only that any psychological state could be reduced to a physical state but also the more controversial thesis that there was a *unique* reduction of a psychological state to a physical state). But he did believe that he had enough of a sense of what the reduction would be like, and what the fact of reducibility tells us, to be able to construct a psychological theory of human behavior (which is also empirically confirmable) to be used later in his political argument. Consider Hobbes's explication of sensation:

The cause of Sense, is the Externall Body, or Object, which presseth the organ proper to each Sense, either immediately, as in the Tast and Touch; or mediately, as in Seeing, Hearing, and Smelling: which pressure, by the mediation of the Nerves, and other strings, and membranes of the body, continued inwards to the Brain and Heart, causeth there a resistance, or counter-pressure, or endeavour of the heart, to deliver it self: which endeavour because *Outward,* seemeth to be some matter without. And this *seeming,* or *fancy,* is that which men call *Sense.* [*Lev,* 1, 4, 3]

Hobbes then uses the idea that external affectation of bodily organs is responsible for our images of external objects in an attempt to offer a materialist explanation of human motivation. After distinguishing between "vitall" motion, or the internal movements of our bodily parts (e.g., movement of the blood), and "voluntary" or "animal" motion, that is, the external movements of the body (e.g., movement of a limb), he explains the origin of voluntary motion by showing its connection with our perceptions and ideas:

conceptions and apparitions are nothing really, but motion in some internal substance of the head; which motion not stopping there, but proceeding to the heart, of necessity must there either help or hinder that motion which is called vital; when it helpeth, it is called DELIGHT, contentment, or pleasure . . . but when such motion weakeneth, or hindereth the vital motion, then it is called PAIN. . . . [*EL,* I, vii, 1, 28; see also *Lev,* 6, 1, 23]

Then, Hobbes continues, either the vital motions that initiate an image in the brain increase, in which case one experiences pleasure and initiates voluntary motion toward the object, or else these vital motions decrease, in which case one experiences pain and begins voluntary motion away from the thing sensed. The former is called man's appetite, desire, or love for that object; the latter is man's hatred of or aversion to it.[8]

8 See *Elements of Law* (I, vii, 2, 22) and *Leviathan* (6, 2, 23). In *Leviathan,* Hobbes also defines what he calls "endeavours," which are "the small beginnings of [voluntary] motion" (*Lev,* 6, 1, 23). Watkins (1965a, chap. vii) discusses this rather nonmaterialist concept and its influence on Leibniz.

Hobbes goes on to distinguish two kinds of appetite and aversion, corresponding to two of the properties we have already defined. The first is "intrinsic":

Of Appetites and Aversions, some are born with Men; as Appetite of food, Appetite of excretion, and exoneration, (which may also and more properly be called Aversions, from somewhat they feele in their Bodies). . . . [*Lev*, 6, 4, 24]

The second kind (accounting for the vast majority of desires) is "interactive":

The rest, which are Appetites of particular things, proceed from Experience, and triall of their effects upon themselves, or other men. For of things wee know not at all, or believe not to be, we can have no further Desire, than to tast and try. [*Lev*, 6, 4, 24]

And because human bodies and their environments are variable, interactive desires will differ between human beings and will vary within a given human being over time:

And because the constitution of a mans Body, is in continuall mutation; it is impossible that all the same things should alwayes cause in him the same Appetites, and Aversions: much lesse can all Men consent, in the Desire of almost any one and the same Object. [*Lev*, 6, 6, 24]

In this way Hobbes accounts for the great variety of desires among human beings.

GLORY AND SELF-PRESERVATION

The bulk of Chapter 6 of *Leviathan* and Chapter XI of *De Homine* are taken up with using this materialist psychology to explain the origin and nature of various passions and emotions.

Because of its prominence later on in Hobbes's argument, I want to introduce briefly his account of our passion for glory. In fact, Hobbes defines two kinds of "glorying" — a healthy sort, and an unhealthy sort:

Joy, arising from imagination of a mans own power and ability, is that exultation of the mind which is called GLORYING: which if grounded upon the experience of his own former action, is the same with CONFIDENCE: but if grounded on the flattery of others; or onely supposed by himself, for delight in the consequences of it, is called VAINE-GLORY. [*Lev*, 6, 19, 26–7]

And, as we shall see, he goes on to implicate vainglory, grounded on flattery rather than reality, in his explanation of violence in the state of nature. It appears from the tone of the discussion of glory in Chapter 6 that Hobbes means us to understand it as a desire for personal advancement that is somehow biologically intrinsic and that is so strong in us that when we cannot see it satisfied by the reality of our own powers and abilities in the world, we lie to ourselves and inflate those powers and abilities. Yet the intrinsic nature of this passion is certainly questionable, because glorying seems to presuppose a comparison of oneself with other human beings, which would make it a passion that could only develop in a social context. In Chapters 2 and 3 we shall be discussing at some length the question whether the desire for glory can be understood as intrinsic or only as interactive and socially developed.

However, I want to concentrate here on the desire for self-preservation, which is the more important of the two desires insofar as it is critical both to Hobbes's account of human warfare and to his justification of absolute sovereignty. This desire is clearly intrinsic, and Hobbes grounds its importance to us in the fact that we are naturally averse to anything that hinders our internal vital motions, above all, death, insofar as it is the complete cessation of vital motion:

> necessity of nature maketh men . . . to avoid that which is hurtful; but most of all that terrible enemy of nature, death, from whom we expect both the loss of all power, and also the greatest of bodily pains in the losing. . . . [*EL,* I, xiv, 6, 71; see also *DH,* xi, 6, 48]

It is important to be clear on the fact that although all people pursue self-preservation, they do not all desire the same object. Each person wants his own self-preservation above all else, not the self-preservation of everyone. And because each person has a different object of desire, conflicts between people as they pursue these different goals are, in Hobbes's eyes, inevitable. Indeed, Hobbes's belief that these conflicts would be pervasive and greatly damaging to each person in the state of nature is, as we shall discuss, one of the most important tenets of his political argument.

It is undeniable that this aspect of Hobbesian psychology is crude and overly simplistic. Although normal human beings clearly have a very powerful desire to preserve themselves, it seems implausible for Hobbes to insist that this desire is *always* prior to *all* other desires in *everyone.* Moreover, it is unclear how Hobbes wants us to understand this desire for life. Is it really plausible to suppose that we are interested in the length of life alone, and not the quality of that life? Imagine having to make a choice between two actions, the first of which will give you enormous pleasure and allow you thirty more years of life, whereas the second will allow you thirty-one years of life but will cost you that pleasure and also bring you considerable pain. Might not many, even most, people prefer a rich, pleasure-filled life to a longer but pleasureless and/or painful existence?

Even Hobbes seems prepared to accept that this might be a better account of most people's psychological predilections, because he qualifies the primacy of the desire for life over death in *De Homine*:

> though death is the greatest of all evils (especially when accompanied by torture), the pains of life can be so great that, unless their quick end is foreseen, they may lead men to number death among the goods. [*DH,* XI, 6, 48–9]

Hobbes is acknowledging here that there are situations in which people will naturally favor death rather than life. However, the situation he describes is highly unusual, one in which a person's body is undergoing torturous pain, either because of disease or because of the actions of others. Nor is the sort of choice described in the previous paragraph commonly presented to us. It would seem to be Hobbes's position that in most, although not all, circumstances, our fundamental desire to enhance our bodily motions is one that will lead us to avoid "that terrible enemy death."

Nonetheless, Hobbes does little to make more precise or sophisticated his psychological view that this desire is usually (but not universally or continually) of primary importance to human beings. And Watkins (1965a, 166–8) worries that one might judge Hobbes's entire political theory as unsound on the basis that it appears to be founded on the unqualified and thus implausible psychological assumption that death is always feared above all else by the normal human being. However, such a judgment is premature at this stage. Even if the notion that all people primarily desire their self-preservation in all circumstances is implausible, it is undeniable that this desire is frequently a very important one for almost all of us; so perhaps this kind of significance is all Hobbes needs (and wants) the desire to possess in order for his arguments to be effective. However, in later chapters we shall be concerned to see if this is true, that is, whether Hobbes can assume a milder and thus more plausible view of the importance of this desire for us, or whether he needs an implausibly strong assumption of this desire's importance in order to derive his political conclusions, such that his argument can be declared unsound.

However, we are required on Hobbes's behalf to elaborate on and make more sophisticated this psychological assumption in one important way, for otherwise he will not even be able to get his argument for the institution of an absolute sovereign off the ground. If the primacy of the desire for self-preservation is understood to be a kind of side constraint on human action, then human beings would be creatures who would never do anything to risk their lives if faced with a choice between a risky course and a safe course of action. And yet Hobbes believes this is manifestly false. As we shall discuss in Chapters 2 and 3, Hobbes argues in Chapter 13 of *Leviathan* that precisely because people desire to preserve themselves, they will deliberately go to war with others if they believe that doing so will enable them to gain greater material advantages. But this means he believes that people will indeed be prepared to risk their lives in the short run (even when they have a nonrisky course of action available to them) in order to further the security of their lives substantially in the long run. To use the terminology of Jon Elster (1979, chap. 1), Hobbes makes the assumption that human beings are "global" maximizers, not "local" maximizers. A local maximizer is one who is capable only of maximizing some quantity in a specific choice. But a global maximizer can do something more: Specifically, if faced with two alternatives, one can choose the nonmaximal course of action now in order to put oneself in a position that will allow one later to reap even more of the quantity one desires than the short-term maximal option would have allowed. Hobbes assumes that when human beings pursue their self-preservation, they will do so as *global* maximizers, able to take one step backward in order that later they can go two steps forward. Specifically, they are prepared to place their lives in jeopardy in the short run for the sake of gaining greater security of life in the long run.

Of course, not every risk of life would be worth taking for a Hobbesian individual. Placing one's life in some degree of jeopardy for the sake of achieving this goal strikes Hobbes as reasonable, but too much jeopardy he regards as craziness. Unfortunately, *Leviathan* contains no explicit account of precisely when risk taking is rational; yet, as we shall see time and again in later chapters, Hobbes continually needs such an account in order to explain and appraise not only the generation of war in the state of nature but also the rationality of living under a sovereign rather than remaining in the state of nature. The most natural account of risk taking to attribute to him is the Bayesian account, represented by the expected-utility calculation. According to this view, one should perform that risky action among available alternatives whose expected utility is greatest, where that expected utility is calculated by multiplying the utility of each possible outcome of the action by the probability of that outcome occurring, and then adding the products. This calculation expresses our intuition that the rationality of taking a risk is dependent on how much one stands to gain, how much one stands to lose, and how likely it is that one will lose. Indeed, these intuitions seem to be shared by Hobbes, because in his story of the development of

the goal of "identifying and destroying invader cells" to human B cells in the immune system and that it is legitimate to convict the B cells of making "errors" in their pursuit of this goal. Similarly, Hobbes is committed to attributing the goal of pleasure pursuit and pain avoidance to the human biological system, and he does not assume, as Bentham seems to do, that this attribution can be made only if the goal is regarded as an object of conscious (or even unconscious) desire. As we shall see, one of the real advantages of the Hobbesian variant of psychological monism is that it allows him to escape having to espouse a position that has classically been called psychological egoism.

IS HOBBES A PSYCHOLOGICAL EGOIST?

If Hobbes is best understood as one who is, or at least tends to be, a psychological monist, doesn't that mean he must also be understood as a psychological egoist?[10] What exactly is that label supposed to designate? As a first approximation we might say it means that human beings always do what they desire to do. Certainly this thesis is a necessary component of psychological egoism, because any theorist, such as Kant, who maintains that reason can move us to act is also able to say that we can act contrary to our own self-interest when we act from reason. But prefiguring Hume, Hobbes insists that only desires can move us, and his remarks on deliberation and "willing" make this particularly clear:

When in the mind of man, Appetites, and Aversions, Hopes, and Feares, concerning one and the same thing, arise alternately; and divers good and evill consequences of the doing, or omitting the thing propounded, come successively into our thoughts; so that sometimes we have an Appetite to it; sometimes an Aversion from it; sometimes Hope to be able to do it; sometimes Despaire, or Feare to attempt it; the whole summe of Desires, Aversions, Hopes and Fears, continued till the thing be either done, or thought impossible, is that we call DELIBERATION. [*Lev*, 6, 29, 28]

This description of deliberation is not in any sense Kantian; that is, deliberation is not understood as involving a debate between practical reason and desire about how we should act. On the contrary, the debate in a deliberation appears to be between or among desires *alone,* and Hobbes's sketchy remarks suggest two different ways in which this debate might go: Either we are simply weighing the strengths of competing desires or we are trying to determine the best means to an end defined by a given desire. In either case, reason's only role in the deliberative process is to help determine how to achieve a goal set by desire — it does not itself dictate a goal nor motivate us to pursue it.

Reason's inertness is once again implicit in Hobbes's remarks on the will. We are said to will to do something following a deliberation only insofar as a desire is moving us to act:

Will therefore *is the last Appetite in Deliberating.* And though we say in common Discourse, a man had a Will once to do a thing, that nevertheless he forebore to do; yet that is properly but

---

10 See the discussions of this traditional label by Gert (1978) and by Watkins (1965a, 107–15).

an Inclination, which makes no Action Voluntary; because the action depends not of it, but of the last Inclination, or Appetite. [*Lev*, 6, 33, 28]

That is, a *decision* to do action *x* is simply a *desire* to do *x* that is the final desire of a deliberation about whether or not to do *x*. So we are moved only by desires, not by reason, even if we deliberate before acting. Clearly, the Humean view put forward in Book II of *A Treatise of Human Nature* that only passions can move us to act is prefigured in this Hobbesian account of willing.[11]

But because Hume criticized Hobbes as a psychological egoist, he must have believed that there was more to this view than just the assertion of this principle, which he himself held. Indeed, Hume's criticisms suggest a second interpretation of psychological egoism that goes as follows: Not only do desires alone move us, but, more important, all the desires that move us have a certain content; they are what C. D. Broad (1978, 111–18) has termed "self-regarding" rather than "other-regarding." For example, if I see you bleeding on the street and I run to your aid, the psychological egoism I am now defining would insist that this action is done by me in order to pursue an object that is "for me." For example, I might be doing it to get a good reputation, or to feel important, or to place you in my debt. Hume tries to convict Hobbes of holding psychological egoism in this sense in the following passage from *An Enquiry Concerning the Principles of Morals:*

An Epicurean or a Hobbist readily allows, that there is such a thing as friendship in the world, without hypocrisy or disguise; though he may attempt, by a philosophical chymistry, to resolve the elements of this passion, if I may so speak, into those of another, and explain every affection to be self-love, twisted and moulded, by a particular turn of imagination, into a variety of appearances. [1975b, 296–7]

Many critics have followed Hume in this assessment, and Hobbes gives us plenty of reason to think the charge might be correct. Chapter 6 of *Leviathan* certainly appears to be a chapter designed to resolve the various passions that seem other-interested into passions of self-love. And Aubrey tells a story about Hobbes in his *Brief Lives* that provides amusing anecdotal evidence that Hobbes was a psychological egoist:

One time, I remember, goeing in the Strand, a poor and infirme old man craved his almes. He, beholding him with eies of pitty and compassion, putt his hand in his pocket, and gave him 6d. Sayd a divine (scil. Dr. Jaspar Mayne) that stood by — 'Would you have donne this, if it had not been Christ's Command?' — 'Yea', sayd he. — 'Why?' quoth the other. — 'Because', sayd he, 'I was in paine to consider the miserable condition of the old man; and now my almes, giving him some reliefe, doth also ease me.' [1898, 352]

Perhaps most significant of all is the way in which, in *The Elements of Law*,[12] Hobbes defines pity, clearly an other-interested emotion, as the "imagination or fiction of future calamity to *ourselves,* proceeding from the sense of another man's present calamity." (*El*, I, ix, 10, 30–1; emphasis added) This is clearly an egoistic "conversion" of what would seem to be an other-interested passion.

Yet, following Bernard Gert (1978) and J. W. N. Watkins (1965a), I shall argue

---

11 These views on "willing" set up Hobbes's compatibilist position on freedom and necessity that prefigures Hume's compatibilist position. Compare *Leviathan* (21, 4, 108) with Hume's *Enquiry Concerning Human Understanding,* Section vii (1975a, 80–103).

12 This is discussed by F. McNeilly (1969, 118).

that psychological egoism understood as a statement about the content of our desires cannot be pinned on the Hobbes who wrote *Leviathan*.[13] Pity, in that book, is "Griefe, for the Calamity of *another*" and "ariseth from the imagination that the like calamity may befall himselfe; and therefore is called also COMPASSION, and in the phrase of this present time is a FELLOW-FEELING." (*Lev*, 6, 26, 27; emphasis added; see also *DH*, XII, 10, 61)[14] Note that in this definition, Hobbes says that when we feel pity we feel concern for another human being. He does not try to twist it into some form of self-love as he did previously in the *Elements of Law* passage; pity is simply "Griefe, for the Calamity of another." But he goes on to explain the origination of the passion by appealing to the action of our imagination — specifically our imaginative idea of what it would be like if we were in an unfortunate person's shoes. And this imaginative identification, which explains the origination of pity, should not be taken for a characterization of the passion itself. When I feel pity for another, I am not feeling pity for *myself* imagined in those circumstances; rather, I am feeling pity for the other person, but that pity has been created in me by an imaginative identification with her plight. Many philosophers have found this a plausible account of the origination of compassionate feeling[15] — particularly David Hume, whose theory in the *Treatise* (II, i, xi) about how the operation of "sympathy" produces in us benevolent emotions and desires is remarkably similar to Hobbes's account of how imaginative identification works.

Hence, psychological egoism in this second sense is not a view Hobbes held at the time he wrote *Leviathan*. Moreover, we should be properly appreciative of the fact that the way in which he includes other-interesting passions into his psychology in *Leviathan* does not threaten his radical individualism. A theory of the origination of certain other-interested passions as arising out of a process of imaginative identification is a way of construing those passions as *interactive* rather than *intrinsic*, and, in particular, a way of construing them as *socially* developed insofar as they originate only after interaction with other members of the species (as a result of certain features, in particular, the ability to identify imaginatively with another person, which presumably is intrinsic to that species). They would not exist in human beings in a state of nature, because such people would not, by hypothesis, be

---

13   However, my reasons for rejecting the idea that Hobbes is a psychological egoist do not include (as Gert would believe they should) the idea that Hobbes is in fact putting forward an objectivist ethical theory in *Leviathan* and that he has an Aristotelian account of reason (Gert, 1978, 13ff.). Much of my discussion in this chapter is meant to show why that appraisal of Hobbes is wrong.

14   The *De Homine* definition of 'compassion' is rather ambiguous: "To grieve because of another's evil, that is, to feel another's pain and to suffer with him, that is, to imagine that another's evil could happen to oneself, is called compassion." (*DH*, XII, 10, 61) It is not clear from this passage if compassion is a concern for another created in one by imaginative identification with him or if it is concern for oneself created by that same process. The words 'that is' in the passage make it hard to decide which interpretation is correct, but because of the context of the passage, I prefer the former reading, in particular because Hobbes speaks of compassion as involving feeling another's pain and suffering with him.

15   For example, Aristotle, in *Rhetoric* (1941b, 1385b, 13–16), and Bishop Butler, in sermon V of *Works* (1896, 79ff.). Their views are discussed by Watkins (1965a, 114).

interacting with one another enough (or in the right kinds of ways) to allow the process of sympathetic indentification to produce these other-interested passions. The interactive nature of these passions would also appear to explain why Hobbes does not take them seriously as significant springs to action after the creation of human society, for how could they be powerful enough to compete with the intrinsic self-regarding desires that drive human beings *as a species*? Hobbes manages in a few brief remarks to find room for other-interested desires in his philosophical system without threatening his radical individualism and without threatening his claim that the state of nature is a state of total war.

Thus, Hobbes differs from Hume only insofar as Hobbes does not believe that one can explain the generation of *any* social group — not even the family, and certainly not political society — by relying in any substantial way on these interactive passions. For him, society is a necessary condition of the passions, not the reverse. It is perhaps for this reason that we should consider Hobbes's views more "pessimistic"[16] than the views of those philosophers who, like Hume, are willing to grant far more power and scope to other-interested desires — more pessimistic, perhaps, but not structurally different. However, the pessimism is so strong in *Leviathan,* and Hobbes says so little about other-regarding passions, that calling him a psychological egoist in this second sense is not an unreasonable mistake, especially because elsewhere in *Leviathan* he makes statements that seem to be explicit admissions of this interpretation of psychological egoism. For example: "of the voluntary acts of every man, the object is some *good to himself." (Lev,* 14, 8, 66; the emphasis is Hobbes's own.) Moreover, for purposes of his political argument, he might as well be a psychological egoist in this sense, because other-interested desires play no role whatsoever in his justification or explanation of the formation of the state. Nonetheless, although I admit placing a great deal of emphasis on these few sentences, they do exist, and we should not attribute to him a crude and probably false psychological view of all human motivation when his text suggests a better alternative.

But we still are not finished with our effort to determine whether or not Hobbes was a psychological egoist, because there is a third way in which this label can be understood. It can be descriptive not of the *content* of our desires but of the way in which these desires are *generated.* Granted that Hobbes believes we can have other-interested objects of desire, nonetheless, insofar as he understands our desires as generated by our inherent biological pursuit of pleasure, he makes the mechanism creating our desires fundamentally self-interested, and this might be sufficient for some people to label him a psychological egoist after all.

Consider what Hobbes understands a desire to be. It is an "endeavour" toward an object to which the body is responding with an increase in vital motions, where this increase is the physiological correlate of the psychological experience of feeling pleasure. So, for example, if I want an apple because I am hungry, not only is my desire self-regarding, but my motive for pursuing the apple is self-interested. The object of my desire is to ease my hunger with this apple, but this object is desired by me because it will increase my vital motions (i.e., give me pleasure). Hence, the cause of my

16   Gert (1978, 5) uses this phrase to describe Hobbes's psychology.

pursuing *any* object of desire is my nature as a biological creature who pursues pleasure for itself and seeks to avoid pain.

The same point can be made about the cause of my acting to achieve other-regarding objects of desire. Consider Hobbes giving alms to the beggar. Why did Hobbes perform this action? Let us say that he did it because he genuinely desired a certain other-regarding object (i.e., helping the beggar), where this desire was created in him by the process of imaginative indentification with the beggar's plight. But next we ask: What was the underlying physiological/psychological reason for his wanting this other-regarding object of desire? And we get what one would naturally describe as a self-interested answer: It is because doing so was a way for him to enhance his pleasure and decrease his pain; it "eased his distress" caused by seeing the beggar's plight.

This third sense of psychological egoism therefore depends on making a sharp distinction between desires, on the one hand, and the cause of desires, on the other hand. To see this, let us define more precisely the three types of psychological egoism presented thus far:

PE¹: the position that all of my actions are caused by my desires.

PE²: the position that all of my actions are caused by my desires and that they are in pursuit of a self-regarding *object of desire*.

PE³: the position that all of my actions are caused by my desires and that my desires are produced in me by a *"self-interested" bodily mechanism*.

Notice how the second and third interpretations are different. The second thesis concerns the content of human desires, and I have argued that Hobbes did not hold it. However, the third thesis characterizes the underlying physiological cause of a human being's desires. Hence, critical to the third view is a distinction between desires and the biological mechanism creating them. As discussed in the last section, this is a distinction Hobbes seems to respect. He never characterizes pleasure as something we desire; instead, he presents it as an experience we are biologically programmed to pursue and which the attainment of certain objects will cause. Hence, the biological pursuit of pleasure is for Hobbes part of the causal story explaining why we have desires for certain objects, but it is not itself a desire.

Bentham, who regards pleasure as the ultimate object of our desires, deliberately obscures this distinction, and if Hobbes had done so he would indeed be a psychological egoist in the second sense of that term, because even our pursuit of other-regarding objects would have to be understood as a means to an ultimate self-regarding object — our own pleasure. But the advantage of Hobbes's position is that he can maintain simultaneously that people are able to pursue other-regarding objects for their own sake (Hobbes wanted to help the beggar, not himself), but do so because these objects are pleasure-producing or pain-avoiding (the causal explanation of his wanting to help the beggar makes reference to the way in which attaining this desired object eases his pain). It is also a position that has, in my view, more intuitive appeal than Bentham's. I might badly want to help a beggar, but I might also be completely unaware that the desire for this object has been created in me because my body "gets high on it," so why attribute to me (or, for that matter, any animal) the unacknowledged and unconscious desire to get pleasure? And why distort the phenomena by saying that what I *really* want when I go after the alleviation of another's pain is the alleviation of my own distress? I may or may not be conscious of the physiological sources of desire, but I do know what I desire, and this is the distinction Hobbes's psychology respects.

Indeed, now we see how close our third definition of psychological egoism is to the first characterization of the view. Any philosopher who, like Hobbes, makes desires the sole motivators for our actions will hold psychological egoism in this third sense as long as that philosopher explains the generation of desires in the same way Hobbes did. But this means that Hume must himself be a psychological egoist in this sense, because Hume explains the generation of desires in a remarkably Hobbesian way. Consider this passage from the *Treatise* (1978, 574):

> The chief spring or actuating principle of the human mind is pleasure or pain; and when these sensations are removed, both from our thought and feeling, we are, in great measure, incapable of desire or volition. The most immediate effects of pleasure and pain are the propense and averse motions of the mind; which are diversified into volition, into desire and aversion, grief and glory, hope and fear, according as the pleasure or pain changes its situation. . . . [*Treatise*, III, iii, 1]

In order for Hume to avoid espousing the third form of psychological egoism, he would have to present either an other-interested mechanism for desire formation in us or else, at the very least, a mechanism for desire formation that is neither self-interested nor other-interested in nature. Whether or not Hume does so is something I leave for Hume scholars to debate; but on the face of it, it does not appear that he does. Indeed, I know of no modern philosopher who can be considered uncontroversially to have given a clearly worked-out conception of an other-interested or non-self-interested mechanism of desire creation. Hence, it does not seem that we are finding Hobbes or Hume guilty of holding an implausible psychological view when we call them psychological egoists in the third sense.

So, because the label 'psychological egoism' is dangerously ambiguous, I am reluctant to use it again in the course of mounting Hobbes's argument. Hence, in subsequent chapters I will describe Hobbes's psychological view of the *content* of our desires as "largely (but not exclusively) self-regarding," and I will describe his psychological/physiological view of the cause of our having desires for certain objects as "exclusively self-interested."

1.4 HUMAN EQUALITY

From his individualist and materialist conception of human beings, Hobbes draws the conclusion that human beings are equal, that is, roughly similar in terms of strength and mental ability. Because he believes that all human beings have roughly the same basic physiological construction, he refuses to recognize any qualitative or significant quantitative differences in ability, either mental or physical, among people. He points out that the weakest person is still strong enough to kill the strongest, and he believes that the least in mental ability can become, through experience, as prudent and learned as the greatest.[17]

17 See *Leviathan* (13, 1–7, 60–2), *De Cive* (*EW* ii, 1, 3, 6–7), and *Elements of Law* (I, xiv, 1–2, 53–4).

Even more interesting, however, is the fact that Hobbes derives individuals' freedom from political subjugation in the state of nature from the assumption of their rough equality with one another. This derivation strikes twentieth-century readers as very odd; we do not assume that personal equality implies freedom from political domination. The fact that Hobbes and a good many others in the sixteenth and seventeenth centuries made this inference[18] shows that during that period political subordination was conceived as subordination to a person or a group of persons. Assuming this notion of political subordination, one concludes from the fact that people are roughly equal to one another in the state of nature that no one has the superior abilities and strengths required to dominate over the others, meaning that everyone is free of "political" dominance. Since the late eighteenth century, however, Western thinkers have made a clear distinction between government as such and rulers holding governmental office, and they have regarded political subjugation as subjugation to the former, that is, to the "rule of law."[19] On this way of thinking, equality does not imply freedom from political subjugation, although it does imply freedom from personal subjugation. However, such a distinction between personal and political subjugation was not clearly made in the sixteenth and seventeenth centuries. The memories of the recent feudal past, when political power was almost completely personalized, were too strong. Whether one was a divine rights theorist or a social contract theorist during that period, one would perceive the institution of a ruler as synonymous with the creation of government.

Hobbes's assumption of human equality may strike modern readers as implausibly strong. But it is important to see that Hobbes does not need to say or even intend to say that there are no large differences in the intellectual and physical abilities among human beings; rather, he is trying to make the point that our differences are never so great as to make some of us natural slaves and others natural masters in a state of nature. Whatever differences in ability or strength or talent differentiate us, they have no *political* significance. Indeed, in *Two Treatises of Government*, Locke endorses this same conception of equality:

Though I have said . . . *that all Men by nature are equal,* I cannot be supposed to understand all sorts of Equality: *Age* or *Virtue* may give men a just precedency: *Excellency of Parts and merit* may place others above the Common Level: *Birth* may subject some, and *Alliance* or *Benefits* others, to pay an Observance to those whom Nature, Gratitude, or other Respects may have made it due; and yet all this consists with the *Equality* which all men are in, in respect of Jurisdiction or Dominion one over another, which was the equality I there spoke of, as proper to the Business in hand, being that *equal Right* that every Man hath *to his natural freedom,* without being subjected to the Will or Authority of any other Man. [2*T*, 54, 346]

18 I have found it in the works of Grotius (1925), Pufendorf (1934), and Lawson (1657) and in Locke's *Second Treatise,* where he writes that the state of nature is "A *State* also of *Equality,* wherein all the Power and Jurisdiction is reciprocal, no one having more than another: there being nothing more evident, than that Creatures of the same species and rank promiscuously born to all the same advantages of Nature, and the use of the same faculties, should also be equal one amongst another *without Subordination or Subjection.* . . ." (2*T*, 4, 309; last emphasis added).

19 One can see this as early as 1791 in Burke's "Appeal from the New to the Old Whigs." More recent political theorists have clearly made this distinction which is especially marked in the work of H. L. A. Hart (1961).

Hobbes's and Locke's point is that because no one is so superior mentally or physically as to be able to establish rulership quickly and securely over everyone else *without* their cooperation, we must be treated from a political standpoint as equal to one another—which means we are naturally subordinate to no one. Hobbes probably overstates the degree to which we are similar, but although we might want to acknowledge greater differences among us than he does, most of us agree with him (and some of us deeply so) that the differences among us are not great enough to have any political significance. We, too, reject the idea that there are natural masters and natural slaves, and we, too, believe that rulers must be chosen, because they are not naturally made. This defiant anti-Aristotelian, antimedieval position has penetrated deep into the psyche of Western society, driving movements designed to achieve political equality for racial minorities and for women. And it is a critical premiss of any social contract theory that seeks to explain political power and political subordination as something *unnatural*, something created by human beings and maintained with their consent.

Whereas Hobbes's materialism and moral relativism provoked great opposition from members of all the rival groups in England's civil wars, his egalitarian beliefs and his individualism were highly appealing to the radicals. As we shall see in Chapter 7, supporters of absolutism, like Sir Robert Filmer, found it very disconcerting to see Hobbes arriving at the royalists' conclusions by using the premisses of their opponents. Lord Clarendon called Hobbes's egalitarianism a "levelling fancy" (1676, 71), thereby linking Hobbes's beliefs with those of the Levellers, a collection of radicals who opposed the king, supported Parliament, and advocated popular control of the government and extensive suffrage.[20] Hobbes, of course, wanted to dissociate himself from all such radical "leftist" political solutions to the problems of his day. But he did agree with the radicals that there was no such thing as a natural hierarchy of men, and that neither the commands of God nor the philosophy of Aristotle could be successfully invoked to support the notion that the social and economic stratification of England was natural. In *The Elements of Law* he contends that

The question, which is the better man, is determinable only in the estate of government and policy, though it be mistaken for a question of nature, not only by ignorant men, that think one man's blood better than another's by nature; but also by [Aristotle]. [*EL*, I, xvii, 1, 87–8]

Indeed, Hobbes goes on to say that this belief in a natural hierarchy promoted by Aristotle is one of the causes of rebellion and sedition in a society. (See *EL*, I, xvii, 1, 18.) It encourages in people the sin of pride, that is, the belief that they are innately superior to others and thus are born to dominate others; and that, in turn, causes men to fight one another—even over "trifles, as a word, a smile, a different opinion, and any other sign of undervalue." (*Lev*, 13, 7, 62)

Furthermore, although Hobbes advocates absolute sovereignty, he does not support continuation of the nobility's power. His remarks on human value, worth, and honor in *Leviathan* (10, 1–35, 41–3) imply that only those people whose elevation can serve

20 Discussion of the Levellers' beliefs can be found in Hill (1975, chap. 7) and Macpherson (1977, chap. 2). See also A. S. P. Woodhouse (1966) for a collection of Leveller writings.

the nation should be so elevated by the sovereign.[21] And with a Calvinistic enthusiasm for merit and ability, he attacks the aristocrat's dominance in court:

> Good Counsell comes not by Lot, nor by Inheritance; and therefore, there is no more reason to
> expect good Advice from the rich, or noble, in matter of State, than in delineating the
> dimensions of a fortresse. [*Lev*, 30, 25, 184]

No wonder Clarendon chided Hobbes for "his extreme malignity to the Nobility, by
whose bread he hath bin alwaies sustain'd." (1676, 181–2)

Hobbes's egalitarian beliefs and his radical individualism show, I believe, how
antifeudal his conception of human beings is. By insisting on human individuality,
human equality, and the importance of self-interest in motivating us, he is rejecting
the old medieval world of natural hierarchies, fixed social roles, and static social places
and accepting instead a new characterization of human beings as (at least potentially)
economically independent and competitive people who conceive of themselves not as
members of guilds or manors or other social groups but as *individuals*. It was a picture
of humanity to which any nonconformist would be drawn, insofar as it emphasized
one's responsibility for one's own well-being in the world. And it would naturally
appeal to the rising commercial classes, anxious to destroy the remains of the old
world of status in order to develop a society allowing unfettered individual participation in the marketplace.[22]

However, whereas the Puritans and the more radical religious and political sects in
England during the 1640s used these ideas to argue for a limited, representative
government, Hobbes used them to argue that only institution of an absolute sovereign
could secure social peace. Political conservatives were appalled that he should use
these radical foundations at all. As we shall see in later chapters, they had good reason
to be worried.

1.5 HOBBES'S ETHICS

CRITICAL QUARRELS

One of the hallmarks of the nonsystematic approach to interpreting Hobbes's *Leviathan* is the claim that Hobbes has a deontological ethical position that does not rest on
his materialist psychology and that must therefore be severed from that psychology in
any successful reconstruction of his argument for absolute sovereignty. It is amazing
that a book that incited fury in the seventeenth century (and was even burned at

---

21   Indeed, in *Leviathan* (30, 16, 180), Hobbes appears to sympathize with the angry attacks
      on the nobles by the poor: "The honour of great Persons, is to be valued for the benefi-
      cence, and the aydes they give to men of inferiour rank, or not at all. And the violences,
      oppressions, and injuries they do, are not extenuated, but aggravated by the greatnesse of
      their persons; because they have least need to commit them. The consequences of this
      partiality towards the great, proceed in this manner. Impunity makes Insolence; Insolence
      Hatred; and Hatred, an Endeavour to pull down all oppressing and contumelious great-
      nesse, though with the ruine of the Common-wealth."
22   Christopher Hill (1969a, 269–79) has a nice discussion of this point. See also C. B.
      Macpherson (1977).

Oxford) because critics thought it argued for the primacy of self-interest in directing human action[23] should in the twentieth century be taken to espouse a strict deontological moral position. These strikingly different interpretations of the book strongly suggest that the ethical position Hobbes is espousing in *Leviathan* is neither clear nor simple; hence, one must move slowly and carefully through the thickets of his text to ensure than one gets Hobbes's view right.

Let us start by introducing the two fundamentally different kinds of critical interpretation of Hobbes's ethical remarks.[24] First, there is the subjectivist interpretation offered by those "systematic" critics who take seriously Hobbes's claim that his ethical views are based on his psychological and physiological theories of human behavior. On this interpretation, Hobbes supposedly understands 'good' objects or states of affairs as defined by all or some of a person's desires, and 'right' or 'rational' actions are understood instrumentally, as those actions that are the most effective ways of attaining the good (i.e., desired) objects or states of affairs. This sort of ethical view rests solidly on Hobbes's psychology and is clearly consistent with his materialist metaphysics. It presupposes no nonmaterial moral objects or qualities and no strange prescriptive powers associated with moral commands. Indeed, it presupposes only the objects of psychology, such as desires and aversions, which Hobbes believes can be reduced to talk of matter and motion. One is even able to say that this sort of moral philosophy can be "derived" from Hobbes's psychology, because it is really just a part of that psychology — specifically, the part that is concerned with what we desire and shun. And in his chart describing the relationships of the different sciences in *Leviathan,* Hobbes himself insists that ethics is simply a branch of psychology, which is itself a branch of physics (*Lev,* 9, p. 41).

This interpretation of Hobbes's remarks was certainly the one overwhelmingly adopted by Hobbes's contemporaries.[25] More recently, Peters (1956), Goldsmith (1966, 93–109), Barry (1972), Watkins (1965a, chap. 5 and chap. 7, sect. 29), and Nagel (1959, 68ff.) have offered interpretations of Hobbes's ethical remarks along these lines. These critics attribute this view to Hobbes not only on grounds of consistency but also because textual evidence from a number of Hobbes's writings supports that attribution. Consider the following important passage from Chapter 6 of *Leviathan:*

But whatsoever is the object of any mans Appetite or Desire; that is it, which he for his part calleth *Good:* And the object of his Hate, and Aversion, *Evill;* And of his Contempt, *Vile* and *Inconsiderable.* For these words of Good, Evill, and Contemptible, are ever used with relation to the person that useth them: There being nothing simply and absolutely so; nor any common Rule of Good and Evill, to be taken from the nature of the objects themselves. . . . [*Lev,* 6, 7, 24]

---

23 The University of Oxford denounced Hobbes's book and burned it, because, they said, Hobbes claimed that "self-preservation is the fundamental law of nature and supersedes the obligation of all others." From "Judgement . . . of the University," in D. Wilkins (1737, 610–12), quoted by Quentin Skinner (1972, 139). And Bishop Bramhall concluded that "where [Hobbes's] Principles prevaile, adieu honour, and honesty, and fidelity, and loyalty: all must give place to self-interest." (1658, 519)

24 These are discussed by W. H. Greenleaf (1972).

25 See Quentin Skinner (1972, esp. 138–40), John Bowle (1951), and Samuel Mintz (1969) for more discussion of contemporary reactions to Hobbes's ideas.

In this passage Hobbes is clearly defining 'good' as "what we desire," and 'bad' as "what we are averse to." Note that whereas Aristotle said that we desire what is good and hate what is evil, Hobbes says exactly the opposite: What is good is simply what we desire, and what we hate is simply what is bad.

That this is a baldly subjectivist ethical understanding of 'good' is something Hobbes seems not only to admit but also to welcome. In Chapter XI of *De Homine*, when he speaks of the profusion of desires that continue throughout one's lifetime, he contends, in opposition to Aristotle, that "one cannot speak of something as being *simply good;* since whatsoever is good, is good for someone or other. . . . Therefore good is said to be relative to person, place, and time." (*DH*, XI, 4, 47) So Hobbes is saying that, strictly speaking, when we use the word 'good' we must use it relative to an individual or set of individuals at a particular time. And despite the fact that neither of these passages expressly tells us how to define 'right' or 'rational' action, it seems reasonable to suppose that Hobbes (who was not using our more careful twentieth-century linguistic distinctions in moral terminology) means the passage to espouse a thoroughgoing ethical subjectivism. This reading is supported by the fact that in the first passage he says that there is no "common *Rule* of Good and Evill, to be taken from the nature of the objects themselves" (*Lev*, 6, 7, 24; emphasis added), suggesting that rules of action are also to be defined relative to a person's time- and place-dependent desires in an instrumentalist way. As we shall explore later, there are other passages in Hobbes's writings that support this subjectivist interpretation of 'right' or 'rational' action.

However, several critics in the twentieth century, chief among them A. E. Taylor and Howard Warrender, have steadfastly refused to attribute this conception of morality to Hobbes; they have insisted, even in the face of the textual evidence cited here, that Hobbes was an ethical objectivist, that is, one who believes we have objective and necessary moral duties known by reason that are not derived from our contingent desires. These critics have textual support of their own for this view. Consider, for example, Hobbes's definition of 'obligation' in Chapter 14 of *Leviathan:*

> when a man hath . . . abandoned, or granted away his Right; then is he said to be OBLIGED, or BOUND, not to hinder those, to whom such Right is granted, or abandoned, from the benefit of it: and that he *Ought*, and it is his DUTY, not to make voyd that voluntary act of his own: and that such hindrance is INJUSTICE. [*Lev*, 14, 7, 65]

What quotation from Kant's work could be more deontological-sounding than this? This passage shows that Hobbes is certainly prepared to use talk of rights, duties, justice, and obligation in his argument, and these concepts would seem to be the moral tools of the ethical objectivist, not those of a subjectivist of the sort Hobbes's critics have traditionally taken him to be. Moreover, this passage appears in the midst of Hobbes's attempt to define nineteen "laws of nature" that he calls "immutable and eternal" (*Lev*, 15, 38, 79), and this enterprise would certainly appear to place Hobbes in the objectivist natural law tradition.

Critics in this second objectivist camp, however, disagree with one another about what sort of objectivist view Hobbes actually held. Taylor (1965, 37ff.) argues that Hobbes was a proto-Kantian and explores a number of Kantian-sounding passages in Hobbes's writings, especially *De Cive*. Warrender's interpretation (1957, 220) is backward-looking; he sees Hobbes as a member of the divine natural law tradition going back to the Middle Ages. Finally, Bernard Gert's objectivist interpretation (1978, 15–17) is even more backward-looking; he would have us see Hobbes as an Aristotelian who argues that human reason has a goal of its own that includes the moral goal of pursuing the well-being of the society of people in a state.

I do not wish to go further into the relative merits of these different objectivist interpretations of Hobbes's ethical remarks right now, because we need to consider the more general issue whether Hobbes was endorsing *any* objectivist view at all or was in fact a subjectivist, as other critics have traditionally claimed. Of course, a thorough examination of the textual evidence is important in deciding this issue, and we shall undertake such an examination later in this chapter. But there are other kinds of evidence that I want to bring to bear on this question at this point. It seems methodologically unsound to attribute to Hobbes an ethical view that is inconsistent with the premises of his political argument or that in some way prevents him from drawing his political conclusions, if we can avoid doing so. Hence, I want to start by considering which type of ethical theory best fits with Hobbes's overall political argument.

Taylor and Warrender both admit that the objectivist ethical view they attribute to Hobbes does not sit well with his materialist psychology, particularly with his desire-based theory of human motivation. Certainly that ethical position cannot be derived from his psychology. Yet, in every one of his books, Hobbes characterizes his political argument as a "demonstration," in the style of geometry, in which his political conclusions are derived from his psychological theories, which in turn can be derived from his physiological theories of human behavior. Indeed, this is simply a consequence of his reductionist views about the relationship between "moral philosophy" and "physics" that we discussed in Section 1.3.[26] So one of the first "costs" one must pay if one attributes to Hobbes an objectivist ethical interpretation is dismissal of his own characterization of the relationship between his "Science of Moral Philosophy" (*Lev*, 15, 40, 79) and his psychology. Some critics of the Taylor-Warrender approach have been quite unwilling to pay that cost.

But an even more serious issue raised by critics of the objectivist interpretation of Hobbes's ethics is whether or not that view is straightforwardly *inconsistent* with the foundational premises of Hobbes's argument, especially with Hobbesian psychology. Although one might be able to argue successfully that regardless of what Hobbes says, his ethics and political philosophy should not be understood to be derived in any strict sense from (or reducible to) his materialist psychology, it seems much more difficult to make a plausible argument to the effect that Hobbes espoused an ethical view that was actually inconsistent with that psychology. Surely Hobbes, the philosopher who admitted to Aubrey (1898, 332) of being "in love" with geometry, would have been aware of and would have renounced such blatant inconsistency in his thought.

Yet the Taylor-Warrender thesis is certainly inconsistent with Hobbes's materialist metaphysics. On their view, a nonnatural and nonmaterial quality of "rightness" is

---

26 See *Elements of Law* (I, i, 1, 1): "The true and perspicuous explication of the elements of *laws natural and politic* dependeth upon the knowledge of what is *human nature*." (Also see *De Cive*, pref., xiv–xx; *Lev*, intro., 1–4, 1–3; "Six Lessons," *EW* vii, 184; *DH*, ep. ded., 35–6; *De Corp*, *EW* i, I, 6, 6, 72–3.)

supposed to attach to certain actions (presumably in virtue of God's commanding them) that is not reducible to any material object, certainly not to any physiological feature of human beings. Hence, this view would commit Hobbes—a philosopher with strong nominalist tendencies—to admit the reality not only of a certain property but also of a *nonmaterial* property. And there is plenty of evidence throughout Hobbes's writings that he would be loath to do any such thing; consider, for example, his rejection of nonmaterial moral objects such as the summum bonum and the golden mean postulated by Aristotelian moral theorists (*Lev,* 11, 1, 47, and 15, 40, 80). Neither Taylor nor Warrender defends attribution of this objectivist ethical view to Hobbes in the face of this inconsistency.

However, Taylor and Warrender have attempted to answer, in a very interesting way, the charge that the objectivist theory they want to attribute to Hobbes is inconsistent with his psychological views. Both insist that Hobbes's ethics and his psychology are two discrete theoretical systems that have "no logically necessary connection" with one another (Taylor 1965, 37). And both insist that these theories provide mutually consistent answers to two different kinds of questions. As Taylor puts it, the reason that one acts as one does is explained by the Hobbesian psychology, and the reason that one *ought* to act in a certain way is explained by the Hobbesian ethical theory (Taylor 1965, 36–7). Warrender elaborates further. He argues that Hobbes's psychological theory is based primarily on the assumption that the desire for self-preservation is our primary motivation, whereas the ethical theory is based on our obligation to obey God's laws. The latter theory is consistent with the former, however, because the actions that we are morally obliged to take are also actions that our self-preservation motivates us to perform. Self-preservation is a "validating" condition of moral obligation, not the source of moral obligation; that is, it explains how we are motivated to act in a certain way, but it is not the source of the moral justification for the actions we perform.[27]

Does this approach succeed in showing how Hobbes's ethical objectivism is consistent with his psychology? Thomas Nagel (1959, 68–83) argues that it does not. Specifically, he argues that Taylor's and Warrender's resolution of the consistency problem succeeds only at the price of rendering Hobbes's moral theory otiose and destroys the very notion of moral obligation that those critics are so concerned to save on Hobbes's behalf. Suppose that a person described by Hobbes's psychology must decide whether or not to keep his contract with his neighbor. According to that psychology, he will not do so if keeping the contract is counter to his best interests, but he will do so if it promotes those interests. But this means that morality cannot dictate his actions; only his (primarily) self-regarding desires dictate what he does (and sometimes this leads indirectly to the pursuit of a moral goal). Whatever moral ideas he might have in his head are ultimately irrelevant to explaining why and how he performs any action.

27 Bernard Gert's approach differs. According to Gert (1978, 15), Hobbes believed that reason has a goal of its own that includes the moral pursuit of the well-being of people in political society. But Gert notes that given Hobbes's desire-based psychology, reason is unable to motivate us to act; so he suggests (although basing this suggestion on virtually no textual evidence) that Hobbes believed that reason uses certain passions to motivate us to act where these passions just happen to have the same goals as reason.

Hence, Nagel (1959, 74–5) is right to conclude that Warrender's admission that, for Hobbes, no man can ever act voluntarily without having as an object his own personal good destroys the notion of moral obligation. On this view, morality can be only an intellectual activity, a way of looking at and evaluating events and actions in the world that can have no motivational effect on human action. Yet to strip morality of all its motivational power is to destroy in a fundamental way the essence of the concept of moral obligation and to lose a critical element of an objectivist moral theory that Warrender is most concerned to keep on Hobbes's behalf. When my judgment that "I ought to do x" can have no power to get me to do x, then there is no sense in which I can do x solely because I know I ought to do it. Or, to put it in Kantian terms, there is no way that I can do my duty for duty's sake; I can act only *according* to duty, and not *from* duty. Indeed, I can act only *from* desire.

Nagel's argument suggests another and perhaps more serious problem for the Warrender interpretation. Given Hobbes's psychology, the descriptive role that remains for morality to play on that interpretation is largely without point in Hobbes's political argument. In *Leviathan*, Hobbes is concerned with getting people to act in certain ways; in particular, he wants them to institute and maintain an absolute power. Given his psychological theory, people will do this only if they believe it is in their self-interest. Hence, self-interest is all that can yield obedience to the laws of nature and political obedience to the sovereign. But if this is so, then why should Hobbes bother to talk about any of these actions in purely descriptive moral terminology? Indeed, there would seem to be as little point in his describing them in moral terms as in aesthetic terms—either description would have no role to play in an argument designed to motivate people to institute a sovereign.

Even Warrender sometimes talks as though he is reluctant to attribute to Hobbes a deontological moral theory that has no motivational power. In a paper written to defend his interpretation, Warrender indicates that one reason why he believes a deontological moral theory must be attributed to Hobbes is that without it, Hobbes cannot secure the following concept of political obedience that, according to Warrender, people must be able to follow in order for the sovereign to remain in power, namely: "obey the sovereign to the point of suicidal risk." (1965, 96–7) According to Warrender, self-interest alone cannot bring a person to obey a sovereign to this extent, but given that Hobbes has a deontological moral theory, Warrender argues that whenever

ordinary self-interest breaks down, he can still say that the citizen has an *obligation* to uphold constituted authorities, though in Hobbes's case not to the point of extreme risk of death. And so a man may rebel to save his life, but not simply for gain, and the ordinary citizen has a duty to thwart the rebel, short of taking suicidal risks. [1965, 96]

But, quite clearly, Warrender is here attributing to Hobbes a concept of moral obligation that not only is able to motivate people to act but also can successfully combat the dictates of "the ordinary principle of mundane self-interest" (1965, 96) telling them to rebel. Such a view of moral obligation is a clear violation of Hobbesian psychology. If a Hobbesian person determines that his desires are better satisfied outside the state than in it, then given Hobbesian psychology there is nothing that can stop those desires from motivating rebellion. Certainly the mere thought that what he is doing is immoral cannot stop him; Hobbes insists that thoughts and reason are inert. So, given that Warrender believes that Hobbes's principle of political obedience is a "prescriptive principle" that "could never be derived from ordinary self-interest of the individual alone" (1965, 97), he is forced either to declare Hobbes's political argument a failure, in that it is unable to justify this principle, or to attribute to Hobbes a view that is inconsistent with his psychology, namely, that morality is objective and does have motivational power such that this prescriptive principle of political obedience can be saved. Either way, Hobbes's political argument is rendered invalid, and on the second interpretation he is convicted of holding (unaware?) a clearly inconsistent position.

It is important to appreciate that, given Hobbes's psychology, *any* objectivist interpretation of ethics, be it Aristotelian, Kantian, or a natural law view, will face the same problems plaguing Warrender's interpretation. Any such moral theory, if it is made consistent with Hobbesian psychology, will be without motivational force and a perspective that is both irrelevant to Hobbes's argument and powerless to secure any political principles; and if it is given a motivational force, it will be inconsistent with that psychology. In the end, Hobbes's insistence on espousing a largely egoistic psychology is, as Nagel appreciated, the ruin of any attempt to incorporate a moral theory into his argument in which moral action is both objective and opposed to self-interest.

But suppose we interpret Hobbes as an ethical subjectivist along the lines of the traditional interpretation. By doing so we succeed in giving him an ethical theory that not only is consistent with his psychology but also, as we discussed earlier, can be derived from it. However, we are now faced with new problems. First, how can we make sense of this view as an ethical theory at all? Second, how can we attribute this view to Hobbes and still account for the many deontological-sounding passages in Hobbes's political writings? And finally, how can this subjectivist ethical theory supply a foundation firm enough to allow for derivation of the political principles Hobbes supports?

In the rest of this chapter I want to offer at least preliminary answers to the first two questions; I want to accept in large part the traditional interpretation of Hobbes's moral theory, but in a way that will make sense of the many passages in his political writings in which moral terminology is used and that also will allow him *a kind of objectivity in ethics,* although not the kind that Kant or Aristotle tried to attribute to moral commands. In addition, although I do not subscribe to this sort of ethical theory, I shall be concerned to defend it, on Hobbes' behalf, from the charge that it is only a descriptive theory, not a truly *moral* theory.

I shall not, however, answer the third question in this chapter, because the rest of this book is an attempt to investigate and answer it. Warrender is, I believe, justifiably worried whether or not self-interest can supply an adequate foundation for Hobbes's political conclusions, and at least one seventeenth-century critic of Hobbes's work had the same worry (Filmer 1652, pref.). It is also important to note that many of the passages Taylor and Warrender find the most deontological-sounding also appear in Hobbes's discussions of political obligation. Does this kind of moral tone signal failure of Hobbes's geometric deduction of absolute sovereignty based on his largely egoistic psychology? That is one of the most important questions I shall try to answer in this book. But in the rest of this chapter, let me present and argue for the ethical subjectivism that I believe Hobbes's various remarks on ethics intend to establish.

THE WAY IN WHICH HOBBES'S MORAL VIEWS ARE SUBJECTIVIST

A moral subjectivist has a subjectivist theory of value, and we have already quoted two passages, one from *Leviathan* and the other from *De Homine*, in which Hobbes quite clearly defines 'good' in a subjectivist way. In fact, however, Hobbes's understanding of the word 'good' is a bit more sophisticated than these passages suggest. After preaching the subjectivist gospel in *De Homine*, he goes on to distinguish between two ways of using the word 'good', first, to refer to what only *seems* good to a person in a particular place and time, given his desires, and second, to refer to what *really is* good for that person, given those desires:

good (like evil) is divided into *real* and *apparent*. Not because any apparent good may not truly be good in itself, without considering the other things that follow from it; but in many things, whereof part is good and part evil, there is sometimes such a necessary connexion between the parts that they cannot be separated. . . . Whence it happens that inexperienced men that do not look closely enough at the long-term consequences of things, accept what appears to be good, not seeing the evil annexed to it; afterwards they experience damage. And this is what is meant by those who distinguish good and evil as *real* and *apparent*. [DH, XI, 5, 48]

Hobbes is making a complicated point. To say that something is good because it is desired is not to say that this object is necessarily known by the desirer to be an object of her desire. If I have a bacterial infection and I desire to get well, then I would desire an antibiotic drug if I knew that it would effect the result I wanted (i.e., an end to my disease). But if I don't know that an antibiotic is a means to that end, then I might in fact desire a certain herbal medicine that I believe will cure me but that in fact will not. In this case, the herbal medicine is only an apparent good; the antibiotic drug is the real good. But note that both are defined by reference to my desires: *In fact* I desire the herbal medicine because of a false belief I have that this is a means to another desired end, but the antibiotic drug is what I *would* desire if I had knowledge about how to effect a cure. Hobbes's point is that we can speak about a person's "real good" without become Aristotelians as long as we note that this concept is defined solely by reference to what a person would desire if the person had true beliefs.

In addition to defining what 'good' means, Hobbes also says a great deal in the early chapters of Leviathan about those things that human beings call good, given the desires that their physiological constitutions produce. Various intrinsic and interactive desires are supposed to define 'good' objects for us. But Hobbes's belief that human beings desire above all else to "avoid that which is hurtful; but most of all that terrible enemy of nature, death" (*EL*, II, xiv, 6, 71) means that self-preservation will be their greatest good, and death their greatest evil (*DH*, XI, 6, 48).

Some critics think that Hobbes is making a normative statement when he says that self-preservation is a good for us. Indeed, Gert takes Hobbes to be a kind of Aristotelian who credits our reason with defining self-preservation as our "greatest good" (Gert 1978, 13). Yet for us to attribute such a view to Hobbes not only would be to run into the sorts of problems Nagel posed for any objectivist ethical interpretation of Hobbes's position but also would be to ignore both Hobbes's blatant attacks on the Aristotelian summum bonum [e.g., his insistence in *Leviathan* that "there is no such *Finis ultimus,* (utmost ayme) nor *Summum Bonum,* (greatest Good) as is spoken of in the books of the old Morrall Philosophers" (*Lev,* 11, 1, 47)] and his insistence that 'good' is defined solely by reference to what we desire. A better interpretive strategy would seem to be to regard the Hobbesian insistence that we desire most our self-preservation as biologically based rather than ethically based. As Gert admits, Hobbes argues in *De Cive* that human beings strive to avoid death "by a certain impulsion of nature, no less than that whereby a stone moves downward." (*DC, EW* ii, 1, 7, 8) And, as we discussed in Section 1.3, Hobbes's physiological views were designed in part to explain why the passion for self-preservation should be so dominant in the human species.

Whether or not this is the correct interpretation of Hobbes's position depends on how we understand Hobbes's conception of what right or rational action is. Hobbes clearly links the notions right and rational; he says in *De Cive,* "that is done by right, which is not done against reason." (*DC, EW* ii, 1, 1, 15) So, for Hobbes, a right action is a rational action, and if he were a subjectivist he would define such action as that which would help to attain or maximize a desired object (i.e., good). Rationality would therefore be regarded by him as having instrumental value; a rational man would be one whose reason would serve his desires well by determining correctly how those desires could be satisfied. Hobbes's writings are filled with this characterization of right reason in the moral and political sphere. For example, after defining the nature of our rational deliberations in Chapter 6 of *Leviathan* in the following way,

the Appetites, and Aversions are raised by foresight of the good and evill consequences, and sequels of the action whereof we Deliberate; the good or evill effect thereof dependeth on the foresight of a long chain of consequences. [*Lev,* 6, 37, 29]

Hobbes goes on to contend that rational men are those who are very good at developing these chains of consequences:

he who hath by Experience, or Reason, the greatest and surest prospect of Consequences, Deliberates best himself; and is able when he will, to give the best counsell unto others. [*Lev,* 6, 37, 29]

Moreover, in *De Cive,* Hobbes makes his instrumentalist notion of reason crystal clear: "in the state of nature, profit is the measure of right." (*DC, EW* ii, 1, 10, 11) This instrumentalism is also implicit in his account of the role of reason in deliberation; reason aids a deliberator in determining causal connections, but it does so in the service of that person's passions, which alone can move him to act. And once we add a Bayesian theory of risk taking to Hobbes's view as a way of clarifying his intuitions in *Leviathan* about when risk taking is rational, we complete Hobbes's position on exactly how reason operates as an instrument of the passions.

But attributing to Hobbes a straightforward instrumentalist view of reason is problematic, because, as critics such as Gert have appreciated, Hobbes frequently uses the notion of rationality to condemn people who do not pursue their self-preservation. And how can an instrumentalist say that pursuing any good is contrary to reason? As Hume puts it, if one accepts the idea that reason is the slave of the passions, then

'Tis as little contrary to reason to prefer the destruction of the whole world to the scratching of my finger. 'Tis not contrary to reason for me to chuse my total ruin, to prevent the least uneasiness of an *Indian* or person unknown to me. 'Tis as little contrary to reason to prefer even my own acknowledged lesser good to my greater. [*Treatise,* II, iii, iii; 1978, 416]

Hume's point is that whereas a theorist espousing an instrumentalist conception of reason will think it contrary to reason to maintain that x causes y when x does not, he also will refuse to see that *any* preference for an object is contrary to reason, because reason does not, for such a theorist, have a goal of its own to oppose to the preference. So how can Hobbes have an instrumentalist conception of rationality when he is prepared to label as irrational those people who don't act to pursue their self-preservation?

He can have such a conception if that label's meaning is roughly equivalent to 'imprudent,' that is, if the label is critical of such people not because they are pursuing an object other than self-preservation but because they are perceived to be pursuing self-preservation *badly.* Such people would be regarded as having made a mistake in their reasoning about how to cause the desired effect, and Hobbes's condemnation would thus convict them of an error in their reasoning, not an error in what they were desiring. This would mean that Hobbes could not be taken to espouse what might be called "primitive instrumentalism," that is, the view that "any act is rational if it is one an individual determines he should take in order to fulfill his present desires." At the very least, Hobbes would have to be interpreted as espousing a more sophisticated position, which might be called "true belief instrumentalism," that is, the view that "any act is rational if it is one an individual *would* determine he *should* take to fulfill his present desires *if* he had true beliefs."

Indeed, Hobbes's distinction between "real" good and "apparent" good supplies evidence for the idea that he was prepared to call wrong (and thus irrational) those actions in pursuit of an object that an individual mistakenly believes to be the best way to achieve a desired end. Moreover, there are several passages in which Hobbes seems to be using the concept of irrationality in this way. Perhaps the most striking is a passage in *De Cive:*

since all do grant, that is done by *right,* which is not done against reason, we ought to judge those actions only *wrong,* which are repugnant to right reason, that is, *which contradict some certain truth collected by right reasoning from true principles.* [*DC, EW* ii, 2, 1, 15–16; emphasis added]

In this passage, Hobbes does not say that acting against right reason is acting against a certain desire; on the contrary, he says it is acting against "a certain truth" that reason can discern, and presumably a truth about how to effect one's desired goal. Following this passage, Hobbes presents his laws of nature, which (as I shall argue in the next subsection) he defines as causal laws about what actions are necessary for peace, itself a goal that is a means to self-preservation. These laws are "dictates of right reason" (*DC, EW* ii, 2, 1, 16), and thus acting against these dictates even while trying to pursue self-preservation is, in Hobbes's eyes, irrational, that is, imprudent. Hobbes surely doesn't mean that one must have full information about how to pursue one's goals in order to be rational, but he does seem to believe that, at the very least, one cannot be rational if one pursues a goal incorrectly in circumstances in which one could have gained access to the information one needed about how to achieve that goal. Exactly how this kind of counterfactual constraint on rationality should be structured is something Hobbes doesn't pursue. Nonetheless, in order to understand Hobbes's project in *Leviathan*, one must appreciate that his appraisal of the rebels of his day as irrational is based on his view that they did not know how to achieve what they really wanted, whereas they *could* have known how to do that if they had reasoned well:

How many kings, and those good men too, hath *this one error*, that a tyrant king might lawfully be put to death, been the slaughter of! How many throats hath this *false position* cut, that a prince for some causes may by some certain men be deposed! And what bloodshed hath not *this erroneous doctrine* caused, that kings are not superiors to, but administrators for the multitude! [*DC, EW* ii, pref., xi–xii; emphasis added]

Hobbes's point here is that the rebels were irrational not because they desired something other than self-preservation but because they failed out of ignorance to realize a state of affairs that would promote their self-preservation. (See also *DC, EW* ii, pref., xiii–xiv; and *Lev*, 29.) *Leviathan* is meant to correct that ignorance by showing how to deduce correctly the appropriate peace-producing behavior.

But there are passages in *Leviathan* in which the notion of irrationality is used in a way that cannot clearly be given this instrumentalist interpretation, and critics such as Gert therefore conclude that Hobbes must be espousing some kind of Aristotelian position in which the goal of one passion (i.e., self-preservation) is also made the goal of reason. For example, in Chapter 11 of *Leviathan*, Hobbes makes a survey of the things that dispose men to live in peace and those that dispose them to war with one another. And whereas ignorance is blamed frequently for actions leading to war and civil strife, vainglory is also made a culprit of conflict. For example:

all men that are ambitious of Military command, are enclined to continue the causes of warre; and to stirre up trouble and sedition: for there is no honour Military but by warre; nor any such hope to mend an ill game, as by causing a new shuffle. [*Lev*, 11, 4, 48]

Clearly, part of the point of this and similar passages on vainglorious men is to condemn them for their actions that threaten self-preservation. But if these people truly desire glory more than self-preservation, how can their actions be anything but right, prudent, and rational if they are intended to achieve this end, even at the expense of bringing about harm or death? Isn't Hobbes assuming that self-preservation is the goal of reason here?

No. Not only would such an interpretation be blatantly at odds with Hobbes's frequent condemnations of Aristotle's moral philosophy, with his subjectivist definition of 'good,' and with his desire-based motivational psychology, but also it would not fit the text well. This is not to say that Gert is wrong to think there is a conception of rationality at work in *Leviathan* that is not captured by the "true belief instrumentalism" I defined earlier. However, an examination of the text shows that Hobbes's actual conception of rationality is still, in an important sense, instrumentalist, and certainly not an Aristotelian conception.[28]

---

28 I am indebted to discussions with Thomas Hill and David Gauthier for helping me to clarify Hobbes's conception of rationality at this point.

Derek Parfit has recently defined a conception of rationality that is quite close to (although, as I shall argue later, not exactly like) the conception that I want to argue Hobbes espoused; Parfit calls it the "Deliberative Theory of Rationality":

What each of us has reason to do is what would best achieve, not what he *actually* wants, but what he *would* want, at the time of acting, if he had undergone a process of 'ideal deliberation' — if he knew the relevant facts, was thinking clearly, and was free from distorting influences. [1984, 118]

On this view, rationality is still understood as an instrument of the passions, but only when it is functioning correctly. This view holds that our actions are "really," as opposed to "apparently," rational (to borrow the terminology Hobbes employed to define 'good') not only when we have true beliefs but also when we take those actions after properly using those beliefs in syllogistic reasoning that is valid.

The best evidence that Hobbes actually embraced something like this conception of rationality comes from a passage in *De Cive* in which he contends that reason "is no less a part of human nature, then any other faculty or affection of the mind [and] is also termed natural." (*DC, EW* ii, 2, 1, 16) If reasoning reduces to a physiological process, then this physiological process can become disrupted in a human being by abnormal bodily motions, or what we would call a disease, and her rational pursuit of self-preservation can thus become disrupted. When this disruption occurs, it would seem appropriate to call her actions irrational insofar as they are not the best means to the objects she desires.

The group of people who behave irrationally when their reasoning processes have been disrupted in this way would certainly seem to include the mentally ill or insane, and Hobbes himself explicitly calls insane those who try to commit suicide, insofar as he believes that this sort of action is a sign that the person's normal bodily processes have been disrupted:

I conceive not how any man can bear *animum felleum*, or so much malice towards himself, as to hurt himself voluntarily, much less to kill himself. For naturally and necessarily the intention of every man aimeth at somewhat which is good to himself, and tendeth to his preservation. And therefore, methinks, if he kill himself, it is to be presumed that he is not *compos mentis*, but by some inward torment or apprehension of somewhat worse than death, distracted. [*A Dialogue of the Common Laws, EW* vi, 88]

And in *Leviathan*, Hobbes defines madness as "too much appearing Passion" (*Lev*, 8, 23, 36), in the context of trying to get across the idea that a mad person is one who has been beset by certain extreme bodily motions causing strong passions that usurp the rational pursuit of his predominant, ruling passion for his own preservation. A body whose vital motions produce the desire to harm itself or kill itself is different from the usual, indeed, so different that we call it sick. Suppose a dog tried to wound itself, or a cat sought to drown itself; something would be seriously abnormal about such creatures. We would think them diseased or sick, and Hobbes's reaction to human beings who strive to kill themselves is the same. And it would seem that little or nothing such people do while they are in this diseased state — in which appropriate syllogistic reasoning is perverted or completely disrupted — can be called 'rational.'

But what is particularly interesting for our purposes is the fact that Hobbes puts people who only *occasionally* threaten their self-preservation through pursuit of glory in the same class as the totally insane! Although a glory-prone individual is not totally crazy, Hobbes still contends that this sort of person suffers from bouts of madness:

The Passion, whose violence, or continuance maketh Madnesse, is either great *vaine-Glory;* which is commonly called *Pride,* and *selfe-conceipt;* or great *Dejection* of mind. [*Lev*, 8, 18, 35]

Similarly, in *De Homine,* Hobbes says that

Excessive self-esteem impedes reason; and on that account it is a perturbation of the mind, wherein a certain swelling of the mind is experienced because the animal spirits are transported. [*DH*, XII, 9, 60]

In this last passage Hobbes adds to this descriptive statement a remark that at least *appears* to be normative: "Proper self-esteem, however, is not a perturbation, but a state of mind that ought to be." (*DH*, XII, 9, 60–1) It is the 'ought' here that is puzzling. But I would argue that Hobbes meant the 'ought' merely to signify that this sort of body is one we consider "normal for nature," that is, working as nature intended and not diseased in any way, such that correct syllogistic deliberations can take place. And his use of 'rational' to describe those who effectively pursue self-preservation rather than competing objects such as glory rejects the idea that reason is only a handmaiden to the passions when it is functioning properly.

Indeed, we also use the word 'rational' in this sense. David Pears has recently defined what he calls 'motivated irrationality,' from which weak-willed and self-deceiving people are supposed to suffer; it is, in his words, the "failure to make proper use of material already in the mind." (1984, 6) Proper use, for Pears, means, at least in part, prudent use. And one of the styles of explanation Pears discusses for why a weak-willed person would fail to make proper use of his reason sounds very Hobbesian: Such people are prevented from effectively pursuing what they "really" want by the intervention of a powerful "wish" that perverts the normal functioning of their reason in pursuit of their primary goal, where the wish "works like an expert in demolition" (1984, 157, and chap. 2). Hobbes would certainly accept the gist of this explanation of why glory-prone individuals are irrational, while expressing it differently. He would say that such people are prevented by a physical disorder from deliberating properly, meaning that they are unable to arrive at the correct action to further self-preservation (glory perverts their deliberations, acting "like an expert in demolition").[29]

Still, Gert seems to be right that many of these passages critical of glory-seeking people appear to be critical of the desire itself, and not merely critical of how people reason when they are afflicted by the desire. Yet I want to propose that these passages are still consistent with Hobbes's instrumentalist conception of reason if we take Hobbes to be suggesting that an action is irrational if it is taken from desires (such as the desire for glory) that are themselves produced by a diseased and abnormal physiological state, such that these people cannot rationally pursue the object they *naturally* want when they are not in this diseased state. I am contending that Hobbes embraced a conception of rationality that is related to but nonetheless slightly different from the "deliberative" conception defined by Parfit. I call it the "healthy deliberation" con-

---

29 Nonetheless, Hobbes does think glory-prone people are not so sick that they cannot pursue self-preservation when the threat to life is severe enough (*Lev*, 11, 12, 49).

ception of rationality: *What each of us has reason to do is what will best achieve not what he actually wants, but what he would want, at the time of acting, if he had undergone a process of "ideal deliberation" in which a) he knew all the relevant facts (where he "could have" known these facts, in some relevant sense of that phrase), b) his reasoning was free from distorting influences, and c) he was not affected by desires produced in him by diseased physiological processes.* On this conception of rationality there are actually three ways in which a person can go wrong such that he acts irrationally [whereas Parfit's definition isolates only two ways, equivalent to (a) and (b) being false]. A person can reason using incorrect beliefs and arrive at an incorrect conclusion, or he can fail to reason properly insofar as physiologically he is subject to "perverting influences" (e.g., a "swelling of the animal spirits"), or he can have desires that are themselves produced in him by abnormal bodily motions indicative of disease that, although not destroying his ability to deliberate syllogistically, nonetheless render impotent his normal primary desire (i.e., the desire for self-preservation) to effect action. The desire for glory, which Hobbes describes as a kind of madness reflecting a physiological perversion, is an example of a disease-produced desire. But can Hobbes criticize a sick person's desires in this way while still preserving his instrumentalist conception of rationality and his subjectivist commitment to desires as determiners of the good?

He can do so in two ways. First, if he assumes that diseased people don't want to be diseased but desire instead the state of health, then he can also attribute to them a higher-order desire to have the desires of a healthy body rather than the desires of a sick one. This would mean that a manic-depressive's desire to commit suicide defines only an *apparent* good rather than a *real* good if he has a higher-order desire not to have the desire to commit suicide. Hence, to the extent that a person wants not to have certain (disease-produced) desires, the goods defined by these desires are also unwanted, and his pursuit of these objects that are not real goods can legitimately be criticized as irrational on the sole basis of what he desires.

Most sick people do want to be healthy, as our crowded health care systems attest. But not every sick person desires to get well; some are so sick that they resist treatment, maintaining that sickness or death is what they really want. If Hobbes persists in saying that such people really want health, despite their protestations to the contrary, isn't he being an Aristotelian?

Not necessarily. Hobbes can say that people who are diseased and who have desires to remain sick or to die are victims of a *biological* mistake produced by the disease itself. Their bodily motions are so disrupted that they become completely incapable of recognizing what will increase their vital motions (i.e., give them pleasure), and it is in virtue of this massive biological misfiring that they are called irrational.

Moreover, this use of the word 'irrational' can still be called instrumentalist, because by using it Hobbes is saying that sick people are making a mistake about how to pursue pleasure, although they do not make a cognitive error in pursuit of an object of desire, but a completely noncognitive biological "error" in the process of forming a desire. It is not that such people don't know how to attain their desired goods, nor even necessarily that their reasoning processes have been disrupted by desire, but rather that they have been rendered incapable of properly forming desires for objects because their physiological processes involving pleasure pursuit have been disrupted by disease. In other words, the disease has disrupted the "desire-formation mechanism," such that the desires that get produced are "wrong" — indicative only of the fact that these people are sick. So we attribute to a delirious person who resists medical treatment the desires of a healthy body, rather than the desires such people actually have, because we think their actual desires "spurious" in virtue of the fact that the desires are the products of a disease. They are, in an important sense, not desires that these people really have.

So, on this conception of rationality, reason is to be considered the instrument of only real desires, not spurious desires. Or, to put it another way, an action is rational only if it is in pursuit of an object we really want, not one we want only because we are in some way sick, or physically damaged, such that this desire represents a biological mistake. Hobbes would contend that this is why we regularly dismiss certain (and sometimes even all) desires of diseased people.

This "healthy deliberation" conception of rationality is also not an Aristotelian conception of reason. Hobbes is not saying that reason has a goal of its own that we "ought" to pursue. Rather, he is presupposing that in other to call something a "real good" (as opposed to an "apparent good"), that object must be the product of a certain kind of passion, namely, one that is produced by a healthy human body, not by just *any* desire. Desires still define what is good, but only certain desires define what is a real good, namely, those desires that one will have when one has true beliefs, a well-functioning reasoning process, and a well-functioning desire-formation mechanism.

However, this way of talking presupposes that we can distinguish between normal and abnormal physiological states and that we can define a physiological state that "ought to be." Is there anything illicit about a subjectivist such as Hobbes presupposing these ways of talking? I think not — any doctor tries to make these distinctions on strictly biological grounds (and thus assumes they can be made) in her daily practice and continually tries to transform sick patients into healthy ones. And the doctor is not making a moral evaluation of her patients when she calls them sick; rather, she is making a biological categorization of them based on her knowledge of standard physiological processes in the human organism. Similarly, Hobbes would insist that his medical use of 'sick' or 'non compos mentis' or 'irrational' is no more morally evaluative than the doctor's and rests on the same biological categorization. Indeed, I would even contend it is a notion of rationality that twentieth-century thinkers should take seriously. It offers a "naturalistic" way to criticize desires without making what many would consider to be the implausible claim that some desires are "inherently" irrational, or that reason has goals of its own.

Indeed, it is not this conception of rationality that is likely to disturb readers so much as Hobbes's assumption, as he uses this conception, that healthiness invariably consists in desiring to preserve one's life above all else, such that anyone in whom this desire is not preeminent is automatically supposed to be diseased. This medical description betrays the same implausibly strong commitment to self-preservation as the "normal" pursuit of human beings in all circumstances that we have already noticed in other passages of Hobbes's political writings. But, as I said previously, whether Hobbes needs such an implausibly strong physiological view to argue successfully for the sovereign's institution, or whether he can be content with a milder reading of the physiological naturalness of the desire for self-preservation (such that someone can be physiologically normal and healthy but still prefer death to self-preservation in certain circumstances) is an issue we shall be exploring later in this book.

I have spent a great deal of time on Hobbes's subjectivism not only because it is important to get Hobbes's meta-ethical views straight but also because it allows us to see that Hobbes has three ways of criticizing people as irrational: People can do the wrong thing because they have mistaken beliefs, because their reasoning processes have been disrupted, or because the mechanism of desire formation in their bodies is diseased. These distinctions will be critically important in Chapters 2 and 3 as we strive to determine why Hobbes believes that the state of nature degenerates into a state of war.

HOBBES'S OBJECTIVE SCIENCE OF MORAL PHILOSOPHY

In order to understand the force of Hobbes's moral imperatives, we need to understand in what sense he claimed to have a "science of moral philosophy." Unfortunately, there appear to be maddening inconsistencies and confusions throughout Hobbes's writings on the nature of science and scientific methodology that probably rest, in the end, on an equivocation about the nature of truth.[30] But his predominant view of science rests on a correspondence theory of truth, and it is important for us to understand this view so that we can correctly interpret what he calls his "science" of moral philosophy. Moreover, by doing so we shall also gain insight into his motivations for writing *Leviathan* and the method of argument he used in that book. Finally, although this view of science is undercut by another and inconsistent conception associated with a "retreat" to a conventionalist view of truth, even the muddles that this inconsistency creates have interesting implications for our understanding of his moral and political views.

Much historical work has yet to be done to learn how Hobbes was affected by the skeptical views of the men with whom he frequently discussed philosophy during his sojourns in Paris, among them Mersenne, Gassendi, and Descartes (Popkin 1982, 133–48). In the skeptical environment of seventeenth-century Paris, these and other thinkers questioned the extent to which we had criteria for determining what was true, and their questioning involved not only the kind of "radical doubt" characteristic of Cartesian methodology but also more quotidian worries about positions that seemed far less well founded than the existence of the external world, including

---

30 However, I believe at least some of the confusion surrounding Hobbes's philosophy of science is generated by us rather than by him. Were Hobbes's views on science to be read in the context of the philosophy of science of his day, we would have a much better understanding of his position. For example, he occasionally shows signs of espousing the hypothetico-deductive model of scientific methodology [see McNeilly's discussion (1969, 71–6)]; yet, insofar as Hobbes's use of the word 'hypothesis' is taken as evidence for this espousal, we should be sure that Hobbes was not using the word in its Aristotelian sense to mean a "statement that posits the existence or inexistence of something." [See Roberto Torretti (1978, 5ff.) for a discussion of the terminology of Aristotelian and Euclidean science.] For if he was, then the methodology he espouses would have to be understood to be Aristotelian, not hypothetico-deductive as we understand that phrase. Other passages in *De Corpore* also suggest that Hobbes was influenced by the Cartesian scientists of his day. We await a definitive study on this aspect of Hobbes's thinking.

Aristotelian physics (attacked, for example, by Mersenne and Charron) and, most important for our purposes, the idea that there is an established and objective body of moral truths. Several thinkers, among them François de La Mothe Le Vayer, followed Michel de Montaigne in putting forward skeptical positions on the existence of moral truths that made use of the fact that men in different cultures and at different times had disagreed dramatically on questions of what was right and wrong.[31]

Nonetheless, these skeptics' intentions were not merely destructive. Descartes was concerned to sweep away all that could be doubted in order to find a foundation on which to build true theories of the world. Likewise, Hobbes was concerned in all of his writings to sweep away the cobwebs of false and outmoded theories — particularly what he called the "filth and fraud" in Greek philosophy (*De Corp, EW* i, ep. ded., ix) — in order to make room for science (or philosophy, for he uses these words interchangeably). In the Epistle Dedicatory to *De Corpore*, he celebrated Copernicus, Galileo, and Harvey as men who established new doctrines of knowledge in modern times, and he perceived himself to be one of this small company of scientists whose use of reason was helping us to achieve *certainty* [that is his word (*De Corp, EW* i, ep. ded., xiii–ix)] in our knowledge of the world. Indeed, when reading *Leviathan* or *De Corpore*, one is struck by Hobbes's supreme confidence that human beings can ascertain the truth about the world through the use of reason, and it is partly this confidence that drives his own encyclopedic project. That confidence, however, was sometimes shaken. As we shall see, a kind of skeptical despair occasionally creeps into *Leviathan* that causes him to wonder if any sense can be made of the confusing and chaotic world in which we live. But generally Hobbes maintains what seems an almost naive faith in the power of human reason to penetrate the mysteries of the world, a faith that was certainly pervasive among many intellectuals of his day.

How is it that modern thinkers are to attain knowledge of the world? According to Hobbes, the key to its penetration is the proper use of reason:

Philosophy seems to me to be amongst men now, in the same manner as corn and wine are said to have been in the world in ancient time. For from the beginning there were vines and ears of corn growing here and there in the fields; but no care was taken for the planting and sowing of them. Men lived therefore upon acorns; or if any were so bold as to venture upon the eating of those unknown and doubtful fruits, they did it with danger of their health. In like manner, every man brought Philosophy, that is, Natural Reason, into the world with him; for all men can reason to some degree, and concerning some things: but where there is need of a long series of reasons, there most men wander out of the way, and fall into error for want of method, as it were for want of sowing and planting, that is, of improving their reason. [*De Corp, EW* i, I, 1, 1, 1]

But what is right reason? Hobbes seeks to define it in *Leviathan*. He starts in Chapter 3 simply by defining mental activity or thinking, which he claims is always regulated "by some desire or designe" (*Lev*, 3, 4, 9): "From Desire, ariseth the Thought of some means we have seen produce the like of that which we ayme at; and from the thought of

---

31 See de La Mothe Le Vayer's "Discours pour Montrer que les Doutes . . ." (1669, 115–20) and Montaigne's "Apologie de Raimond Sebond" (1922, 147). Montaigne used the practices of the savages of America, cases in ancient literature, and the mores of contemporary Europe to question the existence of any objective moral knowledge in the world. Popkin discusses this (1979, 51), as well as de La Mothe Le Vayer's views (1979, 94).

that, the thought of means to that mean; and so continually, till we come to some beginning within our own power." (*Lev*, 3, 4, 9) Hobbes goes on to explain that there are two kinds of "regulated" means—ends thinking: One involves going from the effect or the goal to the cause or means to produce it, and this is a form of thinking that both animals and humans can do; the second involves going from the cause or the means to all the effects or goals that can be produced by it, something that only humans can do (*Lev*, 3, 5, 9).

Next, Hobbes goes on in the same chapter to define 'prudence' as the ability to determine what effects will be brought about by one's actions.[32] But what is important for our purposes is that in Chapter 5 he distinguishes between prudence and genuine reasoning by saying that reasoning must involve the use of language, whereas prudential thought need not: "For REASON, in this sense, is nothing but *Reckoning* (that is, Adding and Subtracting) of the Consequences of generall names agreed upon, for the *marking* and *signifying* of our thoughts." (*Lev*, 5, 2, 18) So, when we reason, we are simply carrying out, using language, more sophisticated cause-and-effect chains of thinking:

The Use and End of Reason, is not the finding of the summe, and truth of one, or a few consequences, remote from the first definitions, and settled significations of names; but to begin at these; and proceed from one consequence to another. [*Lev*, 5, 4, 19]

In the end, reason is barely, but nonetheless importantly, distinguishable from mere prudence; they are different because reason is not

gotten by experience onely; as Prudence is; but attayned by Industry; first in apt imposing of Names; and Secondly by getting good and orderly Method in proceeding from the Elements, which are Names, to Assertions made by Connexion of one of them to another; and so to Syllogismes, which are the Connexions of one Assertion to another, till we come to a knowledge of all the Consequences of names appertaining to the subject in hand; and that is it, men call SCIENCE. [*Lev*, 5, 17, 21]

But what is the "apt imposing of Names," and why is it so important?

One point Hobbes is certainly trying to make is that a language user has the capacity to reason syllogistically and thus to arrive at conclusions that are logically necessary and are true provided that the premises of the syllogism are true. A syllogism "is nothing but a collection of the sum of two propositions, joined together by a common term, which is called the *middle term*." (*De Corp, EW* i, I, 4, 6, 48) If two names are copulated in a proposition, and the second name is copulated with a third name in another proposition, then the first and third names can be copulated in a third proposition that is true provided the first and second propositions are true. Hence, a scientist is a person who reasons logically about the world after rightly naming and defining the world around him:

a demonstration is a syllogism, or series of syllogisms, derived and continued, from the definitions of names, to the last conclusion. And from hence it may be understood, that all true ratiocination, which taketh its beginning from true principles, produceth science, and is true demonstration. [*De Corp, EW* i, I, 6, 16, 86]

32 Given that this would seem to involve the second kind of regulated thought (going from causes to effects), which only humans have, it is strange to see Hobbes maintaining that animals have prudence as well as humans.

However, not only does Hobbes perceive science as a discipline that follows a logical method to yield *logically necessary* truths, he also sees it as having a certain *content,* in which necessity of a very different and *causal* sort is made manifest. The official Hobbesian definition of "Philosophy" or "Science" goes as follows:

PHILOSOPHY is such knowledge of effects or appearances, as we acquire by true ratiocination from the knowledge we have first of their causes or generations. [*De Corp, EW* i, I, 1, 2, 3]

Similarly, Hobbes insists in *Leviathan* that "Science is the knowledge of Consequences." (*Lev,* 5, 17, 21) In other words, science seeks to know about a world that is experienced by us as filled with change — objects move, they degenerate or generate, and they affect one another in many ways. Hobbes argues in *De Corpore* that the foundation of such a world can be revealed to us "without method," for the causes of such changes "are manifest of themselves, or (as they say commonly) known to nature" — and he contends that the cause of all change is *motion* (*De Corp, EW* i, I, 6, 5, 69). Hence, the first principles of science must explain and reveal the causal connection of objects in the world by appeal to certain *laws of motion,* one of which Hobbes is prepared to state, namely, Galileo's law of inertia (*De Corp, EW* i, II, 9, 7, 124–5; see also I, 6, 6, 70–73).

Moreover, when Hobbes speaks of the causal connection of objects that follow these laws of motion, he characterizes this connection as necessary:

And seeing a necessary cause is defined to be that, which being supposed, the effect cannot but follow; this also may be collected, that whatsoever effect is produced at any time, the same is produced by a necessary cause. For whatsoever is produced, in as much as it is produced, had an entire cause, that is, had all those things, which being supposed, it cannot be understood but that the effect follows; that is, it had a necessary cause. [*De Corp, EW* i, II, 9, 5, 123]

This necessary connection clearly is not logical; indeed, it is inexplicable unless we believe with Hobbes that such necessity is simply "manifest" in experience. Hume's attack on this notion of causal necessity fairly leaps from the pages of *Leviathan* and *De Corpore,* and yet Hobbes himself was too committed to the concept of causal necessity even to question the notion in any of his works.

Note that the picture of science that emerges from these passages is one that presupposes the correspondence theory of truth. A true scientific proposition is one that corresponds to the way the world is. In science, objects are correctly described, and causal connections are correctly drawn and are derivable from first principles that we *know* describe the world, because they are, in Hobbes's words, "self-evident" or "manifest."

After setting out his conception of science in *Leviathan* and *De Corpore,* Hobbes goes on to explain in both works the purpose of science. It is his view that we do not engage in this descriptive project solely or even primarily because we value the acquisition of truth about the world for its own sake. Instead, he believes that true scientific descriptions of causes and effects are valuable to us because they are *useful* to us:

The *end* or *scope* of philosophy is, that we may make use to our benefit of effects formerly seen; or that, by application of bodies to one another, we may produce the like effects of those we conceive in our mind, as far forth as matter, strength, and industry, will permit, *for the commodity of human life.* [*De Corp, EW* i, I, 1, 6, 7; emphasis added]

Reminiscent of Bacon,[33] Hobbes asserts that the search for knowledge is the search for power: "The end of knowledge is power . . . the scope of all speculation is the performing of some action or thing to be done." (*De Corp, EW* i, I, 1, 6, 7) Thus, science, for Hobbes, has a prescriptive role as well as a descriptive role. It not only describes the world but also gives us the information we need to control it in order to satisfy our desires. If we want to shoot a cannonball to destroy our enemy in battle, or if we want to change our body chemistry to kill bacteria, science gives us the causal information we need to do these things.

Having seen how Hobbes understands the nature of science, we are now in a position to appreciate how significant it is that he calls his body of ethical views a "science" at the end of Chapter 15 of *Leviathan*. After completing his definition of nineteen moral laws of nature, he maintains that "the science of them is the true and onely moral philosophy." (*Lev*, 15, 40, 79) Because science previously had been defined as "knowledge of consequences," is he saying that these nineteen laws give us causal knowledge about the world?

Indeed he is, as he goes on to explain. Repeating his subjectivist definitions of 'good' and 'evil' from Chapter 6, he says:

For Morall Philosophy is nothing else but the Science of what is *Good*, and *Evill*, in the conversation, and Society of mankind. *Good*, and *Evill*, are names that signifie our Appetites, and Aversions; which in different tempers, customes, and doctrines of men, are different. . . . [*Lev*, 15, 40, 79]

At this point, Hobbes's moral philosophy sounds like little more than an anthropological study — it certainly would appear to be wholly descriptive rather than a prescriptive enterprise. But this is a premature conclusion. He goes on to note that although men differ greatly in what they desire, "all men agree on this, that Peace is Good." (*Lev*, 15, 40, 80) In *De Homine*, Hobbes calls this type of good (i.e., one that all human beings want and that they can all share) a "common good"; economists today would say that such a good is in perfect joint supply. But recall that Hobbes also distinguishes between two sorts of desired goods: real and apparent. The former is what a person would desire if he had true beliefs as well as a rightly functioning reason and desire-formation system in his body; the latter is what a person actually desires given the beliefs that he has and the physiological state he is in. Therefore, when Hobbes speaks about moral philosophy as the science of what is good in the conversation of mankind, he is not being completely clear. He is not interested merely in what people actually seek, given their desires, as means to achieving those desires; he is also interested in what they *should* seek as means to achieving them (i.e., the correct or most effective way to realize the object they are pursuing). Peace is, in his eyes, a "real" common good insofar as it actually does lead to the furtherance of what people desire most — their self-preservation. Moreover, he also believes that peace is actually perceived by all men as a good — the apparent and the real coincide in this case. But what is not so manifest to all men is that if peace is good, then also

---

33 Hobbes was Bacon's secretary as a young man and had philosophical discussions with him (Aubrey 1898, 331).

the way, or means of Peace, which (as I have shewed before) are *Justice, Gratitude, Modesty, Equity, Mercy,* & the rest of the Laws of Nature, are good; that is to say *Morall Vertues;* and their contrarie *Vices,* Evill. [*Lev,* 15, 40, 80]

Hobbes believes that the laws of nature assert a causal connection between these cooperative forms of behavior and self-preservation, insofar as these forms of behavior effect peace (although they do so only in certain circumstances that he specifies when he defines them), and peace in turn helps to effect longer life.

Thus, when Hobbes calls his laws of nature "Conclusions, or Theoremes concerning what conduceth to the conservation and defence of [people]" (*Lev,* 15, 41, 80), he is saying that they are statements of causal connection between a common desired object and certain cooperative actions. So moral science, just like any other science, gives us causal knowledge about the world, and it is useful to us in the same way as any other science; that is, it supplies us with the causal information (in this case, about how to attain peace) we need in order to get what we want. Indeed, its results amount to *prescriptions* concerning how we are to behave to achieve peace. They are what Kant would call hypothetical imperatives,[34] of the following form: *If one wants x, one ought to do y, where x is peace, a common instrumental goal desirable insofar as it is necessary for self-preservation, and y is the action that, when performed in conjunction with others' performance of the same action, will help to effect the achievement of peace.* So Hobbes's moral science is as much a prescriptive enterprise as any other science. Just as a metallurgist who sees a group of people trying unsuccessfully to create an alloy can help them by giving them the causal information they lack, Hobbes believes that he can help the people of his day accomplish their ultimate goals by giving them information that will enable them to avoid pursuing only apparent goods rather than real goods. Thus, he perceives his role to be one that any good scientist plays, that is, the role of giving people the causal information they lack so that they can achieve what they desire:

the utility of moral and civil philosophy is to be estimated, not so much by the commodities we have by knowing these sciences, as by the calamities we receive from not knowing them. Now, all such calamities as may be avoided by human industry, arise from war, but chiefly from civil war; for from this proceed slaughter, solitude, and the want of all things. But the cause of war is not that men are willing to have it; for the will has nothing for object but good, as least that which seemeth good. Nor is it from this, that men know not that the effects of war are evil; for who is there that thinks not poverty and loss of life to be great evils? The cause, therefore, of civil war is, that men know not the causes neither of war nor peace, there being but few in the world that have learned those duties which unite and keep men in peace, that is to say, that have learned the rules of civil life sufficiently. Now, the knowledge of these rules is moral philosophy. [*De Corp, EW* i, I, 1, 7, 8]

In other words, Hobbes perceives his theorizing to be valuable, because whereas people in the past had been willing to pursue peace because they knew that it was a real good, they did not know how to achieve this goal, and thus ended up performing actions that resulted in war rather than peace. I shall be arguing in this book that Hobbes's argument in *Leviathan* is meant to demonstrate the truth of a certain critical piece of causal information, that is, that the institution of a sovereign is necessary to

---

34 Watkins (1965a, 75–99) also invokes Kant's phrase to describe Hobbes's laws.

achieve peace. I shall also be saying a great deal more in Chapter 3 about the structure of all his laws of nature and how they dictate peace.

Would that I could stop here, confident of having adequately represented Hobbes's view of science in general and moral science in particular! But the confusions in Hobbes's thinking in this matter do not make interpretation so easy. Intermixed with this view of science as an enterprise concerned with deriving causal propositions from first principles of motion that are true insofar as they correspond with the world is a rather different picture of scientific methodology resting on a conventionalist account of truth. There is a side to Hobbes that seems to have given up on the prospect of attaining true representations of the world, and instead believes that we can only construct a science based on first principles that are "made" true by convention.[35]

This conventionalism has a tendency to affect not only his characterization of science but also his view of moral philosophy.[36] The subjectivist definition of 'good' in Chapter 6 (*Lev*, 6, 7, 24) of *Leviathan* as "whatever a person desires" can be read as a way of saying that there is no "natural" definition of these terms that all men can accept, and the sovereign is frequently presented as necessary in order to define moral truths that do not exist naturally, as when Hobbes says that "the makers of civil laws, are not only declarers but also makers of justice and injustice." (*Lev*, 42, 107, 306; quoted by Watkins 1965a, 154; see also *Lev*, 18, 9, 91; 26, 4, 137; 29, 6, 168; and 42, 78, 295) Indeed, Hobbes defines his own project in *De Cive* as demonstrating

that there are no authentical doctrines concerning right and wrong, good and evil, besides the constituted laws in each realm and government. [*DC*, *EW* ii, pref., xiii]

And this demonstration certainly seems to presuppose showing that there are no *natural* doctrines of right and wrong, good and evil, capable of being discerned (e.g., by reason) and accepted by human beings inside or outside a civil society.

I shall argue in later chapters that the sovereign does have a considerable role to play in defining moral rules by convention. However, I also believe that just as it is a mistake to think that conventionalism is Hobbes's dominant position on truth, it is a mistake to think that moral conventionalism per se is the dominant position on moral truth in Hobbes's political writings. I do want to argue (and shall do so in Chapter 3) that for Hobbes morality is "convention-based" in the sense that the cooperative actions dictated in the laws of nature are rational for individuals to perform — and indeed will produce peace — only if others in society perform them also, that is, only if a convention exists about performing these actions. But I do not think that these laws of nature are themselves true by convention. The laws of nature are meant to describe what in fact is necessary for peace to be realized: namely, the institution of certain conventions disposing men to act cooperatively. The necessity of these conventions for the achievement of peace is not, however, conventional; for

---

35 See discussions of this by McNeilly (1969, chap. 3 and 4); and Watkins (1965a, sect. 28).
36 See Watkins (1965a, sect. 29) for a discussion of this point. It is odd that Watkins believes Hobbes to have eschewed conventionalism in physics but to have adopted it in the area of morality, given that Watkins is sensitive to the fact that Hobbes regards morality as a branch of physics and thus as inextricably tied to it. My view is that Hobbes usually embraces a nonconventionalist position in both areas, but occasionally, in despair, slips into a conventionalist position in both areas.

Hobbes, their institution is causally necessary, given the way the world is, for the attainment of this end.

Indeed, the very fact that Hobbes wrote *Leviathan* is evidence that, in the end, he rejected the idea that moral truths could be only conventional. *Leviathan* presents, after all, an elaborate argument in defense of the second law of nature, commanding people to institute a sovereign in order to attain peace. The truth of this law is not conventional; rather, it is true because it describes correctly the causal connection between peace and actions bringing about the sovereign's institution. And this causal connection is supposed to be important to us insofar as (almost) all of us agree that peace is desirable. So if there could be no moral truths outside of those conventionally established, Hobbes's project in *Leviathan* would be impossible. The considerable moral chaos about which he worries would be complete and irremediable, because the ultimate peace producer, the sovereign, could not be instituted. It is Hobbes's deepest faith that he can show a *necessary causal connection* between at least one cooperative project (i.e., the institution of the sovereign) and peace.

If we stop for a moment to take stock of the virtues of Hobbes's "moral science," we can appreciate, I think, why he should have regarded it so proudly as an intellectual achievement equal to those produced by Galileo, Harvey, Kepler, and Copernicus.

First, Hobbes's moral science has a way of accounting for why the moral laws of nature are true. The traditional moral theorist claimed to issue moral commands that were objectively true; yet such a theorist always found it difficult to explain how this was so, sometimes doing so only by postulating strange moral objects or strange moral properties that had prescriptive powers. However, Hobbes's explanation of the truth of moral laws is easy and straightforward; the moral laws are true to the extent that they state correctly what actions will effect longer life. That is, they are true in the same way as any conditional cause-and-effect proposition in a physical science. Indeed, Hobbes can even regard himself as a "moral objectivist" of sorts, because he has shown that moral propositions can be understood to be objectively true and necessary if they are interpreted as assertions of a causal connection between certain actions and a desired common goal. Of course, this is not the sort of objectivity a Kantian or Aristotelian wants, particularly because Hobbes's objectively true moral prescriptions can move someone to act only if that person happens (contingently) to desire that common goal. But for Hobbes this is the only kind of objective truth that *any* proposition, including moral propositions, can have. The attraction of this approach to moral objectivity has persisted to the present day.[37] Indeed, what this shows is that we should beware of the terms 'subjective' and 'objective' in moral theory, because they do not necessarily mark the right distinctions. Hobbes is a subjectivist in the sense that he defines value as subjective preference: For him, there is no objective good or right, but only, as he puts it, what is "good for someone or other." (*DH*, XI, 4, 47) But he is an ethical objectivist in the sense that his moral propositions are statements of causal connections that purport to be true. However, because the phrase 'ethical objectivism' has traditionally been used to describe deontological moral theories such as those espoused by Kant, I will continue to call Hobbes an ethical subjectivist in virtue of his subjectivist theory of

37 David Gauthier (1986) has presented a moral theory in which moral propositions are true insofar as they give correct causal information about how to effect desired goals.

value. But the reader should note that Hobbes is a subjectivist who nonetheless seeks to espouse objective moral principles.

Second, Hobbes not only explains how moral propositions are true but also explains why they have prescriptive power. One of the most disturbing questions plaguing the moral deontologist is: Why should I act morally? But Hobbes maintains that the answer to this question is simple: One should do the moral thing because it will advance one's self-interest (and avoid such behavior when it will not). It is an explanation that, in his view, far and away outstrips previous explanations of the prescriptivity of moral behavior, for example, the account offered by Aristotle:

> the Writers of Morall Philosophie, though they acknowledge the same Vertues and Vices; Yet not seeing wherein consisted their Goodnesse; *nor that they come to be praised, as the meanes of peaceable, sociable, and comfortable living;* place them in a mediocrity of passions: as if not the Cause, but the Degree of daring, made Fortitude; or not the Cause, but the Quantity of a gift, made Liberality. [*Lev*, 15, 40, 80; emphasis added]

So Hobbes believes that his self-interested deduction of the virtues both preserves and explains the prescriptivity of moral commands. We ought to act morally in the same way that we ought to take our medicine when we are sick; both actions are necessary causes of desired effects.

This passage also reveals a third feature of Hobbes's moral science of which he was proud. It explains why human beings have perennially been pleased by and promotive of more or less the same cooperative actions, whether their cultural background was Athens of the fourth century B.C. or seventeenth-century England. Moral philosophers "acknowledge the same Vertues and Vices" because of their causal connection with peace. (See also *DC, EW* ii, 3, 32, 48–9.) This explanation is, in Hobbes's eyes, far more sensible than the Aristotelian explanation, which maintains that these virtues are valued insofar as they represent a "mediocrity of the passions." As we shall discuss in Chapter 3, Hobbes did indeed believe that there is such a thing as "too much virtue," but he also believed that his moral science would offer the correct account of the limits of virtuous action.

Finally, there is a fourth feature of Hobbes's moral science that he appears to have regarded highly. As we have seen, throughout *Leviathan* Hobbes seizes on traditional moral words and phrases, such as 'good,' 'right,' and 'law of nature,' draining them of their traditional objectivist meanings and then infusing them with subjectivist meanings of his own. Hobbes is not merely announcing his subjectivism in these passages, but also showing how moral terms must be defined so that they refer. In a passage already quoted, Hobbes insists that scientific reasoning must presuppose the "apt imposing of Names" (*Lev*, 5, 17, 21); otherwise, assertions will be false. In *De Corpore*, Hobbes explains that one way in which we err when we reason is to use names that denote only phantasms (*De Corp, EW* i, I, 5, 4, 59), and he counsels that the way to detect false propositions is to resolve terms in these propositions into their definitions so as to determine whether or not the terms actually refer. Clearly, he believes that moral objectivists such as Aristotle use moral terms, such as summum bonum, that do not refer.[38]

---

38 Hobbes would likely agree with John Mackie (1977, ch. 9) that apart from anything else, they are too "queer" to exist.

So what does one do with these words? Mackie has suggested in his own defense of ethical subjectivism that we retain these moral words and their objectivist meanings and allow the making of false moral assertions using them so long as such assertions are useful.[39] However, Hobbes does not even consider the possibility that an entire body of discourse that is judged to be false can have any value in our search for knowledge and power. However, he opposes the junking of moral discourse entirely. His project in *Leviathan* is to keep moral discourse by changing the reference of moral terms so that they refer. For example, 'good' no longer refers to the nonexistent summum bonum but to the collection of objects desired by a particular person in a particular place and time. Therefore, the unwary reader who does not appreciate the radical revisionist project under way in the early chapters of *Leviathan* will substantially misunderstand in the rest of the book not only the Hobbesian ethical position but also the Hobbesian argument for absolute sovereignty that presupposes that position.

So Hobbes is a powerful revisionist. And as I shall discuss next, he is at his most powerful when he is putting revisionist meanings of 'rights' and 'moral obligation' to work in *Leviathan*.

RIGHTS AND OBLIGATIONS

In trying to understand Hobbes's use of the notion of a right and its connection with his subjectivist meta-ethics, we must begin by making use of the well-known analysis of this notion by the American legal theorist Wesley Hohfeld. In *Fundamental Legal Conceptions* (1919), Hohfeld distinguishes four meanings of the word 'right' — or, perhaps better, four different concepts that the word has been stretched to cover: the notions of right as (1) a claim, (2) a privilege or liberty, (3) power, and (4) immunity. For our purposes, the first two meanings of the word are important.

The notion of a right as a claim is perhaps the most common and natural concept that the word 'right' has been taken to cover. It is the idea that a person has a "moral claim" to some thing or some act or some kind of treatment, and it is correlated with a duty that others have to respect (or provide) that thing, that act, or that treatment to which one has a claim. If Alice has a right not to be murdered, Bill has a duty not to murder her. If Bill has a right to a piece of property in Los Angeles, Alice has a duty not to interfere with or intrude on Bill's land without Bill's permission.

It is easy to mistakenly assume that Hobbes uses the word 'right' in this sense. But he does not; in fact, his use of the word shows that he endorses the second conception of 'right' outlined by Hohfeld — the idea that a right is a privilege or a liberty. 'Right,' in this sense, is the opposite of a duty. If I have a liberty to use land in a certain way, I may do so or not, as I desire; in no way am I morally required to do so. Moreover, 'right' in this sense is correlated with what Hohfeld calls (for lack of a better term) a "no-right." If I have the privilege or liberty of boating on Lake Mead, other people have a "no-right" (i.e., no basis of claim — the 'right' in the term is

---

39 This appears to be Mackie's position in *Ethics*, Part I (1977); however, in Part III, Chapters 5 and 9, he appears to be in favor of modifying at least some moral discourse fairly substantially.

being used in its first sense) that I shall or shall not go boating on Lake Mead. They cannot demand that I do, and they cannot demand that I do not. They can demand nothing in this regard; hence the term "no-right."

What is particularly interesting about the notion of right in this second sense is that people do not have any duty to respect or help one another to carry out what each has the "right-liberty" to do, and this can place them in a position of legitimate competition. If I have logging privileges in a national forest and you do also, I am under no obligation to help (or hinder) your efforts; likewise, you are under no obligation to help (or hinder) mine. And if we both exercise our "right-liberties" in this forest, we will be competing for timber, perhaps to the detriment of one or both of us. So neither of us has a duty to refrain from trying to prevent the other from exercising that liberty. Only if each of us has, in addition to this right-liberty, a claim right blocking the other from interfering with exercise of the right-liberty are we morally required to refrain from impeding each other's logging efforts.

Hobbes's use of the word 'right' is roughly similar to the Hohfeldian notion of a right-privilege or right-liberty. Indeed, in Chapter 14, Hobbes begins by explicating a person's fundamental right of nature as a "liberty":

THE RIGHT OF NATURE, which Writers commonly call *Jus Naturale*, is the *Liberty* each man hath, to use his own power, as he will himselfe, for the preservation of his own Nature; that is to say, of his own Life; and consequently, of doing any thing, which in his own Judgement, and Reason, hee shall conceive to be the aptest means therunto. [*Lev*, 14, 1, 64; second emphasis added]

And this liberty we have to preserve ourselves is not something that other people are obliged to respect, nor do they have any obligation to help or hinder our preservation efforts. So these different liberties come into competition with one another. And after each person claims a "right to all things," that is, the liberty to appropriate and control every object for one's own benefit, each one of them will come into direct conflict with every other person who also claims a right-liberty to do the same. And, of course, Hobbes's famous "war of every one against every one" in the state of nature is the result.

We also get a nice sense of the way in which a no-right is correlated with Hobbes's rights in Chapter 21, on the liberty of subjects in a commonwealth. For example, when Hobbes gives people who have already (unjustly) rebelled against the sovereign the right to continue in their rebellion efforts, he is certainly not saying that the sovereign is obliged to respect that right!

in case a great many men together, have already resisted the Soveraign Power unjustly, or committed some Capitall crime, for which every one of them expecteth death, whether have they not the Liberty then to joyn together, and assist, and defend one another? Certainly they have: For they but defend their lives, which the Guilty man may as well do as the Innocent. [*Lev*, 21, 17, 112–13]

And Hobbes is concerned to point out that none of the liberties that he attributes to subjects in a commonwealth, all of which arise out of their fundamental "right of nature" to preserve themselves, in any way limit the sovereign's power, that is, they do not place upon him any obligation to respect these liberties:

Neverthelesse we are not to understand, that by such Liberty, the Soveraign Power of life and death, is either abolished, or limited. [*Lev*, 21, 7, 109]

Correlated with the subjects' liberties is a no-right on the sovereign's part: He does not have to help or hinder any of their preservation efforts, but if their preservation efforts in some way interfere with his, then his liberty to preserve himself will be "engaged," subject and sovereign will be in competition, and given his power the sovereign will probably win out.

However, it would be highly unlikely that use of the word 'right' in the twentieth century would exactly match this seventeenth-century philosopher's use of the word, and in fact the two do not match. Twentieth-century thinkers who talk about liberty-rights will normally link a *claim-right* to a person's liberty-right such that other people have a moral obligation to respect the exercise of the liberty-right. If a person has a liberty-right to log in a national forest, we tend to assume that her competitors cannot steal or overtly prevent her logging efforts (although they have a right to take timber if they get to it before she does). In other words, her competitors are under an obligation to respect her claim-right to compete with them in the exercise of her liberty-right to log in the forest. However, Hobbes the ethical subjectivist assumes no such natural linkage between people's liberty-rights and moral claim-rights in the state of nature. Indeed, he makes a point of giving no objectivist moral reasons for attributing liberty-rights to human beings in the state of nature such that a claim-right would have to be linked to the exercise of them, and Hobbes accords a person liberty-rights only because of the subjectivist ethical position he espouses.

This conclusion is a bit complicated; so let us go slowly. As I said earlier, I call Hobbes's ethical position 'subjectivist' because he defines 'good' as an object or state of affairs desired by any individual in a particular place and time, and because he defines a right or rational action as one that is instrumentally valuable to that individual in attaining the objects of her desire. This instrumentalist conception of rationality involves, as we saw, both true beliefs and healthy physiological processes, but let us ignore the second component of this conception for the time being and consider how Hobbes can consistently accord individuals liberty-rights using a "true belief" instrumentalist conception of right action. Insofar as an action is a means to a desired object, it not only can be described with the adjectives 'right' and 'rational' but also can be characterized as an action that is done "with right," or an action that the individual has a 'right' to take. This last use of 'right' makes it a noun that indicates that the action is allowed by prudential rationality. This noun can also be used in conjunction with objects; thus, to say that one has a right to an object means that the object is a necessary means to one's desired end. So a subjectivist can incorporate a liberty-right into his ethical position by attributing that right to a person in connection with objects or actions that are instrumentally valuable. On this view, a person has a liberty-right to an object or action when reason determines that this object or action is necessary to accomplish his desired ends.

This is the understanding of rights that Hobbes ought to hold if he is a subjectivist. But does he actually hold it? Happily, there are two important passages in *De Cive* and *Leviathan* in which 'having a right' is defined in exactly this way. In *De Cive*, Hobbes contends that

It is . . . neither absurd nor reprehensible, neither against the dictates of true reason, for a man to use all his endeavours to preserve and defend his body and the members thereof from death and sorrow. *But that which is not contrary to right reason, that all men account to be done justly, and with right. Neither by the word right is anything else signified, than that liberty, which every man hath to make use of his natural faculties according to right reason.* [DC, EW ii, 1, 7, 8–9; emphasis added][40]

In other words, Hobbes is saying that we can be said to "have a (liberty) right" to do or to have whatever reason determines it is right (i.e., prudent) to do or to have. And given the preeminence of self-preservation in Hobbes's psychology, the primary content of people's liberty-rights in the state of nature are objects and actions that are necessary for their self-preservation, insofar as that is our preeminent good. Similarly, in Chapter 14 of *Leviathan,* Hobbes accords people a "right of nature" whose content is to do or to have anything instrumentally valuable to furthering self-preservation:

THE RIGHT OF NATURE, which Writers commonly call *Jus Naturale,* is the Liberty each man hath, to use his own power, as he will himselfe, *for the preservation of his own Nature* [emphasis added]; that is to say, of his own Life; and consequently, of doing any thing, which in his own Judgement, and Reason, hee shall conceive to be the aptest means thereunto. [*Lev,* 14, 1, 64]

Some readers have worried whether or not Hobbes's use of the word 'right' ever implies that there are certain actions people "ought not" to do or certain objects they "may not" appropriate given their right to preserve themselves, where 'ought not' and 'may not' are understood in some sort of morally objectivist way. This worry, however, misunderstands the subjectivist way in which Hobbes uses the noun 'right.' Anyone who appropriates an object or performs an action in order to attain self-preservation would be described by Hobbes as "having a right" to appropriate or perform that action. If Hobbes said that this person "had no right" to do what she did, that phrase could only mean that the person's action was not an effective means to her desired end — it was imprudent or irrational. So, if Hobbes said, for example, that a person had no right to an object, that would only mean that it was irrational or imprudent for her to appropriate it — a judgment that the person who made the appropriation would be in a good position to contest, given what she knew of her own desires and objectives. But their quarrel would only be about the *prudence* of the appropriation, not whether or not it should have happened in some deontological sense of the word 'should.'

However, this cannot be the whole story. Hobbes is willing to let the word 'rational' describe not just a prudent action but also a physically healthy action, that is, one that is taken by someone who is healthy and thus who desires self-preservation above all else. A man who effectively pursues his own destruction may be prudent, but for Hobbes he is still "irrational" in the sense that his actions are insane and a manifestation of a physical disorder. Hence, I suspect (although Hobbes does not actually say this anywhere in his writings) that because someone could not be acting from right reason if he, say, procured a knife to kill himself, Hobbes would not consider this man to have a right to the knife, despite the fact that it would *seem* to be instrumentally valuable to him. So, to a reader who asks Would Hobbes ever say about someone who desired an object that would lead to his destruction (e.g., glory) that he nonetheless did not have a right to do or to procure something that would achieve this goal? my answer is, probably yes. Hobbes's "healthy deliberation" conception of right reason would lead him to endorse the idea that we "have a right" only

---

40 This passage is discussed by Gauthier (1979, 550ff.) in somewhat the same way.

to actions or objects that are not in pursuit of a crazy goal (e.g., suicide) prompted in us by a physical disease. It is probably because right reason is defined partly in a medical way that Hobbes persists in attributing liberty-rights only to healthy individuals for whom self-preservation is their premier good.

Nonetheless, the medical overtones of Hobbes's attribution of rights solely to these healthy individuals are still consistent with his ethical subjectivism. "Having a right" to an object depends on that object being an effective means to an end that one either does or would desire if one were healthy. This definition presupposes that we can criticize some people's goals as physiologically mistaken and/or goals that they do not really want insofar as they want to be healthy. It does not presuppose the existence of an objectivist moral object or property.

But whereas we have been able to see the connection between Hobbes's use of the word 'right' and his subjectivism, it is much harder to reconcile his use of the word 'obligation' with his subjectivism.

Given that subjectivism, Hobbes cannot link the notion of obligation with any objective moral claim-rights individuals have. Yet in *Leviathan* it sometimes seems as if he does so. In Chapter 14, he argues that obligations result from the renouncing or the transferring (via contract or gift) of a liberty-right:

> Right is layd aside, either by simply Renouncing it; or by Transferring it to another. By *Simply* RENOUNCING; when he cares not to whom the benefit thereof redoundeth. By TRANSFERRING; when he intendeth the benefit thereof to some certain person, or persons. And when a man hath in either manner abandoned, or granted away his Right; then is he said to be OBLIGED or BOUND, not to hinder those, to whom such Right is granted, or abandoned, from the benefit of it: and that he *Ought*, and it is his DUTY, not to make voyd that voluntary act of his own: and that such hindrance is INJUSTICE, and INJURY, as being *Sine Jure;* the Right being before renounced, or transferred. [*Lev*, 14, 7, 65]

Is Hobbes saying in this passage that after renouncing a liberty-right, we have a duty to others, correlated with a claim-right that they have over us, to the effect that we do not try to exercise the liberty we have renounced? It certainly sounds like it — the thrust of the passage seems to be that whether we like it or not we are obliged not to exercise a renounced or transferred right. And Warrender is quick to use this and similar passages to support his deontological interpretation of Hobbes's ethical position. Yet in Chapter 15 when Hobbes explains to the "fool" who questions the rationality of contract keeping why we should keep our contractual promises, his explanation does not invoke any normative obligation that we have incurred by promising to transfer our right. Instead, he invokes self-interest, and specifically the benefits we will receive subsequent to keeping our contract because of the reputation of trustworthiness we shall acquire:

> in a condition of warre . . . there is no man can hope by his own strength, or wit, to defend himselfe from destruction, without the help of Confederates; . . . and therefore he which declares he thinks it reason to deceive those that help him, can in reason expect no other means of safety, than what can be had from his own single Power. [*Lev*, 15, 5, 73]

In essence, Hobbes is contending that because contract keeping can build the trust required for formation of strong, protective confederacies, then if a person fails to keep his contractual promise, he is alienating himself from others, thereby seriously endangering his own survival. Hence, for this *self-interested* reason, Hobbes argues that keeping contracts and not breaking them is the way to further one's own preservation.

This suggests that there is a subjectivist way to interpret the passage on obligation and duty quoted earlier from Chapter 14. Hobbes can be taken to be defining in Chapter 14 what it means to be obliged or duty-bound to do something by linking this state to a person's surrender of her right; but in Chapter 15 his explanation for why one should do one's duty is that this is the prudent thing to do, whereas reneging is imprudent. In other words, Hobbes defines the words 'duty,' 'obligation,' and 'justice' in the Chapter 14 passage by reference to the action of laying down one's right, but goes on to argue that in fact doing one's duty (defined in this sense) is right or rational only insofar as that action is prudent.

But what if it isn't prudent? What if it turns out that doing what one ought after the surrender of one's right will damage rather than further one's best interests? Would Hobbes still counsel men to do their duty anyway? He would not. Indeed, given his psychology, he cannot. However, all of Chapter 21 of *Leviathan* is devoted to explaining when it is right (i.e., prudent) for subjects in a commonwealth to renege on their contract creating the sovereign. And in that chapter he repeats (*Lev*, 21, 11, 111) what he had insisted on previously in Chapter 14, namely, that "A covenant not to defend myselfe from force, is always voyd." So, for Hobbes, self-interest explains not only why we should do what we ought but also when our obligations arising from the surrender of right in a contract cease:

For (as I have shewed before) no man can transferre, or lay down his Right to save himselfe from Death, Wounds and Imprisonment, (the avoyding whereof is the onely End of laying down any Right,) and therefore the promise of not resisting force, in no Covenant transferreth any right; *nor is obliging*. [*Lev*, 14, 29, 69–70; emphasis added]

This means that, according to Hobbes, *contractual obligations exist only insofar as it is in our interest to perform them.* To be precise, Hobbes defines two conditions that must be met in order for an obligation to exist: First, there must be a renunciation or transfer of a right to another; second, it must be in the interest of the renouncer or transferrer to respect that renunciation or transfer. So Hobbes defines the nature and extent of our obligations such that our performance of them can never conflict with self-interest.

Hobbes's conception of obligation as it is presented in Chapter 14 is, as Gauthier notes (1969, 60–61), a peculiar one. So, as Plamenatz says (1965, 75; cited by Gauthier 1969, 94), given that our standard notion of obligation is such that "when someone is morally obliged, there is something he ought to do, whether it is to his advantage or not," Hobbes cannot and indeed does not endorse obligation in this sense. But Hobbes would heartily disagree with Gauthier's conclusion (1969, 98) that this shows that he does not really have an account of obligation at all and that his psychology has been "destructive" of his ethics. Hobbes's entire ethical project (which is supposed to be derived from his psychology) involves rejecting the idea that categorical imperatives are capable (inexplicably) of moving us to act against our self-interest. The point, for him, of connecting any virtuous action with peace is to make this action *instrumentally valuable* and thus to render hypothetical the "ought" in any moral proposition that commands one to act virtuously. Thus, to say that Hobbes has no real ethical view because he is unwilling to recognize that we can have obligations to act against our self-interest is simply to refuse to recognize the validity of his philosophical project attempting to give a self-interested deduction of any moral "ought," whether the "ought" is as in "you ought to do your duty and keep your contractual obligations" or in "you ought to be grateful, and equitable, and merciful." Yet this project excited many seventeenth-century philosophers.[41] And some philosophers in the twentieth century, for example, Phillipa Foot (1978, 157–73), have also been intrigued by the way this approach offers a powerful answer to the question, Why be moral?

Perhaps this approach to justifying morality is wrong. Perhaps Hobbes's insistence that morality be based on self-interest is ruinous of what we believe is the true nature of moral reasoning and moral action. We shall be considering these questions as this book continues, particularly in Chapter 3, where we shall discuss the laws of nature constituting Hobbes's moral theory. But another way, indeed a very Hobbesian way, of evaluating the acceptability of this moral theory is to determine whether or not Hobbes can really dispense with a categorical 'ought' and other objectivist moral notions in his justification of absolute sovereignty. In later chapters I shall argue that his justification based on this moral theory fails. And I shall note that Hobbes slips into deontological-sounding language at certain critical and problematic points in his argument. So although I have argued against Taylor's and Warrender's interpretation of Hobbes's ethical views in this chapter, I do not think they are wrong to have heard deontological strains in *Leviathan* — particularly in those passages where he speaks of an obligation to obey the sovereign — that signal that there is no consistent argument for absolute sovereignty based on self-interest in *Leviathan*. They are wrong, however, to think that the language in these passages represents a conscious or even unconscious attempt to mount a full-blown deontological moral theory in *Leviathan*.

41 Spinoza's derivation of ethical imperatives in his *Ethics* was profoundly influenced by this approach to understanding morality. In 1688, Samuel Pufendorf claimed to present a deduction of morality from self-interest in his *De jure Naturae et Gentium,* and in 1672 Richard Cumberland boasted that his deduction of ethical imperatives from self-interest in *De Legibus Naturae* was entirely successful. Even Locke shows signs of being attracted to this type of ethical view. See the *Second Treatise,* Section 57, where he suggests that the fundamental law of nature is valid insofar as it will bring about a mutually advantageous situation for each (as well as for all). In later unpublished writings, Locke even experimented with constructing a self-interested deduction of morality. See his "Of Ethick in General" and "Thus I Think" (1972, 308–23, and 306–7, respectively). See also von Leyden's discussions of these essays in his Introduction to Locke's *Essays on the Law of Nature* (1954).

CHAPTER 2

What Is the Cause of Conflict in the State of Nature?

Who of you is ignorant that the nature of things has been such, that at one time men, before there was any natural or civil law fully laid down, wandered in a straggling and disorderly manner over the country, and had just that property which they could either seize or keep by their personal strength and vigour, by means of wounds and bloodshed. And there is no point in which there is so much difference between this manner of life, polished by civilization, and that savage one, as the fact of law being the ruling principle of the one, and violence of the other.

Cicero, *For Publius Sestius*[1]

Having presented the premises of Hobbes's argument for absolute sovereignty, we now move to discuss the theorems that Hobbes says are derived from those premisses and that he uses to justify the sovereign's institution. Clearly, the first of these theorems is that the state of nature is a state of war. Hobbes's well-known characterization of the life of man in the state of nature as "solitary, poore, nasty, brutish and short" ends a passage containing a particularly graphic description of the violence and loss suffered by men in that state (*Lev,* 13, 9, 62). However, although Hobbes is good at describing the welfare in the state of nature, he is not nearly so good at explaining it. In fact, *Leviathan* seems to present at least two different accounts of what sort of "natural behavior" is responsible for this warfare, and the accounts are inconsistent with one another. It will be the purpose of this chapter, first, to cull from the text of *Leviathan* the two accounts most obviously suggested by the text; second, to persuade the reader that these accounts are inconsistent with one another; and, finally, to show that both of these accounts have problems serious enough to force a Hobbesian to reject them. By doing so we will lay the groundwork for our discussion in the next chapter of the kind of explanation of warfare he needs (and may even have intended) not only in order to mount his argument for absolute sovereignty effectively but also to explain the nature of the validity of his laws of nature.

2.1 THE RATIONALITY ACCOUNT OF CONFLICT

The first account of conflict in the state of nature is presented in Chapters 11 and 13, and parts of the same explanation surface in Chapters 14 and 17. Its major premiss is that the dominant passion in human beings is the desire for self-preservation. And, says Hobbes, the desire to live means the desire to satisfy constantly arising needs and wants generated by a living body:

1 The passage is cited by Samuel Pufendorf (1934, 156).

the Felicity of this life consisteth not in the repose of a mind satisfied. For there is no such . . .
Summum Bonum. . . . Nor can a man any more live, whose Desires are at an end, than he,
whose Senses and Imaginations are at a stand. Felicity is a continuall progresse of the desire,
from one object to another; the attaining of the former, being still but the way to the later. The
cause whereof is, That the object of mans desire, is not to enjoy once onely, and for one instant
of time; but to assure for ever, the way of his future desire. And therefore the voluntary actions,
and inclinations of all men, tend, not only to the procuring, but also to the assuring of a
contented life; and differ onely in the way. [*Lev*, 11, 1, 47]

Hobbes calls the search for means to satisfy desires the search for power (*Lev*, 10, 1,
41) and maintains that because each man's desires are unending as long as he lives, so,
too, is his search for power constant and unending:

I put for a generall inclination of all mankind, a perpetuall and restlesse desire of Power after
power, that ceaseth onely in Death. And the cause of this, is not alwayes that a man hopes for a
more intensive delight, than he has already attained to; or that he cannot be content with a
moderate power: but because he cannot assure the power and means to live well, which he hath
present, without the acquisition of more. [*Lev*, 11, 2, 47]

Some commentators[2] have taken this passage to show that Hobbes is attributing to
human beings an infinite number of desires, an attribution that is certainly implausible. But careful consideration of what Hobbes actually says shows that this is not so.
He is maintaining that human beings will have desires for objects as long as they live,
that their desires will never cease during their lifetimes. This is surely a reasonable
position — until our dying breath we will have certain needs and wants, some of
which will concern the acquisition of goods to satisfy needs that will develop only in
the future (e.g., my need tomorrow to eat food). Hence, all he is saying here is that
we are beings who, as long as we live, will have many desires related to achieving that
goal, but not an infinite number of them. Moreover, by his unorthodox use of the
term 'right,' Hobbes accords each person a "natural right" to search for and appropriate those means that conceivably will help to satisfy his desires in the future. Thus,
note that at this early stage in his argument Hobbes does not impute to people the
right to all things, but it is clear that he believes that each person regards his right as
extending over an indefinitely large number of objects in the world.

   Because each person desires and believes he has the right to so many objects, people
will inevitably come to desire and try to appropriate the same object. But, says
Hobbes, because there is rough equality of strength and mental ability between
people in this state, no one is ready to acknowledge another's superior right to an
object by virtue of this other person's superior strength or superior claim to it, and
competition for it is created. Hence, says Hobbes, competition is the first cause of
conflict; that is, it "maketh men invade for Gain" (*Lev*, 13, 7, 62):

if any two men desire the same thing, which neverthelesse they cannot both enjoy, they
become enemies; and in the way to their End, (which is principally their owne conservation,
and sometimes their delectation only,) endeavour to destroy, or subdue one an other . . . if
one plant, sow, build, or possesse a convenient Seat, others may probably be expected to
come prepared with forces united, to dispossesse, and deprive him, not only of the fruit of his
labour, but also of his life, or liberty. And the Invader is in the like danger of another. [*Lev*,
13, 3, 61]

2   For example, Leo Strauss (1952, 10ff.) and C. B. Macpherson (1968, 36–7).

And, clearly, insofar as Hobbes is assuming that competition for goods will exist in the state of nature, he is assuming that there will be in that state a "moderate scarcity of goods," which Hume tells us in *A Treatise of Human Nature* (III, ii, ii) is no more than to assume that the circumstances that make justice necessary actually prevail in this state.

The realization that others are competing for the goods that one has seized or will want to seize breeds "diffidence," that is, distrust. Each person realizes that to prevent attempts at gaining possession of the goods he has seized to further his own preservation, he must amass as much power as he can; thus, he makes preemptive strikes, using "force, or wiles, to master the persons of all men he can, so long, till he see no other power great enough to endanger him: And this is no more than his own conservation requireth, and is generally allowed." (*Lev*, 13, 4, 61) This distrust therefore constitutes a second cause of conflict, based on a desire to preserve oneself; that is, it causes a person to invade in order to secure a good defense against his enemies.

It is only at this point that Hobbes says that a person in the state of nature begins to claim a right to all things. The dangers of attack on his person, and the advantages of power seen in preventing attacks on himself and his property and in allowing him to make such invasions against others, mean that there is nothing that could not help him to further his own life:

because the condition of Man, (as hath been declared in the precedent Chapter [Chapter 13]) is a condition of warre of every one against every one; in which case every one is governed by his own Reason; and there is nothing he can make use of, that may not be a help unto him, in preserving his life against his enemyes; *It followeth*, that in such a condition, every man has a Right to every thing; even to one anothers body. [*Lev*, 14, 4, 64; emphasis added]

However, once people begin to claim this right, there is competition for every object, and conflict between them can only escalate in frequency and intensity.

Before moving on, I want to emphasize the rather late appearance of the "right to all things" in Hobbes's argument for total war in Chapters 13 and 14 of *Leviathan*. In both of his earlier books, Hobbes inserts this right much earlier into his account of the causes of conflict and consequently leans on it more heavily than he does in the *Leviathan* account to explain the creation of warfare. For example, in *The Elements of Law*, after arguing that "it is not against reason, and therefore right for a man, to use all means and do whatsoever action is necessary for the preservation of his body" (*EL*, I, xiv, 7, 72), he goes on to contend that "every man by right of nature is judge himself of the necessity of the means, and of the greatness of the danger." (*EL*, I, xiv, 8, 55) Thus, he concludes that "Every man by nature hath a right to all things, that is to say, to do whatsoever he listeth to whom he listeth, to possess, use, and enjoy all things he will and can," proving it as follows:

For seeing all things he willeth, must therefore be good unto him in his own judgement . . . and we have made him judge thereof . . . it followeth that all things may rightly also be done by him. [*EL*, I, xiv, 10, 55]

And Hobbes puts forward a very similar argument in *De Cive*, Chapter I, Section 10.

As I have reconstructed it, Hobbes's account of conflict in *Leviathan* departs from these earlier accounts in the following way. Because men have a right to their own preservation and a right to judge what will be conducive thereof, they have a right to whatever they think will lead to their self-preservation, but this right, while being very extensive, will not extend over *all* things. Only after warfare has begun and competitive struggles and preemptive strikes are in full swing does Hobbes say that one can plausibly claim that an individual would think he could really use every object that exists — and thus have a right to all things.

The reason for the change in *Leviathan* is most likely that Hobbes wished to make his account of conflict more plausible and persuasive. It seems very strained to maintain that before warfare has begun every human being will conclude that all things in the world are useful to him in his efforts to survive, and thus that he should have a liberty-right to all things. The advantage of his *Leviathan* account in Chapter 13 is that he can start from a much more limited entitlement claim — the right over many goods and objects that the individual will judge to be necessary for survival — and then, through the demands of competition and fear in that state, transform this right into a right to all objects in that state. Even at this point, however, the right to all things seems a bit implausible: Does one have to claim a right to every blade of grass, every grain of sand, in order to preserve oneself? Hobbes surely exaggerates, but it is an exaggeration of the more reasonable claim to possess vast amounts of objects after the war of all against all has begun.

Hobbes could stop here if he liked, having established two inevitable causes of invasion and quarrel (i.e., competition and fear) based solely on the rational pursuit of self-preservation by each person. However, he adds one more reason for invasion that is not based on this passion, that is, invasion for glory's sake. A man, says Hobbes,

looketh that his companion should value him, at the same rate he set upon himself: And upon all signes of contempt, or undervaluing, naturally endeavours, as far as he dares, . . . to extort a greater value from his contemners, by dommage; and from others, by the example. [*Lev*, 13, 5, 61]

This desire for appreciation and praise is clearly a different motivating power than the passion for self-preservation. A person who seeks glory is not seeking an object that directly satisfies his present or future survival needs. Indeed, this search may conflict with his desire to preserve himself. In addition, because the previous two causes of conflict arising out of the desire to preserve oneself are powerful enough to explain between them the development of *total war* in the natural state, this third reason is really not a necessary part of Hobbes's argument in Chapter 13 that the state of nature is a state of total war. Hobbes could easily have done without it. And, clearly, in Chapter 13, self-preservation is made the key reason for the carnage and destruction in this situation. So perhaps citing glory as the third reason for invasion is just a harmless addition to the Chapter 13 argument — just a way of making the argument more persuasive to the reader. We shall see.

It has naturally occurred to recent commentators on Hobbes's works that, given the account of conflict in Chapter 13, the dilemma all people face in the state of nature can be pictured using game-theoretic tools, in particular the device of the prisoner's dilemma matrix.[3] Suppose we consider two people *A* and *B* in the state of nature.

---

3 Many have had the idea of using the prisoner's dilemma matrix to interpret Hobbes's remarks in *Leviathan*. For example, see John Rawls (1971, 269), Michael Taylor (1976, chap. 6), and Brian Barry (1965, 253–4). David Gauthier (1969, 76–89) challenges this interpretation on the basis of Hobbes's remarks in his "answer to the fool" in Chapter 15 of *Leviathan*, and Edna Ullmann-Margalit (1977, 62–73) also discusses that passage. I will be dealing with both of these discussions in Section 2.3 of this chapter.

Figure 2.1

	B	
	Not invade	Invade
A		
Not invade	2,2	4,1
Invade	1,4	3,3

Each person has seized a number of goods, wants more, and hungrily eyes the goods seized by the other. Each has the choice of invading in order to seize the goods or refraining from doing so. They reason as the payoff matrix in Figure 2.1 indicates. Each person has a choice of performing one of two actions, and the numbers in the quadrants of the matrix correspond to their preference orderings (4 is lowest, 1 is highest) for the state of affairs represented by that quadrant. A's preference orderings are on the left; B's preference orderings are on the right. Let us consider A's preference orderings first. A reasons that if A and B do not invade one another's territories, both will be able to hold on to the goods they have thus far procured, a situation that A rates with a 2 (the upper left quadrant). But A also appreciates that if A does not invade, but B does, then A will most likely be without any of A's former goods, enslaved to B, with A's self-preservation seriously endangered, a situation A rates with a 4 (the upper right quadrant). On the other hand, if A invades but B does not, A will be the master and B the loser, with A's power significantly augmented; this is A's favorite outcome (rated 1, the lower left quadrant). If both invade, the situation is poor — the life of each is endangered, but war is at least better than total domination in that each has a chance of "winning it all," whereas if the other is the victor, everything is lost, and death is a likely possibility (therefore rated 3, the lower right quadrant). And if we consider B's preferences for the various outcomes, we see that they are symmetric with A's. But this means (assuming the players make standard subjective judgments of probability) that *no matter what the other person does, it is rational for each person in this situation to be uncooperative.* If B cooperates, then A gains more if A does not cooperate. If B does not cooperate, once again A gains more by not cooperating. Thus, in game-theoretic language, each person in the state of nature finds that the action of invasion "dominates" over the action of noninvasion, insofar as it maximizes one's security level. The matrix pictures the way in which the predominant cause of invasion is each person's *rational* pursuit of self-interest. Nor does Hobbes think that this unbridled rational action is "wrong" or "unfair" in the natural state: "To this war of every man, against every man," he writes, "this also is consequent; that nothing can be Unjust. . . . Where there is no common Power, there is no Law: where no Law, no Injustice. Force, and Fraud, are in warre the two Cardinall vertues." (*Lev*, 13, 13, 63) Such behavior is "virtuous" and "right" because it is required if each person is to maximize his own preservation. Thus, because this account of conflict explains warfare as the result of rational action by rational men, I shall call it the Rationality account of conflict.

It follows from this account of the causes of warfare in the state of nature that contracts in the natural state are always void, something Hobbes mentions often in *Leviathan*. If two people in the state of nature make a contract, and the first party to perform keeps his part of the bargain even though there is evidence that it is rational (i.e., in the second party's best interest) for the second party not to perform, the first party is foolishly exposing himself to danger and weakening his chances of survival. Let us use as an example an agreement between two people, *A* and *B*, not to invade one another's territories. If *A* did keep the promise and did refrain from invading *B*'s territory, *B*'s self-interest would dictate the action of invasion of *A*'s territory, because the material advantages *B* would gain from this invasion would be significant. Consequently, there is no rational person who, if a contract were made in these circumstances, would perform his part of the bargain first:

If a covenant be made, wherein neither of the parties performe presently, but trust one another; in the condition of meer Nature, (which is a condition of Warre of every man against every man,) upon any reasonable suspicion, it is Voyd. . . . For he that performeth first, has no assurance the other will performe after. . . . And therefore he which performeth first, does but betray himselfe to his enemy; contrary to the Right (he can never abandon) of defending his life, and means of living. [*Lev*, 14, 18, 68]

If such bargains were ever struck in this state, they would be void for the same reason that any intention to commit an act that one subsequently discovers will threaten one's own life is void. A rational person cannot be understood to intend his own destruction (*Lev*, 14, 8, 65–6). In Hobbes's state of nature, where everyone is motivated solely by self-interest, promises to do or refrain from doing something that is against one's self-interest mean nothing.

2.2 THE PASSIONS ACCOUNT OF CONFLICT

Although the rationality account of conflict arises naturally from certain portions of the text, it is not the only account of conflict suggested in *Leviathan*. Indeed, one sees many commentators on Hobbes's work (including Strauss and Gauthier) maintaining that human passion, not human rationality, generates warfare in the natural state. This account of conflict is not as well articulated in the text of *Leviathan* as is the rationality account, and it will take us some time to fully delineate its structure.

There is a reason that many critics have naturally interpreted Hobbes as blaming certain passions for violence. Consider the fact that Hobbes calls the laws of nature "Immutable and Eternal" moral truths (*Lev*, 15, 38, 79). But if this is so, then why don't people in the state of nature follow them, such that the state of nature becomes a state of relative peace? This question puzzled Hobbes's contemporaries. For example, the Earl of Clarendon writes:

How should it else come to pass, that Mr. Hobbes, whil'st he is demolishing the whole frame of Nature for want of order to support it, and makes it unavoidably necessary for every man to cut his neighbors throat . . . I say, how comes it to pass, that . . . he would in the same, and the next Chapter, set down such a Body of Laws prescribed by Nature itself, as are *immutable and eternal?* that there appears, by his own shewing, a full remedy against all that confusion, for avoiding whereof he hath devis'd all that unnatural and impossible Contract and Covenant? [1676, 37]

And note that my interpretation of the laws as hypothetical imperatives does not help to answer Clarendon's question. If the laws of nature are true ("Immutable and Eternal") hypothetical imperatives correctly directing people about how to achieve the common good of peace, then why doesn't the self-interested population of Hobbes's state of nature follow them?

There is a very natural answer to this question: People don't follow these laws because their ability to do so is disrupted by passion — in particular, by the passion for glory. Although the laws of nature are rational for all people to follow, nonetheless these laws are not universally followed, because many people are irrational in the second or third sense we defined in Chapter 1. That is, people become "mad" or diseased as these passions swell up inside them, rendering them incapable of pursuing their self-preservation, either by perverting their reasoning processes or by damaging the desire-formation mechanisms in their bodies.

Can we find this account of conflict in the text of *Leviathan?* In order to do so, we must look for the two central components of the view: first, the idea that it is rational for all people to follow the laws of nature in the state of nature, including the law directing them to keep their contracts; second, the idea that certain passions are responsible for people's failure to follow these laws. And in fact we can find both of these ideas in the text.

It may seem remarkable that in the midst of Hobbes's repeated assertions that contractual promises are void in the state of nature he should nonetheless have an argument that keeping them is rational. However, he does, and it occurs in Chapter 15 of *Leviathan* in the context of a discussion of the validity of the third law of nature, that is, "That men perform their Covenants made."[4] (*Lev,* 15, 1, 71) And it contains Hobbes's argument against "fools" who dispute the rationality of this imperative:

The Foole hath sayd in his heart, there is no such thing as Justice . . . seriously alleaging, that every mans conservation, and contentment, being committed to his own care, there could be no reason, why every man might not do what he thought conduced thereunto: and therefore also to make, or not make; keep, or not keep Covenants, was not against Reason, when it conduced to one's benefit. [*Lev,* 15, 4, 72]

But Hobbes contends that "This specious reasoning is neverthelesse false,"

For the question is not of promises mutuall, where there is no security of performance on either side; as when there is no Civill Power erected over the parties promising; for such promises are no Covenants: But either where one of the parties has performed already; *or* where there is a Power to make him performe; there is the question whether it be against reason, that is, against the benefit of the other to performe, or not. And I say it is not against reason. [*Lev,* 15, 5, 73; emphasis added]

I have emphasized "or" in this passage to stress that here Hobbes says that it is rational to keep covenants *in the state of nature* if one party has already performed. Clearly, as Hobbes points out, it is not against reason to keep one's contracts in a commonwealth — the sovereign's enforceable laws make it in one's interest to do so.

---

4   In the rest of this chapter and in subsequent chapters I will use the word 'contract' and the word 'covenant' interchangeably, although Hobbes distinguishes their meanings (*Lev,* 14, 11, 66). In Chapter 6, I will be discussing why the distinction is unimportant for our purposes.

Presumably the fool would have no problem with this — Hobbes is maintaining that one should not keep contracts if keeping them means not doing what conduces to one's benefit, and when there is a sovereign to enforce them, keeping contracts nearly always conduces to one's benefit.

But in this passage Hobbes is also maintaining that it is rational to keep contracts in the state of nature if one party has already performed, and it follows from this position that it is rational for any party to a contract to keep his part of the bargain in the state of nature. That is, Hobbes's argument for keeping one's contractual promises in the state of nature if the first party has already performed implies that it is also rational for the first party to perform, even if the second party has not yet done so, which means it is rational for both parties to keep "promises mutuall" in a state of nature. To see this, suppose Alice and Bill make a contract to exchange Alice's horse for Bill's cow. If Alice is to be the first to perform, she will reason (provided she accepts Hobbes's argument in the answer to the fool) that it is rational for Bill to give her the cow if she keeps her part of the bargain by first turning over the horse to him. But if this is so, then it is also advantageous for her to perform. Provided that Bill is rational, giving Bill the horse will allow Alice to reap the benefits of the bargain — Bill's cow. Hence, provided it is rational for the second party to perform, given the first party's performance, it is also rational for the first party to perform.

As we discussed in Chapter 1, the argument[5] Hobbes gives in his answer to the fool to establish the rationality of contract keeping goes as follows:

> in a condition of warre . . . there is no man can hope by his own strength, or wit, to defend himselfe from destruction, without the help of Confederates; . . . and therefore he which declares he thinks it reason to deceive those that help him, can in reason expect no other means of safety, than what can be had from his own single Power. [*Lev*, 15, 5, 73]

Thus, in essence, Hobbes is contending that because contract keeping can build the trust required for formation of strong, protective confederacies, then if a person fails to keep his contractual promise, he is alienating himself from others, thereby seriously endangering his own survival. For this reason, Hobbes argues that keeping contracts and not breaking them is the way to further one's own preservation. Hobbes's answer to the fool is remarkable, because it directly contradicts the position taken in the chapters we have previously discussed in which Hobbes appears to adopt the fool's position to explain the failure of contracts in the state of nature. The prisoner's dilemma matrix representing the decision-making process associated with the keeping of a contractual promise dictates that for either party the action of breach is the rational one. However, in his answer to the fool, Hobbes reaches the opposite conclusion; that is, understood correctly, it is always rational (i.e., in one's self-interest) to keep covenants.

5 Hobbes seems to give another, question-begging argument in his answer to the fool. Although his prose is obscure, he appears to argue that even though keeping a contract might not seem to be conducive to one's preservation, one might be wrong in one's calculations, and therefore one ought to keep the contract. Clearly, the fool can respond to Hobbes that if one does perform the correct calculations, then keeping the contractual promise will not be rational, and he can use the PD matrix to prove this. Only Hobbes's second argument in this passage actually challenges that matrix; hence, this is the one I discuss.

Therefore, if keeping mutual promises in contractual situations is rational, does his answer to the fool commit Hobbes to admitting that the state of nature is really a state of peaceful cooperation, in which contracts are frequently completed? Hobbes does not address such a question in Chapter 15, but a natural Hobbesian response is that it does not, that contracts are in principle possible and that in practice contracts continually fail in the natural state because *contract makers either act irrationally or justifiably fear that their partners will act irrationally*. This is, in fact, what Gauthier takes the passage to imply:

Hobbes argues that if a covenant is made for the sake of preservation, then we must always expect preservation to be furthered by keeping the covenant, and so we do always have reason to keep it. But although this provides a motive for keeping covenants, mistaken reasoning and strong occurrent passions may keep this motive from being operative. [1969, 86–7]

Strauss (1952, chap. 11) agrees with Gauthier that the textual evidence clearly points toward passions such as glory-seeking as the disrupters of cooperation. For example, we have already noted that in Chapter 13, Hobbes credits an occurrent passion, the desire for glory, with the power to generate conflict, warfare, and distrust in the natural state. And this is just the sort of passion that could play a role in causing another party to renege on his part of the bargain. Moreover, earlier, in Chapter 11, Hobbes blamed the desire for "honour" as the spark of war: Men who wish to prove their honor will aggress against their fellows (*Lev*, 11, 6, 48). Hobbes even maintains in this chapter that the desire for honor has been the continual cause of warfare throughout Germany's history (*Lev*, 11, 51, 45–6).

In addition, Hobbes says in Chapter 14 that even the reasonable suspicion of a motivation that will prevent the other party from carrying out his part of the bargain is enough to cause the self-interested person to refrain from performing his part of the bargain first. And in this passage he appears to indicate that the motivations that men fear their partners harbor are the "irrational" desires that disrupt a person's rational pursuit of self-preservation:

he that performeth first, has no assurance the other will performe after; because the bonds of words are too weak to bridle mens ambition, avarice, anger, and other Passions, without the feare of some coercive Power. [*Lev*, 14, 18, 68]

Moreover, at the opening of Chapter 17, Hobbes appears to endorse the fool's idea that rational acts by rational people precipitate the conflict in the natural state, saying

The finall Cause, End, or Designe of men . . . is the foresight of their own preservation . . . that is to say, of getting themselves out from that miserable condition of Warre, *which is necessarily consequent (as hath been shewn) to the naturall Passions of men*. . . . [*Lev*, 17, 1, 85]

But in the very next sentence he names those "natural passions," and they are "partiality, Pride, Revenge, and the like" — that is, "irrational" passions related to the desire for self-glorification and capable of disrupting rational efforts at achieving one's own preservation. Finally, in his explication of why creatures like ants and bees are more sociable than human beings (Chapter 17, 6–12, 86–7), Hobbes never once invokes the "natural" passion for self-preservation as the cause of human conflict, but instead constantly blames "vain-glory," in particular, human competition for honor and dignity, the relishing of what is "eminent," the desire to prove oneself wiser than

Figure 2.2

	Keep	Renege
Keep	1,1	4,2
Renege	2,4	3,3

the rest, the sophistical talent of using words to transform evil into good (for personal advancement), and the ease with which people are personally offended, thus implying that this "irrational" passion (or others' fear of it) is the chief cause of conflict and noncooperation among human beings.

Hobbes's earlier works place particular emphasis on the disruptive role of the desire for glory in the rational pursuit of our self-preservation. In *The Elements of Law,* the reason for "diffidence" is that the vainglorious people among us will attempt to subdue the more moderate people, thus producing distrust among all and generating a climate of violence (*EL,* I, xiv, 3, 54). People who compare themselves with others and find the comparison unflattering

must needs provoke one another by words, and other signs of contempt and hatred, which are incident to all comparison; till at last they must determine the pre-eminence by strength and force of body. [*EL,* I, xiv, 4, 54]

And whereas in *De Cive* we find passages supporting both this account of conflict, resting on the irrationality of acting to obtain glory, and the rationality account, the emphasis is clearly on the glory account. Indeed in Chapter 1 of *De Cive,* Hobbes concludes that in human beings there is a "natural proclivity of men, to hurt each other, which they derive from their passions, but chiefly from a vain esteem of themselves. . . ." (*DC, EW* ii, 1, 12, 11)

However, we must be careful here. This account of conflict actually cites two motivations for uncooperative behavior in the state of nature: first, the irrational passions, which disrupt the right reasoning of many (although not most) people; second, the legitimate fear by the majority (who are themselves rational) that their partners' reasoning will be disrupted by these passions. As Hobbes says in *De Cive,*

though the wicked were fewer than the righteous, yet because we cannot distinguish them, there is a necessity of suspecting, heeding, anticipating, subjugating, self-defending, ever incident to the most honest and fairest conditioned. [*DC, EW* ii, pref., xvi]

So the irrational passions prevent some people from understanding the advantages of cooperation, and legitimate fear of these passions' disruptive effects causes the rest to behave uncooperatively in order to avoid getting hurt. But in both cases the irrational passions are held to be the cause, either directly or indirectly, of the warfare in the state of nature.

This account of conflict would therefore have us accept a matrix very different from the PD matrix in Figure 2.1 as representative of the inhabitants' reasoning in the state of nature. This matrix is represented in Figure 2.2. The game represented by the matrix has been called by Amartya Sen the "assurance game" (1967, 112–24; 1973;

1974, 54–67). Let us assume once again that the choice of actions open to A and B is either to keep or to renege on a contractual promise to the other. As the matrix indicates, if A and B both know that the other is rational, the rational action of each of them will be the action of keeping the contractual promise. The advantages that come from the act of keeping one's promise mean that reneging on the contract will never put one in the most desirable situation. Unlike the situation in a prisoner's dilemma matrix, the payoff to the contract breaker when the other party keeps his promise is quite high, but it is not the most desirable situation the contract breaker could be in (compare the payoff in the upper left quadrant with those in the upper right and lower left quadrants). Although the party in breach would gain the benefits of the bargain without having to "pay" the other party for them, he would nonetheless damage his reputation and lose the chance of gaining confederates, benefits that come from the act of keeping one's promise. Therefore, if the first party does perform his part of the bargain, as this matrix indicates, it is rational for the second party to keep his promise also.

However, what is important about this game is that there is no dominant strategy, that is, no strategy that a player should take no matter what the other player does. Although each player is disposed to keep the promise, each will not do so if there is great fear that the other will renege. So if Mary suspects that John will behave irrationally as a result of strong occurrent passions, and hence suspects that John will not choose the action furthering his preservation, but rather the action of breach, then it is rational for Mary to renege. If she performs her part of the bargain first and he reneges, then she is in the worst possible position, her efforts to preserve herself hampered, perhaps seriously. Therefore, if Mary has, as Hobbes himself puts it, a "reasonable suspicion" (*Lev,* 14, 18, 68) that John will behave irrationally, then unless John *proves* his rationality by performing his part of the bargain, the action of breach is the most rational action to choose.

2.3 EVALUATING THE TWO ACCOUNTS

These two accounts of the reason for conflict and failure of contracts in the state of nature are inconsistent with one another. Whereas the rationality account makes rationality a force disruptive of cooperation in the state of nature, the passions account would have us think reason actually counsels cooperation, but is itself either disrupted by irrational passions, such as the love of glory, or overruled by rational fear of those passions' disruptive influence over one's cooperative partner. Clearly, if the revisionist reader had her way, one of these accounts would be expunged from the text.

But how do we choose one of these accounts in the face of textual evidence supporting both? We do so by determining which account (if either) fits well into Hobbes's argument for absolute sovereignty. Therefore, one of the questions we must ask is, Which position best fits with the psychological, ethical, and metaphysical premises discussed in Chapter 1? I will certainly answer this question at some point in this chapter. However, I also want to determine the answer to another query, namely, Which account will best allow Hobbes to argue that the institution of an absolute sovereign is necessary to achieve peace? Answering this second question is a

Figure 2.3

	Keep	Renege
Keep	1,1	2,3
Renege	3,2	4,4

way of determining which account of conflict will allow Hobbes to draw the political conclusion he wants.

It is because Hobbes's text fails us that we are forced to evaluate these inconsistent accounts using this strategy. The text's confusion prevents us from simply describing or explicating Hobbes's argument as he himself presents it. Instead, we must do philosophy *with* him, using our philosophical skills to work through this part of the argument more clearly than he did himself in order to determine what his best position is. The geometric deduction of absolute sovereignty is flawed; so if we want to know if Hobbes's argument can work, we have to determine whether or not this flaw can be "fixed."

2.4 PROBLEMS WITH THE PASSIONS ACCOUNT OF CONFLICT

In appraising the passions account of conflict, let us start by trying to answer the second query raised earlier: Does this account of conflict allow Hobbes to draw the political conclusion that he wants? In fact, we shall see that it does not, because the account fails to establish total warfare in the state of nature. Indeed, we shall see that if contract keeping is said to be rational, and noncooperation irrational, in the natural state, that state has to be considered a situation in which frequent cooperation and successful commerce occur; in other words, it becomes a state of nature very similar to Locke's, and the Lockean remedy for noncooperation produced by irrationality — institution of a ruler with limited power — makes much more sense than the Hobbesian remedy. So, in the end, I will be contending that the dangerous political implications of the passions account are what primarily force a Hobbesian to reject the view.

In order to show this, let us assume that Hobbes's confederacy argument for the rationality of contract keeping in Chapter 15 of *Leviathan* is correct. We previously presented the matrix in Figure 2.2 as the model of the deliberation process that the passions account suggested. However, this is not the only matrix those remarks suggest. Consider the matrix in Figure 2.3. Whereas in Figure 2.2, in the case of unilateral breach, the party who reneges on his part of the bargain is better off than he would have been had he kept his promise and his partner had reneged (the situation in the upper right and lower left boxes), the matrix in Figure 2.3 has the preference orderings reversed in this situation, making the action of promise keeping dominant over the action of breach, no matter what the other party does. And despite the fact that Hobbes needs something like the deliberation model in Figure 2.2 to explain the failure of contracts in the state of nature, a deliberation situation like that represented

Figure 2.4

	Keep	Renege
Keep	1,1	3,2
Renege	2,3	4,4

in Figure 2.3, where contract keeping is always rational, is also suggested by his remarks in the answer to the fool. If, as Hobbes wants us to believe, the benefits that derive from keeping a contract and gaining a reputation of trustworthiness are considerable, there might be situations in which the partner who keeps his part of the bargain gains more from his action of promise keeping than he would if he had reneged. A simple commodities exchange provides a good example. If A and B make a contract to exchange A's horse for B's cow, and A hands over her horse to B, then if B reneges on his promise and keeps his cow, it could still be the case that A is glad she kept her promise, simply because the benefits she obtains from her reputation of trustworthiness could be greater than the benefits she would have obtained from possession of either or both of the animals. Although B can enjoy the benefits of the horse as a result of A's trustworthiness (hence explaining why the preference orderings in the lower right quadrant are the lowest), A is still in the more enviable position in the unilateral-breach situation.

Hobbes's remarks also suggest the matrix in Figure 2.4. Like the matrix of Figure 2.2, this matrix represents the parties in the case of a unilateral breach preferring to be in the position of the contract breaker rather than the contract keeper, but as in Figure 2.3, the benefits arising from keeping the contract are high enough to make this action dominant over the action of breach.

For example, in a land-exchange contract, each party might prefer to be a contract breaker holding two plots of land rather than a contract keeper left with only a good reputation. Nonetheless, if each also believed that a good reputation was worth more than the plot of land he originally held (making the preference ordering in the lower right quadrant the lowest), the action of keeping the contract would dominate over the action of breach, as Figure 2.4 indicates.

Judging from Hobbes's enthusiasm (in his answer to the fool) for the great benefits generated by the action of contract keeping, it seems that the matrices in Figures 2.3 and 2.4 together represent two common types of deliberation situation in the state of nature. I call the agreements that produce this type of deliberation situation low-risk contracts, because the losses suffered by the "trustworthy" party in the unilateral-breach situation are low enough to make his position in this situation preferable to his position in the situation in which both parties renege (as in Figure 2.4), and maybe even preferable to the reneger's position in the unilateral-breach situation (as in Figure 2.3). In these low-risk contracts, the action of keeping always dominates over the action of breach, so that a rational person, even if he knows there is a good chance that his partner will renege, will always keep his part of the bargain, because no matter what his partner does, he stands to gain more if he keeps his promise than if he breaks it. Thus, the confederacy argument

Hobbes advances in his answer to the fool is so strong that completion of all low-risk contracts is possible not only in principle but also in practice, because the fear that one's partner is irrational cannot disrupt the completion of this type of contract. And this means that total conflict will not prevail in the state of nature, because this form of peaceful cooperation can and will occur between rational men.

However, if the losses suffered by someone who kept his part of the bargain while his partner reneged were severe enough, the situation would be that represented by the matrix in Figure 2.2. I call the contract that produces this kind of situation a high-risk bargain, because when such a bargain is struck, the high losses suffered by the contract keeper if there is a unilateral breach make his position the least preferable. This means, as we have discussed, that although the best state of affairs in such a situation occurs when both parties to the contract keep their respective parts of the bargain, if there is some uncertainty whether or not the second party will perform (e.g., if his rationality has not yet been established), then the first party has to decide if it is rational to take a chance and keep the bargain. If the potential harm to be incurred by the contract keeper if his partner reneges is enormous (e.g., involving serious maiming or death), then a party could well decide (irrespective of the chances of reaping great rewards if the contract should be completed) to choose the action of breach in order to minimize the losses he would suffer should the worst possible outcome occur. This amounts to using the maximin rule to decide how to resolve this situation; Elster suggests doing so (1979, 20ff.). But many critics would believe, even in high-stakes situations, that this rule is inferior to the use of an expected-utility calculation,[6] and this is especially true in situations in which the stakes are not so high. In this case, it is sensible for a party to perform an expected-utility calculation (assuming some kind of cardinal measure of utility) in order to determine if it is rational to renege or to keep the contractual promise:

1. The expected utility (EU) for A if she keeps her promise:

$$EU = p(u_1) + (1 - p)(u_2)$$

2. The expected utility for A if she reneges:

$$EU = p(v_1) + (1 - p)(v_2)$$

where p is the probability B will keep, $(1 - p)$ is the probability B will renege, u_1 is the cardinal measure of the benefit to A if she keeps and B keeps, u_2 is the cardinal measure of the benefit to A if she keeps and B reneges, v_1 is the cardinal measure of the benefit to A if she reneges and B keeps, and v_2 is the cardinal measure of the benefit to A if she reneges and B reneges. In short, what A will be asking is whether

$$p(u_1 - v_1) + (1 - p)(u_2 - v_2) \lessgtr 0$$

Hence, if

$$p > \frac{v_2 - u_2}{(u_1 - v_1) + (v_2 - u_2)}$$

6   Even when it is impossible to calculate probabilities, one can use this method of calculation if the principle of insufficient reason is used to estimate probabilities.

then A will keep her promise. And if

$$p < \frac{v_2 - u_2}{(u_1 - v_1) + (v_2 - u_2)}$$

then A will renege on her promise. Clearly, if the probability that B will renege is high enough, the expected-utility calculation dictates that A should renege. But equally important is the harm that will be suffered by A if B reneges and A keeps her promise. If the harm is great enough, it will be rational for A to renege even if there is a fairly low probability that B will also renege. On the other hand, if the harm suffered by A if B reneges and A keeps her part of the bargain is not particularly severe, then even given a fairly high probability that B will renege, it could still be rational for A to keep the contract. For example, that will be the case if the benefits enjoyed by A if she and B both keep the contract are very high. But this means that there are times when it is rational to keep one's part of the bargain even in high-risk contract situations, making it possible in practice for such contracts to be successfully completed between rational people in the state of nature.

Hence, Hobbes is on dangerous ground. It looks as if his argument for the rationality of contract keeping, in his answer to the fool, when combined with the irrationality thesis of conflict, establishes the failure of only certain high-risk contracts in which at least one of the parties has a good chance of reneging and/or in which the loss suffered by one party if the other reneges will be severe. All other high-risk contracts and most low-risk contracts have a good chance of succeeding.

It is not yet clear that this is true, and we shall consider in a moment a Hobbesian argument that it is not. But before doing so, I want to make clear why it would not be good news for Hobbes that his state of nature is really quite a nice place after all. In order to argue for the necessity of an absolute sovereign, Hobbes must reject all characterizations of the natural state and the behavior of its inhabitants that would make that state anything less than a violent anarchy. The complete argument for this contention will be given in detail in Chapter 4, but a few words can be said now that will make the contention plausible. Consider that if the confederacy argument for the rationality of contract keeping is accepted, and the passions account is used to explain why certain contracts fail to be completed, Hobbes's state of nature will look remarkably similar to Locke's. In this state of nature, men and women are able to cooperate, make contracts, and thereby implicitly recognize private property. Why do these reasonable creatures need an absolute sovereign? Locke persuasively argues that they do not. And, as we shall discuss in Chapter 4, it is impossible for Hobbes to avoid these Lockean conclusions if his sovereign is needed only to police human interactions and punish irrational people. A radical political solution for disorder, such as the institution of an absolute sovereign, is needed only if radical division among people prevails, and insofar as the passions account of conflict implies that frequent cooperation and contractual exchange will occur in the state of nature, it does not make the conflict between people deep-seated enough to warrant the drastic solution Hobbes proposes. In such a situation, one needs a ruler only to enforce the already existing patterns of cooperation; one does not need an absolute sovereign to *create* those patterns of cooperation.

So, is there any way that Hobbes could salvage the passions account so that it could generate total warfare and thus allow him to draw the political conclusion he wants? To do so, he would first have to argue that the matrices in Figures 2.3 and 2.4 (in which the benefits of a trustworthy reputation outweigh any losses that a reneging party could inflict) are rarely representative of people's reasoning in the state of nature, so that it is rarely rational for one party to keep his contract even if his partner reneges (or is believed to be planning to renege). In order to make this argument, Hobbes would have to maintain that the benefits of confederacy are so low that it is almost never possible for them to outweigh even small losses, and if we accept his argument in his answer to the fool, this would seem to be implausible.

But even if Hobbes could argue successfully that the matrices in Figures 2.3 and 2.4 are almost never correct representations of people's reasoning in the state of nature, he still would have to argue, in order to salvage this account, that the matrix in Figure 2.2, although it is the correct representation of people's estimations of possible states of affairs, will almost never lead them to cooperate with one another. As we have just discussed, Figure 2.2 depicts a situation that is risky, and Hobbes would have to argue that affairs in the state of nature will invariably be such that cooperation will not be worth the risk (i.e., that an expected-utility calculation will almost always counsel against cooperation). How could Hobbes argue this point? He would have to maintain that even when the losses associated with noncooperation are relatively small, the probability that one's partner will renege is very high. But such a high probability will mean a high incidence of these disruptive passions in the population. And if action from these passions is frequent and widespread, self-preservation would seem not to be the dominant desire Hobbes says it is. Hence, this way of fleshing out Hobbes's passions account would conflict with his psychology of human beings.

But does Hobbes have to be wedded to the psychological characterization of human beings as persistent pursuers of their self-preservation? Yes. Hobbes argues that instituting an absolute sovereign will promote one's self-preservation by bringing about peace. And if people are so frequently moved by passions contrary to self-preservation that almost total warfare is generated, how can there be general agreement on instituting an absolute sovereign? The passions disrupting cooperative activities in general in the state of nature would also seem to disrupt the creation and completion of the contract to institute the sovereign. After all, creating the sovereign by surrendering one's right to all things is the content of Hobbes's second law of nature. And if the other laws of nature are rendered invalid by these passions, then why isn't the second law also made invalid by them? So if these passions are so deep-seated as to generate total war, it would seem that rational pursuit of self-preservation will not be powerful enough among enough of the population to bring about peace. It is to preserve the almost universal applicability of his hypothetical imperative to institute an absolute sovereign that Hobbes credits people with the predominant desire to preserve themselves, and this means that the psychology with which this interpretation of the passions account conflicts cannot be abandoned in favor of that account.

So, no matter which way we move as we try to salvage this account, we face impalement on one horn or the other of a mean dilemma. If we accept that account, either we also accept Hobbes's psychology, in which case we end up with sufficient cooperation in the state of nature to obviate an absolute sovereign, or we postulate the

existence of powerful and widespread passions disrupting people's pursuit of self-preservation, in which case we not only abandon that psychology but also endanger the
applicability of Hobbes's hypothetical imperative to institute the sovereign.

There is, however, one further problem with the passions account that some philosophers have raised. Because that account of conflict relies heavily on the disruptive
passion of vainglory, critics, including Rousseau (1950b, 222), have charged that it
presupposes the operation in the state of nature of what for all the world looks like a
social passion. What is the desire for glory but the desire for high esteem from one's
fellow human beings? Even in Chapter 6 of *Leviathan*, Hobbes bases vainglory on "the
flattery of others" (*Lev*, 6, 19, 27). When we crave glory, do we not crave social
recognition, social esteem, a valuable reputation?

Yet, if this is so, the desire for glory in human beings would seem to presuppose
the existence of a human *community*, a state of affairs in which human beings peacefully interact with and talk about one another, such that reputations can be formed
and people held in high or low esteem. Certainly the state of nature is not such a
peaceful human community, and the last thing Hobbes would want to do is attribute
to human beings a passion that is based on a desire to be socially interrelated in a
particular way to other human beings. Doing so would destroy not only Hobbes's
radical individualism but also that argument's conclusion that an absolute sovereign is
a necessary condition for all social interaction and development.

So it seems we must conclude that the passions account of conflict cannot be
accepted by Hobbes. Either we construct the account so that it is consistent with
Hobbes's psychological claims about the dominance of the desire for self-preservation
in human beings, in which case it establishes too much cooperation in the state of
nature to allow him to argue that only a ruler with absolute power is necessary for
peace, or we construct the account so that it generates almost total war in the state of
nature, making institution of a ruler with absolute power necessary to end it, but at
the price of positing a high probability that other passions (at least one of which
appears to be "postsocietal" in nature) will disrupt one's pursuit of self-preservation.
And this is not only inconsistent with Hobbes's psychological claim that "crazy"
behavior endangering one's life is unusual, but also inconsistent with an assumption
that limits the applicability of the hypothetical imperative to institute the sovereign.
So, in the end, the passions account of conflict must be rejected because it makes the
sovereign's institution either unnecessary or else impossible.

2.5 PROBLEMS WITH THE RATIONALITY ACCOUNT OF CONFLICT

It is perhaps because Hobbes appreciated the political implications of the passions
account of conflict that he abandoned that account, which clearly was present in *De
Cive* and *The Elements of Law*, in favor of the rationality account in *Leviathan*. It
appears that this new account of conflict fits into Hobbes's argument very well,
because it generates total warfare, which the conclusion of his argument requires, by
relying on the predominance of the passion for self-preservation, which is nicely
consistent with Hobbes's psychology.

But on closer inspection, this account is just as problematic for Hobbes's argument
as the passions account. First, accepting this account means abandoning the idea that

there are valid hypothetical imperatives dictating cooperative action, and this amounts to jettisoning Chapters 14 and 15 of *Leviathan*. Provided that the prisoner's dilemma (PD) matrix describes the game-theoretic situation underlying the choice whether or not to perform the actions dictated by these laws, then if we are in the state of nature, no matter what our fellow human beings do, we are right not to cooperate with them. Reneging is always our dominant strategy. If they keep their bargain with us, we are right to renege. If they do not keep their part of the bargain with us, again we are right to renege. But whereas Hobbes did indeed want to say that no one should follow these laws in the state of nature, he still maintains in Chapter 15 that they are "*in foro interno*" valid, although "*in foro externo*" not valid. These words are rather mysterious, and we shall be pursuing their meaning later, but suffice to say here that accepting the rationality account would simply mean abandoning the idea that the laws of nature have any validity whatsoever. The fool's position would have to be Hobbes's own. Clearly, Hobbes was terribly uncomfortable with this, and we should try not to give him an account of conflict that forces us to attribute to him the fool's position on the rationality of total noncooperation.

But there is another reason for abandoning the rationality account, and this reason may well explain Hobbes's insistence in Chapter 15 that it is wrong. That reason is that the account does not seem to be true! It would be true if people really were in one-time PD game situations in the state of nature, but a number of critics have argued that they are not, and that they are in fact in multiplay PD games.[7] And because any PD game they are currently in is likely to be part of a series of these situations extending into the future, rather than a one-time occurrence, it is no longer the case that noncooperation is clearly the best strategy for them to take. To present this argument, let us use the action "keeping a contract" as an example of a cooperative venture. If we were sure that the contractual PD game would be played by two parties in the state of nature only once, the action of reneging on the contract would be the most rational action for both. But in this case the parties to the bargain in the natural state know that they will have occasion to contract with each other in the future, and although they know that the action of breach is rational in the short run (i.e., in the first game), they know that in the long run the breach will deprive them of benefits from future bargains by creating distrust between them and putting the action of breach in equilibrium. Hence, the argument is that because contractual activity between people in the state of nature is likely to be frequent and open-ended,[8] the keeping of a contract is always rational, because in addition to supplying each with the benefits of that particular bargain, it acts as a signal to each party that the other party will keep contracts in the future and thus enables both to reap the long-term profits of constant contractual activity.

Even if one of the parties behaves irrationally by breaking his contractual promise in the first game (or successive games), this "iterated PD game" argument counsels that the long-run benefits accruing from faithful contract keeping will prompt the other party to continue to keep his part of the bargain for a time in order to try to "teach" the breaching party to choose the promise-keeping act. The idea is to make

7 For an argument to this effect, see Gregory Kavka (1983a, 291–310).
8 See the discussion of this idea by R. D. Luce and H. Raiffa (1957, 98–9).

the breaching party realize that it is in his best interest to reward rather than punish his partner's cooperative act, because otherwise he will be forcing his partner to renege in subsequent games, and a pattern of contractual breaches will be established that will deprive both of them of the benefits of future bargains. As Luce and Raiffa argue in their classic text on game theory,

> in the repeated game of repeated selection of (α_1, β_1) [in our discussion, the action of keeping the contractual promise] is in a sort of quasi-equilibrium: it is not to the advantage of either player to initiate the chaos that results from not conforming, even though the non-conforming strategy is profitable in the short run (one trial). [1957, 98]

So the argument would have us conclude that the Chapter 13 account of conflict is wrong, that rationality counsels cooperation rather than conflict.[9] Not only does this iterated PD argument for the rationality of contract keeping seem correct, it may even be right to say that it is a plausible interpretation and development of Hobbes's remarks in his answer to the fool. As we have discussed, Hobbes appeals to the benefits of confederacy in this passage in order to persuade us that contract keeping is rational, and these benefits will certainly be among the present and future contractual benefits that the iterated PD argument relies on in order to establish the rationality of keeping any particular bargain. Indeed, modern critics like Michael Taylor (1976, 112ff.) and Edna Ullmann-Margalit (1977, 62–73) have interpreted Hobbes's remarks on the benefits of confederacy in this passage as an attempt at making the iterated PD argument.[10] In any case, the natural way in which the argument links cooperation with self-preservation makes it fit well with Hobbes's psychology, so that it seems to be an argument he should have made, even if he didn't clearly see how to do this in Chapter 15.

Yet, if Hobbes accepts the iterated PD argument, he must accept the idea that reason dictates cooperation, and this means that conflict must be a function of people's irrationality, not their rationality. That is, if the iterated PD argument is correct, the matrix in Figure 2.2 generally describes the nature of people's deliberations in this type of situation, and it can only be that people's failure to be rational and others' constant fear of that failure cause people to behave uncooperatively. So it seems that accepting this argument forces Hobbes to fall back on the passions account of conflict to explain why self-interested people do not behave cooperatively. But, as we have discussed at length, the passions account of conflict is unable to generate enough conflict in the state of nature to justify institution of a sovereign, provided that we accept Hobbes's psychology. Indeed, it is even more difficult to generate that conflict by relying on passion if the iterated PD argument is accepted, because according to that argument, fear that the second party might renege on his part of the bargain should not be sufficient by itself to cause the first party to renege. It is arguably sufficient in a very high-risk situation, in which one might suffer crippling

---

9   Robert Axelrod has conducted computer experiments using different strategies for dealing with iterated PD games and has found that cooperative strategies amass considerably more utility points than noncooperative strategies (1980a, 3–25; 1980b, 379–403).

10 In addition, Gregory Kavka (1983a) discusses this argument, viewing it correctly as a criticism of the Chapter 13 account of conflict, but not seeing how it provides a good interpretation of Hobbes's remarks in the answer to the fool.

losses if the other party reneged, such that one would be unable to absorb the losses that one's "educative efforts" might involve. An expected-utility calculation here would tell one not to risk the chance that one's partner is irrational, but to play it safe by reneging oneself, even if the probability that one's partner is irrational is quite small. (Or, as noted earlier, one might even justify reneging in this situation using the maximin rule.) But in situations of lesser risk, it appears that it is rational for each party to cooperate initially, even if one party fears that the other will not do so this time, as a way of educating the other to be cooperative on future occasions, or as a way of getting cooperative benefits from other people. And this means that the iterated PD argument for the rationality of contract keeping, like the confederacy argument (which is simply a weaker version of it), must be rejected by Hobbes because of the implications of its success.

So, can Hobbes resist the plausibility of the iterated PD argument and salvage the idea that rationality dictates war rather than peace in the state of nature? He might try to deny that the iterated PD argument implies that the state of nature is relatively peaceful by claiming that the number of irrational, crazy people in the state of nature is very high, such that there will be many people in that state incapable of the prudent reasoning necessary for completion of contracts. However, as we have already seen, this is a denial that Hobbes simply cannot make, because the presence of a large number of crazy people in the state of nature threatens the validity of his psychological characterizations of human beings, and, more important, it threatens the applicability of his hypothetical imperative to institute the sovereign.

Some have suggested that he could make use of a different strategy[11] against the iteration argument if he could persuasively establish that it is common knowledge in the state of nature just how many future contractual interactions between the inhabitants there will be (a big "if"). That strategy goes as follows: If we know that there will be some number n of cooperative situations (i.e., prisoner's dilemmas), then we also know that we should not cooperate in the nth (i.e., last) game (there can be no future benefits to tempt us to cooperate; so the situation must be treated as a single-play PD game, and the action of reneging dominates). But if we know that we shall renege in the nth game of the iteration, then we also know that a cooperative move on the $(n-1)$st game will not teach or produce cooperation on the nth game; so again we have reason not to cooperate on the $(n-1)$st game. But knowing we shall renege on the $(n-1)$st game means that we have no reason to cooperate on the $(n-2)$nd game. And so it goes, back to the very first game.

Where is the flaw in this rather irritating argument? Luce and Raiffa (1957, 98–9), as well as Kavka (1983a, 303), have tried to find one, without success. For our purposes, however, we can dismiss the argument, because its premiss that cooperation among people in the state of nature would have a definite bound and that the number would be commonly known is ridiculously strong. Indeed, we do not know in this society how many times we will be in a position to cooperate with one another. So how could people in the state of nature be able to determine this fact? Indeed, how could it become *common* knowledge? (There might be unusual situations in which it

---

11   See, for example, Kavka (1983a, 303), who does not think this counterargument works, and Luce and Raiffa (1957, 98–9).

would be obvious that a game was the last game of the series, e.g., a situation in which one of the parties was two minutes away from dying. In that situation it would be rational for the healthy party to renege, and the dying party probably would be too preoccupied to care.) Thus, an important epistemological problem in the state of nature (one it would seem that only the Delphic oracle could remedy) makes cooperation in iterated PD games possible.

So Hobbes appears to be in a real jam. The rationality account of conflict that it seems that he needs in order to draw his political conclusions is an account that does not follow from the premises of his argument; consistent with his psychology, reason should dictate cooperation rather than conflict. And when the passions account (presupposing the iterated PD argument) is interpreted such that it is consistent with those premises, it does not, in turn, allow him to draw these political conclusions. All of this provides us with an interesting lesson in the trials and hazards of philosophical theory building: Hobbes's premises motivate the answer to the fool and thus the passions account of conflict; Hobbes's conclusion appears to presuppose the account of conflict (generating total war) in Chapter 13 that is inconsistent with those premises.

However, there is an additional problem with the rationality account of conflict. As we have noted, one of the advantages of this account is that it generates total warfare, such that Hobbes can argue that only a ruler with absolute power can bring about peace. But if reason gets people into this state, how can reason get them out? To say that reason generates total conflict seems to involve saying that conflict is inescapable. So it is no accident that in the context of a discussion of how people in the state of nature escape from the state of war, Hobbes should try to answer the fool and revert to the passions account of conflict. The answer to the fool follows Hobbes's statement of the third law of nature: "That men performe their Covenants made":

From that law of Nature, by which we are obliged to transferre to another, such Rights, as being retained, hinder the peace of Mankind [i.e., the second law of nature], there followeth a Third; which is this, *That men performe their Covenants made:* without which, Covenants are in vain, and but Empty words; *and the Right of all men to all things remaining, wee are still in the condition of warre.* [*Lev*, 15, 1, 71; final emphasis added]

Note that Hobbes is saying here that it is because of the validity of the third law of nature that people are able to leave the state of nature and institute a sovereign. Why? Consider the fact that the sovereign is instituted by a *social contract.* When the contract is made, each party to it agrees to surrender his right to all things to the sovereign; but unless each person keeps his promise and actually obeys all the sovereign's commands, the contract will be void and the sovereign never established. The fool, who says there is no such thing as justice, is saying, consistent with the rationality account of conflict and contractual failure, that it is irrational to keep covenants in the state of nature, and thus that reason does not dictate this law. But this means that the social contract (and hence the commonwealth by institution) is impossible, because this contract, like any other, can never occur in the state of nature. Hence, the rationality account of conflict, which the fool essentially accepts, would seem to make it impossible for people to escape from the state of nature.

In Chapter 15, I believe that we see Hobbes trying to escape from this jam by abandoning the rationality account of conflict. That is, by arguing in Chapter 15 that contract keeping is in principle rational, and implying that generally it does not occur only because of people's irrationality, Hobbes has the room he needs to argue that it is possible for the social contract to occur. That this is the right interpretation of Hobbes's aim is confirmed by looking at the ways he ends his answer to the fool: "He therefore that breaketh his Covenant, and consequently declareth that he thinks he may with reason do so, *cannot be received into any Society* that unite themselves for Peace and Defence. . . ." (*Lev*, 15, 5, 73; emphasis added) Hobbes appears to be saying here that only those people who recognize the rationality of contract keeping will be good citizens of a commonwealth, because only they will comply with the contractual agreement such that a commonwealth can be created.[12]

2.6 SUMMARY

Let us review the ways in which the two accounts of conflict that we have developed from the text of *Leviathan* have failed.

The passions account fails on two counts:

1. If it is interpreted consistent with Hobbesian psychology, it does not generate sufficient conflict in the state of nature to allow Hobbes to derive the necessity for an absolute sovereign.

2. If it is interpreted in a way that is inconsistent with that psychology, it is then able to generate sufficient conflict for that conclusion, but it does so at the cost of threatening the widespread applicability of his hypothetical imperative to institute a sovereign (perhaps even relying on a postsocietal passion in the process).

The rationality account fails for two reasons:

1. It contends that uncooperative behavior is rational, when in fact it seems, consistent with his psychology, that reason would frequently dictate cooperative behavior rather than warfare.

2. It makes conflict so deep-seated that it is impossible to see how people can escape it. In particular, if people are unable to keep contracts in the state of nature, it would seem to be impossible for them to keep a contract to institute a sovereign.

So, do we conclude that Hobbes's argument for absolute sovereignty fails at this very early stage? Not yet. I want to develop a third account of conflict in the next chapter, bearing traces of both the rationality and passions accounts, that seems to do a better job of fitting both Hobbes's premises and his political conclusions than either of these two accounts has done.

12 At least one of Hobbes's contemporary critics also suspected that it was to save his social contract that Hobbes introduced the third law of nature and wrote his answer to the fool. See Ralph Cudworth (1845, 499–502).

CHAPTER 3

The Shortsightedness Account of Conflict and the Laws of Nature

Everyone in our unit thought we would beat the Japanese inside six months. It just goes to show that man's egotism is exceeded only by his stupidity.

U.S. Army veteran of World War II

What if we could come up with an account of conflict that had all of the advantages of the rationality and passions accounts but none of either account's disadvantages? Such an account would fit with Hobbes's psychological premises and yet generate sufficient warfare in the state of nature to make institution of an absolute sovereign necessary to end it. Moreover, it would explain this conflict while still making it possible for Hobbes to argue that people would be able to carry out that institution. I shall try to construct such an account, which I call the shortsightedness account, in this chapter. And I believe there is enough textual evidence to indicate that Hobbes not only would welcome this account of conflict but may even have been confusedly trying to present it himself in both *De Cive* and *Leviathan*.

The discussion of conflict in this chapter will also have another purpose. Although Hobbes characterizes the natural state as war-prone, violent and insecure, he nonetheless argues that people in this state will recognize the validity of certain "laws of nature" dictating moral behavior. As noted in Chapter 1, ever since the publication of *Leviathan*, Hobbes's readers have been mystified as to why the existence of valid moral laws does not render the state of nature relatively orderly and peaceful, rather than chaotic and violent. So we shall be using this account of conflict to explain why these laws' peculiar "validity" in the natural state does not render that state peaceful. Indeed, the success of the shortsightedness account in providing an interpretation of Hobbes's rather obscure remarks on the validity of these laws strongly suggests that he was somehow trying to promulgate that account in *Leviathan*.

3.1 CONFLICT ARISING BECAUSE OF SHORTSIGHTED PURSUIT OF SELF-PRESERVATION

We have already seen the way in which the argument for the rationality of contract keeping in iterated PD game situations fits well with Hobbes's psychological premisses; so let us accept what seemed inescapable before — that given those premises, this argument is correct. But can we say that in the state of nature people will nonetheless tend to mistakenly treat PD games as one-time occurrences rather than as members of a series? If we could do so, we would be acknowledging the soundness of the iterated PD game argument for cooperation, but still endorsing, in the main, Hobbes's Chapter 13 account of conflict! This would mean reconciling Hobbes's remarks in Chapter 13 with his answer to the fool in Chapter 15. Let us see what this argument looks like.

There is, quite clearly, one circumstance that would force people to take a single-play perspective. As we discussed in Chapter 2, in high-risk situations, in which one can suffer crippling losses if the other party reneges and takes advantage of one's cooperation, it would seem irrational to engage in a strategy of cooperating in order to teach one's partner to do the same, because one would be unable to absorb the loss that might be involved in the teaching. But in the last chapter it seemed that if we accepted the iterated PD argument, we could predict pervasive conflict only in these high-risk situations; cooperation in situations of lesser risk would, it seemed, be rational. The only disrupters of rationality in these situations appeared to be passions competing with self-preservation (such as the passion for glory), and if we postulated that these passions were prominent and pervasive enough to generate almost total warfare, we would be contradicting Hobbes's psychological description of human beings and endangering the widespread applicability of his hypothetical imperative to institute a sovereign.

But our acceptance of the iterated PD argument does not commit us to the passions account of conflict we previously rejected. There is something other than disruptive passions that could force a person to take a single-play perspective in a low-risk iterated PD situation: *shortsightedness*. The account would contend that many people fail to appreciate the long-term benefits of cooperation and opt instead for the short-term benefits of noncooperation, and the rest are legitimately fearful enough of this shortsightedness afflicting their partners to doubt that cooperation would have any educative effects. This worry could then force even a farsighted person to take a single-play orientation, with the result that the uncooperative action would dominate.

There is important textual evidence in *De Cive* that we are on the right track in attributing this account of conflict to Hobbes. In that work, Hobbes offers the following explanation for why people fight with one another in the state of nature:

because men cannot put off this same irrational appetite, whereby they greedily prefer the present good (to which, by strict consequence, many unforeseen evils do adhere) before the future. . . . [*DC, EW* ii, 3, 32, 48]

And in the same work he invokes shortsightedness to explain why people do not obey the laws of nature:

most men, by reason of their perverse desire of present profit, are very unapt to observe these laws, although acknowledged by them. . . . [*DC, EW* ii, 3, 27, 45]

This "perverse desire of present profit" seems to be the irrational grasping at short-term advantage. Hobbes labels it "greed" in the first passage, and greed is frequently cited as a cause of conflict in *Leviathan*, as when he blames "avarice" in Chapter 14 for failure of contracts in the state of nature (*Lev*, 14, 18, 68). It is also significant that Hume, whose *A Treatise of Human Nature* shows a deep indebtedness to Hobbes's

Leviathan in so many ways, should have espoused what appears to be the main outline of this account to explain the generation of violence in a state of nature:

> You have the same propension, that I have, in favour of what is contiguous above what is remote. You are, therefore, naturally carried to commit acts of injustice as well as me. Your example both pushes me forward in this way by imitation, and also affords me a new reason for any breach of equity, by shewing me, that I should be the cully of my integrity, if I alone shou'd impose on myself a severe restraint amidst the licentiousness of others. [*Treatise*, III, ii, vii; 1978, 535]

Perhaps Hume developed this account because he was influenced by the suggestive passages from *De Cive* and *Leviathan* just quoted.

But what would lead people to take a shortsighted perspective in their pursuit of self-preservation? Hobbes does not say, and we must be careful to attribute to him an explanation that neither threatens nor contradicts his ethical subjectivism and the instrumentalist notion of reasoning following from it. For example, Hobbes cannot simply condemn people for being shortsighted if it turns out that they want short-term benefits and do not care about the future. If I want to live for the moment, how am I wrong or irrational to do so, given that, according to Hobbes, what is good for me is what I desire?

However, given his "healthy deliberation" theory of rationality, which we discussed in Chapter 1, Hobbes can condemn the people in the state of nature as irrational by convicting them of *a mistake in reasoning*, not a mistake in what they desire. In particular, he can contend that their noncooperative actions further their self-preservation only in small, short-term ways, while putting their lives in considerable danger in the long term. In fact, we can isolate on Hobbes's behalf two plausible ways in which people could incorrectly interpret the situation in the state of nature, and these incorrect interpretations, creating false beliefs, are both natural enough and plausible enough that between them they could generate substantial shortsighted reasoning in this state.

First, the iterated nature of the PD game might not be obvious to some of the less intellectually talented inhabitants of this state, who either never realize that they should take a multiplay perspective or are not mentally acute enough to work out the long-term benefits of cooperation. Such people would prefer the short-term advantages of noncooperation simply because they would not understand that the long-term advantages of cooperation would be much greater.

Second, and more important, even if it did occur to them that they might be in an iterated PD game in which substantial long-term benefits make cooperation rational, they might decide, nonetheless, to reject such a characterization of their situation on the grounds that the prospect of future contractual interactions with their present partners is too remote to warrant it. Remember that in the state of nature, people are supposed to be independent of *all* society. And it would be natural in such a situation for a person to treat a PD game as a one-time occurrence, given the small chances of interacting with the same partner again and the overall uncertainties of this state. In other words, establishing future cooperative ties would seem too unlikely to make a multiplay perspective rational. Indeed, such calculations do not seem badly wrong. Proponents of the iterated PD argument would insist, of course, that they *are* wrong, because even if accidental meetings with other human beings were rare, the vicissitudes of this state would make it rational for them to *seek out* cooperative interactions with one another so as to better deal with the natural and man-made problems of living. (Consider, for example, the benefits of forming a confederacy contract.) The reasoner in this state believes incorrectly that the chances of her interacting again with her fellows are independent of what she does; she does not appreciate that she can and should pursue cooperative interactions with her fellows that, if successfully completed, could benefit her and them substantially (for example, building bridges over streams, or engaging in joint hunts for game). It does not, however, occur to her that the chances of future cooperative interactions with others in this state are in large part up to her, and this does seem to be a very reasonable mistake, making it plausible that many people in the state of nature will make the mistake. This error will lead a person not to cooperate with her partner, fully believing noncooperation to be the rational course of action in what she regards as, to all intents and purposes, a single-play PD game.

For these two reasons, and especially for the second, it would be plausible (or at least arguable) for Hobbes to claim that shortsightedness would be very common in the state of nature, particularly because the belief that one will not interact frequently with one's fellows in this asocial state is not obviously wrong. (What would you think if you were in this state?) However, Hobbes does not have to take the unreasonable position that *everyone* suffers in the state of nature from some sort of shortsightedness in order to explain the origination of widespread conflict. Those who are good calculators of their long-term self-interest and who therefore do recognize the rationality of cooperation established by the iterated PD argument will rarely find it rational to cooperate if this shortsightedness is common in others. As Hume notes in the passage previously quoted, if each party to a contract knows that there is a high probability that his partner is too shortsighted to be able to be "taught" to cooperate, he will not think his cooperative action overly likely to bring him benefits of future bargains. Instead, he will think there is a very good chance that his partner will fail to understand his strategy and thus end up believing him to be a "sucker" in this (from the partner's perspective) single-play PD game. Nor will he think that, as a rational member of the state of nature, he has much chance of developing a "trustworthy" reputation in others' eyes that will enable him to reap future contractual benefits with them, because the prospective partners in any future contracts will be more likely to see any previous contract keeping as establishing his reputation as a sucker rather than as a trustworthy promise keeper.

These considerations mean that cooperative action is risky in the state of nature. Whether or not one should take the risk depends on the probability that one's partner will renege, the extent of the damage his reneging will inflict, and the probability, if he does renege, that he can be educated by one's cooperation to cooperate himself in the future. Clearly, as we have said, in high-risk situations, contract keeping will be too dangerous for a person who is committed to self-preservation. And in low-risk situations, Hobbes could insist that the widespread shortsightedness of the natural state's inhabitants will make the probability of one's partner reneging and failing to learn anything from one's own cooperative act high enough that an expected-utility calculation likely will dictate against cooperation.

But the situation is actually worse than this. I might believe that you are rational, and I might also be rational and thus willing to cooperate, but I might fear that you think that I am shortsighted. This fear will then cause me to worry that you will take a single-play perspective and behave uncooperatively in self-defense, leading me to take the same single-play perspective and thus to behave uncooperatively. In other words, in order for cooperation to be ensured, either there must be common knowledge among the partners in a cooperative situation that each of the others is rational, or each must believe that the probability of her fellows believing her rational is quite high, so that an expected-utility calculation will dictate cooperation. Hobbes would certainly argue that this "common-knowledge" or "common-belief" assumption is very strong and unlikely to be present among many collections of people in the state of nature.

Note also how any tendency toward substantial risk aversion can cause one to overestimate the probabilities that one's partner is shortsighted and thus to conclude incorrectly that cooperation is irrational after an expected-utility calculation.[1] Indeed, such overestimates can be innocently but incorrectly made by normally risk-averse people; evidence of the extent of one's partner's farsightedness might, after all, be hard to come by in this state.

There is another effect that knowledge of the widespread existence of shortsighted people can have on the rational reasoners in the state of nature. The more convinced I am that shortsightedness is common in this state, the less interested I will be in actually seeking out interaction with my fellows with an eye toward actively cooperating with them, because I will fear that by doing so I would only be foolishly exposing myself to the dangers of exploitation and/or open conflict. But the less inclined I am to seek out interactions with my fellows, the lower the probability that I will interact with any of them again, and thus the less likely it will be that I can expect any long-term benefits from cooperation with them. These calculations dispose me, once again, to take a single-play perspective and hence not cooperate with my partners in PD games.

Hobbes might also cite two other causes of shortsightedness: the tendency to discount future benefits because they do not seem to be as "fully real" as present ones, and the tendency to be abnormally risk-averse, and thus to grab present benefits rather than risk them (even when the risk is more than worth it) for more. These causes of shortsightedness would not be traceable to false beliefs resulting in mistakes in reasoning; they are more like diseases, or perhaps "congenital deformities" in one's reasoning ability. Hobbes could not plausibly argue that they are powerful or widespread in the population, and thus he could not argue that they can produce any substantial amount of conflict in the state of nature. But they are useful supplemental causes for shortsightedness in this state, and their occurrence in the population increases the chances that any given person will be shortsighted in this state.

Note that among right-reasoning people there might be situations in which correct estimation of probabilities and utilities would be such that an expected-utility calculation actually would dictate cooperation. Hence, this account of conflict cannot, like the rationality account, rule out the possibility of cooperation in the way the latter account does unless it presupposes that shortsightedness is universal — an implausible

---

1   I am indebted to Don Hubin for suggesting this point.

assumption. But as long as the argument makes this kind of fallacious reasoning only very common, the dangers of cooperation would seem to be enough to make conflict even in low-risk situations very widespread, making the state of nature *almost* a state of total war, and this is probably good enough for Hobbes's purposes. Although this account admits that a few people will establish patterns of cooperation among themselves in the state of nature, it maintains nonetheless that the vast majority will not do so and will be disposed to fight with one another in the way that, as Hobbes himself puts it, "foul weather" tends to result in rain (*Lev,* 13, 8, 62). This means that genuine peace can be achieved in this state only by a ruler with the power to create the possibility of cooperation, not by one with only the limited power to police preexisting patterns — for almost none exist.

So this account of conflict cites both shortsightedness and the (rational or irrational) fear of it in one's partner as the reasons that people in this state of nature generally behave exactly as Hobbes characterizes them in Chapter 13, despite the correctness of the iterated PD argument about which he (at least) hints in Chapter 15. How is this account more successful at generating conflict than the passions account previously sketched? The problem with the passions account was that either the passions disruptive of cooperation were taken to be pervasive in the population, in which case we purchased warfare at the price of a description of human beings at odds with Hobbes's psychology that endangered the applicability of his hypothetical imperative to institute a sovereign, or these passions were understood to be no more common than Hobbes's psychology would have us believe, in which case there would be far too much cooperation in the state of nature to make a ruler with absolute power necessary for achievement of peace. The shortsightedness account of conflict, however, explains conflict by reference not to disruptive passions but to fallacious reasoning, and this can be held to be extremely common among the inhabitants of the state of nature without in any way endangering Hobbes's psychological characterization of human beings, because it is a mistake that people who are predominantly concerned about their self-preservation not only can but naturally will make.

But even if this account explains conflict consistent with Hobbesian psychology, does it endanger the applicability of the hypothetical imperative to institute the sovereign? Because this account does not challenge Hobbes's psychology, instituting a sovereign can be understood to advance the primary interest of both shortsighted and farsighted people alike: their self-preservation. The only concern this account raises is whether or not shortsighted people will be able to understand this point. What Hobbes has to do later in his social contract argument is to contend successfully that because shortsightedness is widespread, instructions about the benefits of cooperation will not work (shortsightedness, in other words, is difficult, if not impossible, to cure), but that both shortsighted and farsighted people will come to realize that the rational way to deal with this deep-seated irrationality precipitating warfare is to institute an absolute sovereign who will make it in one's short-term best interest to cooperate. Finally, Hobbes has to be able to say that people are just rational enough to be able to institute such a sovereign. That is, although they are not able to live peacefully and cooperatively on their own, they are just rational enough to be able to cooperate "once," as it were, in the institution of the sovereign. This project at least sounds possible, although it is by no means clear that Hobbes can pull it off, and that is what we shall evaluate in later chapters. However, that the project sounds plausible is enough to assure us at this stage that the shortsightedness account of conflict is a good account for Hobbes to incorporate into his argument for absolute sovereignty.

Indeed, if Hobbes can use this account to show that cooperation in the institution of a sovereign is possible but still difficult, his argument would seem to have the virtue of being historically accurate. Recall his contention in *De Cive* that it was "bad reasoning" that plunged the England of his day into civil strife (*DC, EW* ii, pref., xi–xii) and that it was his purpose to use "most firm reasons" (*DC, EW* ii, pref., xiii–xiv) to demonstrate the necessity of a ruler with absolute power (*DC, EW* ii, pref., xiii–xiv). Such remarks square nicely with an account of conflict that says that warfare results mainly from mistaken (or distorted) reasoning and that such warfare can be cured only by an absolute sovereign whose institution by human beings is difficult but not impossible.

Note that this account can be nicely supplemented by an explanation for conflict that blames glory for at least some of the warfare in the natural state. Hobbes's psychology recognizes that we can become "diseased" and be moved by other desires that disrupt our rational pursuit of self-preservation. As long as these disease-produced desires are not held to be very prominent or powerful among the population generally, Hobbes can invoke them to supplement the previous two causes of conflict. Indeed, perhaps this is what he meant to do in Chapter 13. Perhaps he meant to say that people's believing, either rightly or wrongly, that they are in a one-shot PD game is the chief source of conflict in the state of nature, whereas irrational passions such as the desire for glory are minor, although not unimportant, disrupters of cooperation in that state. Given that our new interpretation of the Chapter 13 account of conflict does not establish total conflict and does not implicate rationality as the sole source of conflict, there is no theoretical obstacle preventing Hobbes from blaming passions like glory for at least some of the conflict in the natural state.

Indeed, Strauss seems correct in holding that Hobbes is persistently attracted to this passion as a force disruptive of cooperative behavior. We have already detailed many of the passages in *Leviathan* and elsewhere in which this passion is blamed for civil strife. However, we have also discussed Rousseau's contention that glory is a *postsocietal* passion that should not be playing any role in the generation of conflict in the natural state. If this is true, Hobbes cannot use it at all as a cause of conflict in the state of nature. So can the desire for glory be understood in a way that does not presuppose comparison of oneself with others in a social community?

It can. Hobbes's definition of glory in Chapter 6 suggests that it is better understood as a desire to "win" or "prevail" over all things, rather than a desire to climb to the top of some social ladder:

Joy, arising from imagination of a mans own power and ability, is that exultation of the mind which is called GLORYING. [*Lev*, 6, 19, 26–7]

This passage suggests that when we are "glorying" we are taking satisfaction in our great power and ability allowing us to predominate in the world, so that the desire for glory is the craving for that power that allows us to "have our way." Indeed, Hobbes suggests that this craving is sometimes so strong that we are disposed to lie to ourselves about the extent of our power in order to believe it satisfied:

vain-glory . . . consisteth in the feigning or supposing of abilities in our selves, which we know are not. [*Lev*, 6, 21, 27]

Hobbes's discussion also suggests that the desire for glory will manifest itself in different ways in different situations. In a philosophical argument, for example, it might manifest itself in a desire to be right; in a political or athletic contest, it might become a desire to win the contest; in certain social settings it might well take the form of social ladder climbing if this were a way to gain power and precedence. However, in a presocial situation like the state of nature, the desire for precedence would take none of these forms; instead, people would crave the power to predominate over whatever came their way in that state — be it people or animals or inanimate objects. Readers might still be suspicious of the idea that this craving to be "first" and superior to all things is a presocial passion. I do not want to mount an elaborate defense of Hobbes's claim that the desire for glory is presocial. My remarks here are meant only to show that Hobbes at least has a good case for making this claim, and the way in which "me-first" thinking generally prevents cooperative interaction among human beings, both young and old, is certainly grist for his mill that the passion is both presocial in its nature and antisocial in its effects.

The desire for glory can be used not only to supplement the shortsightedness account of conflict but also to bolster it. As Hobbes says in *The Elements of Law,* people who suffer from vainglory "hope for precedency and superiority above their fellows." (*EL*, I, xiv, 3, 54) And because we want and even need to see ourselves as powerful and superior, even though we are not, we are liable to underestimate our opponent's powers and overestimate our own. Thus emboldened, we are more likely to think it reasonable to wage war with our opponent. To put it more exactly, it affects the probabilities of our expected-utility calculation. We tend to overestimate the probability of our winning a conflict and underestimate the probability of being beaten by our opponent, and that makes our calculation more likely to favor warfare. Like the army veteran whose remark was quoted at the start of the chapter, people tend to believe not only that their side will win but also that their victory will be swift.

Moreover, people's fears that the effects of glory pursuit may lead their partners to make this kind of miscalculation will make them less likely to trust their partners, and more likely to turn to violence themselves. As Hobbes says in *De Cive,*

All men in the state of nature have a desire and will to hurt, but not proceeding from the same cause, neither equally to be condemned. For one man, according to that natural equality which is among us, permits as much to others as he assumes to himself; which is an argument of a temperate man, and one that rightly values his power. Another, supposing himself above others, will have a license to do what he lists, and challenges respect and honour, as due to him before others; which is an argument of a fiery spirit. This man's will to hurt ariseth from vain glory, and the false esteem he hath of his own strength; the other's from the necessity of defending himself, his liberty, and his goods, against this man's violence. [*DC, EW* ii, 1, 4, 7]

If you know that your partner is disposed to think herself more powerful than she is, and thus is disposed to think she can win a confrontation with you, you are fearful of making yourself prey to her violence, and thus become disposed to "defensive" violence yourself. Thus, the desire for glory has another important effect on the expected-utility calculation concerning the advisability of cooperation. It "feeds" the fear that one's partner is shortsighted and thus makes it appear all the more plausible that one should not cooperate with one's fellows in this state.

To conclude, we should ask how plausible this entire explanation of conflict really is. We do Hobbes no favor if we attribute to him an explanation of warfare and a view of human behavior that, no matter how consistent with his psychology, few would find believable. However, I think this account is at least arguable. The crux of the account is its claim that shortsightedness will be common, although not ubiquitous, in this state. And our discussion has shown that Hobbes can make a fairly good case for the claim that the rationality of cooperation is sufficiently difficult to understand that the number of people who will reason badly and who thus will fail to cooperate is high enough to make cooperation generally too risky. However, I have not meant my remarks to be a full-scale defense of this account of conflict as *true*. All that I have tried to suggest is that the account is at least arguably true, such that we can, in good conscience, insert it into Hobbes's argument for the clearly deficient rationality and passions accounts. In Chapter 7, after we have finished presenting Hobbes's complete argument for absolute sovereignty, we shall have reason to look at this account with a more critical eye. In particular, we shall have cause to wonder about the "despair" this account attributes to rational people in the state of nature of ever being able to educate their shortsighted partners. Moreover, it is important to keep in mind that the shortsightedness account of conflict is the key to Hobbes's claim that the state of nature does not match Locke's description of it. Thus, it carries a dangerous amount of weight in his argument. In particular, if one could show that the shortsightedness account of conflict fails to generate extensive warfare, Hobbes would be stuck with an account of conflict necessitating a more Lockean political remedy, not his own. We shall see that this is not the only time that Lockean ideas come dangerously close to intruding into Hobbes's argument.

3.2 REVIEW OF THE SHORTSIGHTEDNESS ACCOUNT OF CONFLICT

Let us now review the explanation of conflict we have just constructed:

1. The iterated PD game argument establishes that although it is not rational to cooperate in single-play PD games, many and perhaps even most cooperative situations in the state of nature are multi-play PD game situations in which it is in one's long-term best interest to cooperate.

2. The complexities of life in the state of nature are such that many people will reason, mistakenly, that it is rational not to cooperate in iterated PD game situations. This fallacious reasoning will be common, but not ubiquitous, in the state of nature.

3. The fear that one's partner is too shortsighted to appreciate the long-term benefits of cooperation, or the fear that one's partner will believe that one is shortsighted, will lead one (a) not to cooperate in high-risk cooperative ventures (as dictated either by the maximin rule or by an expected-utility calculation), and (b) not to cooperate in many (although not all) medium- and low-risk cooperative situations, as dictated by an expected-utility calcu-

lation (where the probability that one's partner will behave uncooperatively is generally high).

4. The desire for glory, understood as the desire to have the power and ability to get one's own way, is a powerful but subsidiary cause of conflict; and insofar as it encourages the belief that one is superior to one's fellows, it leads one to overestimate one's chances of winning a conflict, and this encourages the conclusion among people in this state that [as defined in 3(a) or 3(b)] it is rational not to cooperate.

Henceforth in this book I will refer to this entire four-step explanation of conflict in the state of nature as the shortsightedness account of conflict.

3.3 THE LAWS OF NATURE[2]

I have tried to show, in a variety of ways, how the desire for self-preservation (supplemented by the desire for glory) suggests an explanation of conflict that not only fits neatly with Hobbes's argument for absolute sovereignty but also is suggested in the text of *Leviathan*. But this explanation has at least one other significant advantage: Unlike the rationality and passions accounts of conflict, it does an excellent job of explaining how and why Hobbes's laws of nature are not fully valid in the natural state.

As we have already discussed, Hobbes characterizes his laws of nature as hypothetical imperatives, that is, conclusions or theorems designed to specify actions that will be means to one's self-preservation. However, he is very hazy about the nature of these laws' validity:

The Lawes of Nature oblige *in foro interno;* that is to say, they bind to a desire they should take place: but *in foro externo;* that is, to the putting them in act, not alwayes. For he that should be modest, and tractable, and performe all he promises, in such time, and place, where no man els should do so, should but make himselfe a prey to others, and procure his own certain ruine, contrary to the ground of all Lawes of Nature, which tend to Natures preservation. [*Lev,* 15, 36, 79]

This qualification of the laws' validity is vague and very puzzling in light of the strong statements Hobbes makes immediately following this passage concerning the force of the laws' obliging power:

The Lawes of Nature are Immutable and Eternall; For Injustice, Ingratitude, Arrogance, Pride, Iniquity, Acception of persons, and the rest, can never be made lawfull. For it can never be that Warre shall preserve life, and Peace destroy it. [*Lev,* 15, 38, 79]

Hobbes even concludes Chapter 15 by saying that the laws of nature have the status of laws because they are "delivered in the word of God" (*Lev,* 15, 41, 80), making them divine commands. But readers from the seventeenth to the twentieth century have

---

2   The numbers and formulations of the laws of nature vary in Hobbes's three political works, but in substance the laws remain the same. In this book, I shall be using the final formulation of the laws given in *Leviathan*. M. M. Goldsmith (1966, 245–7) gives a detailed comparison of the different formulations of the laws of nature in Hobbes's three political works.

been confused by these various characterizations of the natural laws.[3] If the laws are immutable, eternal, and commanded by God, why are they not binding in the natural state? And even if we consider them to be only prudent "theorems," dictates of right reason, why should Hobbesian self-interested people not follow them, given that they are supposed to want above all else to further their self-preservation?

Clearly, it is to caution his readers from thinking that these laws provide a full remedy for the warfare in the state of nature that Hobbes qualifies the laws' validity, saying that some of them are only *in foro interno* valid, not *in foro externo* valid. But what do these peculiar terms mean? From Hobbes's remarks in Chapter 15 we know that the peculiar validity of these laws has something to do with not making oneself a "prey" to others. And in Hobbes's statement of the second law of nature there is a "directive" *built into the law itself* to determine the willingness of one's partner to perform the peaceful action before deciding to do so oneself. It is right, he says,

That a man be willing, *when others are so too*, as farre-forth, as for Peace, and defence of himselfe he shall think it necessary to lay down this right to all things; and be contented with so much liberty against other men, as he would allow other men against himselfe. [*Lev*, 14, 5, 64–5; emphasis added]

These two passages therefore suggest that the laws have the following structure:

If you seek peace (which is a means to your preservation), then do action x, provided that others are willing to do x.

In other words, the laws of nature are to be understood as hypothetical imperatives, with a rider attached to each of them specifying the conditions under which doing x is rational.[4]

Exactly why this rider must be attached to each of these laws is explained by the disruptive role that the account of conflict just developed assigns to our shortsightedness. According to this account, the rider has to be attached to these laws because only then will they be *true* hypothetical imperatives. Each of the actions mentioned in the laws leads to peace and involves cooperation with others. But each action will lead to peace only if not only we but also our cooperative partner(s) engage in the action. According to the iterated PD argument, if we can determine that our partner appreciates this point now, or will appreciate this point in the future after a little educative help from us, her willingness to perform these peaceful actions should cause us to perform them also. Doing so will generate a cooperative equilibrium, and a state of peace, rather than a state of competitive violence. Thus, the iterated PD argument helps us to understand the mysterious phrase "*in foro interno* valid"; Hobbes uses it to endorse the laws as *true* hypothetical imperatives. They correctly describe to us how we can preserve ourselves by telling us ways of achieving peace, ways that will be effective means to this goal provided that a certain condition is fulfilled — specifically, the willingness of others to perform these peace-producing actions also.

But the shortsightedness of human beings and their occasional tendency to seek glory before anything else explain why these laws are *in foro externo* invalid in the state of nature. That phrase simply means that the actions that the laws direct ought not to

3   Recall Clarendon's puzzlement, discussed in Chapter 2, Section 2.2 (1676, 37).
4   Warrender also speaks of "validating conditions" of the natural laws in somewhat the way I am doing (1957, chap. 5, esp. 87–93).

be performed in the state of nature, because the shortsightedness account explains why the rider attached to these laws will not be satisfied in this state. According to this account, although cooperation is rational, the prevalence of shortsighted and glory-prone people will mean that one usually cannot risk cooperation oneself because one cannot be sure enough in most cooperative situations that one's partner will be cooperative (or will learn to cooperate). So the fact that the rider to these laws will rarely, if ever, be satisfied will mean that the actions dictated by the laws should not be performed. And remember that this is precisely the explanation for people not following the laws of nature that Hobbes gives in *De Cive:* "most men, by reason of their perverse desire of present profit, are very unapt to observe these laws, although acknowledged by them. . . ." (*DC, EW* ii, 3, 27, 45)

So the shortsightedness account of conflict developed on Hobbes's behalf in this chapter provides us with a neat and effective interpretation of Hobbes's remarks on these laws' validity, whereas neither the rationality account nor the passions account succeeds as well. If we accept the passions account of conflict, we are maintaining that the actions dictated by the laws of nature, such as "contract keeping" or "mutual accommodation," are rational (i.e., actions that will further one's self-preservation), but cannot be followed in practice because people have no way of assuring that others' passions will not disrupt their reasoning processes. But this characterization of *in foro interno* validity is not successful, because if we grant that following any of these laws is in principle rational, and if we accept Hobbes's psychology, we are also forced to grant that most of the time people will want to follow them in practice, thus making the laws of nature *in foro externo* obliging in the state of nature.

The rationality account does a bit better. The PD matrix explains why, in the end, the actions that would bring about this improved state of affairs are irrational for state-of-nature inhabitants to perform in practice, making the laws *in foro externo* invalid. However, as we discussed briefly in the last chapter, the problem with the rationality account is that it does not give an adequate account of *in foro interno* validity. Hobbes maintains that the validity of these laws, understood as hypothetical imperatives, is bound up with others' willingness to do the actions in question. Yet, if the rationality account is correct, others' willingness to cooperate gives one an excellent reason not to cooperate, because one can gain significant advantages as the reneger in a unilateral-breach situation. Indeed, the rationality account of conflict would seem to dictate against acting peacefully, especially when one's partner is disposed to do so.

Therefore, only an account of conflict that blames shortsightedness for most of the conflict, while allowing glory to be a subsidiary cause of warfare, can show how the laws of nature are true hypothetical imperatives (i.e., *in foro interno* valid, but, in general, not *in foro externo* valid).

It is important to note, however, that only laws three through twenty fail the *in foro externo* validity test on this account of conflict. As Hobbes would wish, the first and second laws presented in Chapter 14 are *in foro externo* binding in the state of nature. The first law of nature is

That every man ought to endeavour Peace, as farre as he has hope of obtaining it; and when he cannot obtain it, that he may seek, and use, all helps, and advantages of Warre. [*Lev,* 14, 4, 64]

The latter half of the law, as Hobbes says, is merely "the sum of the right of nature" (*Lev*, 14, 4, 64), that is, a directive to do those things that will further one's self-preservation, and it is simply a fact, in Hobbes's view, that rational people do exercise the "right" to pursue their self-interest in the state of nature. The first half of the law, the willingness to seek peace, also has to be an accurate description of at least the people's state of mind in this state, insofar as peace is supposed to be a means to one's self-preservation. In addition, the second law of nature, that is, "*That a man be willing, when others are so too, as farre-forth, as for Peace, and defence of himselfe he shall think it necessary, to lay down this right to all things,*" must hold *in foro externo* if Hobbes is going to make his argument for the desirability of civil society under a sovereign. And if Hobbes's argument works, it will hold.

But what about Hobbes's third law? Should that be valid in the natural state? It would appear not. If the shortsightedness account of conflict is correct, people in that state will almost never be willing to keep their part of the bargain, whether they be the first or the last to perform. But if this is so, how can Hobbes successfully argue that the social contract instituting the absolute sovereign can be completed in the state of nature? This question, which presents a dangerous challenge to the success of Hobbes's entire deduction of the absolute sovereign, will be the topic of Chapter 6 of this book.

3.4 HOBBES'S SCIENCE OF MORAL PHILOSOPHY REEXAMINED

How successful is Hobbes's doctrine of the laws of nature as a moral theory? He would argue, I think, that it is very successful. First, it offers an intriguing explanation of how actions have an important conventional status in society. We think that we are "supposed to" keep contracts, be merciful, and so forth. Why do we embrace these norms? Consider that the rider to each of these imperatives in the natural laws indicates that the actions dictated by the laws are rational for any person to follow only when and if others are willing to perform them also. Thus, from the Hobbesian standpoint, it would be rational for societies (such as the ones in which we live) to develop conventions dictating these actions. Widespread participation in these conventions (i.e., widespread interdependent adoption of and action on the idea that one is *supposed to* keep contracts in the same way that one in *supposed to* drive on a particular side of the road) will mean that people will come to expect that when they deal with one another in particular cases, the rider will be satisfied such that it is rational for each of them to cooperate. This "conventional side" to Hobbesian thought might warrant us calling him the father of the kind of "moral contractarianism" developed by such twentieth-century thinkers as Harman (1977) and Gauthier (1985).[5]

Still, is this the kind of conventional, rule-based analysis of the natural laws sufficient for us to call Hobbes's theory a *moral* theory? Indeed, given the self-interested justification of these laws, is Hobbes not simply a sophisticated kind of ethical egoist? There has been some confusion on this point. Gregory Kavka, who has put forward a structural interpretation of the laws of nature similar to my own, claims

---

5   However, Gauthier's views are importantly different from Hobbes's views, in part because Gauthier does not believe that Hobbes's approach represents a truly moral theory.

that Hobbes's theory counts as a moral theory because it is what Kavka calls "rule" egoism:

Hobbes is not . . . an ethical egoist in the straightforward sense that he believes that one should always perform the act that best promotes one's interest in the particular situation one is in. Instead he is a *rule-egoist* who holds that right and wrong conduct is determined in particular cases by appeal to more general moral rules, the laws of nature. These rules, in turn, are justified by the fact that following them generally best promotes the agent's long run interests. [1983b, 127]

But it is not exactly clear what Kavka means by the term 'rule-egoist.' Is the only difference between this kind of egoist and an ethical egoist the fact that the former takes proper account of his long-term best interest, whereas the latter does not? If so, the rule egoist would only be smarter and more appreciative of the long-term benefits of cooperation than the ethical egoist. But Kavka's terminology suggests that he means something different — specifically, that the rule egoist is prepared to follow a cooperative rule contained in a law of nature, the performance of which is generally justified as conducive to one's self-preservation, even in those particular cases in which it is not. Kavka seems to recognize something about these laws of nature that Hobbes does not: In certain circumstances, following them can pose a free-rider problem. We will be discussing at length the precise game-theoretic structures defining this problem (one of which is PD-like) in Chapters 6 and 8. Suffice it to say here that this problem exists whenever the rider to a law is satisfied (one's partners are willing to perform the cooperative action), but it is still individually rational to renege insofar as the payoffs from reneging are greater than the payoffs from cooperating.

In such cases, performance of the cooperative action would not be individually rational, even given that the rider was satisfied. Would Hobbes counsel a person to follow the law of nature anyway? I do not see that he would, or could, given his psychology. Hobbes insists that people desire above all else their self-preservation, and he describes his laws as "Conclusions or Theoremes concerning what conduceth to the conservation and defence of themselves." (*Lev*, 15, 41, 81) Given this description of the laws, and given his psychology, Hobbes would appear to endorse following them only insofar as they really are conducive to self-preservation. If a medicine that normally cures me of a disease will actually make me sicker when I take it in certain circumstances, I should not take it. And if a cooperative action that normally advances my long-term self-interest will actually hurt that self-interest on a particular occasion, then, as a person concerned above all else with advancing that self-interest, I should not perform it. Nowhere in *Leviathan* does Hobbes, given his psychological views, endorse the rationality or even the possibility of an individual described by that psychology performing the cooperative action in the law anyway. Such behavior would strike him as inexplicable rule worship.

Indeed, were people able to follow the law in free-rider situations, it would seem that they could also follow the law even in one-time PD situations. After all, if they can perform collectively rational but individually irrational actions in the one case, why can they not do so in the other case? Hobbes's refusal to admit the rationality of doing so in one-time PD situations is decisive evidence that he would not regard it as rational to do so in free-rider situations. Note, however, that this means that his laws of nature must have a more sophisticated structure in order to be true conclusions or theorems concerning what will lead to the preservation of human beings: The rider to these laws must be supplemented by a directive not to follow them, even when others are willing to do so, when nonperformance results in greater benefits (in the short term and long term) than performance.

But, as we discussed in Chapter 1, some readers might conclude that this means that Hobbes's doctrine of the laws of nature cannot be a truly moral theory because it neither counsels nor even admits as possible other-interested action taken against one's self-interest — the kind of action that seems quintessentially moral. In their eyes it might indeed be a theory that puts far too little distance between itself and ethical egoism. For Hobbes, morality never commands us, after we have taken proper account of our long-term self-interest, to put ourselves in jeopardy, or to act "on faith" for the good of others, or to risk our self-interest for the good of others, or to perform a collectively rational but individually irrational action.

But does this mean that Hobbes's theory cannot be the right account of what moral action is? Indeed, does it fail even to deserve the name 'moral'? I see no point in denying that title, although I can see a lot of reason in arguing against it as a *wrong* account of what morality is. But those who, like myself, want to say that moral action does involve performing other-interested actions that are against one's self-interest have the burden of proof of showing how we can understand the force of moral commands such that, even given their opposition to self-interest, they are authoritative for us. Or, to put it another way, we have the burden of proof of showing why Hobbes is wrong to believe that morality should never demand of us that we make ourselves "prey" to others or risk the satisfaction of our desires for their good. It is not clear that there has been any theorist who has succeeded in carrying out this project. We are thus forced, however much we might dislike doing so, to take Hobbes's analysis of morality seriously.

3.5 GOD AND THE LAWS OF NATURE

Before we conclude our discussion of the laws of nature, I want to consider what part God might play in making these laws valid. At the conclusion of Chapter 15, Hobbes says that

These dictates of Reason, men use to call by the name of Lawes; but improperly: for they are but Conclusions, or Theoremes concerning what conduceth to the conservation and defence of themselves; whereas Law, properly is the word of him, that by right hath command over others. But yet if we consider the same Theoremes, as delivered in the word of God, that by right commandeth all things; then are they properly called Lawes. [*Lev*, 15, 41, 80]

In this passage, Hobbes calls the laws "Theoremes" but he goes on to say that they can be called laws only insofar as "the same Theoremes" are delivered in the word of God. But what does that mean?

Suppose it means that God commands the laws *as hypothetical imperatives*. That is, he says to humankind: "If you want to preserve yourself, pursue peace by performing the following action, provided that others are willing to do so too." Such a "command" is strange, but perhaps that is what Hobbes means when he says that "the same Theoremes" are delivered in the word of God. However, we might take Hobbes to mean something very different. God, he might be saying, commands the action and the rider, but not the antecedent of the conditional. That is, the action dictated in the law will come in the form "Do *x*, provided condition *c* applies" — which would seem to be a categorical rather than a hypothetical imperative. Note that if this is so, Hobbes can still argue that we are not commanded by God to perform the actions dictated by these laws if we are in the state of nature. If, when God commands the laws, he also commands the rider to these laws, he is doing so because he does not wish us to be cooperative when that would make us prey to the self-interested people around us. Hence, even if we regard the laws as God's categorical rather than hypothetical commands, they still do not provide a "full remedy" to the warfare and violence in this state.

Hobbes is also making a rather simple "definitional" point when he says that these theorems can be called laws only insofar as they are commands of God. Given his positivist definition of law in Chapter 26 of *Leviathan* as a rule made by a commander, these theorems are "properly" laws only insofar as they are understood to be rules commanded by God.

But why should Hobbes bring God into this at all? When the laws are described only as theorems conducive to our self-preservation, it is self-interest, based on the desire to survive, that motivates us to follow them when conditions are right. But when the laws are described as commands of God, it certainly appears as if Hobbes is introducing a different motivation, one that seems "moral" rather than self-interested, connected to some sort of powerful duty of obedience owed by us to God, our creator. This moral motivation is certainly something that both Taylor and Warrender "hear" in Hobbes's words at the end of Chapter 15, and it is a critical component of their reconstruction of the Hobbesian argument in *Leviathan*. But does Hobbes introduce a moral motivation for obeying the laws of nature when he labels them divine commands?

He does not, as a careful reading of the later chapters of *Leviathan* shows. Consider what Hobbes says in Chapter 31:

The Right of Nature, whereby God reigneth over men, and punisheth those that break his Lawes, is to be derived, not from his Creating them, as if he required obedience, as of Gratitude for his benefits; but from his *Irresistible Power*. [*Lev*, 31, 5, 187]

We do not obey God, says Hobbes, because we owe him obedience and worship, we obey him because he is mightier than we are. Whereas on earth we must create an absolute sovereign via a contract or pact because we are all roughly equal and none of us can (like some superman) claim mastery in the war of all against all, we obey God because he is powerful enough to do with us what he likes:

To those therefore whose Power is irresistible, the dominion of all men adhereth naturally by their excellence of Power; and consequently it is from that Power, that the Kingdome over men, and the Right of afflicting men at his pleasure, belongeth Naturally to God Almighty; not as Creator, and Gracious; but as Omnipotent. [*Lev*, 31, 5, 187]

What is it that this omnipotent God can do to us that causes us to perceive him as our final and ultimate master? In Chapter 38, Hobbes describes in great detail the "Eternall life" we shall receive from God if we obey him, and the "Eternall torment" we shall be subjected to if we do not. Earthly sovereigns can promise us only preservation of our lives on this earth, and natural death if we disobey their rulings.

But *"Eternall life* is a greater reward, than the *life present;* and *Eternall torment* a greater punishment than the *death of Nature. . . ."* (*Lev,* 38, 1, 238) So, because God can give us more and hurt us more than any earthly sovereign, his commands must be obeyed prior to all others. But this means that our self-interested concerns motivate our obedience to God just as much as they motivate our obedience to a king or queen. Hobbes even speaks of the divine reward as "life eternall," and if the desire for self-preservation is understood broadly enough, this desire can be understood to support both our motivation to obey God and our motivation to obey our ruler! This self-interested explanation of our obedience to God is the most serious obstacle to the Taylor-Warrender thesis.[6]

Moreover, we need never worry about our self-interested motivation to obey God conflicting with our self-interested motivation to obey our ruler (which would be a conflict between securing future life on earth and securing "life eternall"). In Chapter 43, Hobbes admits that if there existed such a conflict, then, given the severity of God's punishment, "it were madnesse to obey" the earthly sovereign's command (*Lev,* 43, 2, 321). But the bulk of the chapter is taken up with showing that God's premier command (embodied in the second law of nature) is to obey unconditionally our earthly sovereign — no matter what that sovereign orders us to do.

Nonetheless, despite a lengthy discussion of the religious warrant for his political conclusion in Part III of *Leviathan,* Hobbes emphasized the secular understanding of these laws' warrant in that work. And it is likely that he did so because he believed it would provide a more powerful and a more universal argument for their *in foro interno* validity. Whether or not one believes in God, and whether or not one thinks it is a real possibility that one can go to hell (and who does?), Hobbes argues that there is a tremendously powerful earthly motivation to follow these laws in certain circumstances.

6   Nagel (1959, 78ff.) discusses this point.

CHAPTER 4

The Argument for Absolute Sovereignty

Monarchy hath bin crucified (as it were) between two Theeves, the *Pope* and the *People;* for what *principles* the *Papists* make use of for the power of the *Pope* above Kings; the very same by blotting out the word *Pope* and putting in the word *People,* the Plebists take up to use against their soveraignes. If we would truly know what Popery is, we shall find by the Lawes, and Statutes of the Realme, that the main, and indeed, the only point of *Popery is the alienating and withdrawing of Subjects from their obedience to their Prince, to raise Sedition and Rebellion:* if *Popery* and *Popularity* agree in this point, the *Kings* of *Christendom* that have shaken off the *power* of the *Pope* have made no great bargain of it, if in place of one Lord abroad, they get many Lords at home within their one Kingdoms.

Sir Robert Filmer, *The Anarchy of a Limited or Mixed Monarchy*

Once Hobbes has established that the state of nature is a state of total war in which it is irrational for one to follow a natural law dictating peaceful cooperation with one's fellows, the next step in his argument is that, in these circumstances, it is rational to institute an absolute sovereign, thereby creating a commonwealth. This chapter will be devoted to exploring the justification for this step in his argument. Specifically, what we will be asking is why Hobbes argues that only a ruler with *absolute* power can end the violence in the state of nature. As we shall see, Hobbes's argument that an absolute sovereign is not only a sufficient condition but also a necessary condition of peace is based on the fact that the state of nature is an almost complete state of war. Later in this chapter we will explore the implications of this argument for his support of monarchical government and for his positivist theory of law, then conclude by discussing the argument's historical context.

One warning to readers: I shall be presenting what I call Hobbes's "regress" argument for the necessity for an absolute sovereign as powerfully and as forcefully as I can in this chapter. This is not because I endorse the argument; on the contrary, I think it is badly wrong. Nonetheless, ever since the publication of *Leviathan*, critics have tried to refute this Hobbesian argument, while failing to appreciate both its power and its structure, with the result that their attacks have failed to kill their target. I do not want to make the same mistake. So in this chapter I will be doing my best to take Hobbes's side in the matter. By the time we get to Chapter 7, however, this sympathetic approach should pay off, because by then we will be in a position to see exactly where and how the regress argument fails. Readers are therefore counseled to be patient.

4.1 HOBBES'S REGRESS ARGUMENT FOR ABSOLUTE SOVEREIGNTY

Hobbes's support for absolute sovereignty as the sole remedy for warfare in the natural state is deeply rooted in a powerful "logical" argument for its necessity in a genuine political union. It is used in *Leviathan,* Chapters 19, 20, 22, and 29, but Hobbes states it best in *De Cive:*

> It is therefore manifest, that in every city there is some one man, or council, or court, who by right hath as great a power over each single citizen, as each man hath over himself considered out of that civil state; that is, supreme and absolute, to be limited only by the strength and forces of the city itself, and by nothing else in the world. For if his power were limited, that limitation must necessarily proceed from some greater power. For he that prescribes limits, must have a greater power than he who is confined by them. Now that confining power is either without limit, or is again restrained by some other greater than itself; and so we shall at length arrive to a power, which hath no other limit but that which is the *terminus ultimus* of the forces of all the citizens together. That same is called the supreme command; and if it be committed to a council, a supreme council, but if to one man, the supreme lord of the city. [*DC, EW* ii, 6, 18, 88][1]

Hobbes is saying here that if there is a limited power in a well-ordered, "perfect" civil society, it must be limited by a greater power. If that greater power is in turn limited, the limits must come from a still greater power. And the search for the greatest power in such a commonwealth will come to an end only when we come to a power that limits all others but that itself has no limits — and this, he says, is the sovereign power.[2] Hence,

> whosoever thinking Soveraign Power too great, will seek to make it lesse; must subject himselfe, to the Power, that can limit it; that is to say, to a greater. [*Lev*, 20, 18, 107]

In essence, Hobbes is arguing that a *government* comes into existence only when a ruler with absolute power is instituted.

As M. M. Goldsmith (1980, 33–50) has pointed out, Hobbes's argument aims to show that civil society can be truly *unified* (and hence a genuine *state*) only when it is a "closed system" having a single validating authority built into it beyond which no subject can appeal. But Goldsmith notes that H. L. A. Hart (1961, 97–107) and Hans Kelsen (1945, 110–16)[3] have discussed how a system can be "closed" without there being a simple and indivisible power residing in a *person* or *assembly of persons*. These theorists would maintain that Hobbes conflates the idea (which is correct) that an independent political regime must be a closed decision-making entity with the idea (which is false) that there must be a final *human* decision maker (or body of such decision makers) in this regime. Hart and Kelsen argue persuasively that a system can be closed even when there is no such final human authority, as long as the "final decider" is a set of rules that, for example, might establish several "human deciders"

---

1   See also *Leviathan* (19, 10–18, 98–100; 20, 18, 107; 22, 1–5, 115–16; 29, 9, 169) and *Elements of Law* (II, viii, 6 and 7, 136–8).
2   This same argument is suggested, although not explicitly made, by Grotius, who writes "That power is called sovereign whose actions are not subject to the legal control of another, so that they cannot be rendered void by the operation of another human will." (1925, 102) Bodin's definition of sovereignty also suggests this argument (1962, 102ff.).
3   See also Ivor Wilks (1969).

with mutually exclusive jurisdictions over different areas and issues, with each human decider being "final" in his own jurisdiction. And, indeed, their argument would seem to be a welcome one, explaining how a political regime need not be purchased at the costly price of making one or more human beings supreme in power and unchallengeable in authority. Goldsmith concludes that Hobbes simply made a mistake here, that he did not realize that his argument for absolute sovereignty claimed more than it was entitled to claim, because he confused the need for finality in a political regime with the need for a final human authority.

However, I believe that such confident modern refutations have really missed the force of the Hobbesian argument, as well as the central premiss on which this argument rests. Hobbes explicitly recognizes in his political writings the possibility of "Hart-like" systems of government whose ultimate deciders are sets of rules — for example, a divided sovereignty or a government with a human ruler constitutionally limited in power by laws that are designed to be "final deciders." The regress argument cannot show and is not designed to show that these governments are *theoretically* impossible; instead, its point is that, given the nature of human beings and given the fact of moral relativism, such governments are impossible *in practice*.

Therefore, what modern readers must appreciate is that the regress argument successfully justifies absolute sovereignty only insofar as it includes a vitally important Hobbesian theorem: *Because human beings are unable to establish any substantial cooperation among themselves and, in particular, are unable to agree on any rules of private property, no law or set of laws can be the final decider in a political regime. And this means that a human being or assembly of human beings must act in this capacity.* How does Hobbes argue for this theorem, which is an implicit premiss in the regress argument? He does so by making four distinct subarguments against four kinds of challenges to the theorem:

1. To those who say that a state can rest on a set of ultimate *moral* rules that limit a ruler's power and that act as the final deciders in that political regime, Hobbes simply denies that such moral rules exist if they are understood as necessarily true categorical imperatives. Of course, he cannot be a complete moral relativist; he must admit that there are laws of nature that are hypothetical imperatives (indeed, true ones), dictating certain actions when certain conditions are satisfied for those who accept the goal of self-preservation.[4] But he can and does argue that these hypothetical laws are not, as it were, "strong enough" to act as final deciders in a political regime. First, as stated, they are certainly vague enough to be completely unsuitable as a clear-cut and precise legal guide for a commonwealth. He says in Chapter 26 that

All Laws, written, and unwritten, have need of Interpretation. The unwritten Law of Nature, though it be easy to such, as without partiality, and passion, make use of their naturall reason, and therefore leave the violators thereof without excuse; yet considering there be few, perhaps none, that in some cases are not blinded by self love, or some other passion, it is now become of all Laws the most obscure; and has consequently the greatest need of able Interpreters. [*Lev*, 26, 21, 143]

---

4 Thus, my interpretation of why moral laws cannot bind a sovereign is importantly different from those interpretations [such as the one offered by Watkins (1965a, sect. 29)] that presuppose that Hobbes believes there are no moral facts. Such interpretations fail to take into account the effect of Hobbes's laws of nature on his political argument.

Hobbes's point is that human beings can be expected to come up with a variety of interpretations of these vague laws, given their self-interested bias in pursuit of their different self-regarding goals (particularly self-preservation), that can never be resolved by appeal to any objective and perfectly clear moral rule. Nor can we expect the development of cooperative practices to provide interpretations about what these rules mean, because people are incapable of cooperating with one another (and thus incapable of working out terms of cooperation) in a natural state. Finally, the desire for glory will only encourage the dissension and refusal to cooperate in that it will make each of them reluctant to "back down" and "give in." Of course, their conflicts could be resolved if they could appeal to someone charged with judging what these laws of nature say. But if such a judge were instituted, Hobbes would say this judge is sovereign — the judge has ultimate power in this state, not those natural laws. The point of the regress argument is to show that because all rules, even the natural laws, "have need of Interpretation," human beings with final interpretive power must be the final rulers of commonwealths.

However, more important is the fact that this set of natural laws is "morally" incomplete. In particular, only one of the laws of nature, the ninth law on equity, contains any prescriptions about property (i.e., about who is entitled to what, and why). These prescriptions not only are vague but also fail to deal effectively with many varieties of property disputes. Moreover, because Hobbesian people are incapable of cooperating with one another in a natural state, they cannot be expected to have arrived at any working consensus on how to determine what items belong to whom. Given that many (and perhaps even most) disputes about justice in a society will be disputes about property, the moral void in this area makes the creation of a sovereign who will actually *define* what property rights we have absolutely imperative for the resolution of conflict.

Note that the claim that a state of nature is a state of total war is critical to Hobbes's argument against the viability of rule-based commonwealths. Were people able to establish and maintain cooperative practices in the state of nature, those cooperative practices would themselves constitute conventional rules governing their interactions. How one came to own something, how one could exchange property, how one behaved toward other people's property would all be defined by reference to cooperative practices that would function as norms in the community. Because no such practices can be developed, Hobbesian people could not hope to generate normative rules defining the terms of cooperative interaction that would bring about peace. Nor could they generate practices that could be used to arrive at a common interpretation of the inherently controversial natural moral laws, laws that are invariably the subject of dispute given people's inevitable opposition of interests.

Therefore, the fact that the state of nature is a state of total war means that we live in a world of "moral chaos," so that we need a sovereign to create "objective" meanings for moral words, meanings that human beings cannot develop on their own either by practice or by objective reflection on what actions and policies will further the cause of peace. The "measure of Good and Evil actions, is the Civill Law." (*Lev*, 29, 6, 68; also see *Lev*, 29, 7, 68–9) The sovereign's civil laws define "Good, Evill, Lawfull and Unlawfull" (*Lev*, 18, 10, 91) and the "Rules of Propriety (or *Meum* and *Tuum*)." (*Lev*, 18, 10, 91, and 24, 5, 127) Moreover, the word 'justice' is not a word to which people are able to give any objective moral content naturally; rather, "Laws are the Rules of Just, and Unjust; nothing being reputed Unjust that is not contrary to some law." (*Lev*, 26, 4, 137)[5] Indeed, for the sake of peace, Hobbes maintains that the sovereign is given the power to determine answers to all issues, not just moral ones: "it is annexed to the Soveraignty, to be Judge of what Opinions and Doctrines are averse, and what conducing to Peace." (*Lev*, 18, 9, 91)

Those who would dismiss the need for such final sovereign judges, says Hobbes, "seek no more, but that things should be determined, by no other mens reason but their own," and this, he says, "is as intolerable in the society of men, as it is in play after trump is turned, to use for trump on every occasion, that suite whereof they have most in their hand. For they do nothing els, that will have every of their passions, as it comes to bear sway in them, to be taken for right Reason, and that in their own controversies." (*Lev*, 5, 3, 19) Hence, if people desire to resolve their disputes, they must

by their own accord, set up, for right Reason, the Reason of some Arbitrator, or Judge, to whose sentence they will both stand, or their controversie must either come to blowes, or be undecided, for want of, a right Reason constituted by Nature. [*Lev*, 5, 3, 19; see also *DC, EW* ii, 12, 1, 149–51, and 14, 17, 195–7]

And the institution of a sovereign is essentially the establishment of a judge whose reason will substitute for the "universal reason" (i.e., the shared, correct interpretation of the laws of nature), which does not exist in our world.

2. To those theorists of his day who, like Hart, argue that we can have a state based on a constitution or set of laws that regulate and define the power of government officials, Hobbes will reply that such a constitution is impossible. In Chapter 29, Hobbes specifically rejects the possibility of a commonwealth ruled by a constitution or set of "higher laws," arguing that

to be subject to Lawes, is to be subject to the Common-wealth, that is to the Soveraign Representative, that is, to himselfe; which is not subjection, but freedom from the Lawes. Which errour, because it setteth the Lawes above the Soveraign, setteth also a *Judge* above him, and *a Power to punish him;* which is to make a new Soveraign; and again for the same reason a third, to punish the second; and so continually without end, to the Confusion, and Dissolution of the Commonwealth. [*Lev*, 29, 9, 169; emphasis added]

In this passage Hobbes is assuming that human beings can never agree on one recognized interpretation of this constitution, so that a judge will need to be instituted to interpret and define it for them. But this means that the judge of the constitution will become the sovereign, because he has the final power of decision in

---

5 Yet, on the definition of justice, Hobbes is not consistent. In Chapter 15 of *Leviathan* he gives the concept of justice a determinate meaning without making reference to a sovereign's laws: "the definition of INJUSTICE, is no other than *the not Performance of Covenant.* And whatsoever is not Unjust, is *Just.*" (*Lev*, 15, 2, 71) However, this passage occurs in the midst of an argument for the third law of nature "that men performe their Covenants made." And the suggestion here that 'justice' has this meaning even before the sovereign takes office is related to the fact that in this argument Hobbes is trying to make contract keeping in principle and in practice possible in the state of nature, so that he can explain the validity of the social contract creating the sovereign. In Chapter 6, I will propose a way of explaining the validity of the social contract that does not rely on any objective understanding of justice or the validity of contract keeping.

this commonwealth; and if someone insists that he also be subject to a still higher constitution, Hobbes will again maintain that this constitution must have a judge, and so the regress is generated. And if the constitutionalist tries to argue that the highest laws of the state should be interpreted by the subjects, Hobbes will contend that such a commonwealth will inevitably fall apart, because the total warfare in the state of nature shows that there is simply no way these subjects, who are intensely interested in their own self-preservation and prone to vainglory, can ever come to agree on the interpretation of the constitution or on how well the rulers are performing their constitutional duties (see the subsequent argument 4).

3. To those "Whig sympathizers" who advocate a government with sovereignty divided among different branches, Hobbes once again argues, using the regress argument, that what they want is impossible. "For what is it to divide the Power of a Common-wealth," he writes, "but to Dissolve it; for Powers divided mutually destroy each other." (*Lev*, 29, 12, 170) There are two reasons why such a "commonwealth" will fail. First, the same motivation to "grab all you can get" that guides people in the state of nature is not suddenly going to disappear in the rulers of these different jurisdictions; these self-interested people can be expected to try to enlarge their jurisdictions by taking power from one another, not only because they want that power but also because they want to prevent rulers in other jurisdictions from robbing them of what they already have. Inevitably, civil war will ensue. So the same single-play PD perspective generating conflict in the state of nature will generate conflict among rulers within different jurisdictions of government. Moreover, this power grabbing will be encouraged if any of the rulers in these different jurisdictions is prone to glory-seeking and hence eager to invade to the jurisdictions of the others to obtain precedence and superiority.

Second, even should this scenario of conflict never occur, given that a constitution would be needed to set up the division in sovereignty and to empower rulers in their separate jurisdictions, quarrels would inevitably break out between the rulers concerning who had jurisdiction over areas and issues that were difficult to "classify" using that constitution — quarrels that could not be adjudicated because there would be no higher court of appeal and that would therefore degenerate into armed conflict. Constitutions are, in Hobbes's view, made up of rules that are vague in some way or difficult to apply — rules that need an interpreter in order to work in a society. But if an interpreter is established for these rules, then that interpreter is the sovereign. If not, and if sovereignty is divided up into legislative, judicial, and executive branches, then we have

not government . . . not one independent Common-wealth, but three independent Factions; nor one Representative Person, but three. In the Kingdome of God, there may be three Persons independent, without breach of unity in God that Reigneth; but were men Reigne, *that be subject to diversity of opinions*, it cannot be so. [*Lev*, 29, 16, 172; emphasis added]

Once again we see Hobbes maintaining that what destroys this sort of constitutional regime is the impossibility of agreement on the interpretation or enforcement of moral rules or principles of any kind.

4. Finally, to those who, like Locke, maintain that there can be a contract between ruler and people that will contain terms limiting the ruler's power, Hobbes will say

that this is merely a recipe for disorder and war, not for peaceful order and government. Suppose, he says, that the people make such a contract with their ruler. The problem with this arrangement is that

if any one, or more of them, pretend a breach of the Covenant made by the Soveraigne at his Institution; and others, or one other of his Subjects, or himselfe alone, pretend there was no such breach, there is in this case, no Judge to decide the controversie: it returns therefore to the Sword again; and every man recovereth the right of Protecting himself by his own strength, contrary to the designe they had in the Institution. [*Lev*, 18, 4, 89]

Hobbes realizes that in essence a contractual relationship between sovereign and subject will establish a set of higher laws directing the ruler's actions that the subjects have a right to interpret. But quarrels and infighting will break out among the subjects about how the sovereign should act, whether or not he is acting in accordance with the intentions and goals of their authorization, and so on, leading to warfare and a return to the state of nature. Hence, Hobbes maintains that if the union of the many into the one is to survive, the sovereign must be the *sole judge* of whatever is necessary for the peace and defense of his subjects (*Lev*, 18, 8, 90–1), and thus the subjects must give up their right of judging his actions. So, as we shall discuss in Chapters 5 and 6, what makes Hobbes's theory an *alienation* social contract theory is that there is no such contractual arrangement between sovereign and subject. Instead, the ruler holds power because every one of his subjects has alienated power to him.

Having presented in detail these four arguments against the four different types of limited, rule-based regimes, we are now in a position to see that there is a pattern to Hobbes's arguments against them. All of these regimes require rules to set up the limitations on the ruler's power (or the power held by particular ruling branches of power), where these rules are understood to be natural, or contract-created, or constitutional. But Hobbes invariably points out in his arguments that rules are never completely clear and require interpretation, and the interpretation that any one individual will put on these rules will likely be different from the interpretations one's fellows put on them, mainly because each individual is self-interested and hence will have a biased judgment about what any of them means. So in a commonwealth in which the ruler is limited by such rules, the rules will need to be interpreted, and who will interpret them? If the ruler is charged with judging them, then in fact she is not limited by them, because she has the power to declare that they mean whatever she wants them to mean, making her absolute sovereign. However, if the people are charged with judging them, then they will inevitably disagree with one another and with the sovereign about what these rules mean, and because these conflicts cannot be resolved peacefully, the peace of the commonwealth will be destroyed through violent attempts at resolution, and the state of nature will return. So what goes wrong in these commonwealths, according to Hobbes, is that they do not set up one human judge to determine the answers to all disputed issues in the commonwealth.

In order to make Hobbes's regress argument for absolute sovereignty as clear and perspicuous as possible, let us consider the following reformulation of it:[6]

6 This reformulation is based on Ivor Wilks's construction of the regress argument (1969, 200–1), although Wilks's formulation is without the critical step 1.

1. Because no commonly interpreted and accepted body of moral laws exists or can be established through agreement or cooperative practice, then no set of laws (either natural or artificially created) can be the final, ultimate decision maker in a state, because they will require a human interpreter to be effective in resolving disputes.
2. It is evident that there are individuals or groups in a unified civil society who have the right to decide issues and who have the power to enforce these decisions.
3. An infinite regress of such decision and enforcement bodies is impossible.
4. Therefore, there must exist in civil society a person or group whose right to decide and enforce its decision is unlimited.
5. This person or group is the sovereign.

As we have just seen, step 1 is critical to this argument. Without it, Goldsmith is right that the argument fails, because without it, the possibility of there being a rule that is a nonhuman final decider of all issues in a commonwealth is not barred. But Hobbes's argument that a state of nature is a state of war establishes the extreme pervasiveness of human conflict based on the natural opposition of interests among individuals. This opposition of interests and the resulting conflict mean that it is impossible for a community to arrive peacefully at a common interpretation of any such rule or to develop communal practices constituting such rules. So the regress argument with step 1 included is a way of establishing the practical impossibility of any government except one headed by a *human will.*

Having appreciated the structure of the regress argument, we are now able to define one of the most important concepts in *Leviathan,* that is, the concept of absolute sovereignty. Indeed, this definition will be extremely important to us in our evaluation of the Hobbesian argument in subsequent chapters. For Hobbes, an absolute sovereign is not merely a very powerful ruler but one who has two characteristics (where the second is actually implied by the first, but is important enough to single out):

An *absolute sovereign* is a person or group of persons who (1) has the power to decide, in the last analysis, all questions in the commonwealth and (2) because of having the power to decide all questions in the commonwealth, has the power to decide the most important question in the commonwealth: namely, whether or not the sovereign shall remain in power. This means that the absolute sovereign who wishes to retain her power holds that power permanently during her lifetime, and not conditionally. The sovereign will rule for as long as she lives or for as long as she does not choose to abdicate power to another.

As we shall discuss in the next chapter, Hobbes makes no bones about accepting what seems obvious from this definition of sovereignty, namely, that the relationship between an absolute sovereign and her subjects is exactly the same as a master/slave relationship. For Hobbes, war is ended only when all but one of us are made slaves to that one's commands: The price of peace is the destruction of all but one will.

However, one note of caution: Even while Hobbes supports absolute sovereignty, he is not a supporter of Orwellian totalitarian regimes. It is his view (a view that most of us in the twentieth century probably find, at best, sadly naive) that concentration of power in the hands of one person will bring about benevolent rather than tyrannic rule (*Lev*, 19, 4, 96); he never advocates a regime that would terrorize and radically constrain its citizens. He does, however, believe that only a complete concentration of power in one individual or group of individuals will produce peace. It will be the principal task of Chapters 7 and 8 to determine if his argument for this conclusion is correct.

4.2 CAN ABSOLUTE SOVEREIGNTY BE INVESTED IN ALL OR SOME OF THE PEOPLE?

Although, in *Leviathan,* Hobbes says explicitly that absolute monarchy, that is, sovereignty invested in one person, is the best form of government, he also maintains that sovereignty can be invested in a group of people (an aristocracy) or in all of the people (a democracy). Yet readers have generally taken the book to be a defense of one-man rule rather than of democratic or aristocratic rule. And this misreading is not discouraged by Hobbes, who makes quite plain in all of his political works his own very strong preference for monarchy. But in every one of those works, he offers only reasons for preferring monarchy, not arguments designed to prove that it is the best structure of government. And in *De Cive,* Hobbes openly laments the fact that he cannot provide such a proof:

I have endeavoured, by arguments in my tenth chapter, to gain a belief in men, that monarchy is the most commodious government; which one thing alone I confess in this whole book not to be demonstrated, but only probably stated. . . . [*DC, EW* ii, pref., xxii]

Nor does he attempt to argue that absolute monarchy is the only satisfactory form of government such that people either must create an absolute monarchy or watch their commonwealth dissolve into the state of nature.

In this section, I want to advance a proof for this second, stronger claim that absolute monarchy is not only the preferable but also the necessary form of government for a commonwealth, and I will use Hobbesian ideas advanced in his regress argument to do so. In the end, I will argue that the reasons Hobbes gives for rejecting governments with sovereignty divided between different branches of government are also reasons for rejecting governments with sovereignty divided between two or more people.

Recall again that Hobbes says we must reject the idea of a divided sovereignty because "what is it to divide the Power of a Common-wealth, but to Dissolve it; for Powers divided mutually destroy each other." (*Lev*, 29, 12, 170) As we discussed, this inevitable destruction will be either the result of attempted power grabs (motivated by either vainglory or self-perservation) by members of each branch or the result of jurisdictional fights between the different powers over which of them has the right to adjudicate a particular conflict.

But we can imagine that these same two kinds of problems will attend a government in which the sovereign power is divided among people, rather than branches of government. Suppose we invest it in three people, making an aristocracy. Will not each of them be prone to power grabbing, either to advance her own glory or to increase her chances of preserving herself? And will there not be fights between the three as each seeks to resolve legislative or juridical disputes that might well end up producing violent conflict among them, given that there are no commonly accepted moral laws to arbitrate such disputes? (And note that if one of them is made "final decider" of these jurisdictional questions, then she will be sovereign.)

Even if, *per impossible,* the ruling oligarchs could accept or agree on an interpretation of a constitutional rule specifying how they should share power, there could be no refusal by one or more of them to cooperate if the group together decided to institute a policy that somehow would threaten the self-interest of one of the members of the ruling junta. Given Hobbes's account of human motivation and his moral subjectivism, we have as little reason to expect this kind of harmonious cooperation among rulers sharing power as we do among individuals in the state of nature, but every reason to expect violent confrontation if the self-preservation of one of the rulers is threatened.

Finally, would not the investing of power in all of the people in a democracy make violent conflicts stemming from power grabbing and jurisdictional disputes even more likely? It seems very improbable that Hobbesian people could hope to leave the state of nature by constructing a "commonwealth" that would allow each one of them to have a share in ruling. If their self-interested pursuits made peaceful anarchy impossible, it would certainly seem that these pursuits would also make collective rulership impossible. If they could not cooperate outside of government, how could we expect them to cooperate inside a government?

Therefore, to paraphrase Hobbes's remarks on the division of power in a commonwealth: If we divide power among people (rather than among branches of government), we shall have "not government . . . not one independent Common-wealth, but . . . independent Factions" (*Lev,* 29, 16, 172), and as many independent factions as there are people.

Given that this proof for absolute monarchy as the sole legitimate form of government follows naturally from Hobbes's arguments against constitutional rule and divided or mixed monarchies, it is interesting to speculate why he never actually put forward this argument in any of his political works. Perhaps he simply did not see it. It could be that because the argument against all forms of rulership other than absolute sovereignty is not presented in a clear, orderly fashion in *Leviathan* (pieces of it are all over Part II, although primarily in Chapter 29), Hobbes was not as familiar with the structure of that argument as he should have been, and thus missed its implications for the issue of the preferability of monarchical government.

However, I suspect that a different explanation is more plausible. Given that, prior to Hobbes's day, governments that certainly looked like aristocracies and democracies had existed and survived as well as any absolute monarchy, the argument we have reconstructed on Hobbes's behalf that they are "impossible" looks a bit foolish, to say the least. Perhaps Hobbes was willing to endorse an argument to the effect that absolute monarchy was better than other forms of government, but was reluctant, for these historical reasons, to put forward or endorse any argument that democracies and aristocracies could *never* be viable regimes. Yet the argument I have just given for their impossibility arises naturally out of Hobbesian premises about the nature of human beings — their self-interested motivations and their inevitable conflicts — and it is difficult to see how Hobbes can reject that argument without rejecting critical components of his main justification for absolute sovereignty. Certainly, from our point of view, the unnaturalness of the conclusion that democracies and aristocracies are impossible casts serious doubt on that justification.

4.3 HOBBES'S LEGAL POSITIVISM

Hobbes clearly takes a position on the nature of law that has traditionally been called positivist:

I define Civill Law in this manner. CIVILL LAW, *Is to every Subject, those Rules, which the Common-wealth hath Commanded him, by Word, Writing, or other sufficient Sign of the Will, to make use of, for the Distinction of Right, and Wrong; that is to say, of what is contrary, and what is not contrary to the Rule.* [*Lev*, 26, 3, 137]

This is a positivist position, because law is understood to depend on the sovereign's will. No matter what a law's content, no matter how unjust it seems, if it has been commanded by the sovereign, then and only then is it law.

Because Hobbes defined law in this way, he opposed the chief competing theory of law during that period: the natural-law view. A natural-law theorist maintains that it is neither necessary nor sufficient for something to be a law that it be commanded by the sovereign; rather, for something to be law, it must be part of (or derived from) a set of "natural laws" known by human reason. To quote the natural-law theorist Thomas Aquinas:

As Augustine says, *that which is not just seems to be no law at all.* Hence the force of a law depends on the extent of its justice. . . . Consequently, every human law has just so much of the nature of law as it is derived from the law of nature. But if in any point it departs from the law of nature, it is no longer law but a perversion of law. [1945, 21]

It is quite clear why Hobbes does not endorse the natural-law view. To do so would be to say that the ruler's power is limited by a set of natural and seemingly deontological rules, which would make them the source of law, rather than the sovereign's will. But, in Hobbes's view, human beings cannot establish a state in which the ruler is supposedly bound by moral laws that command him irrespective of his desires, not only because such laws do not exist but also because no law can rule human beings without interpretation by a human judge. Thus, his support for a positivist conception of law is derived from his support for absolute sovereignty. To say that instituting a state involves only instituting a ruler with absolute power is to say that the sole source of law in a state must be the sovereign's will.

However, the modern legal theorist H. L. A. Hart, who is no more sympathetic to a natural-law view than Hobbes, has argued against the sort of legal positivism that Hobbes endorses (although, generally, Hart's target is the positivist position espoused by John Austin). According to Hart, anything that we would want to call a legal system cannot be analyzed as resting on a final human authority, as Hobbes or Austin would insist, but in fact must rest, ultimately, on a set of rules that Hart calls "rules of recognition," which are "second-order" laws allowing us to recognize "first-order" laws, that is, the primary legal obligations we have in a society. Whereas Hobbes says we must look to a human being or group of human beings to know these primary obligations, Hart insists that in the end we must look to a set of "constitutional" second-order rules that identify who can make these primary legal rules and how they can make them. Hart contends that these rules entitle rulers to wield political power and are used by both rulers and subjects to justify obedience to the government. And he maintains that only if they are understood to constitute the foundations of the state can we explain critical features of a legal system.

We have already discussed the way in which such constitutional rules must be present in an oligarchic or democratic form of government, and for that reason we rejected, on Hobbes's behalf, those forms of government as viable, given Hobbes's arguments against constitutional rule in Chapter 29 of *Leviathan*. But Hart maintains that even in an absolute monarchy, certain second-order constitutional rules must exist in order for this monarchy to be a state, that is, a genuine legal system. In other words, Hart does not merely attempt to show, as Goldsmith contends, that a state need not have a single and indivisible power residing in one person or assembly in order to be a state; rather, he argues that a state cannot have such a power. So Hart's position is that what we call Austinian or Hobbesian legal positivism is wrong, because the "sovereign-based" state on which these theories of law rest is impossible.

Hart (1961, 50) puts forward two arguments to support this conclusion, the most powerful of which is that the brand of legal positivism that both Austin and Hobbes endorse cannot explain the authority to make law possessed by the successors of the first absolute sovereign.[7] In some sense, Hobbes's entire social contract justification is an attempt to answer this very serious charge. Thus, I want to postpone a presentation of Hobbes's reply to it until Chapter 5, and postpone an evaluation of the effectiveness of that reply to Chapter 7, where we will be taking a long and detailed critical look at the validity and soundness of Hobbes's argument. However, I would like to discuss here Hart's second charge against this kind of legal positivism, namely, that it cannot explain the persistence of laws over many generations of lawmakers.

Consider the conviction of a woman for the crime of witchcraft by an English court in 1944 using a statute from 1735. The sovereignty model of the state makes a sovereign's will the source of law. But how, Hart asks, can law made by an earlier legislator, long dead, move us to act in a certain way now? Hart concludes that there is no reason that it should, and that only if we admit that there is a secondary rule identifying that old law as still valid today will we be able to understand how its legal force persists over many generations of legislators.

Yet, after making this argument, Hart admits that Hobbes has an answer to it:

Is it possible to dispense with this complexity, and by some ingenious extension of the simple conception of others backed by threats show that the persistence of laws rests, after all, on the simpler facts of habitual obedience to the present sovereign?
One ingenious attempt to do this has been made: Hobbes, echoed here by Bentham and Austin, said that the legislator is he, not by whose authority the laws were first made, but by whose authority they now continue to be laws. [1961, 62; he paraphrases *Lev*, 26, 9, 139]

In this passage, Hart notes that Hobbes's strategy for explaining the persistence of laws over many generations of legislators would be to regard a deceased legislator's

---

7 Hart also gives two other arguments against absolute sovereignty that are weaker, but they are designed to show only that rule-based states are possible, not that they are the only possible sort of legal system we can create.

law as law under a new legislator only if it is either tacitly or explicitly endorsed by the new legislator. This is, in fact, how Hobbes explains the fact that the "customary" English common laws have persisted as laws over hundreds of years. In Chapter 26, he maintains that any kind of "customary" or "common" law in a society is law not because it has long been in use but because the current sovereign has given his (tacit) consent to it:

When long Use obtaineth the authority of a Law, it is not the Length of Time that maketh the Authority, but the Will of the Soveraign signified by his silence, (for Silence is sometimes an argument of Consent). [*Lev*, 26, 7, 138; see also *Lev*, 26, 9, 139]

As Hart appreciates, this passage can also be used to explain why laws passed by previous legislators are still laws today:

[According to Hobbes,] as a matter of history the source or origin of a law such as the Witchcraft Act was the legislative operation of a past sovereign, its present status as law in twentieth century England is due to its recognition as law by the present sovereign. This recognition does not take the form of an *explicit* order, as in the case of statutes made by the now living legislators, but of a *tacit* expression of the sovereign's will. This consists in the fact that, though he could, he does not interfere with the enforcement by his agents (the courts and possibly the executive) of the statute made long ago. [1961, 62]

However, Hart goes on to interpret Hobbes's position as one that says that the witchcraft statute passed by a previous sovereign is not really law under the new sovereign until the courts, who are the sovereign's delegates, decide to enforce it. And this, he says, is absurd: We do not think that the courts are making new law when they convict witches under this statute; rather, we think that they are enforcing a statute that is already law and is defined as such by a secondary rule validating any statute as law when it has been passed by the appropriate legislative body, no matter when the legislation was enacted.

I will argue in a moment that Hart is making a mistake in thinking that Hobbes's position commits him to the view that courts remake law rather than enforce preexisting law. But even if we think that Hobbes is so committed, how do Hart's remarks in this passage constitute an argument against this position? Clearly, Hart and many others do not find this understanding of the nature of law intuitively plausible, but why should that necessarily constitute a decisive refutation of this position, especially given that Hobbes could also contend that the analysis of law on which Hart relies is counterintuitive according to his lights? Assertions of implausibility do not show that a position is wrong.

But Hobbes would neither endorse nor believe himself committed to the view Hart attributes to him that old laws are remade rather than simply enforced by courts acting as agents of the new sovereign. Remember that Hobbes says that customary laws are laws insofar as they are tacitly commanded by the sovereign. But this tacit consent should not be understood to come into existence only when a court under the sovereign's jurisdiction actually uses the customary law (without being censored for doing so). On the contrary, the fact that the sovereign does not at any time after taking office revoke the customary law is enough, on Hobbes's view, to allow us to regard it as law. His silence is a sign of his tacit consent that the customary rule is still law under his regime:

For whatsoever Custome a man may by a word controule, and does not, it is a naturall signe he would have that Custome stand. [*Lev*, 19, 21, 100]

And so, whenever a court applies a customary rule in a case, it is applying a preexisting law that is derived from the sovereign's will.

Applying these Hobbesian remarks on customary law to the issue of the legal status of "old" laws is straightforward. Hobbes would say that in the same way that customary rules become laws under a new sovereign through his silence, which we interpret as his tacit consent to them, so do laws passed by previous sovereigns become laws under the new sovereign when by his silence he allows them to stand, thus making them available for use by the courts. And those old laws that he does not want to let stand he will "repeal"; that is, he will announce that they are no longer law under this regime. Therefore, the positivist position Hobbes actually takes in *Leviathan* allows us to understand him to take what Hart regards as the sensible view that a court enforces a preexisting law when it uses a statute originally enacted under a previous sovereign's reign.

Hart might still contend that the Hobbesian view I have just outlined is counterintuitive, that courts' and lawyers' intuitions about the nature of law match better the model of law Hart endorses. But even if Hart is right, why should this trouble Hobbes? In both *Leviathan* and *A Dialogue Between a Philosopher and a Student of the Common Laws of England,* he frequently despairs at the bad legal reasoning that, in his view, flourished in the courts of his time. And he meant his own remarks on law to provide a replacement for what he considered to be the faulty and irrational "natural-law" thinking prevalent in legal circles. Hence, he would reject the idea that we should use the actual reasoning of courts and lawyers concerning legal matters in any argument purporting to show what the nature of law really is.

No doubt many readers will intuitively prefer Hart's explanation (I certainly do), but Hart does nothing to show that Hobbes's explanation is simply *wrong,* and insofar as the Hobbesian explanation connects up with a variety of other political and legal positions that Hobbes would contend are both correct and plausible, Hobbes would argue that we have good reason to endorse his explanation of the persistence of laws and thus good reason to "get over" any feelings we might have that it is an unintuitive or unnatural position.

4.4 THE HISTORICAL CONTEXT OF THE REGRESS ARGUMENT

I believe we can understand why Hobbes found the regress argument for absolute sovereignty persuasive and why he was so attracted to legal positivism if we consider the historical context in which Hobbes wrote.

As we have discussed, Hobbes's regress argument is designed to attack the idea that sovereignty can be divided. And the events taking place in England and elsewhere in Europe during the first half of the seventeenth century were clearly in his mind when he made that argument.[8] He was concerned to attack both the efforts of the lawyers to

8 Christopher Hill (1969a, 277ff.) discusses the way in which Hobbes perceived that the "overriding problem of seventeenth-century politics" was "Who was to interpret conflicting customs — King or Parliament, Lords or Commons?"

split power between the court system and the crown[9] and the efforts of the church (whether Roman or Episcopal or Puritan) to share power with secular government.[10] But clearly his major target of attack was the position of the parliamentarian rebels that power should be shared between the king and Parliament. This is his main target in *Behemoth* (especially in Part II), where he agrees with Filmer's sentiments quoted at the beginning of this chapter (Filmer 1648, pref.) that religious ideas fomented the belief that the people had the right to judge their ruler's performance and take part in the operation of government.[11]

The civil war that arose in England by the end of the 1640s between Parliament and the king was, for Hobbes, proof of the general proposition that "Powers divided mutually destroy each other." (*Lev*, 29, 12, 170) Nor was Hobbes alone in his diagnosis of the nation's ills. Even left-wing supporters of Parliament like George Lawson believed the lesson of the 1640s was that a civil society cannot be truly united if sovereignty is divided:

One supreme will directed by one judgement, and strengthened with one force of the sword, must command, judge, execute: Otherwise there can be no order or regular motion. [1657, 133]

However, whereas Hobbes preferred to see sovereignty invested in the king,[12] Lawson wanted it invested entirely in Parliament, not sufficiently appreciating that Parliament itself is a representative body. Indeed, he insists, confusedly, that this "undivided sovereignty" should be granted to a parliament (elected by the people), because such a government invests "supreme power . . . in many persons, several and distinct physically, but morally reduced to one by the major part agreeing in one suffrage." (1657, 133) And he even goes on to advocate rebellion against "sovereigns" who commit heinous crimes against the people. The inconsistency of Lawson's position provoked John Dewey to note dryly that

---

9   John Dewey (1974, 17ff.) and J. N. Figgis (1914, 228–9) discuss this point. John Milton is an advocate of the court in *Against Salmasius;* cited by Dewey (1974, 17).
10 See Dewey (1974, 8ff.), who notes that modern theorists ignore this aspect of Hobbes's attack. It is a persistent theme of Part III of *Leviathan* (e.g., *Lev*, 39, 5, 248) and of *Behemoth* (e.g., *EW* vi, 222), and he is chiefly interested in this question in "An Answer to Bishop Bramhall's Book, called 'The Catching of Leviathan' " (*EW* iv).
11 In *Behemoth*, Hobbes cites the availability of translations of the Bible in vernacular languages as one of the causes of the popularity of this idea. He commends the wisdom of Moses, who "suffered no man to go up to hear God speak or gaze upon him, but such as he himself took up with him," because "after the Bible was translated into English, every man, nay every boy and wench, that could read English, thought they spoke with God Almighty, and understood what he said." And Hobbes concludes that "this licence of interpreting the Scripture was the cause of so many several sects, as have lain hid till the beginning of the late King's reign, and did then appear to the disturbance of the commonwealth." (*EW* vi, *Behemoth*, 190–1) Christopher Hill (1975, 93–5, 101, 161–2, 267) seems to agree that this was one cause of the development of politically radical Protestant sects.
12 In *Behemoth*, Hobbes argues that Parliament was originally established only as a body of counsel, not as a legislature, "by which it seems to me, that though they gave [the king] counsel when he required it, yet they had no right to make war upon him if he did not follow it." (*EW* vi, *Behemoth*, 260).

In a situation where a writer sees that the great need is for a unified authority or sovereignty, and yet argues in support of that very principle of private judgement of laws which had been a large factor in bringing about the situation he deplores, Hobbes's case almost states itself. [1974, 17]

And probably the theoretical confusion of his opponents was seen by Hobbes as evidence of the futility of building a government on any "precepts of reason" or "divine law."

However, one contemporary of Hobbes, Philip Hunton, did squarely confront the problems of judgment and definition of law that Hobbes's argument for the necessity of an absolute sovereign raises. Hunton (1643) supported the idea that the monarch could be limited by Parliament, but because he was very worried about the violence of his time, he tried to develop a position that condemned revolution except in dire emergencies. So he simultaneously supported the idea that people could and should create a limited and mixed government by contract, but denied that this creative activity made the ruler the servant of the people such that they could remove him at will:

if I convey an estate of Land to another, it doth not hold that after such conveyance I have a better estate remayning in me then that other, but rather the contrary; because what was in one is passed to the other: The servant who at the year of *Iubile* would . . . give his master a full Lordship over him: can we argue, that he had afterward more power over himselfe then his Master, because he gave his Master that power over him, by that act of Oeconomical Contract[?] [1643, 15–16]

However, Hunton forsees the objections that the royalists will raise to his position. Specifically, if the sovereign's rule is limited, then who decides whether or not he is keeping within the bounds of the authority granted him in the original contract? Hunton considers whether or not any foreign person or state should be allowed to judge, and he rejects this alternative because it would destroy the autonomy of the state. He then considers whether or not to allow the monarch the right to judge, and he rejects this because it would make the monarch absolute in power. Finally, he considers whether or not the people shall judge, *and he rejects this also,* because this would mean that the people would rule and the monarchy would be destroyed. In the end, Hunton says that in a limited monarchy, no one shall judge whether or not the monarch is abusing his powers! This is a remarkable example of intellectual honesty, but it is hardly a compelling or satisfactory position.

Robert Filmer, who wrote a short essay on Hunton's pamphlet, has an easy time attacking that position: "Thus our Author hath caught himself in a plaine *dilemma:* if the King be judge, then he is no limited Monarch. If the people be judge, then he is no Monarch at all. So farewell *limited Monarchy,* nay farewell *all government* if there be no Judge." (1648, 20) Hunton himself realized the unsatisfactory nature of this position, and so he went on to argue that although the people have no legal authority to judge the monarch in a limited monarchy, they do have a moral right to do so:

And this power of judging argues not a superiority in those who Judge, over him who is Judged; for it is not Authoritative and Civill, but morall, residing in reasonable Creatures and lawfull for them to execute, because never devested and put off by any act in the constitution of a legall Government, but rather the reservation of it intended: For when they define the Superiour to a Law, and constitute no Power to Judge of his Excesses from that Law, it is evident they reserve to themselves, not a Formall Authoritative Power but a morall Power, such as they had originally before the Constitution of the Government; which must needs remaine, being not conveyed away in the Constitution. [1643, 18]

So we have come full circle. Subjects in a limited monarchy are slaves to the monarch, and yet they reserve the *moral right* (which they cannot alienate in an original contract) to judge the monarch's performance and depose him if they feel it necessary. And note that although Hunton does not recognize it, this argument also establishes the right of the subjects of an *absolute* monarchy to depose their ruler. Filmer once again attacks Hunton's position:

Thus at the last, every man is brought by this Doctrine of our Authors, to be his owne judge. And I also appeal to the consciences of all mankinde, whether the end of this be not utter confusion, and Anarchy. [1648, 22]

Hunton's dilemma allows us to see that the question "Who shall judge?" was Hobbes's most powerful retort to the protestations of his critics that he would deny men liberty and destroy the courts and the church. The theoretical and actual dilemmas that proponents of these notions had to face show how plausible Hobbes's regress argument for absolute sovereignty was in the seventeenth century. In Chapters 8 and 9 we will attempt to find a satisfactory answer to the question "Who shall judge?" such that Hobbes's argument for absolute sovereignty can be defeated.

CHAPTER 5

Authorizing the Sovereign

Canst thou draw out leviathan with a hook? or his tongue with a cord which thou lettest down? Canst thou put a hook into his nose? or bore his jaw through with a thorn? Will he make many supplications unto thee? will he speak soft words unto thee? Will he make a covenant with thee? wilt thou take him for a servant forever?

Job, 41:1–4

Supposing that the inhabitants of the state of nature accepted Hobbes's regress argument for the necessity of an absolute sovereign, their next move would be to determine how to go about instituting one. Hobbes says that two distinct actions are involved in the sovereign's institution: First, people must agree with one another to create a sovereign; second, each of them must keep her part of the agreement by "authorizing" the individual selected.[1] In the next chapter we will be concerned with what this social contract is and how Hobbes can contend that it is possible for people to keep it. But in this chapter I want to focus on what the action of "authorizing" someone as sovereign is supposed to involve.

My purpose in this chapter is not simply to clarify Hobbes's rather hazy remarks on authorization. Depending on how we clarify these remarks, Hobbes can be interpreted as espousing either a master/slave relationship between a subject and a ruler or a more "Lockean" agent/principal relationship between them. And if we take Hobbes to be espousing the latter, his support of "absolute sovereignty" is not what people have historically taken it to be. Therefore, by analyzing how subjects create an absolute sovereign, we shall reveal Hobbes's view of the sovereign/subject relationship and thus shed helpful light on what an absolute sovereign really is.

5.1 AUTHORIZATION

The concept of authorization can be interpreted, using evidence from the text, in a harsh "Hobbesian" way, such that it generates an "authoritarian" civil union, or it can be given a milder, more "Lockean" reading, from which follows a more "democratic" conception of the state. David Gauthier argues for the more Lockean interpretation of authorization and the nature of civil union in his book *The Logic of Leviathan*

---

1 I say 'individual' here, assuming that my argument on Hobbes's behalf against dividing sovereignty between or among individuals is correct. See Chapter 4, Section 4.2.

(1969).[2] According to Gauthier, the use of the notion of authorization to characterize the content of the social agreement in *Leviathan* shows that Hobbes is departing from the position he took in *The Elements of Law* and *De Cive* on the manner of the sovereign's institution. In both of those earlier works, the future subjects *give up* or *surrender* their right to all things to the future sovereign. Hobbes writes in *The Elements of Law:*

The making of union consisteth in this, that every man by covenant oblige himself *to some one and the same man, or to some one and the same council,* by them all named and determined, to do those actions, which the said man or council shall command them to do. . . . And though the will of man being not voluntary, but the beginning of voluntary actions, is not subject to deliberation and covenant; yet when a man covenanteth to subject his will to the command of another, he obligeth himself to this, that he resign his strength and means to him, whom he covenanteth to obey. . . . And because it is impossible for any man really to transfer his own strength to another: or for that other to receive it; it is to be understood, that *to transfer a man's power and strength, is no more but to lay by or relinquish his own right of resisting him* to whom he so transferreth it. [*EL,* I, xix, 7 and 10, 103–4; emphasis added]

And in *De Cive* he says that

This submission of the wills of all those men to the will of one man or one council, is then made, when each one of them obligeth himself by contract to everyone of the rest, not to resist the will of that one man or council, to which he hath submitted himself. [*DC, EW* ii, 5, 7, 68]

However, Gauthier claims that in *Leviathan,* Hobbes no longer has the subjects surrender their rights, because in his final statement of the content of the social agreement Hobbes writes that

A *Common-wealth* is said to be *Instituted,* when a *Multitude* of men do Agree, and *Covenant, every one, with every one,* that to whatsoever *Man* or *Assembly of Men,* shall be given by the major part, the *Right* to *Present* the Person of them all, (that is to say, to be their *Representative;*) every one, as well he that *Voted for it,* as he that *Voted against it,* shall *Authorise* all the Actions and Judgements, of that Man, or Assembly of men, in the same manner, as if they were his own, to the end, to live peaceably amongst themselves, and be protected against other men. [*Lev,* 18, 1, 88]

The key word in this passage is 'authorization.' Gauthier admits that Hobbes does not give an explicit definition of the term, but notes that the concept is usually defined as the appointment of some man or men to be one's representative, or to bear one's person, or to assume one's authority to do something (1969, 124). And Gauthier believes that this definition makes it clear that for Hobbes

authorization must involve some translation of right. This is evidently not mere renunciation, nor is it transfer, in Hobbes's usual sense. For transfer is nothing more than a limited renunciation; if I transfer my right to some object to you, I merely renounce my right to possess that object in so far as this would interfere with the exercise of your right to the object. Authorization, on the other hand, enables *you* to act in my place, and so with *my* right. [1969, 124]

Thus, says Gauthier, whereas in Hobbes's earlier accounts of the original contract, the sovereign possesses only his own right to all things, made effective because the subjects have lost theirs, in the *Leviathan* account the claim is that the sovereign

---

2 As I will discuss later, Gauthier would disapprove of my characterization of his interpretation of authorization as "Lockean."

possesses new rights that still belong to the subjects and that by contract he is allowed to use.

Although Hobbes does not give an explicit definition of 'authorization' that supports Gauthier's interpretation, certainly that interpretation trades on the normal meaning of the word. In addition, much of what Hobbes says in Chapter 16 of *Leviathan* supports this understanding of the notion. In that chapter, Hobbes calls a person "natural" if his words are ones he makes for his own purposes, and "artificial" if his words or actions are carried out under the direction of, and in the name of, another person. That is, people are "artificial persons" when they

have their words and actions *Owned* by those whom they represent. And then the Person is the *Actor;* and he that owneth his words and actions, is the AUTHOR: in which case the Actor acteth by Authority. . . . So that by Authority, is always understood a Right of doing any act: and *done by Authority,* done by Commission, or Licence from him whose right it is. [*Lev,* 16, 4, 81]

These remarks are not perspicuous, but a natural interpretation of them[3] is that an author is one who owns the actions of an actor because he has given this actor the use of his own right to perform these actions; and insofar as the author owns the right, he owns the actions as well. Because the sovereign is said by Hobbes to be authorized by the subjects in the original contract, it would therefore seem that the sovereign is an artificial person, performing actions that his subjects "own," because those actions are carried out using their rights, which they have lent him.

However, Gauthier advocates this interpretation of authorization not only because of this and other passages in Chapter 16 (e.g., *Lev,* 16, 14, 82) but also because he believes that the relationship of the sovereign to a subject that it generates is superior to the one arising out of the surrender model used in *De Cive.* This latter model, he complains, makes the relationship between ruler and ruled analogous to that between master and servant, and he believes that Hobbes does not really want to make this identification in *Leviathan.* Indeed, he even chides Hobbes for "slipping up" and explicitly making this comparison in his *Leviathan* chapter on commonwealths by acquisition. Gauthier insists that Hobbes cannot mean for us to take this comparison seriously, because if we do,

Hobbes's account begins to assume a totalitarian dimension. And this is quite contrary to Hobbes's intention. He succeeds in misleading both himself and his readers by accepting the comparison between master and sovereign, servant and subject. Indeed, he invites the rejoinder, urged by Locke, that the sovereign is the enemy of his subjects, and an enemy given the strength to overpower and destroy him by their own act in creating him. [1969, 116–17]

The notion of authorization, says Gauthier, presents a new account of the relationship between the ruler and the ruled that, unlike the surrender account, does not make the subjects slaves of the sovereign. Whereas slaves, when they surrender their right of governing themselves, become mere instruments of their master's will, subjects who authorize their ruler only lend their rights to him and thus never lose their self-rulership. Indeed, Gauthier's authorization model represents the sovereign as the instrument of the subjects' wills.

---

3 However, what follows is not the only interpretation of them, as we will see later in this chapter.

However, this interpretation of authorization would seem to make Hobbes into a king of Whig. The idea that the sovereign is the subject's instrument, holding power that the people entrust to him, is a constant theme of Locke's *Two Treatises of Government*. Gauthier denies that the Hobbesian notion of authorization is anything like the notion of "trust" used by Locke to explain the nature of the subject/sovereign relationship (1969, 176). And he steadfastly maintains that although the authorization account establishes a new and nontotalitarian concept of civil union, it does not give rise to a new political theory in *Leviathan*. He writes: "it is the substantive premises about human nature, and not the formal structure of the theory, that determines its absolutist character" (1969, 145). But how can a nonabsolutist account of a sovereign's powers be used to establish an absolutist political theory? Without wanting to mount a direct challenge to Gauthier's material/formal distinction, I do wish to challenge directly Gauthier's interpretation of authorization on both textual and philosophical grounds. Not only does examination of the text of *Leviathan* show that there is a persistent tendency on Hobbes's part to propound the same understanding of authorization as presented in *De Cive*, but, more important, Gauthier's understanding of authorization does generate, despite his denials, a substantive account of political obligation to which Hobbes is adamantly opposed in *Leviathan*, an account that is decidely Lockean. Indeed, this fact would certainly explain why Hobbes is at pains not to use 'authorization' in Gauthier's sense whenever he discusses the creation of the sovereign/subject relationship in Part II of *Leviathan*.

Nonetheless, Gauthier is certainly right that the interpretation of authorization he develops is strongly suggested by Hobbes's use of that word in Chapter 16. So after we show that Hobbes rightly eschews the use of that word in Gauthier's sense in all chapters of *Leviathan* other than Chapter 16, we still must ask why Hobbes suggests it in that chapter.

5.2 THE TEXTUAL EVIDENCE

Despite the textual support for Gauthier's understanding of authorization in Chapter 16, when one reads descriptions of the Hobbesian argument by his contemporaries one finds that they invariably understand his notion of authorization to be renunciation rather than translation of rights.[4] And I want to argue now that his contemporary critics were responding to a number of passages in Part II of that book in which the word is clearly given that sense. For example, in Chapter 14, when Hobbes defines

---

4 I quoted in the last chapter a passage from Cudworth's discussion of *Leviathan* in which he takes 'authorization' to mean "renouncing" or "abandoning" one's right to all things (1845, 499–502). The word 'divest' is used by Clarendon (1676, 39) to characterize what people do with their powers when they institute a ruler. And phrases like "divesting" power, "laying down their Right," and "relinquishing power" are employed by Robert Filmer (1652, 3–4) as interpretations of the authorization act. Indeed, Samuel Pufendorf (1934, 392–3) even criticizes Hobbes's account of authorization precisely because he believes that it relies on the idea that men renounce their rights to all things. Those who advanced or copied Hobbes's political theory also interpreted authorization this way; for example, Spinoza (1951, 302–5) says that the institution of the sovereign occurs when the subjects "forego" their rights or "cede" them to a person or group, thereby "submitting" absolutely to the dominion and will of another.

the second law of nature, he says that the law commands "That a man be willing, when others are so too, as farre-forth, as for Peace, and defence of himselfe he shall think it necessary *to lay down this right to all things;* and be contented with so much liberty against other men, as he would allow other men against himselfe." (*Lev,* 14, 5, 64–5; emphasis added) It is difficult to believe that Hobbes simply slipped up here, forgetting the new account of the original contract based on authorization that he supposedly puts forth in *Leviathan.*

The claim that this passage was not just a "regression" to the old *De Cive* model is supported by examining the concluding passage of Chapter 17, where Hobbes explicitly sets out the "promise" each man gives to the other:

I *Authorise* and *give up my Right* of Governing my selfe, to this Man . . . on this condition, that thou give up thy Right to him, and Authorise all his Actions in like manner. [*Lev,* 17, 13, 87; emphasis added]

Thus, authorization is deliberately identified with the renunciation of rights. Gauthier dismisses this passage by saying that Hobbes mistakenly slipped back into the old *De Cive* terminology, and Gauthier feels justified in calling the language "mistaken" because "Hobbes never characterizes authorization as a procedure for giving *up* right." (1969, 155) But Gauthier admitted earlier that Hobbes never gives an explicit definition of authorization. So there seems no reason not to take this passage as more evidence of what Hobbes really thinks authorization *is,* that is, the surrender of rights to the sovereign.

Moreover, consider how Hobbes prefaces his discussion in Chapter 17 of the liberties of a subject in a commonwealth. In order to understand what those liberties are, says Hobbes,

we are to consider, what Rights we *passe away,* when we make a Common-wealth; or (which is all one), what Liberty we deny our selves, by owning all the Actions (without exception) of the Man, or Assembly we make our Soveraign. [*Lev,* 21, 10, 111; emphasis added]

Shortly afterward, Hobbes calls this surrender of rights and subsequent acceptance of the sovereign's acts as one's own the act of authorization:

Againe, the Consent of a Subject to Soveraign Power, is contained in these words, *I authorise, or take upon me all his actions;* in which there is no restriction at all, of his own former naturall Liberty: For by allowing him to *kill me,* I am not bound to kill myself when he commands me. 'Tis one thing to say, *Kill me, or my fellow, if you please;* another thing to say, *I will kill my selfe, or my fellow.* [*Lev,* 21, 14, 112]

Gauthier interprets this passage such that it will give support to his understanding of authorization: "I take it that Hobbes intends us to understand that by authorizing another man, we do not in any sense forgo our own rights." (1969, 125; see also 141) Gauthier's reasoning is that if authorization produces no restriction of our natural liberty, then it must not be an action that involves the surrender of rights. But before we can be sure this interpretation is correct, we need to understand the force of the adjective 'natural' modifying 'liberty' in the passage. Hobbes begins chapter 21 by distinguishing two senses of the word 'liberty'. There is the 'proper' use of the word, which he calls both "corporall" and "naturall" liberty (see *Lev* 21, 6, 109; and 21, 4, 108): this is defined as as the "freedom from prisons, and chains" and is consistent with fear and necessity. (*Lev,* 21, 2–5, 108–9) Then there is the liberty which men want in political societies and which Hobbes defines as the "exemption from Laws." (*Lev*, 21, 6, 109) Hobbes doesn't name it, so we'll call it political liberty. It is political liberty which men lose in the commonwealth, not natural liberty (unless they are put in chains): "For if wee take liberty in the proper sense, for corporall liberty; that is to say, freedome from chains and prisons, it were very absurd for men to clamor as they doe, for the liberty they so manifestly enjoy." (*Lev*, 21, 6, 109) Hence the thrust of chapter 21 is to explain how much political liberty men lose in a commonwealth. Just before the passage under discussion, Hobbes introduces and defends the idea that one right which we do not "passee away" (Hobbes's language in 21, 10, 111) is the right to defend our life when it is attacked. Because the subject retains this right which can never be transferred by covenant (*Lev* 21, 11, 111), authorization does not make him bound to kill himself when the sovereign commands him to do so, hence the subject retains this political liberty. Finally, Hobbes also notes in this passage that authorization does not restrict in any way one's natural or corporal liberty, so that one is able to resist the sovereign's attacks. But the retention of natural liberty and the right to self-defense appears consistent with the idea that authorization involves the *surrender* of the right to all things.

Moreover, in two other places in *Leviathan* Hobbes both insists that and explains why the sovereign alone retains his entire political liberty after his authorization, and both these passages support the "surrender" interpretation of authorization. In Chapter 28, when he explains the sovereign right to punish, Hobbes specifically uses the idea that when authorizing the sovereign the subjects renounce their rights to all things:

the Subjects did not give the Soveraign that right [to punish]; but onely in laying down [their right to all things] strengthned him to use his own, as he should think fit, for the preservation of them all: so that it was not given, but left to him, and him onely; and . . . as entire, as in the condition of meer nature. [*Lev*, 28, 2, 162][5]

And in Chapter 14 there is a passage that explains why authorization must involve the surrender rather than the translation of rights and why that action leaves the sovereign with "his own former natural liberty." According to Hobbes, when a man transfers or lays down a right, he

giveth not to any other man a Right which he had not before; because there is nothing to which every man had not Right by Nature: but onely standeth out of his way, that he may enjoy his own originall Right, without hindrance from him. . . . So that the effect which redoundeth to one man, by another mans defect of Right, is but so much diminution of impediments to the use of his own Right originall. [*Lev*, 14, 6, 65]

Hobbes is saying here that in the state of nature one man's right cannot be "passed on" or "conveyed" to the other in a contract, because when a man has a right to all

---

5 According to Gauthier, in this passage Hobbes deliberately reverts to the *De Cive* model of the sovereign's creation because he cannot see how the power to punish can be created out of the subjects' loan of their rights to the sovereign. However, this cannot be the problem Hobbes is wrestling with here, because when he presents the problem to his readers he uses the surrender interpretation of authorization; specifically, he notes that "In the making of a Common-wealth, every man *giveth away* the right of defending another; but not of defending himselfe." (*Lev*, 28, 2, 161; emphasis added) Thus, he implies that the problem is to explain how this renunciation of rights by the subject generates the sovereign's right to punish. I will be giving a full interpretation of this passage in Chapters 6 and 7.

things, it is impossible to grant him a right to something he does not already have. Gauthier's interpretation of authorization fails because in Hobbes's state of nature there is nothing one can give the sovereign that he does not already claim to own. Now perhaps Gauthier would reply to this that the sovereign possesses only his own right to all things, not the future subject's right to the same. But how does the possessive pronoun limit this right, such that the subjects' rights can supplement it? We cannot say that when a man grants his own right to all things to the sovereign he has granted the right to make use of all objects, because the sovereign already possesses that right. Nor can we say that the subject makes the sovereign his "agent" in order that the sovereign go out and deliver up to him all those things over which the subject's rights extend — the sovereign certainly does not do that. And to say that the subject gives the sovereign his assurance that he will not challenge the sovereign's right is simply to say that the subject renounces his own right to all things, allowing the sovereign's right to become effective. Therefore, because in Hobbes's state of nature it makes no sense to say that the subject gives something to the sovereign, authorization must necessarily involve the surrender of rights.[6]

Whereas Gauthier contends that Hobbes does not want to encourage the comparison between master and sovereign, slave and subject, Hobbes's most striking uses of authorization occur in his discussions of the institution of master/slave relationships. For example, he maintains that

The Master of the Servant, is Master also of all he hath; and may exact the use thereof; that is to say, of his goods, of his labour, of his servants, and of his children, as often as he shall think fit. For he holdeth his life of his Master, by the covenant of obedience; that is, *of owning and authorising whatsoever the Master shall do.* And in case the Master, if he refuse, kill him, or cast him into bonds, or otherwise punish him for his disobedience, he is himselfe the author of the same; and cannot accuse him of injury. [*Lev*, 20, 13, 104; emphasis added]

So, if servants, like the vanquished in war, give up their rights to the lord whom they fear and thereby *authorize* their lord with this action, then authorization must be interpreted as the surrender of rights, and the same relationship between subject and sovereign that prevails in *De Cive* prevails in *Leviathan* — that is, a relationship between master and servant.

However, one also arrives at this conclusion by noticing how Hobbes characterizes a stable commonwealth. The identification of master with sovereign and slave with subject made frequently by Hobbes in *De Cive* and *The Elements of Law* is just as frequently made in *Leviathan*.[7] For example, following the passage in which Hobbes

---

6   Indeed, Gauthier's use of the word 'translation' to mean loan is very un-Hobbesian. Whenever Hobbes uses the phrase 'translation of rights,' it means the specific surrender of rights to another, so that it is synonymous with both 'transfer' and 'renunciation' (e.g., *Lev*, 14, 16, 67). And Hobbes's explanation for using it in this way would appear to be given by the passage just discussed.

7   For example, see *De Cive* (*EW* ii, 8, 1 and 7, 108 and 111–12) and *Elements of Law* (II, iv, 9, 105). In these passages it is important to note that Hobbes uses the word 'servant' the way we would use the word 'slave.' 'Slave,' for him, is a technical term, designating someone who is literally in bonds, or in prison; whereas 'servant' is one who is vanquished by another but "hath corporeal liberty allowed him; and upon promise not to run away, nor to do violence to his master, is trusted by him." (See *Lev*, 20, 10, 104; *DC*, *EW* ii, 8, 1

says that servants authorize their masters, he maintains that "In summe the Rights and Consequences of both *Paternall* and *Despoticall* Dominion, are the very same with those of a Soveraign by Institution, and for the same reasons. . . ." (*Lev*, 20, 14, 104) And when he speaks of a commonwealth by acquisition, he insists that the only difference between it and the commonwealth by institution is in the way the sovereign powers originated, not in the sovereign powers themselves:

> Soveraignty [by acquisition] differeth from Soveraignty by Institution onely in this, That men who choose their Soveraign, do it for fear of one another, and not of him whom they Institute: But in this case, they subject themselves, to him they are afraid of. . . . But the Rights, and Consequences of Soveraignty, are the same in both. [*Lev*, 20, 2, and 3, 102]

Hobbes is not figuratively comparing subjects to servants and sovereigns to masters; he is identifying one with the other,[8] thus endorsing the *De Cive* position that a sovereign owns his subjects; that is, he "may say of his servant no less than of another thing, whether animate or inanimate *this is mine* [and] he that can by right dispose of the *person* of a man, may surely dispose of all those things which that *person* could dispose of." (*DC, EW* ii, 8, 5, 111)[9]

Hobbes also argues that subjects have no rights that can limit or constrain the sovereign's absolute powers, and he believes that there is nothing the sovereign can do to injure his subjects insofar as they have authorized him as their sovereign:

> For he that doth any thing by authority from another, doth therein no injury to him by whose authority he acteth . . . and consequently he that complaineth of injury from his Soveraigne, complaineth of that whereof he himselfe is Author; and therefore ought not to accuse any man but himselfe. [*Lev*, 18, 6, 90; also see *Lev*, 21, 7, 109–10]

We will be discussing this passage later in this chapter; however, now I wish to bring attention to the way Hobbes uses the word 'authorization' here. He is saying that in surrendering up his right to all things, a person has literally surrendered up himself to

---

and 2, 109–10). There are interesting issues concerning Hobbes's notion of freedom raised by this distinction that I do not have time to explore, and for purposes of the discussion in this section, I will ignore the distinction and use 'servant' and 'slave' interchangeably, because I believe it is important to realize that Hobbes's conception of servitude would cover what we normally think of as slavery.

8 Gauthier argues that Hobbes's remarks on the commonwealth by acquisition contradict his characterization of a commonwealth by institution and thus that "Despotic dominion is an aberration, in terms of Hobbes's later political theory." (1969, 117) Our analysis of authorization and Hobbes's own characterization of both "kinds" of civil union show that this is not quite so. However, in Chapter 6, I will discuss certain inadequacies of the commonwealth-by-acquisition story as a justification of sovereign rule.

9 See also *Leviathan* (24, 5–10, 127–30; 29, 10, 170–1). Hobbes is not the only writer in the seventeenth century to consider the sovereign to be like an absolute property holder, "owning" his subjects and their land. Any advocate of the divine-rights doctrine, including Filmer, derives the monarch's power from his descent from Adam, who was given full domination over "all things" by God. Locke's discussion of Filmer's theory in Book 1 of *Two Treatises of Government* nicely shows how these theorists conceive rulers as owners (see especially Book 1, Chapter vii). Likewise, Bodin (1962, bk. I, chap. 6) and Grotius (1925, bk. I, chap. III, sect. vii, ix, xii; bk. II, chap. vi, 261) compare sovereigns to property-owning masters, although, unlike Hobbes, they are reluctant to completely equate the two. Moreover, this idea has obvious medieval roots.

the sovereign's will, transforming both his body and his goods into instruments of the sovereign's volition. Hence, there is no doubt that Hobbes considers authorization to be an act of enslavement, and the resulting commonwealth to be a union of slaves (albeit willing slaves) within the will of their master.

So a survey of the text shows that although Hobbes does seem to use Gauthier's sense of 'authorization' in Chapter 16, he persistently uses the word in the rest of the book to mean the surrender of rights. Thus, the text is at best ambiguous about the word's meaning, but because it is used to mean the renunciation of rights many more times than it is used to mean their translation, it seems natural to think (as Hobbes's contemporaries did) that the translation meaning of authorization suggested in Chapter 16 is aberrant, and the surrender meaning is standard.

Still, this issue must be finally resolved not by counting supporting passages but on philosophical grounds. In this regard, it is important to note that Hobbes was not the first writer to argue that the institution of a sovereign ruler is accomplished when the people alienate their power to him. As mentioned in the Introduction, medieval commentators on the *lex regia* notion in Roman law advocated this conception of the ruler's receipt of power. More significantly, even *liberal* thinkers in England during the seventeenth century held this view. For example, in the work quoted at the end of the last chapter, Philip Hunton, a proponent of mixed monarchy in the 1640s, argues that even when a limited ruler is instituted in a contract, the people are still mastered by the ruler and do not have "Power above the Power of the Monarch." (1643, 15) So, for Hunton, the election of a limited ruler is conceived as a slavery contract! Why? How is it that even the critics of absolute sovereignty in the seventeenth century had trouble conceiving of a ruler's institution in anything but "surrender" terms?

5.3 THE REGRESS ARGUMENT AND AUTHORIZATION

I believe that Hobbes's advancement of this regress argument shows why he should not be understood to be espousing Gauthier's reinterpretation of the action of authorization as the loaning or the translation of power. As I mentioned in the last section, Gauthier's interpretation of 'authorization' shows that he is giving the word its usual meaning, which is derived from the legal usage of the word current in English since at least the sixteenth century.[10] If we look at uses of this word by both seventeenth- and twentieth-century legal theorists, we can see why Hobbes would not want to invoke this sense of it. The authors of the *American Restatement of Agency* state that

'Agent' is a word used to describe a person *authorized* by another to act on his account and under his control . . . the attorney-at-law, the broker, the factor, the auctioneer, and other similar persons employed either for a single transaction or for a series of transactions, are agents. . . . [1958, sec. 1, 3(e); emphasis added][11]

Through authorization, the "principal" temporarily grants or loans "the agent" his power to do certain actions, as specified by the principal. Therefore, in this relationship,

10 The *Oxford English Dictionary* gives examples of the use of the word in this legal sense going back to 1571.
11 Compare Pufendorf (1934, bk. III, chap. ix, sect. 1, 449).

An agent is subject to the control and direction of the principal. . . . Agency is formed with the thought of constant supervision. . . . [Bogert 1935, 74]

This definition fits the seventeenth-century usage. For example, Pufendorf defines an agent as follows:

Such a person acts . . . like an instrumental cause, in that he not only carries on all negotiations upon the authority of the other, but also acquires no right for himself, and contracts no obligation touching the person with whom he is appointed to treat. [1934, 449]

So the agent/principal relationship has three features. First, it is fiduciary: The principal entrusts the agent with power (*American Restatement of Agency* 1958, 9). Second, it is a fiduciary relationship in which the principal controls the agent, never vice versa: "It is the element of continuous subjection to the will of the principal which distinguishes the agent from other fiduciaries and the agency agreement from other agreements" (*American Restatement of Agency* 1958, 9). As Pufendorf says, the agent "is bound to [the principal] to conduct his affairs with all fidelity." (1934, 449)[12] Third, this fiduciary relationship is generally established by contract:[13] "Agency depends on contract for its existence. The agent must be shown to have accepted the relationship, expressly or impliedly." (Bogert 1935, 72)

These three features of the agency relationship established by authorization make it identical with the fiduciary relationship that Locke says prevails between ruler and subject,[14] and which he argues is created by contract. For example, Locke explicitly evokes the concept of the ruler as agent of the people when he writes that

Though in a Constituted Commonwealth . . . there can be but *one Supream Power* which is the *Legislative*, to which all the rest are and must be subordinate, yet the Legislative being only a Fiduciary Power to act for certain ends, there remains *in the People a Supream Power* to remove or *alter the Legislative* when they find the *Legislative* act contrary to the trust reposed in them. [2*T*, 149, 412–13]

Note that Locke is saying that the powers that a ruler has are granted to him "on condition." He has certain specifiable duties owed to the subjects that mark him as a fiduciary, and like any agent, he is tied to the principal's control—in this case, the control of the subjects—ultimately serving only at their pleasure. Thus, like it or not, by using the word 'authorization' as he does, Gauthier is importing Lockean ideas into *Leviathan*. Specifically, he is introducing the idea that the sovereign is tied to his subjects' control, acting at their behest.

Thus, it should be obvious, given the regress argument, that 'authorization,' in the legal sense, the sense that Gauthier invokes, is a disastrous concept for Hobbes to use in characterizing the sovereign's institution by his subjects. First, if the subjects "authorize" the sovereign in this sense, not only is the sovereign restricted to act in

---

12 Pufendorf and other legal theorists in this period used Roman law as the source of their pronouncements on agency. For example, Pufendorf cites the *Digest* (I, bk. II, chap. xi, sect. 17).

13 But this should be qualified. Other noncontractual agreements can establish an agency relationship. See *American Restatement of Trusts*, Volume 1 (1935, 28). I will be discussing this point in Chapter 8, Section 8.3.

14 In Chapter 8, footnote 18, I discuss why an "agency" rather than a "trust" relationship captures the Lockean view of the ruler/subject relationship.

ways that the subjects have mandated, but, more important, insofar as this action makes him their agent, he is, as the law books say, under their constant supervision and control. For example, suppose, as Gauthier has argued (1969, 147–9), that the sovereign's right to punish is created out of the grant to him of each subject's own right to injure others. In that case, a sovereign could legitimately harm one of his subjects only if that punishment furthered the safety and welfare of every other member of the society. Only then would he truly be acting with *their right*, as he was authorized to do. Yet consider that if this explanation of the sovereign's rights is adopted, the judge of whether or not the sovereign is following his mandate is not the sovereign but the subjects. Insofar as they have lent their rights to the sovereign for specific purposes, it seems the subjects have the right and the responsibility to evaluate whether or not the sovereign has abused the powers of punishment granted him, withdrawing their authorization if he has. But Hobbes specifically denies that the subjects have such a power of judgment:

To resist the Sword of the Common-wealth, in defence of another man, guilty, or innocent, no man hath Liberty; because such Liberty, takes away from the Soveraign, the means of Protecting us; and is therefore destructive of the very essence of Government. [*Lev*, 21, 17, 112]

Hobbes is saying that the sovereign's judgment concerning whom to injure cannot be challenged without challenging the fabric of civil society.

Philip Hunton, whom we quoted in Chapter 4, might present this same problem with the agency model in a slightly different way: A subject is supposed to obey and be subordinate to a ruler; but the agency relationship is the wrong model to use in understanding the subject/sovereign relationship, because, in essence, it reverses the roles of ruler and subject. If the ruler is the subject's agent, then the subject actually rules him (as the owner of the right that the ruler wields), rather than the reverse. This would seem to mean that subordination of subject to ruler does not exist, and given that the ruler must, on this model, answer to the judgment of the subjects, we can expect the chaos and destruction of the state that Hobbes predicts when such judgment is allowed them.

A second and closely related problem with Gauthier's model is that it establishes a contract between subject and sovereign, setting out the duties and obligations that the sovereign-agent owes the subject-principal. However, as we discussed in Chapter 4, in Chapter 18 of *Leviathan*, Hobbes attacks the idea that this kind of contractual obligation exists between subject and sovereign, maintaining that no civil union can be created by such a contract because it would make the subjects the final judges of the sovereign's performance. The inevitable discord that would develop as the subjects sought to determine if the ruler had lived up to his part of the bargain would plunge the commonwealth into a destructive civil war.

Even more important, the third problem with Gauthier's authorization model is that it implies that the subjects are the judges of the sovereign's performance, and consequently the authorization of the sovereign can never be considered permanent. An agent's actions are controlled and supervised totally by the principals, who also have the right to revoke their authorization if they choose. Hence, if, through agreement, people authorize a sovereign for specific purposes, it would seem that through agreement they can revoke that authorization when they believe that their purposes can be better furthered in a different way, or when their purposes change. As masters of the contract with themselves and with the sovereign establishing him as their agent, they become the ultimate masters of the sovereign's authority to act. Although he will have absolute power while his authorization is maintained, insofar as it can be revoked and his actions resisted at the pleasure of the subjects, his power will hardly be permanent, and *his*.

This is clearly a result Hobbes would not want. Permanence of sovereign power is a central feature of the "absoluteness" of the sovereign's rule:

they that have already Instituted a Common-wealth, being thereby bound by Covenant, to own the Actions, and Judgements of one, cannot lawfully make a new Covenant, amongst themselves, to be obedient to any other, in anything whatsoever, without his permission. [*Lev,* 18, 3, 88]

Hence, Hobbes has to reject a model of civil union that places final control over the permanence of sovereignty after its institution in the hands of the subjects rather than in the hands of the sovereign.

Gauthier recognizes the problem his model has in explaining the permanence of the sovereign authority. And he constructs a contract for Hobbes that he believes will allow the philosopher to hold the "new" authorization model and still be able to explain how sovereign rule is permanent (1969, 160). Granted that the action of creating the sovereign does not make his reign over the subjects permanent, perhaps the subjects' contract to create him, a contract that they make among themselves, can be understood so as to render that reign permanent. Suppose, says Gauthier, that there are two people, A and B, who make a contract to authorize C as sovereign. Each promises

1. To keep the bargain as long as the other does so, and
2. Not to release the other from his/her promise in 1 and 2.

As Gauthier puts it, "A then has an obligation not to release B, and B has a similar obligation not to release A. Neither of them may release the other. For A to exercise the right to release B, B would have to release A from his obligation not to release B. But for B to exercise the right to release A from this obligation, A would first have to release B from his obligation not to release A. Thus release is impossible." (1969, 160)

But it is only an illusion that release is impossible here. Suppose that the contract between A and B concerns joint investment of their funds in a company facing impending bankruptcy. Does anyone doubt that if A and B get wind of the bankruptcy they will be able to release each other from their promises such that their joint investment can be ended? No. Whatever "no-release" clauses exist in the promise can always themselves be released, and will be so released by self-interested people if it is advantageous for them to do so. Consider again the promise A and B make to each other:

1. They promise to keep their respective parts of the bargain.
2. They promise (a) not to release each other from the promise in (1) and (b) not to release each other from the promise in (2a).

But note that the promise in (2b) is "unprotected" — neither one has made a promise not to release the other from promise (2b). So if they want to get out of the stock deal, they will release each other from (2b), then from (2a), and then from (1). Would it help to add promise (2c) not to release each other from promise (2b)? No, because that promise (2c) would then be unprotected, and so they could release one another from (2c), then from (2b), then from (2a), and then from (1). Thus, all the no-release clauses in the world will not make the parties any more permanently bound than if they had made a contrct without them.

In any case, aside from the impossibility of Hobbesian people making no-release clauses that would unconditionally bind, there is a more obvious and fundamental reason to reject the idea that the sovereign's reign can be made permanent by the subjects' promising. How can Hobbesian people make and keep promises like this? If they had had this remarkable ability to bind themselves, the state of nature would have been a state of relative peace, and the institution of a ruler with absolute power would have been unnecessary.

But the final argument against Gauthier's model comes from the consequences of accepting it. Suppose we agree with him that the subjects' loan of their rights to the sovereign is permanent. What is the difference between making a permanent loan of one's rights to the sovereign and simply surrendering those rights to him? How is this different from the action of enslavement? I can see no difference, and I submit that there is none. If I "lend" you a right that I can *never* withdraw from you, I have in fact surrendered it to you. I cannot exercise this right, I can make no enforceable demands using it, and I must forever submit to your exercise of it in whatever way you see fit because there is no possibility that I can take it away from you if I disapprove of your use of it. Whatever euphemisms I may want to use in describing what I have done, I have *effectively alienated* that right to you. So Gauthier's interpretation of authorization as a "permanent loan" not only is without substantial textual support outside of Chapter 16 but also would fail to purchase the non-master/slave relationship between sovereign and ruler that Gauthier wants.

Nonetheless, we still have a puzzle on our hands. Given that Hobbes believes (and must believe) that the subjects surrender their rights to the sovereign, why does he use a word like "authorization" to describe this act of subjugation, when this word, in its legal meaning, seems to create the very agency relationship between subject and sovereign that he condemns? Clearly, one answer to this question is that he meant to use the word only in its other, nonlegal senses. According to the *Oxford English Dictionary*, in addition to denoting the establishment of an agency relationship, seventeenth-century English speakers also used 'to authorize' to mean "to set up as authoritative; to acknowledge as possessing final decisiveness . . . to give formal approval to; to sanction, approve, countenance." We sometimes use the word in this manner today, as, for example, in the phrases "no unauthorized parking" or "the authorized version of the Bible." Many passages in *Leviathan* show that Hobbes is using 'authorization' in this sense frequently in order to express the idea that when surrendering his rights, the subject is endorsing the exercise of absolute power by this man or assembly of men and accepting him or them as the final authority on all issues. We find one example of this usage at the opening of Chapter 18, where he says that in choosing a sovereign, "every one, as well he that *Voted for it,* as he that *Voted against it,* shall *Authorise* all the Actions and Judgments, of that Man, or Assembly of men, in the same manner, as if they were his own . . . " (*Lev,* 18, 1, 88), and another example in Chapter 20, where he says that servants have committed themselves to "owning, and authorising whatsoever the Master shall do." (*Lev*, 20, 13, 104)

That this is the correct interpretation of Hobbes's use of the word is supported (as in the passage just quoted) by his frequent linking of 'authorization' with a meaning of the verb 'to own' that is no longer current in English. According to the *Oxford English Dictionary*, in the seventeenth century 'to own' could mean "to acknowledge as having supremacy, authority or power over one; to profess, or yield, obedience or submission to (a superior, a power, etc.)." Note the use of the word in this sense by Hobbes's contemporary, Gerrard Winstanley, in an attack on the concept of private property: "so long as we own Landlords we hinder the work of restoration." (1941, 260) Compare this use of the word with its employment in these passages in *Leviathan:*

. . . Every man giving their common Representer, Authority from himself in particular; and owning all the actions the Representer doth. . . . [*Lev*, 16, 14, 82]

. . . we are to consider . . . what Liberty we deny our selves, by owning all the Actions (without exception) of the Man, or Assembly we make our Sovereign. [*Lev*, 21, 10, 111]

Hobbes is clearly using 'own' and 'authorize' in these passages to mean the acceptance and approval of authority, in order to convey the idea that the subject endorses the sovereign's use of absolute power when the subject surrenders his rights to the sovereign.

However, Hobbes also uses 'authorization' at times to invoke the concept of creation, emphasizing the word's root 'author.' Note how he does this in the following two passages:

. . . he that complaineth of injury from his Soveraigne, complaineth of that whereof he is Author himselfe; and therefore ought not to accuse any man but himselfe. [*Lev*, 18, 6, 90]

. . . nothing the Soveraign Representer can doe to a Subject, on what pretence soever, can properly be called Injustice, or Injury; because every Subject is Author of every act the Soveraign doth. . . . [*Lev*, 21, 7, 109]

By playing on 'author' in this way, Hobbes suggests that because the subjects create the lawmaker, they are also indirectly the creators or authors of the laws he makes. At one point in *Leviathan* he says that "The skill of making and maintaining Commonwealths, consisteth in certain Rules." (*Lev*, 20, 19, 107) This gaming analogy is highly revealing of Hobbes's use of 'authorization.' Those who are the creators of the rules of a game are also the authors of its results, and in the case of the commonwealth, the way the subjects create the rules is to create the rulemaker.

Thus, in a way, Gauthier was correct to contend that by using the word 'authorization' in his mature political work, Hobbes was trying to involve the subjects in a more "positive" way in the sovereign's actions. But Hobbes's use of the word does not signify a change in the structure of his theory. Instead, he uses it to clarify and sharpen the same argument for an absolutist regime put forth in his earlier books. In particular, because the word indicates that we are voluntary creators of the sovereign's absolute powers, and thus that we endorse and accept his absolute and unlimited mastery, it sweetens the bitter truth of the necessity of our total submission to him and encourages in us the idea that an absolutist political regime is justified because we need and would want to create such a sovereign.

It would be nice to end this section on this note, but unfortunately Hobbes himself prevents us from doing so. Although, as we have seen, 'authorization' can be given alternative meanings consistent with the surrender account of the sovereign's creation, one of its most natural meanings in the realm of politics and law is the reading that Gauthier gives it, and it is impossible for Hobbes to use the word without suggesting to his readers Gauthier's translation account of the institution of the sovereign and a "Whig" conception of civil union. Worse yet, some of the language in Chapter 16 appears to use the word straightforwardly in its legal sense, for example when Hobbes says that "by Authority, is always understood a Right of doing any act; and *done by Authority,* done by Commission, or Licence *from him whose right it is*" (*Lev,* 16, 4, 81; last emphasis added), or when he defines an author:

Of Persons Artificall, some have their words and actions *Owned* by those whom they represent. And then the Person is the Actor; and he that owneth his words and actions is the AUTHOR: in which case the Actor acteth by Authority. [*Lev,* 16, 4, 81]

In these passages it certainly sounds as if Gauthier is right that the subjects' rights are actually lent to their sovereign-agent. Now I could try to argue that 'authorization' and 'own' in these passages ought to be interpreted to mean "endorsing, sanctioning, and approving." But I believe that such a reading is forced and artificial and that in the passage the legal meaning of 'authorization' is naturally suggested. There seems to be no way of getting around the fact that Hobbes has deliberately invoked the legal notion of agency in these passages and therefore implied that there is a Lockean fiduciary relationship between sovereign and subject.

Why do these discordant ideas appear in *Leviathan?* Perhaps Hobbes was trying to mislead people into thinking (as Gauthier did) that "permanent loans" of power to a sovereign are somehow different from surrenders of power, thus making the action of authorization appear more palatable. But there are other, more honest and yet more worrying reasons for the appearance of the legal notion of authorization in Chapter 16 that we will be dealing with in Chapter 7.[15] For now, the reader is advised to note that in addition to finding a thesis of conflict in the state of nature that is dangerously close to being Lockean, we have discovered pieces of a Lockean conception of civil union against which Hobbes gives many explicit arguments in *Leviathan.*

5.4 AUTHORIZATION AND HOBBES'S NOMINALISM

As we discussed in Chapter 1, Hobbes has persistent nominalist tendencies; though sometimes admitting the reality of properties, in the main he is reluctant to countenance the existence of universals or abstract objects, committing himself instead to the idea that what exists must be individual and material (Watkins 1965a, 143–60). This being so, what exactly does this nominalist sympathizer believe authorization to be?

One of the advantages of giving up the idea that authorization involves the lending of rights is that we are not saddled with language that seems to violate Hobbes's nominalism by committing him to the existence of something that is either an abstract object or some kind of strange occult power that, when transferred, makes

15 See Chapter 7, Section 7.2, and Chapter 8, Sections 8.2–8.5.

someone a sovereign. Indeed, I quoted previously a passage from *The Elements of Law,* in which Hobbes indicates that nominalist considerations lead one to understand the institution of the sovereign as the *surrender* of rights, because there is literally nothing a subject can give a sovereign (*EL, I,* xix, 10, 104). Thus, an additional reason for rejecting Gauthier's interpretation of authorization is that it is inconsistent with Hobbes's nominalist metaphysics. Note also that although it may be difficult to make sense of the idea of surrendering a moral claim, it is perfectly natural to speak of surrendering a privilege or a liberty.

Still, the understanding of authorization as the surrender of one's right to all things is metaphoric. On reflection, we discover that we do not really understand what a person actually does when he "surrenders his rights" to the sovereign. Watkins (1965a, 160–2) suggests that the subjects bestow on the sovereign their names when they authorize him, but there is no textual support for this way of cashing out the metaphor of surrender, nor does it seem plausible that any such action would be sufficient to create an absolute and permanent sovereign power. Therefore, although we have explained Hobbes's use of the word 'authorization' so as to discover what he believes the sovereign/subject relationship to be, we must still explore the mechanics of authorization in order to understand how this action creates the *right kind* of ruler. In other words, we need to know in concrete terms what men and women actually do when they surrender their rights to all things to the ruler.

This investigation is complicated, and much of Chapter 6, which is devoted to exploring the contractual process for instituting the Hobbesian sovereign, is relevant to this task. But the reader is advised to note that we still do not have a literal rendering of the action of authorization.

5.5 THE PERMANENCE AND CONTINUITY OF SOVEREIGN RULE

Given that the agency model of the sovereign's institution cannot secure the permanence of the sovereign's rule, how exactly does the surrender account of his institution secure it?

Explaining permanence seems straightforward with the surrender account. Remember that if we surrender our right to all things to the sovereign and thereby make his right to all things actual and unchallenged (at least as far as we are concerned), we allow him to have a property right *in us.* We have given up to him our liberty to control our lives, and he now has that right. Hobbes argues in Chapter 18 that any attempt by the people to wrest away from the sovereign his political power is wrong, in the same way that any attempt to wrest away from anyone something that person owns is wrong: "they take away from him that which is his own, and so again it is injustice." (*Lev,* 18, 3, 89)

Moreover, a Hobbesian can use this explanation of the permanence of the sovereign's rule to explain the continuity of political authority over many generations of sovereign rulers. H. L. A. Hart (1961, 51) has argued (against John Austin) that such continuity cannot be explained if sovereignty is invested in one person. And, in *Leviathan,* Hobbes is aware that, on the face of it, the succession of rulers in an absolute monarchy at least *seems* impossible to explain without recourse to some higher-order "rule of succession." He notes that there is no problem of succession in democracy: "In a Democracy, the whole Assembly cannot faile, unlesse the Multitude that are to be governed faile. And therefore questions of the right of Succession, have in that forme of Government no place at all." (*Lev*, 19, 16, 99) And there is not much of a problem in aristocracy either: "In an Aristocracy, when any of the Assembly dyeth, the election of another into his room belongeth to the Assembly, as the Soveraign, to whom belongeth the choosing of all Counsellours, and Officers." (*Lev*, 19, 17, 99) However, in a monarchy, the problem of succession does seem serious:

The greatest difficultie about the right of Succession, is in Monarchy: And the difficulty ariseth from this, that at first sight, it is not manifest who is to appoint the Successor: nor many times, who it is whom he hath appointed. [*Lev*, 19, 18, 100]

Hobbes then says that there are two possible answers to the succession question in an absolute monarchy (neither of which makes reference to any second-order rule of succession). First, we can say that "he that is in possession has right to dispose of the Succession," which is to maintain that the present sovereign can somehow give or will his sovereign power to his successor. Second, we can maintain that after his death, the sovereign power "is again in the dissolved Multitude." (*Lev*, 19, 18, 100)

If we accept the second answer, we say that in an absolute monarchy the commonwealth exists only as long as the ruler lives, and that at his death the commonwealth dissolves. Although this means accepting Hart's contention that one cannot explain continuity in an absolute monarchy, nonetheless, we can still preserve a positivist analysis of the nature of the state. We must simply admit that when the state is structured as an absolute monarchy, it cannot last longer than a single generation of ruler.

However, Hobbes explicitly rejects this way of dealing with the problem of succession in a monarchy because it forces one to maintain that commonwealths are destroyed after the death of the monarch, "which is a returne to Confusion, and to the condition of a War of every man against every man, contrary to the end for which Monarchy had its first Institution." (*Lev*, 19, 18, 100) Thus, Hobbes opts for the first answer. Sovereignty is willed or in some other way passed on by the sovereign to his successor, so that there is never a return to the state of nature between monarchs: "Therefore it is manifest, that by the Institution of Monarchy, the disposing of the Successor, is alwaies left to the Judgment and Will of the present Possessor." (*Lev*, 19, 18, 100) Thus, sovereignty is being understood here as an object to which the person made sovereign is entitled. And even as we say that he can pass on, or will, objects like land or money to another after his death, so can we say that he can pass on his sovereignty to another. But how, one might ask, are we to tell to whom a monarch wills his sovereign power?

And for the question (which may arise sometimes) who it is that the Monarch in possession hath designed to the succession and inheritance of his power; it is determined by his expresse Words, and Testament; or by other tacite signes sufficient. [*Lev*, 19, 19, 100]

Hobbes then discusses in detail various kinds of expressed words and testaments, in word or in writing, and tacit signs of the will, such as the following of custom (e.g., the custom of transferring sovereignty to one's firstborn son), that have been taken as signs of a sovereign's choice of who should inherit his power. Nor are such customs higher-order rules binding a sovereign's choice of successor: "For whatsoever Custome a man may by a word controule, and does not, it is a naturall sign he would have that Custome stand." (*Lev*, 19, 21, 100) Insofar as the sovereign has control over who will possess his power after his death, he also has control over any custom that might speak on this issue. *Contra* Hart, Hobbes puts any rule of succession in the hands of the sovereign.

Hobbes's account of succession therefore rests on the idea that political authority over human beings is no different from a property right in any object, and, as such, it can be willed or passed on to another. Austin, who explained a ruler's power simply on the basis of the people's habit of obedience, is not able to treat that ruler's power as a kind of property right that he can dispose of as he wills. But Hobbes's position does, because once we have "authorized" a sovereign by resigning or giving up our right to all things, including ourselves, we are owned by the ruler. Thus, his right to the subjects and everything else in the commonwealth can be passed on to another, by written will or some tacit sign, in the same way that one's property right to a single object such as a piece of land can be passed on to another by some accepted sign. And Hobbes argues that if the subjects do not accept the valid property right of the original sovereign's hand-picked successor, they "take away from him that which is his own, and so again it is injustice." (*Lev*, 18, 3, 89)

But perhaps this answer to Hart is not as neat as it seems. What does Hobbes mean when he says that one would be "unjust" if one deposed one's sovereign or his successor? Hobbes might simply be saying something descriptive here; that is, given that the sovereign defines justice and injustice, any subject who takes back from that sovereign her right to all things is disobeying the sovereign's will, and hence performing an injustice. However, although that might be part of Hobbes's meaning, I doubt that that is all of it. Hobbes is trying to criticize the rebellious subject. But he surely cannot mean that it would be wrong to take back the right one had surrendered to the sovereign because such an action would violate some kind of deontologically valid natural moral law against stealing, because no such natural law is supposed to exist. The sense of wrong he is invoking here must be *prudential:* It would be wrong because it would precipitate violence and civil strife, endangering the life of each member of the commonwealth. And he might point out that if enough people surrendered their rights to the original sovereign or recognized the legitimacy of the successor's exercise of his political authority, the sovereign would indeed have the power to do with the subjects what he liked, leaving them unable to take back the self-control they originally surrendered to him.

However, if readers are a bit suspicious of these last few remarks, they are right to be so. If the sovereign and his successor really own us, then why is it that Hobbes explains the wrongfulness of our attempt to depose him by appealing to what it is prudent for us to do? Unlike chairs or houses, subjects need some persuasion to be "owned." They have to allow their ruler to own them. Are we on the verge of a major weakness in Hobbes's argument for absolute sovereignty? Is there, as Hart would suspect, a covert secondary rule lurking around in Hobbes's understanding of civil society? I must reluctantly postpone the discussion of this important question until Chapter 7, after we have discussed the contractual process involved in instituting the sovereign. Only then can it be tackled effectively.

CHAPTER 6

Hobbes's Social Contract

Two men, who pull the oars of a boat, do it by an agreement or convention, tho' they have never given promises to each other. Nor is the rule concerning the stability of possession the less deriv'd from human conventions. . . . On the contrary, this experience assures us still more, that the sense of interest has become common to all our fellows, and gives us a confidence of the future regularity of their conduct.

David Hume, *A Treatise of Human Nature*

In Chapter 3, I hinted that Hobbes might have a serious problem explaining the sovereign's institution. According to the shortsightedness account of conflict, Hobbesian people can keep virtually no contracts, but if this is so, how can they keep a "social contract" instituting the sovereign? More generally, if Hobbesian people cannot cooperate on much of anything in the state of nature, how can they cooperate on the sovereign's institution? Unless Hobbes has an effective answer to these questions, his argument collapses, because he will be unable to explain how people escape the state of nature and enter civil society.

In addition to dealing with this issue, I will have a more practical aim in this chapter. We know that instituting the sovereign is supposed to involve "surrendering the right to all things," but this is merely metaphor. What concrete actions have to be performed in order to accomplish this surrender? In the context of discussing whether or not Hobbes's social contract instituting the sovereeign is possible, I will be clarifying what concrete actions people in the state of nature must take to surrender their rights to the sovereign.

6.1 PROBLEMS WITH HOBBES'S SOCIAL CONTRACT

In order to appreciate the precise nature of the problem facing Hobbes's attempt to explain the practical possibility of the sovereign's institution, it is useful to review what tasks a sovereign, once instituted, would be expected to perform.

In addition to threatening and punishing anyone who brought harm to the subjects or to the structure of the commonwealth, the sovereign would also be concerned with the solutions to certain prisoner's dilemmas. As shown in Chapters 2 and 3, keeping a contractual agreement presents a prisoner's dilemma to the partners in that agreement, who either cannot or should not see this agreement as a member of an indefinite series of such contracts. However, even shortsighted people unable to appreciate the long-term benefits of cooperation can at least appreciate the short-term consequences of the sovereign's sanctions against reneging and will therefore find it in their

Figure 6.1

I:		Keep	Renege		II:		Keep	Renege
				transformed after a				
Keep		2, 2	4, 1	$\longrightarrow$	Keep		1, 1	2, 3
				coercive power issues a threat				
Renege		1, 4	3, 3	to both parties	Renege		3, 2	3, 3

Note: The agreed-on action dominates.

best interest in the short run and in the long run to keep their parts of the bargain. As the matrices in Figure 6.1 show, the sovereign's sanctions mean that keeping a contractual promise is no longer a prisoner's dilemma; each contractual partner now has a dominant choice: keeping the promise. The matrix of Figure 6.1 (II) represents what is probably the most common of a variety of transformations of our preferences wrought by legal sanctions. So our sovereign presumably would use his coercive power to mandate those actions that individuals found themselves rationally unable to take on their own.

Our sovereign also would be concerned with another kind of problem that game theorists have argued[1] is structurally similar to a prisoner's dilemma and that has been called the "free-rider" problem. If a certain good can be produced only collectively, but after its production no one can be excluded from enjoying it (either it is impossible to exclude them or their exclusion would be too costly), the production of this good becomes problematic. Suppose[2] we have a group of five people who are considering the production of a collective good of this sort. Suppose further that this collective good will generate a total payoff to the group twice as high as the total cost to produce it. Clearly, each of the five will be benefited if this good is provided, but each would seem to have an incentive, nonetheless, not to pay the cost of producing it, as the matrix in Figure 6.2 indicates. In this matrix, the individual's preferences are compared against the preferences of the group. For our purposes, only the individual's preferences in italics are important. Note that they match the preferences of any particpant of a prisoner's dilemma. Hence, the individual's preferences are such that it is rational for her not to pay, no matter what the others do. And because symmetrical preferences are held by all, it seems that it is not rational for anyone to pay the cost of production.

We will have cause later to question whether or not this PD analysis of free-rider problems is correct. But leaving it unchallenged for the moment, one of the most commonly recommended and apparently sensible solutions to this problem, or indeed

---

1   See, for example, Russell Hardin (1971); reprinted in B. Barry and R. Hardin (1982). The same argument is repeated by Hardin (1982).
2   This supposition is based on Hardin's argument (Barry and Hardin 1982, 124ff.; Hardin 1982, 25ff.).

Figure 6.2

	Collective	
	Pay	Not pay
Individual		
Pay	3, 3	1, 1
Not pay	4, 2	2, 1

any prisoner's dilemma, is the creation of an external coercive force that will attach sanctions to the action of not behaving cooperatively. As a result, the preferences of each individual in the group will change, and the action of producing the good will become dominant, as indicated, for example, in Figure 6.1(II). Thus, the inhabitants of the state of nature would welcome the sovereign not only because he would be able to punish wrong-doers and solve prisoner's dilemmas but also because he could supply the external force necessary to discourage free riding in the production of collective goods. Of course, if the subjects could act from "ethical" as opposed to "self-interested" incentives, they would be able to solve prisoner's dilemmas and free-rider problems without recourse to a sovereign. If, for example, they were able to mutually agree to bind themselves to the collectively rational but individually irrational action, each could trust the other(s) to perform this agreed-on action, thus solving their dilemma without resorting to external sanctions. However, such a binding agreement is simply a type of contract presenting the parties with a one-shot prisoner's dilemma. And Hobbes does not recognize the existence of any "ethical" incentive that could overcome self-interest and consequently motivate these people to perform the cooperative action in this or any prisoner's dilemma. Of course, the iterated PD game argument is supposed to show the long-term rationality of performing the collectively rational act in those prisoner's dilemmas that are part of an indefinite series; but as we discussed in Chapter 3, in most situations too many Hobbesian people are likely to be shortsighted to make it rational for even farsighted people to trust that their partners will be true to their commitments. Thus, Hobbes's argument in *Leviathan* is that, in general, the inhabitants of the state of nature can solve their prisoner's dilemmas and free-rider problems only through the institution of a sovereign.

If instituting a sovereign were itself a prisoner's dilemma, or if his institution in some way involved producing a collective good from which free riders could not be excluded, then Hobbes's argument would seem to be in trouble. To resolve this PD or free-rider problem, he could not appeal to any preexisting sanction by an external force, because no such external force exists in the state of nature. Indeed, it is precisely the need to create such an external force that justifies the sovereign's institution. Nor can the contract instituting the sovereign be enforced by the sovereign. The social contract, if it is completed, *creates* the sovereign, and the sovereign is not able to enforce the very agreement that brings him into existence. Some readers might not appreciate this point, thinking that the sovereign-designate could always use force to coerce any holdout individuals into keeping their promise to authorize his rule. But where would the sovereign-designate get this coercive force? He could get it only from other individuals who were willing to carry out his threats on the holdouts. But what reason would any individual have to carry out the sovereign-designate's threats? There would be no coercive force to persuade them to do so, nor would they be able to keep any contractual promise to do so; and they would not want to assume the serious risks involved in performing such activities unless they were in some way "mad." Hence, the sovereign-designate would be without the power necessary to enforce the social contract purporting to create his sovereignty. He would have no straps to bootstrap himself into power.

In *Leviathan,* Hobbes appears to know this, as we noted in Chapter 2. In the midst of his discussion of the third law of nature (i.e., "that men performe their covenants made") he seems to propose the "confederacy argument" to explain not only the rationality of contract keeping in general but also the rationality of the people keeping the social contract. If we interpret his confederacy argument as the powerful iterated PD argument for the rationality of contract keeping *in principle* (as we did in Chapter 3), does this latter argument allow him to say that keeping one's part of the social contract is rational not only in principle but also *in practice* in the state of nature?

The answer appears to be no. If we are to believe Hobbes's claim that the inhabitants of the state of nature cannot keep most contracts in practice because they cannot trust one another to be farsighted, then why is it that they can trust one another in *this* contract? The shortsightedness that kills off the practical possibility of other contracts would also seem to kill off this one. Indeed, Hobbes maintains that not only individual contracts in the state of nature but also contracts between sovereign and subject *cannot* be completed because "Covenants being but words, and breath, have no force to oblige, contain, constrain, or protect any man, but what is has from the publique Sword. . . . " (*Lev,* 18, 4, 89) And if a contract between sovereign and subject cannot be completed in practice, is not completion of a social contract among the subjects to create the sovereign also impossible in practice? Hobbes's contemporary critic Clarendon writes that Hobbes

may be thought to be too indulgent to his Soveraign Governor, and very neer to contradict himself, that after he hath made the keeping and observation of promises to be a part of the Law of Nature, which is *unalterable and eternal,* and so the ground and foundation of that obedience which the subject must render, how tyrannically soever exacted, yet *all Covenants entred into by the Soveraign to be void; and that to imagine that he is or can be bound to perform any promise or covenant, proceeds only from want of understanding.* [1676, 48]

As Clarendon appreciates, if contracts cannot be completed between people in the state of nature, or between sovereign and subject, Hobbes's insistence that the social contract instituting the ruler can be completed begins to look like a desperate move to salvage his argument.

Moreover, the character of the social contract makes it look like a one-play PD game. Only once are the inhabitants of the state of nature going to be asked to surrender their right to all things. So it appears that the social contract cannot be construed as one member of an indefinite series of similar interactions, and this means it will have all the characteristics of a high-risk, one-play PD game, making it rational for the players to renege on their parts of the agreement.

Perhaps some readers think that Hobbes's distinction between a "covenant" and a "contract" might help him to explain how the social contract is possible. However, the distinction is relatively trivial. Whereas a contract is simply "a mutual transferring of Right," a covenant is a particular *species* of contract, in which "one of the Contractors . . . deliver[s] the Thing contracted for on his part, and leave[s] the other to perform his part at some determinate time after," or in which "both parts may contract now, to performe hereafter." (*Lev.* 14, 9 and 11, 66) So Hobbes's definition does not make a covenant different from a contract; rather, it is a particular type of contract in which there is bilateral or unilateral reliance on promises for a significant period of time. Indeed, Hobbes's contemporary Samuel Pufendorf complains that this Hobbesian distinction between contracts and covenants is unimportant and a misuse of their standard meanings derived from Roman law (1934, 699ff.). The only reason Hobbes makes this distinction is that in a situation (presumably quite rare) in which the parties can perform their parts of the bargain at the same time in full view of one another, they do not need to trust one another to perform their parts of the bargain, and thus completion of the contract is possible (it cannot be derailed by distrust). But Hobbes's social contract *does* appear to involve trusting others to keep their parts of the bargain, which is why Hobbes consistently refers to it as a "covenant" (*Lev*, 17, 13, 88, and 18, 1, 88). Whatever the concrete steps necessary to institute the ruler (and admittedly we still do not know what these steps are), it does not appear plausible to think that they could be accomplished by everyone at the same time, in full view, without dissimulation.

So because Hobbes's social contract does indeed appear to be a "covenant" made to effect a solution to a one-time prisoner's dilemma, the shortsightedness account of conflict, which establishes that other contracts of this form must fail in practice, will also establish that this one must fail in practice. So, just as we feared in Chapter 3, Hobbes's account of conflict seems to generate sufficient strife to make the institution of the sovereign necessary, but too much strife to make that institution possible.

But is this argument for the impossiblity of the sovereign's institution really correct? The reason we gave for saying that Hobbesian people could not complete the social contract was that completing this contract essentially meant performing the collectively rational but individually irrational action in a prisoner's dilemma, something they were unable to do. But had we any reason for assuming that a prisoner's dilemma was in fact involved in the institution of the sovereign? No. We simply took that for granted, primarily because it was suggested by Hobbes's use of the term 'covenant' to characterize the process of instituting the sovereign. But we need to know whether or not there really is a prisoner's dilemma involved in empowering a ruler. If there is, Hobbes's argument fails; if not, and if the problem Hobbesian people face when attempting to authorize a sovereign is soluble, Hobbes's argument can be shown not to fail — at least not here.

So, in this chapter, while being utterly faithful to the premises of Hobbes's argument — in particular, to his conception of the person, to his psychology, and to his account of conflict in the state of nature — I will use these premises to construct the appropriate Hobbesian account of what problems people in the state of nature would face in trying to institute an absolute sovereign, and I will show that these problems are not prisoner's dilemmas but problems that Hobbesian people are able to solve. Such an explanation is not explicit in the text of *Leviathan* or in any of Hobbes's other writings. Given his uncharacteristic unclarity and use of metaphor at this point in his argument, it appears that Hobbes did not see his way clearly enough to give it. But I shall not really be leaving the text, because while I will be theorizing in ways that are not explicit in *Leviathan*, I will be trying to clarify what is implicit in that book and attempting to dispel the clouds of confusion that Hobbes's metaphoric language creates.

However, our detailed analysis of the mechanics of authorization will in fact help to expose *other* critical problems in Hobbes's argument. To the extent that Hobbes was not clear about what authorizing the sovereign involves, he suggested that his argument had a problem that in fact it does not have, but he also managed to cover up the real "fatal flaw" in his argument. So we save Hobbes in this chapter only to set him up for refutation in the next.

In order to clarify the Hobbesian argument at this point, I will use certain concepts and techniques of modern game theory. This may appear to some as an anachronistic approach to Hobbes's seventeenth-century argument, but it is not. As Hobbes himself insists, his argument is meant as an independent, rational structure analogous to a Euclidean proof, and if we as philosophers want to treat this argument as more than a seventeenth-century museum piece, we need to determine whether or not it works and, in particular, whether or not obvious deficiencies in it can be corrected by conceptual or mathematical tools that are consistent with the philosophical premises of his argument. Euclid would feel himself vindicated rather than violated if his faulty proofs were corrected so that his conclusions could be derived from his axioms, and Hobbes would feel the same.

Getting a better statement of Hobbes's social contract theory has implications for understanding other social contract theories. Many historians of political theory have contended that the notion of a social contract is a completely inadequate theoretical tool for accomplishing an explanation and justification of the institution of government.[3] They ask:

If the natural condition of mankind [is one] in which each individual is independent of any formal legal ties, how is it possible for men to perform such complex, apparently unified and obviously legal acts as consenting to the establishment of a sovereign, transferring their authority into his hands and contracting to acknowledge the legitimacy of his laws? [Skinner 1978, 164]

These critics believe that it is logically confused to use a juristic and legal concept to explain the creation of legality. By showing the way in which Hobbes can avoid using this juristic concept to explain the creation of the state, I will be indicating the way in which *every* social contract theorist's argument can be interpreted so that this "logical confusion" is avoided. Hence, the discussion here is meant not only to solve specific problems in Hobbes's argument but also to introduce and tentatively suggest answers to larger issues concerning the nature and structure of any social contract theory, which we will finally be tackling in Chapter 9.

3 For example, see J. W. Gough (1936, 4), and D. G. Ritchie (1893, 144). Moreover, Otto Gierke (1934, 107–11) suggests the idea.

Figure 6.3

A:	*a*	*b*	B:	*a*	*b*	C:	*a*	*b*
a	1,1	2,2	*a*	1,1	4,3	*a*	1,1	3,2
b	2,2	1,1	*b*	3,4	2,2	*b*	2,3	2,2

6.2 AGREEMENTS OF SELF-INTEREST

We have seen that Hobbes's argument assuming the possibility of the sovereign's institution would fail if his institution in some way involved solving a one-shot prisoner's dilemma. However, I will argue that the structure of one of the problems faced by the inhabitants of Hobbes's state of nature is a variant of what is called a "coordination" problem, and this is a problem that can be solved not via a contract but via something called a self-interested agreement. In this section I will analyze this type of agreement so that we shall be able to understand how it can be used to explain the sovereign's institution.

If we follow Schelling's suggestion (1960, 83–118, 291–303; see also Lewis 1969, 24) to "reorient" game theory so that problems of interdependent decisions are understood to range over a spectrum, with games of pure conflict and games of pure coordination at the two extremes, coordination problems can be generally described as those games that will be toward the "pure-coordination" end of the spectrum. To use David Lewis's more specific formulation, they are "situations of interdependent decision by two or more agents in which coincidence of interest predominates and in which there are two or more coordination equilibria." (1969, 24) Coordination equilibria are defined as those situations in which the combination of the players' actions is such that no one would be better off if any single player, either oneself or another, acted differently (1969, 14). The matrices in Figure 6.3 are examples of typical coordination problems. Whereas matrix A is a pure coordination problem, matrices B and C are mixtures of conflict as well as coordination of interest (although a coordination of interests predominates), and hence these matrices will be farther toward the middle of the game-theoretic spectrum. (Note that all three matrices have two coordination equilibria.)

How are these coordination problems solved? One method of solution involves introducing certain incentives (either positive or negative) into the situation and thereby changing people's preferences over the possible outcomes such that all the players in the game straightforwardly prefer only one of these coordination equilibria and thus will independently pursue that equilibrium to both their individual and collective advantage.

But this strategy for solving such dilemmas, while effective, seems unnecessarily hard. If circumstances allow communication among the players in a game of this sort, there seems to be an easier strategy for solving it, namely, *reaching an agreement* to pursue only one of these coordination equilibria. In the situations depicted by matrix A, the agreement would be either that both players would do action *a* or that both players would do action *b*. In the situations described by matrices B and C it would be in the parties' best interest to agree that both would do action *a*. And, as David Lewis says, such agreements work as solutions to these problems of interdependent decision because they give each party the "common knowledge that each prefers to conform to [*a*] conditionally upon conformity by others involved with him in [the game]," which means that "each has all the more reason and propensity to conform — and this, too, is common knowledge." (1969, 83) Once action *a* (or, in situation A, action *b*) is performed by the parties, the coordination of their interests is realized, and this is the first step toward building a convention dealing with the situation if it recurs.

Henceforth I will call such convention-producing agreements "self-interested" or SI agreements. This name identifies one centrally important feature that distinguishes them from contracts: In SI agreements, self-interested rational calculation, rather than the sense of "duty" arising out of a promise or fear of a coercive power, is the motive for each person's performance of the act agreed on. Let us now clarify how the preferences generating the completion of a contract are different from those involved in the completion of SI agreements.

As we have already discussed, the device of the prisoner's dilemma (PD) matrix can be used to illuminate the interactive structure of a contractual situation (Birmingham 1969, 103–17). This means that in a situation (such as Hobbes's state of war) in which there is no law, "one-shot" contracts can be completed only if each party to the contract is able to bind himself to the collectively rational action such that the other party (or parties) believes that he will perform that action. But, as Hume would note, this is just a way of saying that contracts could be completed in the state of nature if people in that state were able to make and keep promises.[4] Just as a sovereign's threats can transform a PD matrix into a matrix in which the cooperative action dominates, so can mutual promising effect that transformation, as Figure 6.4(I) shows.[5] Players who promise to each other to do a certain action are saying that each of them has committed himself to doing that action, such that performance of it is now preferred by them to nonperformance. So a promise has two components to it: A promise maker in a contract situation "commits" himself to the action promised by signaling to the others that this action is now his *dominant choice,* and he makes a speech act to the others in which he communicates that commitment — in particular the preference orderings over the various outcomes that the commitment effects. The point of the speech act is to convince the others (either truly or falsely) that the nonlegal penalties he claims he expects to suffer if he does not keep his promise (e.g., earning a reputation as an evildoer) are substantial enough that he would rather do the promised action than incur those penalties. And the matrices in Figure 6.4 show that such an exchange of promises understood in this way will introduce incentives that

---

4   In what follows, I discuss how promises function in the "economic" practices of life. But I do not mean to suggest that this is *all* that promises are; the word 'vow' might suggest a deeper and morally more sophisticated kind of commitment than the one I am explicating here. I ignore this only because promising per se is not my topic and because Hobbes himself would dismiss any such explicitly deontological notion as nonsense.

5   There are several variants of the two matrices depicted in Figure 6.4 (II) that could also describe the parties' transformed preferences after an exchange of promises. None of these variants, however, is sufficiently different from the matrices depicted as to affect the discussion here.

I:	Keep	Renege
Keep	2,2	4,1
Renege	1,1	3,3

$\xrightarrow{\text{Transformed After the exchange of promises to do action } a}$

IIA:	Keep	Renege
Keep	1,1	2,3
Renege	3,2	4,4

IIB:	Keep	Renege
Keep	1,1	3,2
Renege	2,3	4,4

Figure 6.4

Note: In both IIA and IIB, the promise-keeping action now dominates.

will transform the PD situation into one of two easily solved games with a mutually beneficial solution.

How does this commitment change a person's preference orderings? Historically, there has been a "Humean-style" answer and a "Kantian-style" answer to this question, and we have time here only to sketch them roughly. The Humean answer is that when we make a promise, we signal that we expect to suffer penalties for nonperformance that give us an incentive for our performing the action. In Hume's view, promises "are the conventions of men, which create a new motive, when experience has taught us, that human affairs wou'd be conducted much more for mutual advantage, were there certain *symbols* or *signs* instituted, by which we might give each other security of our conduct in any particular incident." (1978,522) And Hume says that the penalty we invoke on ourselves when we use those signs is never to be trusted again in case of failure (see *A Treatise of Human Nature,* III, ii, vi). Recently, Thomas Schelling has given a similar explanation of promising (1960, 150–1). However, for a Kantian, the commitment made in a promise is affected by the moral law. That commitment does not change what one *desires* to do, only what one *rationally prefers* to do. On this view, one's preference orderings change following a promise not because the commitment has affected one's desires but because the moral law has made the promised action (in this case, keeping the contract) preferable or most "authoritative" in the circumstances.

In the rest of this chapter I take no position on whether the Humean account or the Kantian account of promising is superior (although if Hobbes were to admit the possibility of promise keeping, he would certainly prefer the former). What I do assume is that promising, in some way or other, effects a change in the players' preferences, and the two matrices in Figure 6.4(II) depict the sorts of changes in preference that a promise can effect. Matrix IIA depicts a situation in which the promisor is making an unconditional commitment to do the promised action. That is, she is maintaining that the penalties she expects to suffer on nonperformance will *always* make it more desirable for her to do the action than to renege. In particular, she says that she will be better off as a promise keeper than as a reneger in the unilateral-breach situation, because the penalties she will incur after reneging will be severe enough to more than offset the gains received from the double cross. Moreover, she is also claiming that even if circumstances should be altered such that she will receive *no* benefits of the bargain and even suffer additional losses on performing, she supposedly will suffer even *more* severe penalties if she reneges. So because she says that she will do the promised action even if she knows she will not gain any of the benefits of the bargain, her promise introduces what I will call "moral" incentives for performing the action that *replaces* the incentive to receive the benefits of the contract. In this way, the promised action will always "dominate" in her rational calculations.

However, matrix B depicts a situation in which a person promises to perform an action conditional on receiving some benefits of the bargain. Such a promise maker invokes moral incentives that only *supplement* and do not replace the desire to receive the benefits of the bargain. Because he believes that he is better off as the reneger rather than as the promise keeper in the unilateral-breach situation, he has calculated that the penalties for noncompliance are not severe enough to wipe out the gains he would receive as a reneger from his double-crossing action. This calculation means that his performance of the promised action would be motivated not only by the desire to avoid these (fairly weak) morally induced penalties but also by the desire to receive some of the benefits of the contract. Therefore, this promisor commits himself to performance only insofar as these benefits are forthcoming; otherwise he will find that reneging is his most rational action.

I have given a detailed explication of the roles of promises and legal threats in the keeping of contracts in order to explain how the forging of a contract is different from the keeping of a self-interested agreement. As Lewis notes, a simple "exchange of declarations of present intent" is sufficient to assure the completion of an SI agreement, because in such an agreement "it will be in the interest of each to do just what he has led the others to expect him to do, since that action will be best for him if the others act on their expectations." (1969, 34) SI agreements fundamentally differ from contracts in that the "benefits of the bargain" are sufficient to motivate the parties to perform the actions agreed on. If you and I make an SI agreement, there is no need for me either to appeal to a coercive power or to make promises to you in order to assure you that I will perform the agreed-on action, because it is common knowledge between us that the payoffs in the coordination matrix generating the agreement and the beliefs created in us by the agreement itself provide both of us with sufficient motivation to keep our parts of the bargain.

To illustrate how this is so, let us study an example of the way an SI agreement solves a coordination problem taken (with some modifications) from Hume's *Treatise of Human Nature* (1978, 490); see also Lewis's use of this example (1969, 5–6, 44, 63–4, 86–7). Suppose you and I both need to get across a lake; we have access to a boat, and we can reach the other side only if we row the boat together. Matrix C in Figure 6.3 describes our preferences in such a situation. Those combinations of actions in which both of us row, or in which neither of us rows, are coordination equilibria, and it is in our best interest to realize one — preferably the former. One way to do this is to *agree* with one another that we will both row. But all we have done in such an agreement is to coordinate our future actions such that a mutually beneficial result can be achieved. Given that each of us desires to row if the other will row, we are confident that if we make an SI agreement to row, it will be successfully completed, because the rowing action is in our best interest once it is common knowledge to both of us that the other wants to take that action also.

But after we make an SI agreement, how do I know that you were not lying to me when you told me that you intended to take a certain action? Why do I expect you to remain true to the *intention* you have given me, as your part of our SI agreement, and yet distrust you to keep your *promise* in a contractual situation?[6] There seems to be a kind of *assurance* problem here: It will be rational for me to do action *a* only insofar as I can be assured that you will also do *a*. Indeed, the actual assurance game that has been discussed by Amartya Sen and that we discussed in Chapter 2 (see Figure 2.2 and note 14 in Chapter 2) is analogous to this type of coordination game in that in both games there is no dominant strategy, and an agreement on the best state of

---

6 I am indebted to Isaac Levi for pointing out to me that this question needed answering.

affairs will be completed only if each party can be assured that the others will perform the agreed-on action. Indeed, one might say that *every* coordination game poses a kind of assurance problem to the players involved in it.

So how does an SI agreement resolve this assurance problem? Suppose, in a situation depicted by any of the matrices in Figure 6.3, that *A* and *B* have the following conversation:

> *A:* I'll do *a* if you will.
> *B:* And I'll do *a* if you will.
> *A:* Okay, I'll do *a*.
> *B:* Right, I'll do *a* too.

A and *B* are signaling to one another in this conversation that:

1. Each of them recognizes that their preferences for the various outcomes match those in one of the matrices in Figure 6.3.
2. Each wants to coordinate both of their actions so that one of the coordination equilibria will be realized.
3. Each is willing to perform action *a*, conditional on the other's doing so.
4. Given mutual communication of (3), both know that their conditions for doing *a* have been satisfied, so that they now intend to do *a*.

Let us suppose, however, that after they make this agreement, each of them has second thoughts. *B* thinks to himself: "Maybe *A* is lying; maybe she isn't really going to do *a*." And let us suppose that *A* has the same worries about *B*. Now remember that in prisoner's dilemmas, these kinds of second thoughts caused each party to distrust the other and renege on the agreement. However, such worries cannot disrupt the completion of an SI agreement. To appreciate this point, consider that before reneging, *B* would ask himself why *A* might be lying or trying to mislead him about her intentions to perform *a*. There are three possible reasons:

1. *A* was trying to get *B* to do *a*, but was herself planning to do *b*.
2. *A* was trying to get *B* to do *b*, and was herself planning to do *b*.
3. *A* was trying to get *B* to do *b*, and was herself planning to do *a*.

However, option (1) is easily ruled out: The situation resulting from *B* doing *a* and *A* doing *b* is *worse* for *A* than the situation resulting from both of them doing *a*. Option (2) is also unlikely. If *A* and *B* really are in a situation represented by either matrix B or C in Figure 6.3, then action *a* will bring about the best situation for both of them. So why would *A* think that an agreement on *a* would really signal an agreement on *b*? As she herself would know, her actions are rationally construed as ways of bringing about what is, from her point of view, a superior rather than an inferior state of affairs; so one can assume that she truly intended to perform *a*. And in a situation represented by matrix A in Figure 6.3, where the *a/a* state is just as good for both of them as the *b/b* state, it would be reasonable to think that if *A* wanted to ensure that one of these results would be reached, then she would speak truly about her intention to perform one of these actions, and thus not expect her partner to infer from their agreement to do *a* any *secret* intention or expectation that both of them should really do *b*. Option (3) is perhaps the most ridiculous. *B* would reason that, as long as *A* is rational, it is impossible to think she would intend *B* to think she wanted both of them to perform actions that would bring about, for both of them, a situation inferior to the *a*/*a* state.

So *B* concludes it is highly likely that *A* has been telling the truth about her intention to perform *a*, and *A* herself concludes likewise about *B*. Thus, what is actually happening when they make the agreement to do action *a* is that they are making that action *salient*; after the agreement, it is common knowledge that the action stands out as the action that the other is *likely* to perform, so that when each of them performs an expected-utility calculation concerning whether to do action *a* or action *b*, each will estimate the probability that the other will do *a* to be higher (indeed much higher) than the probability that the other will do *b*, so that the calculation will dictate for each of them the performance of action *a*. To summarize, the strategy of solving coordination problems by making agreements works as follows: The agreement makes it common knowledge for all participants in the game that the agreed-on equilibrium is the one that the others are most likely to perform, such that an expected-utility calculation dictates the pursuit of that equilibrium for each of them.

Moreover, this analysis makes it clear why it is rational not only to make but also to keep an SI agreement. Unlike contracts, such agreements cannot be disrupted by distrust, because each party has very little reason for thinking the other party is lying about the intention to perform the agreed-on action. As long as each party is reasonably sure, first, that the other party is rational, second, that the other's preferences are as have been communicated, and, third, that these preferences will not change, each will determine, using an expected-utility calculation, that it is rational to do what one has said. In these sorts of agreements *it is in each party's self-interest to carry through on the intentions as communicated in the agreement*.

However, David Lewis and others have noticed that coordination problems can also be solved without such an explicit agreement:

Explicit agreement is an especially good and common means to coordination — so much so that we are tempted to speak of coordination otherwise produced as *tacit* agreement. But agreement (literally understood) is not the only source of concordant expectations to help us solve our coordination problems. We do without agreement by choice if we find ourselves already satisfied with the content and strength of our mututal expectations. We do without it by necessity if we have no way to communicate, or if we can communicate only at a cost that outweighs our improved chance of coordination (say, if we are conspirators being shadowed). [1969, 35]

If we cannot or do not need to communicate in order to collectively decide which coordination equilibrium to realize, either we rely on already established mutual expectations about what each of us will do or we aim to bring about that coordination point that is particularly *salient*, that is,

one that stands out from the rest by its uniqueness in some conspicuous respect. It does not have to be uniquely *good*; indeed, it could be uniquely bad. It merely has to be unique in some way the subjects will notice, expect each other to notice, and so on. [1969, 35]

Lewis's point is that when circumstances are such that one cannot make one coordination equilibrium salient by agreeing on it, or when an equilibrium is *already* salient, each party can make use of the "natural salience" of a particular equilibrium in calculating what to do. This will be used in the same way as the natural salience produced by agreement. If it is common knowledge that one of these equilibria stands out in an obvious way, each will estimate the probability that the others will pursue that equilibrium as higher than the probability that they will pursue any of the rest, such that an expected-utility calculation will dictate the pursuit of that equilibrium. In such situations, it is as if there were an agreement on the pursuit of that salient outcome; hence, it is common to hear people speak of there being a "tacit agreement" in these situations. Literally, of course, no one explicitly agreed with anyone on anything, but each did act by making reference to the beliefs and preferences of the others in the pursuit of this particular outcome, just as each would have done if there had been an explicit agreement among them to pursue it. And if this coordination problem persists and is repeatedly solved in this way, the participants have in fact developed (without explicit agreement) a *convention* to solve their coordination problem.

So let us summarize the conclusions we have thus far reached. Coordination games can be solved via two basic strategies: first, by using devices to change the preferences of people in these situations so that one outcome is preferred more than any other by all of them; second, by agreeing on one outcome or otherwise relying on common knowledge of an outcome's "salience" such that the probability of its pursuit by others is greatest and an expected-utility calculation dictates one's own pursuit of that outcome. The diagram below reviews the solution strategies we have outlined:

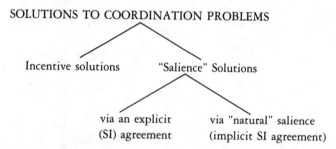

SOLUTIONS TO COORDINATION PROBLEMS

Incentive solutions   "Salience" Solutions

via an explicit   via "natural" salience
(SI) agreement   (implicit SI agreement)

But can we also use an agreement in which there is an exchange of *promises* to solve coordination problems? In principle we could do so, but I want to make clear that were we to adopt this solution, we would essentially be employing the incentive-solution strategy just outlined, not the salience strategy, because whereas in an SI agreement the benefits of the bargain are sufficient to motivate both parties to keep their intentions to perform as they agreed to do, the exchange of promises introduces moral incentives into the situation that either supplement or replace the incentives to receive the benefit of the bargain, so that the game is transformed into one of the easily solved games depicted in Figure 6.5(II). Indeed, we can see here that promising actually destroys the game's character as a coordination dilemma. Hence, SI agreements differ from contracts in being coordinations of intentions to act that are kept by both parties *solely for self-interested reasons*, whereas contracts are trades of *promises* that

Figure 6.5

I:

	a	b
a	1,1	4,3
b	3,4	2,2

transformed by the
exchange of
promises to
do action a
$\longrightarrow$

IIA:

	a	b
a	1,1	2,3
b	3,2	4,4

IIB:

	a	b
a	1,1	3,2
b	2,3	4,4

IIC:

	a	b
a	1,1	2,3
b	3,2	3,3

introduce moral incentives that either *supplement* or *replace* each party's self-interested motivations.[7]

The difference between the two shows up nicely if we examine the fact that coordination problems seem much more easily and naturally solved via self-interested agreements, whereas promise making will be perceived by the parties as a strangely difficult and unnatural way of solving this sort of dilemma. Suppose, in our rowing example, that you made a promise to me, solemnly swearing to row — no matter what. I would find your promise puzzling, given that performing the action was already in your best interest. Indeed, the fact that you made this promise to me would probably make me suspicious whether or not the action really was in your self-interest and might even lead me to doubt your performance of it! My perplexity and doubt would be due to the fact that by promising, you were substituting "moral" incentives for a self-interested motivation that was already sufficient to cause you to complete your part of the agreement once you determined that the probability that I would also do that action was very high. The only reason that might explain why a party would want to change incentives is fear that the SI agreement situation might deteriorate into a prisoner's dilemma. Suppose, in our rowing example, you were afraid that once we got out on the lake, I might decide I enjoyed seeing you row in circles more than I would enjoy reaching the other side of the lake. In such a situation, you might feel that an exchange of promises was desirable because our self-interested incentives, although sufficient to motivate us now, might not be sufficient in the future. But in this case, you would essentially be treating the present coordination problem as a prisoner's dilemma and solving it accordingly — via a contract.[8]

6.3 INSTITUTING THE SOVEREIGN, STAGE 1

Having explicated the notion of a self-interested agreement as a device used to solve coordination problems, I will now contend that from Hobbes's argument for the desirability of instituting a sovereign we can infer that the problem of choosing the sovereign in his state of nature involves only coordination dilemmas, which can be resolved successfully by the people in that state if they use either this device or some

---

7   Much of what Lewis says in *Convention* supports this conclusion. In addition to recognizing the way forceful promising gets rid of coordination dilemmas, he also notes that conventions cannot arise out of contractual trades of promises, because "We have a convention only after the force of our promises has faded to the point where it is both true and common knowledge that each would conform to some alternative regularity R' instead of R if the others did." (1969, 84) Thus, it is surprising to see Lewis maintaining that convention-producing agreements can be an exchange of promises, albeit of a very weak sort. He appears to believe that such "promises" are stronger than declarations of present intent, but weaker than "stronger" promises that effect the transformation depicted in Figure 6.5 (II). But how can they truly be *promises* unless they signal to the other party that the maker claims he has effected the transformation of his preference ordering over the various possible outcomes depicted in Figure 6.4? Because Lewis's "weak promises" do not generate moral penalties that supplement the incentive to receive the benefits of the agreement in any significant way, it is difficult to distinguish them from mere declarations of intent.

8   The law also distinguishes between contracts and what I have called SI agreements, enforcing only the former. For a discussion of this, see Fuller and Eisenberg (1972, chap. 2).

Figure 6.6				Figure 6.7		
		X				X
		Surrender to Z	Do not surrender to Z		Surrender to Z	Do not surrender to Z
Y				Y		
Surrender to Z		2,2	4,1	Surrender to Z	1,1	2,4
Do not surrender to Z		1,4	3,3	Do not surrender to Z	4,2	3,3

other method to establish a convention on how to resolve it. In the rest of this chapter, I will argue for three distinct theses in order to establish this conclusion. First, the fact that people are continually in (what they are forced to regard as) single-play prisoner's dilemmas in the state of nature does not mean that they regard escaping this PD-prone situation as itself posing a prisoner's dilemma for them. Second, there are no PD or free-rider problems associated with choosing which one of them will be sovereign, but only a kind of coordination problem. Third, and most important, these self-interested Hobbesian people are able to solve the problem of how to give this sovereign-elect the power necessary to make him their sovereign. I will also show, at each stage of the argument, that no reasoning is required by Hobbes for the sovereign's institution that shortsighted people would be unable to perform. Shortsightedness makes warfare inevitable, but it does not make the sovereign's institution impossible.

In this section we will start by showing that the people in Hobbes's state of nature would find it not only collectively but also individually rational to escape from this PD-prone situation, which (according to the regress argument) means trying to institute a sovereign. If we consider how Hobbes describes the state of nature and what he says about the reasons people have for instituting a sovereign, his remarks indicate that it is *not* best characterized by the matrix in Figure 6.6, but by the matrix in Figure 6.7. Actually, this matrix represents an idealized version of what I will eventually argue is the real deliberation of the parties regarding the institution of the sovereign, because it assumes that the question of who will be the sovereign is already settled. However, this idealization is useful now because it helps us to clarify what the preferences of the people are for remaining in the state of nature versus surrendering their rights to some person or assembly. In the matrices of Figures 6.6 and 6.7 we are supposing, for simplicity's sake, that there are three people in the state of nature, that one of them, person Z, has already been selected by some process as potential sovereign, and that the other two people, X and Y, are deliberating whether or not to surrender their rights to all things to Z. Suppose that I am individual X and you are individual Y. Would our preferences match those in Figures 6.6 or 6.7? In the PD matrix of Figure 6.5, I reason that I would be better off in a "partial" state of war (where you have surrendered your rights to Z but where I have not) than I would be in either a complete state of war or a complete state of peace. However, this does not seem to be the preference I would actually have if I were deliberating whether or not to surrender to Z; instead, it would seem that I would believe, as the matrix in Figure 6.7 indicates, that I would be *worse off* in this partial state of war than I would be in the total state of war. In the latter state there would exist only individuals (i.e., Y and Z) of strength and abilities roughly equal to my own, who might be deterred from attacking me because they would be uncertain of having sufficient strength to overcome me, or who could be repelled successfully by me, given their attack, if I had a slight advantage in strength. But if you should surrender your right to Z and I did not, there would be a consolidation of powers in this small confederacy, making the group significantly stronger than any single individual like myself. This confederacy would therefore be likely to attempt, and be successful in, an attack against me. But this means I would perceive my life in such a partial state of war to be less secure than in a total state of war, so that I would prefer the latter to the former.

However, as the matrix indicates, I would regard being a member of this confederacy in a partial state of war as preferable to being a lone individual in the state of total war. If I surrendered my right to all things to Z, I would gain additional security because I could rely on the support of Z if I were attacked, and the two of us together would fare better in any preemptive strike against another individual like you because of the strength of our numbers. However, I would best prefer the situation in which both you and I would authorize the same person or assembly of persons as sovereign. My security would be greatest when there were no other individuals or groups who were still at war with me, and this would occur when everyone in the state of nature had authorized the same person as sovereign. Moreover, were we to increase the number of inhabitants of the state of nature to levels far higher than these, the advantages of alliance with Z would be even greater, given the dangers of living as an independent in a state of war with so many opponents.

This reasoning produces the preference orderings in the matrix in Figure 6.7. And there is no portion of this reasoning that requires any sophisticated long-term reasoning ability — even shortsighted people can see the *immediate* advantages of life as under a sovereign, and the immediate disadvantages of life as an "independent" either when others have authorized the sovereign (thereby giving him tremendous advantage in any fight with them) or when others have not done so and the state of war continues. But notice that in this matrix the action of surrendering one's rights to the sovereign straightforwardly *dominates* for each individual in the state of nature. Each person's decision to create a sovereign is not something generated by a contract, agreement, or even a discussion with the others in this state. *No matter what the others do,* in a situation where there is a sovereign-designate, it is rational for each person to transfer his rights to that individual in an effort to begin the process of creating an absolute power. According to this matrix, there is no dilemma of decision regarding the institution of the sovereign in the state of nature — people are clamoring to create an absolute ruler!

Apart from the fact that is seems to do away with the need for an agreement on the sovereign (which we will see in a moment is not true), such a portrayal of the state of nature might well startle the reader accustomed to hearing the people of this state characterized only as violent and aggressive toward one another. But Hobbes would argue that the preference orderings in the matrix of Figure 6.7 are completely consistent with the scenario of conflict generation in Chapter 13 of *Leviathan*. The PD matrix characterizes what people should do, relative to their neighbors, given that there is no sovereign; whereas the matrix in Figure 6.7 represents something different, that is, the preferences for being in such a PD-prone state versus being in a commonwealth (or something in between). Indeed, Hobbes needs to have the inhabitants of the state of nature desire peace and not war so that he can argue for the legitimacy of the commonwealth. As we shall see, this is the core of his justification of the state.

To summarize Hobbes's argument thus far: The people in the state of nature realize that in a world of equals, aggressive, violent behavior toward one another will never enable anyone to achieve total mastery over all things, but will instead render each person's life miserable, insecure, and brief. Therefore, these people desire to end this "no-win" PD situation by actually creating a "winner" (i.e., an absolute master over all things). But do they find that it is also rational to *act* on this desire to create a commonwealth?

6.4 INSTITUTING THE SOVEREIGN, STAGE 2: THE LEADERSHIP-SELECTION PROBLEM

Having shown that each person independently desires to try to institute a sovereign, there is still a problem involving the creation of a commonwealth whose solution *does* require that there be an agreement among them, namely, *Which one of them is going to be sovereign?* If we suppose that everyone would rather be the possessor of the effective right to all things than a subject who has lost this right,[9] their preferences are given in the matrix in Figure 6.8. We are assuming in this matrix that the parties' preferences for the following situations are, for our purposes, irrelevant:

1. the situation in which two of them *exchange* their right to all things.
2. the situation in which one party gives away his right to another, but receives a third man's right.

(Note: the first number in each box of the matrix represents *A*'s preference ordering, the second represents *B*'s, the third represents *C*'s.) Note that in this three-dimensional matrix there are three coordination equilibria, at *AAA, BBB,* and *CCC.* For a population of *n* people in the state of nature, the matrix representing their deliberations will be *n*-dimensional, with *n* coordination equilibria, but that game will be closely analogous to this three-dimensional game.

The deliberation already depicted in the matrix of Figure 6.7 is only an idealization

---

9 This seems a reasonable supposition to make in light of Hobbes's view that "there are very few so foolish, that had not rather governe themselves, then be governed by others." (*Lev,* 15, 21, 77) However, nothing turns on this supposition. Indeed, if only *some* people in Hobbes's state of nature wanted to be sovereign, the dilemma all of them faced would be easier, rather than harder, to solve.

Figure 6.8

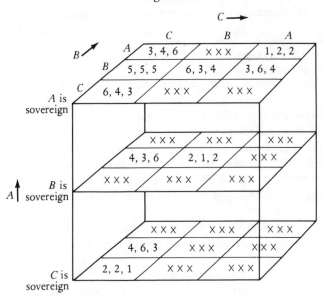

of the actual deliberation process in the state of nature pictured in Figure 6.8. However, this more complex deliberation matrix incorporates the same preference orderings for total war, partial war, and total peace that appeared in the idealized matrix. For example, in the boxes *ABA, ABB, AAC, ACC, BBC,* and *CBC,* the person who has not surrendered his rights to anyone gives this situation the lowest number in his preference ordering, because he is a lone individual in a partial state of war facing a unified group of two. Each rates the partial state of war in which he is a member of a group (either as master or as servant) higher than this, and the highest number in his preference ordering is reserved for life in a commonwealth in a total state of peace. However, the matrix in Figure 6.8 also registers each person's prefer- ence for being master rather than servant in the partial-war and total-peace situations. For example, comparing *ABA* with *BBC,* we see that *A* prefers the former situation because he would rather be leader of the confederacy than a servant in it; most important, in the three coordination equilibria depicting the total-peace situation, each of the individuals would rather be sovereign than subject. But note that the preference of each individual for being subject in a commonwealth with one of them as sovereign is always greater than his preference for being master of a confederacy in a partial state of war. However, the question to be settled is, Who shall reign?

The situation in this matrix is actually a version of a standard "mixed-motive" game much discussed in game-theoretic literature. Luce and Raiffa call this type of situation "the battle of the sexes," after their unfortunately sexist example of a husband and wife who prefer different evening activities (he prefers a prize fight, she prefers a ballet), but each of whom would rather go to the nonpreferred event with spouse than go to the preferred event alone (1957, 90–4, and chap. 6). In order to facilitate discussion of the game, a simplified version of it is given in Figure 6.9.

Figure 6.9

	A is sovereign	B is sovereign
A is sovereign	1,2	3,3
B is sovereign	3,3	2,1

It is very important to note that this type of interaction problem is still a *coordination* problem, because coordination of interest predominates, and there is more than one coordination equilibrium; in Figure 6.8 there are three (*AAA, BBB,* and *CCC*), and in Figure 6.9 there are two (*AA* and *BB*). It is clearly in the interest of all parties to reach an agreement on their actions so that one of these equilibria will be realized. Hence, an SI agreement will solve this coordination dilemma. However, there is also enough conflict of interest to make the reaching of this agreement somewhat in doubt. Although it is in the parties' interest to agree, the relative advantages of the different coordination points could generate enough controversy to prevent them from coming to an agreement.

Examples of this type of dilemma abound: the negotiation between a union and the company that employs its members; various sorts of leadership decisions, such as the one faced by the inhabitants of Hobbes's state of nature; controversies in Congress over things like federal budget cuts that everyone agrees are needed but that are the subject of endless disagreement regarding how the cuts are to be made. And although agreements are usually reached in these sorts of situations, there are also times when they are not. Strikes by labor unions can sometimes go on so long that the company goes bankrupt, damaging the best interests of both the company and the union; reform legislation can take years to achieve because of constant failure to agree on a specific reform proposal.

So the first major problem Hobbesian people face in their efforts to create a commonwealth is a coordination problem with considerable conflict of interest on the issue of who shall be sovereign. I call this the "leadership-selection problem," and given its nature as a coordination problem, a self-interested agreement would seem to be able to solve it. However, although Hobbesian people can certainly keep such an agreement, can they make it? In prisoner's dilemmas, the problem is to *keep* an agreement effecting a solution to the dilemma; in a battle-of-the-sexes dilemma, the problem is to *make* that agreement in the first place.

There are really two components to this leadership-selection problem. First, people must decide how many leaders to elect, and if they want more than one, they must decide how they are to share power, and this means deciding on what form of government they want. Second, they must decide which person or persons to elect as leader. Now, if we believe the implications of the regress argument, the only form of government that will succeed in creating a viable political union is an undivided sovereignty invested in an absolute monarch. Thus, every rational individual in the state of nature should prefer this form of government, and if everyone were rational, there would be no disagreement or battle-of-the-sexes problem on this important question. But at least in the beginning it seems reasonable to suppose that all people will not know that this form of government is superior and will disagree about what form of government to create, so that this disagreement will have to be resolved prior to selecting the leader(s) of that government.

In what follows, I shall provide a detailed argument to show that Hobbesian people can indeed solve this two-part leadership-selection problem. However, doing so will involve investigating the nature of the solution to any battle-of-the-sexes problem. After all, we know we *do* solve them: Legislation in Congress is regularly passed, labor unions and management regularly reach bargaining agreements even after bitter strikes, and leaders are continually selected without major problems in Western democracies. But how are these solutions in the real world accomplished? Does their accomplishment have anything to do with the fact that real people are more other-interested or "moral" than Hobbesian people?

I think not. Although game theorists (e.g., Nash 1950, 1953; Luce and Raiffa 1957, chap. 5, sect. 3, and chap. 6; Bacharach 1976, 84–9, 91ff.) have investigated "fair" solutions to battle-of-the-sexes problems, an interest in and ability to do the *fair* thing (which Hobbesian people do not have) probably are not needed very often in the resolution of these problems, and in any case have very little to do with the resolution of leadership-selection problems. Suppose we have a state of nature filled with people who have self-regarding desires but who are also able to act *purely* for other-regarding reasons. Let us also suppose that each of these people desires an absolute monarchy and will choose a leader purely on other-regarding grounds; that is, each will choose to support that leader among the available candidates whom she believes will be best able to pursue the *group's* well-being. Unless they all decide to support the same sovereign candidate, such people face a leadership-selection problem with a battle-of-the-sexes structure. But in this case, the *moral* concerns of these people are the source of their disagreement over who should rule. And even if we credit these moral people with the ability to perform collectively rational but individually irrational actions, they still will not be able, *using that ability alone,* to resolve their moral disagreement, because each will insist that it will be collectively rational for all the others to support her favorite candidate. When there is a dispute about what it is collectively rational to do, it does not help to resolve the dispute to tell the disputants to do the collectively rational thing. And finally, even if there were an obviously "fair" solution to this sort of problem that these moral individuals might be able to effect, each of them might, for moral reasons, be reluctant to support it, believing that her candidate should win for moral reasons that are more important than doing the fair thing.

So it is likely that these other-regarding individuals will need some kind of device, other than an appeal to fairness, to resolve their leadership disagreement, just as Hobbes's self-regarding individuals do. Other social contract theorists therefore have good reason to be supportive of Hobbes's efforts to find one or more devices to resolve conflict in this sort of situation, because they, too, need such devices to resolve leadership-selection conflicts among their own (perhaps more other-regarding) folk. Having given what I hope is a reason for the reader to root for Hobbes's success in this project, let us consider, first, what sorts of strategies people can, in general, use to solve these dilemmas and, second, what sorts of strategies Hobbesian people could use to resolve their conflict over who should be sovereign.

6.5 SOLVING BATTLE-OF-THE-SEXES PROBLEMS

Recall from Section 6.3 that rational, self-interested people have two sorts of solution strategies for coordination problems with little or no conflict of interest. Either they can introduce incentives into the situation that will change the game-theoretic structure of the game such that it will be easily solvable or they can make one of the equilibrium outcomes salient (e.g., by explicit agreement) such that an expected-utility calculation will tell each participant to pursue that outcome. Clearly, the first strategy would also be an effective way of solving a coordination problem with a battle-of-the-sexes structure. Consider as an example of an n-person battle-of-the-sexes dilemma a modification of the original battle-of-the-sexes example used by Luce and Raiffa in which a family, wife, husband, and two children, have differing preferences about which evening activity the four should attend. The wife might try to solve their problem by introducing positive incentives that would, in effect, "buy the other three out." That is, she might try to give them a payment such that they come to regard going with her to her favorite activity and getting this payment as better for them than going to any of their favorite activities and getting no payment. However, she might also use a "negative selective incentive" to effect the change she wants. For example, she might threaten to inflict some kind of unpleasantness on them if she has to go to any of their favorite activities, so that they come to regard going with her to her favorite activity as better than going with her to any of their favorite activities and suffering the negative incentive. Or, if threats will not work, she might use whatever distaste the others have for wrangling to try to get them to give in. The expected gains of giving in and doing what she wants might be greater than the expected gains of holding out and having to suffer the costs associated with the unpleasantness of wrangling.

However, if the use of positive or negative selective incentives is not an option for any of the family members, they can still try to employ the second strategy for solving coordination problems that we presented in Section 6.3; that is, they can try through an SI agreement to make one of the outcomes salient, such that an expected-utility calculation will tell each of them to pursue that outcome, even when it is not their favorite outcome, in the interest of establishing a convention that will resolve the coordination problem. However, this strategy is more difficult to use in battle-of-the-sexes problems than in coordination problems with little or no conflict of interest, because disagreements over which equilibrium outcome is best will make it difficult to reach any such agreement. Hence, what the participants in this sort of dilemma must do is "negotiate" with one another in various ways until it becomes common knowledge that one outcome has become salient and an expected-utility calculation dictates the pursuit of that outcome to each of them even when it is not the favorite outcome for each.

Depending on the situation, this negotiation could work in a number of ways. Suppose, first of all, that the participants in the dilemma want to negotiate until they actually reach an agreement to pursue one outcome. In the negotiation process, each person engages in one of two strategies:

1. "giving in," conditional on the others doing so; that is, being prepared to pursue an equilibrium *other* than one's favorite on condition that everyone else pursue it, or

2. "holding out," that is, continuing to insist that one's favorite outcome be realized in the hope of persuading the rest to give in and pursue that outcome also.

Moreover, each of these strategies will have an expected utility (EU) associated with it. If a person gives in conditionally and accepts a nonfavorite outcome conditional on others accepting it, then assuming that the others also accept this outcome, she will get utility equal to the gain to her from the realization of the nonfavorite outcome. If she holds out, the situation is risky. Either the others will give in and accept her favorite outcome, in which case she will get even greater benefit from the realization of her favorite outcome, or the others will not give in, with the result that no coordination will be achieved, and the utility of this outcome is lowest. That is:

$$\text{holding out:} \quad \text{EU}_h = p(u_2) + (1-p)\,(u_3)$$

$$\text{conditional giving in:} \quad \text{EU}_g = p'(u_1) + (1-p')(u_3)$$

where u_1 is the utility associated with enjoying the realization of one's nonfavorite coordination equilibrium, u_2 is the utility associated with enjoying the realization of one's favorite equilibrium, u_3 is the utility associated with no equilibrium being realized, p is the probability of getting u_2 if one holds out, $(1 - p)$ is the probability of getting u_3 if one holds out, p' is the probability of getting u_1, and $(1 - p')$ is the probability that not enough others will give in to make coordination on the equilibrium associated with utility u_1 possible. Note that one will want to give in *conditionally* to avoid a situation in which she pursues a nonfavorite equilibrium, but the rest do not, so that her action still does not result in a successful coordination. Hence, one negotiates so as to rule out this sort of thing happening; in particular, one engages in strategies that will result in enough people making a conditional communication of the form "I'll give in and pursue my nonfavorite outcome if you will too" so that it becomes common knowledge that the conditions of giving in have been met for all and the probability that anyone will not pursue the agreed-on outcome is very small. Nonetheless, it is still possible that not enough people will make this conditional communication; if that happens, no coordination will be achieved despite the fact that one has previously given in conditionally. So one's giving in conditionally is no guarantee that coordination will be achieved, and in one's calculations this is taken into account.

Now, at the start of the negotiation when no conditional communications have been made, the expected utility of holding out is likely going to be greater than that of giving in. This is not going to be true when the number of equilibria to choose from is very small *and* where the cost of not reaching an agreement is very high. In this sort of situation, it is possible that one will find it immediately rational to give in to the others (thereby accepting a less than optimal equilibrium in the interest of avoiding the terrible costs of no coordination at all). But where utilities are not that extreme and/or where it is not obvious which of several equilibrium outcomes to accept, *no one* will initially find the expected utility of holding out greater than that of giving in. But the fact that holding out is *initially* rational does not make agreement impossible, because one's own willingness to give in depends on other people's willingness to give in, and their willingness to give in depends, in turn, on one's own willingness to give in. Initial disinclination to accept a nonoptimal outcome on the part of some or all of the members of the group therefore means little, because one's *real decision* in this strategic situation whether or not to accept a certain nonoptimal equilibrium has to be made in concert with the others in the group. Therefore, no one should take the initial expected-utility calculation as final, because everyone knows that people's ultimate dispositions to pursue one of these outcomes will be formed in an interdependent way. So it is rational for all of them to engage in an interdependent decision process with one another to effect a solution to their problem.

What sort of strategies should a person pursue during such a decision process in order to try to make the others give in and pursue her favorite outcome? Clearly, one strategy is to "bluff," that is, to try to convince the others that she will *never* give in, either because she is irrational or because (she says) her preferences are not as they appear. Thus, she tries to persuade the others that the probability that she will give in and accept their favorite outcome is extremely small, so that in the interest of reaching an agreement they become more likely to give in and accept her outcome themselves. Of course, this is a dangerous strategy, because if everyone bluffs successfully, no one will think that anyone else will join with her in the pursuit of one of the nonfavorite outcomes, and so no one will ever give in. Ideally, she wants to be one of the few successful bluffers, convincing the other group members that her bluff makes it necessary for them to give in and accept her favorite outcome. But if everyone bluffs, and everyone suspects that each of the others is bluffing, there will be complete deadlock, and the group members will be rational to use other strategies to break that deadlock and finally coordinate on a solution to their problem.

Another strategy that people in this situation might pursue rests on each of them having different stakes, relative to one another, in getting the coordination problem resolved. To be specific, consider a situation in which people have stakes of unequal sizes in coordination being reached, and where there is a fairly clear deadline to their bargaining. At the start of this bargaining period, each might believe herself rational to hold out. But as the deadline approaches, things change. The probability that there will be no solution to this situation increases, and the probability that one will "win" and have her favorite outcome realized decreases. But those people who have big stakes in *some* solution being reached will find at a certain point that it is no longer rational to hold out hoping to secure a win. Holding out is an action that involves risks. If a person holds out, she might win and have her favorite outcome realized, or she might lose everything because not enough people would accept her outcome and no agreement would be reached. The closer she gets to the deadline, the more likely it is that agreement on some outcome will not be reached; but the bigger her stake in reaching an agreement, the sooner it will be rational for *her*, as opposed to those with lesser stakes, to be willing to give in conditional on enough others doing so, rather than continue to hold out and risk no solution at all. Other people who have large stakes in coordination being achieved will also find it rational, at some point, to make this same conditional communication. Thus, in the course of negotiation, suppose that the participants, say four people, hear the following exchange among the four: "I'll give in and accept this nonfavorite outcome if you will." "Me too." "Me too." "Me too." Then, for those four people, $EU_g > EU_h$, and an agreement on pursuing this outcome has essentially been reached. Notice that the larger one's stake in achieving a solution to the coordination problem, the lower the utility number associated with failure to produce it, and thus *the sooner it will be* that for this person it will be rational to make this conditional communication. Also notice that this process of deciding who should give in is truly *interdependent* and reveals how the solution of this sort of problem must be achieved in an interdependent way.

Why does the probability that a solution will not be reached increase as the deadline approaches, given that the way in which a person's willingness to cooperate is dependent on others' willingness to do so? First, one will have some reason to worry (given the silence of the others) that many or all of them are irrational types who will *never* give in. And, more important, even if one does not believe their bluffs, one will know that as the deadline approaches, the time necessary to effect a solution is running out, making it less likely that the group will be able to do what is necessary to decide on realizing a particular outcome.

Therefore, the strategy for solving this battle-of-the-sexes dilemma is comparable to the strategy for solving the chicken game, even though the two games have different game-theoretic structures. Consider the classic game of chicken: Two people get in their cars and drive straight toward one another; as they approach, time becomes critical to each of them in avoiding death. The closer the cars come to colliding, the less chance there is that each driver will be able to take the appropriate steps to avoid a collision. And it becomes *rational* for each of them to swerve away, in order to avoid a crash, at the point when the probability of crashing becomes high enough that the expected utility of losing the game is higher than the expected utility of crashing. In the wrangling period before the deadline for achieving coordination, something like this game of chicken is going on. And the larger a person's stake in resolving this coordination problem, the sooner one will decide to use the time remaining to give in conditionally and persuade the rest to do so, just as the larger one's stake in staying alive, the sooner an expected-utility calculation will tell one to bail out of a collision course.

Undoubtedly, real-life games of chicken frequently are won by irrational people who decide to "hold out, no matter what." But that is the whole point: People who hold out "no matter what" *are* irrational, whether in a game of chicken or in a deliberation on how to resolve a conflict-ridden coordination problem. It is rational for each person not to hold out after a certain point in these situations. And although irrational people may be able to score wins over others in this situation, they do so only by risking something that at some point it is not rational for them to risk: namely, that the other people in the situation *will* be rational and thus will give in before it is too late. And irrational people in these situations can be big losers: Games of chicken sometimes end up with both drivers dead, and deliberations over which equilibrium to realize can end up with no outcome selected after the deadline for resolving the problem has past. But it is the irrationality of the parties involved that spells failure in each type of situation, whereas rationality will mean success.

Suppose that enough people give in conditionally in this sort of negotiation that one of the coordination equilibria in the battle-of-the-sexes problem can be achieved if each person acts as he says he will. Isn't there still an assurance problem faced by these players? Each is rational to pursue this outcome only as long as he can be assured that the others do so. Do the "conditional givings in" at the conclusion of this negotiation process give each of them that assurance?

They do. Consider, for the sake of simplicity, a battle-of-the-sexes problem with only two players — call them A and B — each of whom has agreed, conditional on the other's doing so, to perform action x rather than action y, with the result that B's favorite outcome will be realized. Consider, too, that they make this agreement as the deadline for agreement is fast approaching. Suppose B is trying to determine whether or not to do x. B might reason as follows: "Why would A do any other action but x? She indicated in the agreement that she would do x; so why should I take it that she meant to do y? Her doing y and my doing x is worse for her than both of us doing x. And her saying to me that she would do x cannot plausibly be construed as an attempt to get me to do y in expectation that she will do the same, especially because the outcome y/y is worse for me than x/x. Hence, it is probable (albeit not certain) that she will do x, in which case I should do x also." A's reasoning will likely be similar. And when both reason in this way, each assigns a high probability to the other's performance of x, such that an expected-utility calculation dictates that each of them should perform this action. Just as in any other coordination game, the agreement following a negotiation in a battle-of-the-sexes problem makes one of the outcomes *salient*, such that it is in each person's self-interest to pursue that outcome (and hence keep the agreement).

It is interesting to note that if, at the start of a wrangling period, everyone knows that there is a person with a particularly large stake in the production of the collective good, then this knowledge can have a desirable effect on the deliberations, encouraging the resolution of the problem. Assuming that all know that it is rational for this person to give in first because of his larger stake in the resolution of the coordination problem, he and the rest know it is likely that he will lose in the deliberation process. But this means that it is rational for this person not to adopt the strategy of holding out initially, because his chances of getting his favorite outcome realized are minimal, so that initially, for him, $EU_g < EU_h$. In other words, in this situation, he is forced to discount the possibility of scoring a win over the others, so that it becomes rational to give in and do the work.

There is another effect on these deliberations that we have not discussed: various degrees of risk aversion. The less happy someone is about taking risks, the less able he will be to adopt the holding-out strategy for very long. Degrees of risk aversion can vary considerably among people we consider "normal." Thus, the more (normally) risk-averse people are, the more likely they will be to give in sooner than less (normally) risk-averse people. Frequently, the sense one has that giving in is a sign of "weakness" is a function of the fact that it is done because of an aversion to the risk involved in the situation. Indeed, sometimes the aversion can be so pronounced that we might be right to believe that a person's giving in because of that aversion was actually irrational, because her chances of scoring a win if she had continued to hold out were still quite good.

It is likely that the majority of battle-of-the-sexes problems will be ones in which people's stakes in getting the good produced will differ such that the people with lower stakes will be able to score a win over the people with higher stakes. But what about the situation in which their stakes are almost equal? Why and when is it rational in this situation for each of them to give in?

Let us start by considering the following situation in which the stakes involved in producing the good are equal, and also very high. Consider the case of ten American soldiers trying to escape certain death at the hands of Nazi soldiers, who are in hot pursuit of them, by rowing a boat across a lake to neutral Switzerland. Suppose that any two of the ten soldiers can row the boat (it has only two oars), and suppose further that rowing involves some danger, because the rowers will be exposed to sniper fire (while the rest huddle in the bottom). Even given the risks of rowing, it is highly unlikely in this situation that the conflict over who should row will fail to be solved, given that death faces them all if it is not. If each performed an expected-utility calculation in this situation, the utility associated with not reaching an agreement would be so low for each of them that even a small chance that an agreement might not be reached would be enough to make it rational for them to give in fairly quickly in the negotiation process, rather than hold out and risk death.

But if everyone is willing to row, how is the group going to agree on which two of them will do so? The exact symmetry of the situation for each of the players means that it might be difficult for them to break it to resolve their problem. However, given that each individual involved in this sort of situation is better off if a solution is reached, it is rational for each of them to support any method that will break that symmetry and allow a solution to be reached.

What are "symmetry-breaking" techniques? We are all familiar with some of the most popular, such as coin flipping and lotteries. These techniques work by inducing in some of the people who are holding out the same kind of "discounting" of the possibility of scoring a win that, as we have already discussed, people with large stakes in the production of a collective good are forced to accept. Suppose, for example, that a group of ten people interested in choosing two of them to drain a meadow decided to use a lottery to determine who would do the work, and they drew names just before the deadline for starting the drainage work. (Suppose the draining was desirable in order to eradicate mosquito breeding grounds. If the mosquito breeding season was one week away, and if it would take two people five days to drain the meadow, then the lottery would be held at the end of the two-day deliberation period.) Those who were selected in the lottery would be in a difficult position. Assuming that time had run out on the wrangling period, each would know that there was no more time to renegotiate about who would do the work, and given that each would also know that as a result of the lottery, everyone would expect the two of them selected in the lottery to do it, then each would be forced to accept that the probability of someone else doing the work instead of him was almost zero, and that the probability of the meadow going undrained if he didn't do the work was extremely high. Thus, for each of them, $EU_g > EU_h$, meaning that it would be rational for them to do the work. Again, doing the work has become their best available option without the introduction of selective incentives. So these devices work to make it common knowledge that one outcome is *salient,* so that an expected-utility calculation will tell all of them (even those who do not like this outcome) that it is rational to pursue it.

However, these devices can work only if the situation is such that (as in the example just given) renegotiation is impossible. When I was a child, coin flipping rarely produced resolution to such problems, because if one of us lost the flip she would simply respond "Okay, make it three out of five flips to pick the loser!" Further flips would always be demanded by the one who lost. In this situation, the resolution produced by the coin flip was never perceived by the loser to be one she *had* to accept. And thus, after the flip, no one had the assurance she needed to pursue the outcome dictated by the flip, given that she could not be confident that the losers of the flip would do the same. Or, to put it another way, the flip in these circumstances failed to make one of the outcomes salient. Thus, to use these devices, circumstances must be such that renegotiation is regarded as unlikely, undesirable, or impossible. (Indeed, selective incentives can be useful here: In our neighborhood, a loser of a coin flip who continually demanded more flips could be persuaded to accept the results of the flip if the others threatened to beat her up if she did not!)

In any case, what is common both to negotiation and to device-produced solutions to battle-of-the-sexes problems is that they accomplish a solution to these problems only when they produce in the participants a common belief that one of the outcomes of the situation is salient, such that the probability the other participants will act to pursue that outcome is high and an expected-utility calculation will tell each participant to pursue that outcome also, even when it is not the favorite outcome for each. Better to effect a desirable, albeit nonfavorite, solution to this problem than to insist on one's favorite outcome and reach no solution at all. And understanding this last point is important in appreciating why, if an agreement on a solution to a battle-of-the-sexes problem is reached, every participant of that agreement will find it rational to keep it. When an agreement on one outcome produced by negotiation or by a randomizing device in this sort of situation creates a common belief in the participants that the probability of the others' pursuit of *this* outcome, as opposed to any other outcome, is high, then an expected-utility calculation dictates keeping the agreement. Indeed, as we discussed earlier, this is the same way agreements produce resolutions in *any* coordination problem.

So, to summarize, battle-of-the-sexes problems can be resolved in one of two ways: either by introducing selective incentives that change the structure of the game such that it is readily solvable, or by using a tactic (e.g., negotiation, coin flipping, etc.) so that an expected-utility calculation dictates its pursuit by all. The following summarizes the results of our analysis:

WAYS OF RESOLVING CONFLICT IN BATTLE-OF-THE-SEXES PROBLEMS

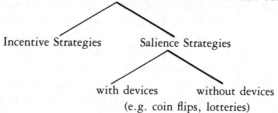

Incentive Strategies   Salience Strategies

with devices   without devices
(e.g. coin flips, lotteries)

However, understanding the solution to these problems is a bit more complicated than this diagram indicates. Battle-of-the-sexes problems are coordination problems, and *the strategies I have discussed are primarily tactics for resolving conflict in these situations, not necessarily tactics for achieving complete coordination.* Of course, salience strategies accomplish both; the use of direct negotiation or certain devices for conflict resolution will achieve full coordination among all the game participants via explicit or implicit agreement. But incentives strategies can be used to resolve conflict in a way that does not, by itself, effect full coordination. In particular, individuals can use positive or negative incentives to gain support from only some of the people for a particular outcome, and if enough support is gained, it will give this outcome a "natural" salience that then will make it the rational choice for everyone else. So certain individuals' judicious use of negative or positive incentives in an "invisible-hand" process of coordination can be an effective way of relying on both incentives and salience to resolve this sort of problem. In fact, this kind of "mixed" strategy is suggested by Hobbes himself as a way to resolve the leadership-selection problem in the state of nature, and we will be examining the details of that strategy later. But first, I want to argue that one of the most natural ways of solving this problem (i.e., voting on a leader) is in fact an example of a device-produced resolution of the conflict in this situation, paving the way for an explicit or implicit agreement that effects the coordination needed to solve the problem. Moreover, I will contend that this device is one that Hobbes suggests is available to people in the state of nature.

6.6 VOTING

In a situation in which people want a leader but disagree over who that leader should be, the use of threats or rewards to resolve that disagreement is usually regarded as politically undesirable, and so people turn to the second strategy for resolving this type of problem (i.e., getting enough people to "give in" such that one leader is selected). But direct negotiation to produce that capitulation is inefficient and, in larger societies, hopelessly impractical. So these societies need a device that, like coin flipping or lotteries, will force enough people to discount their chances of getting their favorite candidates chosen such that an agreement can be reached by everyone on one candidate as leader.

Voting is such a device. Consider the problem facing any political party of selecting a viable candidate to represent the party in a general election. All members of the party realize that it is overwhelmingly in their interest to select someone from among their ranks to represent them, but there is often considerable disagreement about who should be chosen. What political parties like the Democratic party in the United States or the Labour party in Britain do to resolve this controversy is to hold successive elections (either in different geographical areas at different times, or successively at one national party convention), with those who get the majority of the votes staying in contention, and those who get small percentages of support dropping out. As the process continues, there is a gradual "snowball" or "bandwagon" effect, with one person finally emerging as the clear-cut favorite. The process concludes when there is either explicit agreement on this candidate as leader or else substantial independent empowerment actions by enough persons who perceive him as a salient solution to their leadership problem to establish him as leader (such that we might say that there is an "implicit" agreement on him).

The snowball effect in these elections is a clear indication that these are tactics for effecting a solution to a type of battle-of-the-sexes problem. The results of each successive election give each voter a way to determine the probability that one's favorite leader will be able to receive support from the rest of the electorate, thus allowing one to calculate whether or not it is rational to hold out for that leader's selection. And, in particular, those people who find themselves supporting candidates with little or no support from the rest of the electorate will find it rational to switch to a more popular candidate they prefer less in the interest of getting a resolution to this coordination problem.

If this election technique ever fails to effect a solution to a leadership-selection problem, it is because a significant number of those whose favorite candidates lose refuse to accept that their candidates are effectively out of contention for selection, in just the same way that the loser of a coin flip might repudiate that coin flip as a strategy for resolving this sort of problem. Such a refusal in a political context can produce stalemate and even civil war, but the point to note about this refusal is that it is *irrational* insofar as the losing electorate would actually be better off with this nonfavorite candidate as leader than with no leader at all (i.e., insofar as the situation has a battle-of-the-sexes structure).

We must now apply the results of this analysis to Hobbes's argument. As we noted earlier, the leadership-selection problem in Hobbes's state of nature actually has two components. First, people must decide how many leaders to elect, where this essentially means deciding on what form of government they want. Second, they must decide which person or persons to elect as leader. Clearly, Hobbesian people could employ all sorts of strategies to settle these two questions if they disagreed over how to settle them, including the use of coin flips and lotteries.[10] But I now want to argue that it would be both possible and natural for them to use the election strategy just outlined to deal with the leadership controversy in Hobbes's state of nature, provided they could stop fighting long enough to agree to use it! Moreover, I will also argue that Hobbes suggests the use of this strategy in certain passages in which he recounts what he calls his "Commonwealth by Institution" story of the creation of government.

In order to explain how Hobbesian people would use a voting procedure to resolve these two questions, let me concentrate on the resolution of the second question. The disagreement over who should rule will be much more radical than the disagreement over what form of government to institute, insofar as there are only (in Hobbes's eyes) three possible forms of government from which to choose, but as many candidates for sovereign as there are people in the state of nature. So if Hobbesian people can choose a leader using a voting procedure when there are this many choices, the same voting procedure can certainly resolve their less serious disagreement over what form of government to institute.

To help them in choosing a leader to rule them, these people would be rational to employ a voting procedure using successive balloting. On the first ballot, every Hobbesian person would vote for himself, producing a stalemate. However, knowing that this stalemate would have to be resolved in order for coordination on a leader to be achieved, each would do an expected-utility calculation to determine whether or not it would be worth it for him to give in and support another leader conditional on

---

10 It is not implausible to think that in certain situations there would be little disagreement on these questions. Locke suggests how a father in an extended family might be a salient choice for leader in that community: "Thus 'twas easie, and almost natural for Children by a tacit, and scarce avoidable consent to make way for the *Father's Authority and Government*. They had been accustomed in their Childhood to follow his Direction, and to refer their little differences to him, and when they were men, who fitter to rule them?" (2T, 75, 360)

getting the others to support that leader also. However, it is highly probable that these people would have different stakes in becoming sovereign. It is likely that there would be some who would not want to be leader all that much; more important, there would be some who had done particularly badly in the state of war and thus would have a lot more to lose than more successful warriors if resolution of the leadership-selection problem were not achieved and the state of war were to continue. Such people likely would find that the expected gains of holding out would be exceeded by the expected gains of giving in and voting for someone else. So, on the next ballot, these people would find it rational to vote for another, "salient" candidate, that is, someone to whom they would prefer being subjugated and who also would have a reasonable chance of being elected. Thus, the symmetry in the first ballot would be broken in the second primarily because of the differing stakes some of these people would have in escaping the state of war. And in succeeding ballots, front-runners would emerge, and those getting small percentages of the vote would drop out because the probability of them winning would be too small for them to remain in the race, particularly because they would not receive any significant support from the electorate (who would be concerned to find a person on whom all could agree) on the next ballot. Eventually there would be two candidates remaining, and after a final ballot in which one of them got the majority of support, it would be rational for everyone else to agree that he would be leader, because he would have emerged as the salient choice for resolving their leadership-selection problem.

But there is one final and serious question we must consider before we can conclude that this election strategy would be successful in resolving the leadership problem in the state of nature. In the last section's discussion of device-produced resolutions to battle-of-the-sexes problems, I indicated that such devices probably would not resolve the conflict in these situations unless there was some kind of deadline involved in the situation, such that the device could be used immediately before the deadline, thereby making renegotiation impossible. But Hobbesian people do not appear to face any deadline for resolving their leadership-selection problem. So why would any losers in the election believe that their loss was final, such that they had to accept the winning candidate as leader in order to leave the state of nature? Wouldn't they believe that renegotiation was possible and continue to insist on their own candidacies, possibly producing a stalemate and making the creation of a commonwealth impossible?

No. Rational members of the state of nature would appreciate that there was a kind of deadline to the solution of their leadership-selection problem. Remember that each of them would have to return to the state of war unless a resolution of this problem was reached, and for virtually all of them, their chances of remaining alive or healthy for any length of time if that happened would be very small. These people face the following choice: Either they accept the results of the election and subjugate themselves to the winner of the election, whom they did not support, or they hold out for a better deal and risk no solution to the problem and thus a return to the state of war. However, people's fear of this state would be so substantial, according to Hobbes, that no matter who was chosen, they would be rational to subordinate themselves to him, rather than risk a return to that hellish state. In other words, the state of war would be so awful for almost all of them that it would act in place of a time deadline. Hobbes would believe that people in the state of nature were in the same situation as the soldiers escaping from the Nazis in my earlier example. In that example, the short-term consequences of not choosing two rowers clearly were horrible enough to make it rational for any two of them who were selected to row by some selection procedure (e.g., by drawing straws) to accept that selection and not insist on renegotiating the outcome. Hobbes would argue that, similarly, the horrible short-term consequences of continued warfare if the selection of a leader was not achieved would make it rational for the losers in the election to accept the results and not insist on somehow renegotiating the outcome.

Moreover, note that anyone who found himself one among only a handful of holdouts following an election would be faced with the choice of either joining the political confederacy created by the majority or remaining aloof from it and thus having it as an enemy in the state of war. In these circumstances it would be rational for this holdout to conclude that "When you can't beat them, join them." So, although the battle-of-the-sexes dilemmas discussed in the last section were such that one had to be assured that every other person would pursue the agreed-on outcome in order for it to be rational for one to pursue it oneself, this is not true of the leadership-selection problem faced by Hobbesian people. They need only be assured that *most* people will accept the outcome of their election, because if that happens, the power that this large majority will give to the elected candidate should be sufficient to convince any holdout of the rationality of accepting that candidate.

Not only is this resolution of the leadership-selection problem consistent with Hobbes's premises, but also there is textual evidence in at least two of Hobbes's political works suggesting it. For example, in *The Elements of Law*, Hobbes maintains that the institution of a commonwealth involves agreeing with one another on the kind of government to form and the identity of the leader to rule in that government:

Having in this place to consider, a multitude of men, about to unite themselves into a body politic, for their security, both against one another, and against common enemies. . . . The first thing therefore they are to do, is *expressly every man to consent* to something by which they may come near to their ends; which can be nothing else imaginable, but this: that they allow the wills of the major part of their whole number [democracy], or the will of the major part of some certain number of men by them determined and named [oligarchy]; or lastly, the will of some one man, to involve and be taken for the wills of every man. And this done, they are united, and a *body politic*. [EL, II, i, 2–3, 108–9; emphasis added]

In this passage, Hobbes clearly regards the agreement of *every person* on a form of government and on a particular person as leader to be a necessary condition for the creation of the commonwealth. And although he does not go into the details of how people in the state of nature are to reach this agreement, it seems natural to suppose that they would vote in the way I have described in order to resolve any disagreements they might have on these questions and thus clear the way for an agreement on one solution to them.

Thus, voting seems a natural resolution procedure, and Hobbes supports it for this purpose in the next chapter. In particular, he supports it for resolving the question of who shall be leader:

Having spoken in general concerning instituted policy in the former chapter, I come in this to speak of the sorts thereof in special, how every one of them is instituted. The first in order of time of these three sorts is democracy; and it must be so of necessity, because an aristocracy and a monarchy, require nomination of persons agreed upon; which agreement in a great multitude of men, must consist in the consent of the major part; and where the *votes* of the major part involve the *votes* of the rest, there is actually a democracy. [*EL*, II, ii, 1, 118; emphasis added]

In this passage, Hobbes notes that if the people select an oligarchical or monarchical form of government, they will have to select one or more leaders. He also believes that the selection process will involve voting. However, he mistakenly thinks that such a voting process presupposes the prior creation of a democratic political union, such that the majority's vote will determine the selection. But my analysis has shown that this is not so; it has shown that voting is a *precommonwealth* device for solving this problem and that the majority's candidate will win only because of the snowball effect that voting aims to accomplish as a way of resolving this coordination problem. And it is not really the majority who choose a sovereign candidate; it is rather that the candidate who gets a majority of support in a voting process becomes the salient choice for sovereign for all. And only when (virtually) *everyone* makes that choice (as Hobbes admits in the first passage from *The Elements of Law* quoted earlier) does the candidate finally have the power to reign as sovereign.

Explicit talk of the necessity of voting on who shall be absolute sovereign disappears in Leviathan, but Hobbes's remarks on the social agreement creating the absolute sovereign still strongly suggest it. Consider his characterization of the social contract at the beginning of Chapter 18:

A *Common-wealth* is said to be *Instituted*, when a *Multitude* of men do Agree, and *Covenant, every one, with every one*, that to whatsoever *Man*, or *Assembly of Men*, shall be given by the major part, the *Right* to *Present* the Person of them all, (that is to say, to be their *Representative;*) every one, as well he that *Voted for it*, as he that *Voted against it*, shall *Authorise* all the Actions and Judgements, of that Man, or Assembly of men, in the same manner, as if they were his own. . . . [*Lev*, 18, 1, 88]

Although Hobbes suggests that the parties exchange promises in this rather hazy description of the original agreement,[11] thereby implying that they might be acting against their self-interest if they finally authorize a sovereign they did not initially vote for, his remarks show that he does conceive of the dilemma as essentially one of deciding who is to be sovereign, and his language indicates that the dilemma will be solved in an agreement of each with all via the sort of voting procedure we have outlined. Our reconstruction of the circumstances underlying the final agreement on who shall be sovereign shows that Hobbes is not wrong to suggest here that it will be, in part, a resolution of genuine conflict; however, our clarification has shown that this conflict can be resolved successfully in a final agreement that does not involve any party giving *promises* to any other, nor in any way acting against his best interest.

Would Hobbesian people have any particular difficulty using a voting procedure to effect a solution to the leadership-selection problem? Shortsighted reasoners would not; even they could appreciate that it would be in their (immediate) interest to support a salient candidate emerging from the voting process, given what a return to the state of war would mean. However, the desire for glory might well disrupt and destroy this solution. Only one person can be sovereign, and the rest must be willing

---

11 Contemporary critics and readers of *Leviathan* also considered it confusing and obscure; for example, see George Lawson (1657, 4).

to give up their dreams of precedence and superiority in the interest of peace if this one person is to be authorized as ruler. *All but one of them* must therefore accept two things before peace can be secured: first, that the desire for glory cannot be satisfied if they wish to further their self-preservation; second, that a realistic appraisal of the relative strengths and weaknesses of people in this state is such that no one can hope to win superiority over all the others in battle, so that a "winner" must, in effect, be "created" by agreement if peace is to be secured. Thereafter, each must perform expected-utility calculations concerning the wisdom of holding out to be sovereign himself, *realistically* assessing his strengths and assigning probabilities to estimate the likelihood of success. If people reason *rationally* in this way (and note that there is very little farsightedness required from them in this reasoning), use of the election technique will result in selection of one of their number as leader.

Nonetheless, one of the probable reasons that Hobbes returns again and again to the dangers of the desire for glory in securing peace is that it is this desire, rather than shortsightedness or others' fear of it, that is the principal obstacle to creation of the absolute sovereign via an election technique. Indeed, as we discussed in Chapter 3, Hobbes's views in *Behemoth* on the causes of warfare in the Europe of his day reflect his belief that vainglory was responsible for the failure of Europe's religious factions to agree that all but one of them had to give in to the others in order that peace be secured.

But here is where Hobbes's psychological assumptions and his shortsightedness account of conflict stand him in good stead. If we believe his psychology, the desire for glory cannot compete in the long run with the desire for self-preservation: Most of us will not risk our lives for glory. Thus, when Hobbes argues for the practical possibility of instituting the sovereign, he can point to his psychology to show that people's predominant desire will incline them to carry out this institution, and he can show that the *primary* cause of warfare in the state of nature will not prevent them from cooperating on that institution. The only obstacle to this institution is the secondary passion for glory, and that passion can *in practice* be overridden in most people by the desire for self-preservation once they learn that trying to satisfy this desire will mean endangering their lives.

Hobbes does not need to argue that this is an easy lesson for human beings to learn. After all, if the creation of an absolute sovereign to achieve peace were obviously the right and easy thing to do, human history would have been vastly more peaceful than it has been. He could therefore note that by revealing the structure of this situation, we are able to see why people have sometimes had trouble selecting and subjugating themselves to one sovereign, but he would also note that this analysis shows that they are still able to do so.

However, the voting solution is just tenuous enough to make it desirable for Hobbes to have recourse to another plausible strategy to explain how glory-prone people could create a commonwealth. Fortunately he does, and in *Leviathan* he calls it his "Commonwealth by Acquisition" story of commonwealth creation.

6.7 CREATING A COMMONWEALTH BY ACQUISITION

Hobbes insists in *Leviathan* that commonwealths can be created by violent means, and this insistence has tended to puzzle many readers who question the story's soundness and who, in any case, wonder about the legitimacy of a commonwealth created in this way. In this section I will reconstruct Hobbes's acquisition account of commonwealth creation to show that, understood in a certain way, it can be regarded as another plausible account of how the leadership-selection problem can be solved.

Imagine that the state of war has gone on for some time. For those who are still alive, a number of lessons become obvious:

1. Nobody is naturally powerful enough to win battles against every other person, which means that this war could continue indefinitely for each of them until they are all dead. (This follows from Hobbes's conception of "rough equality.")

2. In order for peace to be secured, one of them has to be artificially declared the "winner," such that his right to all things becomes effective. This is just another way of saying that one of them must be made sovereign.

3. Because people's equality with one another is only "rough," there are differences in strength and intelligence among them that enable some of them to do better in the state of war than others.

Note that believing (3) is perfectly consistent with believing (1): As I argued in Chapter 1, Hobbes's equality assumption is meant to establish that no one is so strong that he can hope to win everything through warfare in this state; but Hobbes would not want to deny what is obvious to any student of human nature, that is, the fact that there are very real inequalities in strength and intelligence among us that would allow some to survive in this state of war better than others.

So, in this situation, consider the plight of a very unsuccessful inhabitant. Unless he is badly vainglorious, such a person knows that he will never score a complete win over all the others in this state. Such a person is ripe for the following offer by a more successful inhabitant, whom I will call a "sovereign-entrepreneur." This entrepreneur says: "Look, you're getting nowhere on your own. But if you join forces with me *and do my bidding* (so that I am your sovereign), then you will have more security than you now have." If this person does not accept this rather attractive-looking positive incentive, he might also be "offered" the following negative incentive by the sovereign-entrepreneur: "Do my bidding, or else I'll harm you!" And this threat will be real, because, as we said, the sovereign-entrepreneur is a better warrior.

In general, both of these incentives are important tools for successful warriors to use in attracting subjects. The advantages of submission to this sovereign-entrepreneur are substantial: The subject will receive protection from other members of the confederacy, he will have a greater chance of warding off attacks from outsiders if he is allied with this leader than he would have on his own, and he might receive a share of the spoils of any victory achieved over the forces of these outsiders. Indeed, these advantages of submission might cause someone to submit to a sovereign-entrepreneur willingly, without the need of any encouragement by a negative incentive. However, negative incentives are of great use to a sovereign-entrepreneur as a method of encouraging some reluctant members of the state of nature to give in and accept him as leader. These threats will make it worth their while not to hold out for being sovereign-entrepreneurs themselves, and thus the threats help to resolve the battle-of-the-sexes problem in this situation over who should be made "winner" of the war and declared leader. But even if they submit initially to the sovereign-entrepreneur *solely* because of the negative incentives, the advantages of life under his rule should make them quickly appreciate the positive reasons for maintaining that submission. And this will mean that their continued subjugation will be as much the result of their wanting it as the result of their fear of the sovereign-entrepreneur's threats.

Finally, note that the arrangement between the sovereign-entrepreneur and the weak warrior is not contractual. Out of fear and out of desire to receive future benefits, the weak warrior's *best* move is submission, and as long as he submits, the sovereign-entrepreneur's best move vis-à-vis him is to continue protecting him. We will explore the precise game-theoretic structure of this situation in Chapter 8, but clearly it is not a prisoner's dilemma requiring the completion of a contract, because it is individually rational for each party to do what is required to create and maintain this confederacy.

As entrepreneurs attract subjects in this way, a certain number of powerful confederacies will emerge. But with their emergence will come a real market choice for people in this state. Robert Nozick (1974, 16) noticed this in his own attempt to construct a scenario of the emergence of government.[12] In Nozick's scenario, the forces of two agencies do battle. One of these agencies will emerge as the usual (or continual) winner of these battles. And because the clients of the losing agency are ill-protected in conflicts with clients of the winning agency, they leave their losing agency to "do business" with the winner. Eventually one confederacy emerges as winner over all others and is thus the "best buy" in protection for everyone in this state.

What Nozick is pointing out is that the inhabitants of the state of nature who are looking for a sovereign leader are in a market. Heads of different confederacies essentially say to these inhabitants: "Buy me if you want protection." And the confederacy that wins more often than any other will be the best buy for the people in that state. Moreover, if it is true that absolute monarchies are not only preferable but also the only viable form of government, then confederacies with a single sovereign-entrepreneur should continually be preferred to confederacies with joint rulers, and thus the winning confederacy should be ruled by an absolute monarch.

There are two important points to notice about this scenario. First, coordination on who should be leader is being achieved not via explicit agreement of the inhabitants of the state of nature on who their ruler will be but via a series of independent choices of a salient sovereign candidate by each inhabitant that eventually result in one person as leader. Nozick cited his own invisible-hand explanation of the creation of government to show that he did not have a social contract argument; however, I hope it is clear that he was wrong to say this. What his ability to tell this kind of story does illustrate is that the problem people face in choosing a ruler to lead them is a kind of coordination problem that can be solved either by explicit agreement or by some kind of invisible-hand process.

Second, the negative incentives in this scenario are particularly useful in solving the

---

12 Nozick actually constructs three scenarios, but the second is not relevant to our Hobbesian tale, and the third is impossible for Hobbesian people to perform; so I am invoking only his first story here.

sort of coordination problem that leadership selection presents to people in Hobbes's (or even Nozick's) state of nature. As I said earlier in this chapter, battle-of-the-sexes problems have conflicts that can be resolved either by certain devices, such as an election or a coin flip, that cause one outcome to be rational for all people in this situation to pursue, or by the use of selective incentives that are used to make it rational for enough people to change their preference orderings over the possible outcomes so that coordination is finally reached. When a sovereign-entrepreneur threatens a person in the state of nature to "obey or else," the threat is making that person prefer the outcome in which he gives in and accepts this entrepreneur as ruler rather than the outcome in which he holds out for that rulership position himself. Nor does the sovereign-entrepreneur have to say this to *everyone* in the state of nature. He need say it to only enough people to get a cadre of support enabling his confederacy to dominate in the state of war. Thereafter, his confederacy will be the "best buy" in the state of nature, and as such, it will be the salient choice for subjugation by everyone else. Hence, the acquisition scenario is a nice example of an "invisible-hand, incentive solution" to a battle-of-the-sexes problem, whereas the election scenario is a nice example of a "nonincentive solution" (culminating in either an explicit or implicit agreement on one candidate) to this sort of problem.

Pieces of the acquisition scenario appear in *Leviathan* in two places. First, Hobbes suggests it in Chapter 17, where he discusses the instability of small confederacies:

Nor is it the joyning together of a small number of men, that gives them this security; because in small numbers, small additions on the one side or the other, make the advantage of strength so great, as is sufficient to carry the Victory; and therefore gives encouragement to an Invasion. [*Lev*, 17, 3, 85–6]

Hobbes is arguing here that it is rational for people to move from smaller confederacies to larger ones, because the larger ones have more power over the smaller ones and thus offer more protection and less insecurity. The Nozickean story I have just sketched on Hobbes's behalf explains in detail why small confederacies are unstable: Rational people will continually realign themselves with a winning commonwealth until only one confederacy, and only one sovereign-entrepreneur, remains.

This scenario is also suggested in Chapter 20 of *Leviathan*, where Hobbes contends that a commonwealth can be created by "acquisition":

Dominion is then acquired to the Victor, when the Vanquished, to avoyd the present stroke of death, covenanteth either in expresse words, or by other sufficient signes of the Will, that so long as his life, and the liberty of his body is allowed him, the Victor shall have the use thereof, at his pleasure. [*Lev*, 20, 10, 103–4]

However, critics have long noticed problems with this Hobbesian explanation of the role acquisition plays in the creation of commonwealths. It is clear from the foregoing passage that Hobbes believes the primary incentive for the vanquished person to subjugate himself to the victor is a negative one; the victor "offers" to refrain from inflicting pain in exchange for obedience, and the vanquished individual "accepts" the offer. Hobbes actually talks as if this "coerced contract" justifies the sovereign's rule: "It is not therefore the Victory, that giveth the right of Dominion over the Vanquished, but his own Covenant." (*Lev*, 20, 11, 104) But Hobbes is misleading both himself and his readers by saying this, because a "threat agreement" is interestingly different both from a contract whose game-theoretic structure is a prisoner's dilemma and from an SI agreement. I shall be going into this difference in structure at more length in Chapter 8, but enough can be said here to suggest the nature of Hobbes's mistake. Whereas SI agreements or contracts are solutions that benefit all participants such that all of them *want* to see the agreement not only made but also completed (assuming, in the case of the contract, that they can be assured the other players will not exploit them), in a threat situation the loss that one party has to undergo in order that the other party receive the greatest benefit makes the resolution of the game considerably less than ideal for the first party, one that *he would never have agreed to in advance of the threat*. That is, the victor does not want this agreement to be made or completed. Hence, Hobbes's attempt to make the action of a vanquished person a "consideration" exchanged with the victor for another "consideration" is misleading. Whereas such an exchange does occur in contract situations, and something like it (the coordination of future intentions) exists in SI agreements, a threat situation is essentially a conflict involving not simultaneous exchange but *two separate moves,* the second contingent on the first, with the player who moves first losing out to the player who has manipulated himself, via the threat, into the second-move position. No exchange, or coordination of the actions of both parties, has occurred, but only a "win" scored via the manipulations of one party.

Hobbes is correct in saying that we do not always consider these game resolutions illegitimate in actual life, although sometimes we (and the law) are unhappy enough about them to consider them void.[13] However, he is wrong to say that a threat agreement between subject and sovereign *legitimates* the sovereign's rule. The subject will obey the sovereign only as long as he fears the sovereign's superior strength. However, if circumstances change such that the sovereign is suddenly vulnerable, and effective disobedience of certain laws or a full-scale rebellion is possible, the subject's self-interest that dictated obedience when the threat was believed will now dictate the action of seizing back all or some of his rights. What this shows is that in "commonwealths" created by acquisition, as Hobbes describes them, the subjects give only a *conditional* acceptance of the victor as sovereign — that is, they will obey him only so long as he can threaten them with his power. What the subjects "say" when they surrender their rights to another in this situation is that they do not want to get killed by the ruler; they are not saying they *want* to have an absolute ruler governing them. Locke is right to argue that the situation following a threat agreement is really *a continuation of the state of war between them* and that peace has not been lastingly secured (*2T*, 24, 325).

Hence, what is missing from Hobbes's acquisition story is what the Nozickean story expressly includes, namely, the realization on the part of the subjects not only that they should obey the ruler because they are frightened of him but also that *they should want to have him as a ruler to obey* because they will gain increased security by being subjugated to him. The key to creating a sovereign through the acquisition scenario is something that Hobbes neglected to include in his own presentation of this scenario, that is, the realization on the part of the inhabitants of the state of nature

---

13   This is clearly the case with things like ransom demands or thefts, which in any case offend our views of private property. But any Marxist would contend that coercive situations are often tolerated in markets.

that subjugation is actually a *good thing* for them and that they should be searching for and aligning themselves with the best leader in this state. Hobbes is right, however, to think that threats can play a useful role in creating a commonwealth: Specifically, they help to break the conflict in this situation over who should be sovereign and thus encourage the process of subjugation.

Of course, the failure of the commonwealth-by-acquisition story as *Hobbes himself* presents it is not something Hobbes admits in *Leviathan* — we are correcting his argument here. But there are passages in Hobbes's later political writings that allow us to think that if our correction were presented to him, he would agree with it. Consider, for example, the way Hobbes characterizes the regime of Oliver Cromwell in his essay "Heresy" (*EW* iv). He maintains that the government of England that followed the reign of Charles I was not legitimate because

The parliament having other ends besides the setting up of the Presbyterate, pursued the rebellion, and put down both episcopacy and monarchy, erecting a power by them called *The Commonwealth*, by others *The Rump*, which men obeyed not out of duty but for fear. . . . And in this heat of war, it was impossible to disturb the peace of the state, which then was none. ["An Historical Narration Concerning Heresy," [*EW* iv, 407]

Here Hobbes is explicitly linking a legitimate government with the subjects' *uncoerced consent*, that is, with the subjects' positive desire to be subjugated to that government, and as a result, he is repudiating the legitimacy of the "commonwealth" established by Parliament that did not receive such consent. He also implies in this passage that the state of war was not ended by the creation of such a "coerced union." However, if people had come to accept Parliament's rule (albeit unhappily, wishing that the king had won), Hobbes would have had to admit that Parliament's rule had thereby been secured and legitimized. In these circumstances, they would have regarded it as the "best buy in protection" in the circumstances. Indeed, it is the fact that Hobbes's argument could be used to legitimize governments created by coups and rebellions that outraged Hobbes's royalist critics (and probably pleased Cromwell and his supporters). [14]

There are distinct advantages of the acquisition story (as I have corrected it) over

14   Hobbes's royalist critics frequently charged that *Leviathan* was intended as a justification for Cromwell's rule. Clarendon even contends that he heard Hobbes say in Paris that *Leviathan* was written because "The truth is, I have a mind to go home." (1676, 7–8) Hobbes argued angrily in a tract written in 1662 against John Wallis, called "Considerations upon the Reputation, etc. of Thomas Hobbes" (*EW* iv) that *Leviathan* could not have been a justification for Cromwell's rule because its ideas were drawn from *De Cive* (published in 1642), written long before Cromwell became protector. He also tried to refute the charge that he was an apologist for Cromwell's regime in *Leviathan* by adding a twentieth law of nature: "*That every man is bound by Nature, as much as in him lieth, to protect in Warre, the Authority, by which he is himself protected in time of Peace.*" (*Lev*, review and conclusion, 5, 390) But this law could hardly establish him as a royalist in the eyes of his critics, who also noted that it was a consequence of his argument in *Leviathan* that "The Obligation of Subjects to the Soveraign, is understood to last as long, and no longer, than the power lasteth, by which he is able to protect them [sic]" (*Lev*, 21, 21, 114), and hence that "If a Monarch [is] subdued . . . his Subjects are delivered from their former obligation, and become obliged to the Victor." (*Lev*, 21, 25, 114); see also *Leviathan* (29, 23, 174) for the best statement of this last point. And Hobbes could not deny that his argument in *Leviathan* could be (and was) effectively used by Cromwellians to justify de facto power in general and the Puritan regime in particular.

the previous election scenario, chief of which is the fact that the sovereign's selection in this process is less likely to be disrupted by the desire for glory. The threats from a confederacy leader directed at those who do not support him can be powerful enough to persuade even a glory-prone individual to give in and accept his leadership in a way that his election by the majority might not. However, this method still is not foolproof. A glory-prone confederacy leader still might find it difficult to accept defeat and so extend warfare with the dominant confederacy for years (as Europe's history would seem to attest). Still, the more powerful threats of the dominant confederacy leader and the horrors of war should eventually be sufficient to persuade the supporters of this lesser leader (if not the leader himself) that it is rational to give in and accept defeat.

The violence inherent in this scenario is certainly regrettable, and given the prominence of the institution story in *Leviathan*, Hobbes clearly preferred the more peaceful election process as a way of creating the commonwealth. But either method will do, because either one will enable the subjects to solve their coordination problem over who should be ruler. Indeed, as I noted previously, the fact that we can come up with two scenarios for the sovereign's institution, one of which makes his selection the result of a convention developing over time, also illustrates that the game-theoretic structure of the situation is a coordination problem. This is something Nozick did not appreciate when he gave his invisible-hand scenario of the state's creation. Nozick did appreciate, however, the particular advantages that this story has over an "explicit-social-agreement" story. In my statement of the acquisition story, I attributed to Hobbesian people the *intention* to leave the state of nature and create a winner. But I needed to attribute to them at each moment *only* the intention to subjugate themselves to the best confederacy leader at that moment, and given the structure of that situation, this intention on the part of each of them would inevitably lead to the creation of a confederacy leader with a monopoloy of power. Indeed, even this intention is too strong. I needed only to attribute to people at each moment the intention to do what was in their best interest (as defined by an expected-utility calculation), and assuming they saw (or could be made to see) the advantages of initial subjugation to a sovereign-entrepreneur, their search for the best buy in subjugation would result in the sovereign's creation. And as Nozick points out, insofar as this invisible-hand acquisition explanation of the sovereign's creation need make use of only this limited intention, it has desirable reductionist features:

Invisible-hand explanations minimize the use of notions constituting the phenomena to be explained; in contrast to the straightforward explanations, they don't explain complicated patterns by including the full-blown pattern-notions as objects of people's desires or beliefs. Invisible-hand explanations of phenomena thus yield greater understanding than do explanations of them as brought about by design as the object of people's intentions. It therefore is no surprise that they are more satisfying. [1974, 18–19]

In Hobbes's case, the invisible-hand acquisition story would reveal through its reductionism that *nothing is required for the sovereign's institution that these self-interested people are unable to perform.*

Nonetheless, in *Leviathan*, Hobbes chose to emphasize the institution explanation of sovereign rule that did indeed involve an explicit agreement on a sovereign leader, and I believe he did so because he wanted people to see that it was indeed rational to *have the "pattern" intention* to create a sovereign "winner" in the state of nature. Indeed, that pattern intention is nothing by an intention to act on the second law of nature (i.e., to authorize a sovereign when others are willing to do so too in order to achieve peace). So, because the election scenario is one that affirms and uses the second law of nature to explain the sovereign's creation, it makes clear to Hobbes's readers the rationality of following this law. And because one can help prevent the erosion of stability in a commonwealth by teaching people that instituting an absolute sovereign is rational not only in principle but also in practice, the institution story constitutes Hobbes's main attempt to cure the disease of bad reasoning provoking civil war in the European commonwealths of his day.

6.8 INSTITUTING THE SOVEREIGN, STAGE 3: THE PROBLEM OF EMPOWERMENT

Once we have selected a sovereign leader, is there anything else that remains to be done in order for him to be instituted as sovereign? Oddly enough, the answer to this question appears to depend on which leadership-selection technique one uses. If the people in the state of nature employed the more violent process of leadership selection, they would indeed by finished when one person emerged after potentially violent competition as "top dog" in this state, because he would then have absolute power and authority in that community. But the election technique does appear to leave them with some important unfinished business. After a person has been elected sovereign leader, what power does he have? It seems he has none, so why should anyone who elected him obey any of his subsequent commands? Although it is rational for everyone to engage in this election procedure and to agree with one another after the last ballot to make the winner sovereign, it still does not appear to be rational for them to do what is required to give that person the power he needs to rule. But why? And does the fact that there is an empowerment problem in the first scenario mean that there is a problem of empowerment hidden in the second story after all? In this section, I want to clarify what is required to give a sovereign his power, so that we will be clearer about why people seem to have a problem giving it to him. In the next section, I will be concerned to show not only how this problem can be solved in the election scenario but also how it was implicitly solved (by the use of selective incentives) in the acquisition scenario.

When does a sovereign have power? A person is a ruler only when his subjects do what he says; so people presumably make someone a sovereign (i.e., their master) when they (or at least most of them) obey his commands. Consistent with what we said in Chapter 5 about the creation of a commonwealth, complying with the agreement to institute a person as ruler seems to mean obeying whatever that person says. But this is not quite right. Recall that in Section 6.1 we established that the sovereign is needed to achieve peace, because his *sanctions* are needed to transform prisoner's dilemmas and free-rider problems so that the collectively rational actions will become individually rational. So a sovereign has political power when and only when he has sufficient power to "coerce us out of" prisoner's dilemmas. Instituting an individual as sovereign therefore means *doing whatever is required to give the sovereign punishment power*. And note that once a group of people have done this, each of them seems to have, in effect, surrendered her right to refuse or resist anything else the sovereign orders, because once the sovereign has a punishment cadre on hand, he can order the people to do anything he wants through threats of punishment that the cadre are prepared to carry out.

But how do we give the sovereign punishment power? If it does not involve obeying his every order, what does it involve? Obeying his order to punish oneself? It cannot, because, as Hobbes maintains in Chapter 21, our psychological propensity to preserve ourselves means that we cannot obey such a command:

If the Soveraign command a man (though justly condemned,) to kill, wound or mayme himselfe; or not to resist those that assault him; or to abstain from the use of food, ayre, medicine, or any other thing, without which he cannot live; yet hath that man the Liberty to disobey. [*Lev*, 21, 12, 111–12]

But it *does* make sense to say that compliance involves *obeying his order to punish others*, which Hobbes very definitely thinks we can do. As long as we are all prepared and able to obey the sovereign's orders to punish someone (or not to interfere in the punishment of that person), he has the power he needs to coerce us into doing whatever he likes. Therefore, *complying with the agreement to create a sovereign means obeying his orders to punish others.*

But this understanding of authorization still is not quite clear enough. Let us quote at length from Hobbes's discussion of the sovereign's punishment power:

there is a question to be answered, of much importance; which is, by what door the Right, or Authority of Punishing in any case, came in. For by that which has been said before, no man is supposed bound by Covenant, not to resist violence; and consequently it cannot be intended, that he gave any right to another to lay violent hands upon his person. In the making of a Common-wealth, every man giveth away the right of defending another; but not of defending himselfe. Also he obligeth himselfe, to assist him that hath the Soveraignty, in the Punishing of another; but of himselfe not. But to covenant to assist the Soveraign, in doing hurt to another, unlesse he that so covenanteth have a right to doe it himselfe, is not to give him a Right to Punish. It is manifest therefore that the Right which the Common-wealth (that is, he, or they that represent it) hath to Punish, is not grounded on any concession, or gift of the Subjects. . . . For the Subjects did not give the Soveraign that right; but onely in laying down theirs, strengthened him to use his own, as he should think fit, for the preservation of them all: so that it was not given, but left to him, and to him onely; and (excepting the limits set him by naturall Law) as entire, as in the condition of meer Nature, and of warre of every one against his neighbour. [*Lev*, 28, 2, 161–2]

This passage gets quite specific about what it means to be "willing" to obey the sovereign's punishment commands concerning others, finally making it clear what it means to "authorize" or "surrender one's right to all things" to the sovereign:

1. The subject must give "away the right of defending another" (but not of defending himself) (*Lev*, 28, 2, 161); that is, he must not interfere with the sovereign's punishment of anyone other than himself.

2. The subject must oblige "himselfe, to assist him that hath the Soveraignty, in the Punishing of another" (but not of himself) (*Lev*, 28, 2, 161); that is, the subject must actively assist the sovereign when ordered to do so in punishment and enforcement activities involving others.

3. The subject must be disposed to obey the punishment orders of only the sovereign elected as ruler.

Note that we now have a completely nominalist rendering of what authorizing the sovereign involves. That is, we now know what concrete actions are required of a community of people if they want to institute a ruler.

But would it be possible for Hobbes's self-interested people to perform each of these actions in most if not all situations? In particular, would there be PD or free-rider problems involved in performing any of them?

Regarding the third action, once the subjects have agreed that the person elected as sovereign will be their ruler, none of them will have any self-interested reason for obeying any *other* person's punishment commands. This much is accomplished by the self-interested agreement on one candidate as sovereign ruler after a voting procedure.

Regarding the first action, it would also seem that, in general, Hobbesian people will have no trouble refraining from interfering with the sovereign's punishment of others. Such punishment does not threaten their own well-being, and insofar as allowing it to happen is a way of instituting a remedy to the warfare in that natural state, it is desirable to let it occur.

However, regarding the second action, actively assisting the sovereign in his punishment of others is trickier to explain. In a community of any significant size, the sovereign will need help enforcing his edicts; police, judges, and jailers will all be required to make effective enforcement of the sovereign's laws possible. Therefore, some percentage of persons in the community will have to be willing to carry out these jobs at the sovereign's behest in order that the sovereign have the power to be a sovereign (after all, the sovereign can't do everything by himself). But can they do so? Wouldn't the structure of the situation and their preferences be such that it would be more rational to *refuse*, given that what would be produced by obeying the sovereign (i.e., peace) would be a collective good from which nonproducers could not be excluded? Indeed, in this situation, wouldn't each find it rational to ride free, benefiting from the enforcement but refusing to carry it out? And if each found it rational to refuse to obey the sovereign's enforcement commands, wouldn't this mean that no one would do so, thus leaving the sovereign without sufficient power to be a sovereign? It certainly appears as if empowering the ruler involves creating a collective good, and thus performing collectively rational but individually irrational actions — in this case, punishment actions. And if people are unable to produce collective goods of this sort in the state of nature, inasmuch as their production involves them in a problem analogous to a prisoner's dilemma, how are they suddenly able to produce *this* good? From what Hobbes has told us about the nature and motivations of these people, they will have no way of doing so.

We are now able to see what the agreement among the subjects that makes the winner of the election procedure absolute sovereign actually accomplishes and what it does not. It *does* make it rational for each subject to accept only this individual as sovereign, which seems to mean obeying only this person's punishment commands. But obedience turns out to involve them in additional difficulties that their SI agreement making him ruler does not address. It seems that after this individual has been agreed on as sovereign by the populace, there must be an *additional contractual agreement* in which each future subject says, either to one another or to the sovereign, "I promise to obey the sovereign-elect's punishment commands." But given Hobbes's psychology, people are unable to keep such a contractual promise, and in any case Hobbes explicitly tells us in Chapter 18 that no contract between subject and sovereign can exist in a viable commonwealth (*Lev*, 18, 4, 89).

So Hobbes appears to have a problem: In order to leave the state of war, the people must institute a sovereign. But a sovereign can be instituted only if people are able to follow his edicts, and it appears that they can follow his edicts if and only if either

1. each of them can comply with the sovereign's orders knowing that they are going to be producing a collective good (i.e. punishment force) that cannot be excluded from nonproducers and thus knowing that they will have to perform actions that are only collectively and not individually rational (and, of course, the subjects know they can do neither of these things), or
2. each of them can keep a promise in a social contract, either with one another or with the sovereign, to obey even those sovereign commands ordering assistance in punishing wrongdoers that are opposed to their self-interest (and, of course, the subjects cannot do that).

Can we bail out Hobbes's argument by suddenly bestowing on Hobbesian people the ability to keep a contract? We cannot. Doing so would destroy Hobbes's political conclusions because it would make contractual activity, and thus peaceful cooperation, possible *in the state of nature,* and this would mean that the institution of an absolute sovereign, and hence the social contract creating him, would be unnecessary for the attainment of peace. So if completion of the social contract by Hobbesian people is possible, that contract is also unnecessary for the realization of peace; but if it is necessary for peace, it is also impossible.

If Hobbes cannot have recourse to a contract to explain how the sovereign is empowered, can he accomplish that explanation at all? It would be easy for me to conclude that Hobbes's argument finally fails, even with this revised understanding of what is involved in the sovereign's institution, and thus end this chapter here. But although I certainly believe that Hobbes's argument fails (as I shall argue in the next chapter), I have never believed that it fails *here.* An important indication that it does not fail is that empowerment somehow takes place in the acquisition account of the sovereign's creation. Indeed, when Nozick employs a similar scenario to explain the creation of the state, it never even occurs to him that a protective agency might have a problem receiving power from the people it protects. In what follows, I shall explain why I think Hobbes is able to sail successfully through the shoals of this free-rider problem, and part of my argument is that some of the shoals that this problem is supposed to present are illusory. And, in the process, I will show why neither Genghis Khan nor Idi Amin nor gang leaders in Los Angeles have had to rely on the *morality* of their followers in order to get those followers to obey their commands to inflict violence on others.

6.9 EMPOWERMENT: THE SOLUTION

Suppose that the inhabitants of the state of nature have determined that they need and want a sovereign to end their mutual warfare and have elected a sovereign. This sovereign then proceeds to issue a variety of orders backed by threats, among them an order not to steal another's possessions. Nevertheless, an individual we shall call Joe the Desperado seizes many valuable possessions from one of the subjects of this newly formed commonwealth and heads off into the sunset. The sovereign-elect then calls on her subjects to give her the power to enforce her threat against Joe: "It will take a posse of six people to bring back Joe dead or alive. I have arrived at that number by determining the minimum number of people required to overpower Joe so that the danger to each of them is less than the dangers they would face as individuals in the state of nature from attack by any of their fellows in this state. So I hereby order *you six* [she fingers them] to capture Joe, bring him back here for trial before me, and punish him as I specify if I find him guilty." Will the six obey the sovereign's command, knowing that as yet she has no punishment cadre to back up that command?

We seem to have an instance of the free-rider problem here. The collective good that the posse would produce (i.e., capturing Joe) would be valued by everyone, but each of the six selected to perform this task would prefer avoiding the danger to his life in the posse by letting another person take his place, and so would be disposed not to obey the sovereign's command to capture Joe.

But we would be making a serious mistake if we were to assume that just because these people faced a free-rider problem, they were a fortiori facing a problem with a PD structure. Although the literature on free-rider problems has frequently assumed that the PD structure underlies *all* such problems, we will now see that this is importantly *false;* in particular, we will see that it does not, in general, underlie the production of what are called "step goods,"[15] and minimally effective posses are in fact step goods.

A step good is one whose magnitude is not a linear function of the contributions made to produce it, one that comes into existence only after a very large contribution "step." For example, a bridge over a river is a step good, because unless the entire river is spanned, the bridge does not exist — half a bridge is no bridge at all. Contrast this with clean air: This is what I call an "incremental" good, because each contribution made to produce it brings it into existence to a degree. Any individual can help to clean up the air a *bit* by making his small contribution, whereas an initial small contribution to the making of a bridge will not result in the bridge itself nor any "degree of bridgeness" coming into existence.

What is the game-theoretic structure underlying the production of a step good? Consider a famous example of such a good given by Hume:

Two neighbours may agree to drain a meadow, which they possess in common; because 'tis easy for them to know each others mind; and each must perceive, that the immediate consequence of his failing in his part, is, the abandoning the whole project. But 'tis very difficult, and indeed impossible, that a thousand persons shou'd agree in any such action; it being difficult for them to concert so complicated a design, and still more difficult for them to execute it; while each

15 Russell Hardin (1982, 55ff.) suggests that step goods (which is his name for this type of collective good) do not involve a prisoner's dilemma in their production. There is also a suggestion to this effect by Norman Frohlich, Joe Oppenheimer, and Oran Young (1971, 18–29). I have discussed at length the non-PD structure of step-good production in my article "Free Rider Problems in the Production of Collective Goods."

Figure 6.10a. Preferences represented with ordinal numbers

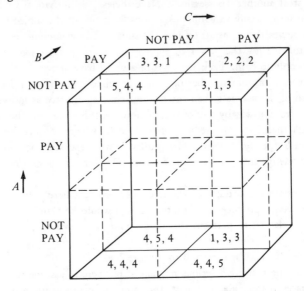

seeks a pretext to free himself of the trouble and expence, and wou'd lay the whole burden on others. [III, ii, vii; 1978, 538]

Hume's remarks suggest that the situation has the following structure:

1. The task to be performed is *minimally* a two-person job, because the gross benefit to one person who does the job minus the total cost of producing the good (i.e., draining the meadow) is less than zero. Or, to use Mancur Olson's formula (1965, 22–36),

$$V_i - C < 0$$

where V_i is the gross benefit to individual i, and C is the total cost of the project. If, for some individual i,

$$V_i - C > 0,$$

then the group is what Olson calls *privileged* (1965, 48–50), and the collective good will be provided. For example, if among a thousand people there is one who will benefit from the draining of the meadow so much as to outweigh the cost to him of draining it *alone*, then this group is privileged, and the collective good will most likely be provided (i.e., by this individual). But we are structuring the example so that there is no individual i for whom $V_i - C > 0$, and because of this we have what Olson calls a *latent* (1965, 48–52) group. However, it is true in this example that if two people do the job, such that each person's cost of producing the good is halved, then

$$V_i - \frac{1}{2}C > 0$$

So if two people share the task, the net benefit they receive from the good will be great enough that it will be in their self-interest to carry it out. In other

Figure 6.10b. Preferences presented with cardinal numbers

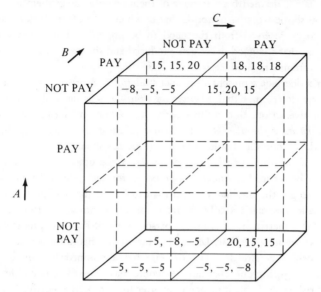

words, life is better for each of them with the meadow drained, even given the cost to them of draining it, than it is without the meadow drained.

2. The good produced is clearly "nonexcludable" and hence "collective" in the sense we have defined.

3. It is a step good. The meadow will not be drained unless both of them contribute to its production, and it makes no sense to say that the drained meadow can be increased in increments of quality or quantity after it comes into existence.

What are people's preferences in this sort of situation? It is incorrect to try to force this situation into a two-person matrix, because it simply is not a two-person dilemma. We would need a 1,000-person matrix to represent it properly, but because I have as little inclination to provide such a matrix as the reader has to see one, I shall make do with a three-person matrix (Figure 6.10a, b), which, as we shall see, is not qualitatively different from a 1,000-person matrix, but importantly different from the me-versus-them PD matrix normally used to represent this type of situation. Each matrix represents *A*'s, *B*'s, and *C*'s actions along each dimension of the box. Inside the large box are eight smaller boxes, each of which contains *A*'s, *B*'s, and *C*'s preferences (in that order) for the situation represented by that box (the preferences are on the top and bottom surfaces of each box). Figure 6.10a gives ordinal preferences; 6.10b describes preferences in terms of (cardinal) utility numbers.

As these matrices show, each player's favorite situation is that in which the other two players drain the meadow and she languishes at home, eventually enjoying the good produced at no cost to her. Next best is the situation in which the three of them share the work to be done, which is better than the situation in which she and only one other player split the work between them (doing half of the work is worse than doing a third of it). But this option is substantially better than the situation in which the meadow is not drained because none of them or only one of them is willing to do it, and of course the worst situation is that in which she puts in work almost equal to the benefit to be received from the good to be produced, but is never assisted by anyone else, so that the good never gets produced and she loses whatever resources she put into the attempt to produce it.

This matrix does not represent a prisoner's dilemma. A prisoner's dilemma is one in which a player determines that *whatever the others do*, it is rational for her to perform the uncooperative action. But in this matrix, it is *not* rational for her to refuse to drain the meadow *whatever the others do*. She should refuse if she thinks that the other two people will do it, but she should *not* refuse (i.e., she should pay the cost of draining the meadow) if she thinks that only one, and not the other, is willing to drain the meadow. It is better for her (indeed, *much* better for her) to help the one other person do the work to get the meadow drained than to let the meadow go undrained. And, of course, she knows that the others' preferences are symmetric with hers.

Therefore, this matrix presents a three-person battle-of-the-sexes problem, a problem with which we are now familiar. Let us therefore apply this to the sovereign's problem of raising a posse to go after Joe. The sovereign has determined the number of members in this posse by figuring out what number would make the risk to one's life in the posse *less* than the risk to one's life if no one went after Joe and people remained in the state of nature. Assuming they accept that her estimate is correct, this means that people regard the risk to their lives in the posse as *less* than the risk to their lives in the situation in which no posse is formed. Nonetheless, they also regard the risk to their lives when a posse is formed, but without them, as *less* than the risk to their lives when they are members of the posse. Finally, the sovereign's determination of the number of people in the posse is such that it is the minimal number necessary to capture Joe, because any fewer people in the posse will mean that the risk to each in the posse is greater than the risk to each in the situation in which no posse is formed. So this posse of six is a step good — unless there are six contributors to it, no enforcement activity will take place, because no one will have the belief stated in item (1).

Thus described, the situation is a battle-of-the-sexes dilemma. Each person knows he is better off taking the risks involved in pursuing Joe than he is taking the risks involved in remaining in a situation in which no one pursues Joe. But each person also knows he is better off if someone else besides him is part of the six-person posse, such that he gets the benefits of Joe's being caught (i.e., the deterrence of not only Joe but also other subjects by the sovereign's threat of punishment next time) without having to catch Joe (and incur risks) himself. So if he believes that others will join the posse instead of him, he is rational not to join it; but if he believes that his joining is critical to the posse's formation, then he is rational to join (being a member of the posse is better than being in a situation in which no posse is formed).

But having analyzed the problem in this way, it should be clear that Hobbes has the room he needs to say that six self-interested people will be able to obey the sovereign's punishment orders for self-interested reasons alone. Compare the situation of people in this Hobbesian world to the situation of the ten American soldiers being pursued by Nazis and trying to escape across a lake in a boat with only two oars. The best situation for each of the ten would be to huddle in the bottom of the boat; the worst situation would be to remain on shore and face certain death at the hands of the Nazis. Being a rower would be better than remaining on shore — one would be only *risking* death, not *expecting* it. But, of course, rowing is inferior to not rowing. Given the nature of the options, we think it highly unlikely that this group of ten would fail to agree on which two of them would do the rowing. But Hobbes would say that this is exactly like the situation in a newly formed commonwealth. Although no one wants to run the risks involved in capturing Joe the Desperado, not doing so means remaining in a state of war and risking death at the hands of *every* inhabitant of the natural state, not just Joe. Obeying the sovereign's commands to capture Joe, however, is the kind of action that finally will help to bring an end to their warfare, and Hobbes would contend that an expected-utility calculation would clearly dictate to each of them that it would be better to participate in the posse than to refrain from doing so, because the advantages of posse membership (like the advantages of rowing) would be substantially greater than the (minimal) advantages of remaining in the state of nature (analogous in the rowing example to facing imminent death). So each would believe, first, that because u_1 (the utility associated with being in the posse) was so much greater than u_3 (the utility associated with no posse being formed), and second, that because the probability of no posse being formed if he did not join was larger than the probability of no posse being formed if he did join, then giving in and joining the posse would be rational; that is,

$$EU_g > EU_h$$

$$p'(u_1) + (1 - p')(u_3) > p(u_2) + (1 - p)(u_3)$$

(Note that the symbols here stand for the relevant instantiations of the notions of utility and probability that the symbols represented earlier in Section 6.6.) However, if each person in this situation finds it rational to join the posse, how does the sovereign get only six people to do it? The solution is easy. The sovereign's selection of six people for this posse is in fact a way of solving the coordination dilemma for the group, even as a commanding officer's selection of two rowers among the American soldiers would also be a way of determining which two of them were to be the "salient" choices for the job. The sovereign is, in a way, the political entrepreneur who organizes the solution to this coordination problem.

Therefore, Hobbes's argument is that the appearance of the free-rider problem in the context of obeying the punishment commands of the sovereign in this situation does not in any way pose a prisoner's dilemma, but only a battle-of-the-sexes dilemma that can and will be solved by self-interested people given the overwhelming advantages (to each) of resolution.[16]

---

16 However, the situation may be more complicated and, as a result, more problematic than I have indicated here if the costs involved in participating in a posse are not retrievable by individual posse members once they have been paid. If they are not, it might be possible for a minority (one or more posse members) to exploit the others by doing only part of the work, such that the others would be rational to pay the minority's remaining cost. Whether or not such exploitation in this situation would be possible and, even if it were, whether or not it would present any problem for the *collective* in getting the posse formed are complicated issues. I ignore the nature of these complexities here because their relevance to the present discussion is questionable, but they are discussed in my article "Free Rider Problems in the Production of Collective Goods."

But suppose people are reasoning badly or shortsightedly such that they believe (falsely) that it is better to refuse to participate in the posse than to participate. In this case, the sovereign-elect can use the prospect of future selective incentives to help resolve the conflict in this situation and defuse the dangers of shortsightedness. For example, the sovereign can try to persuade potential posse members that their production of this public good is linked with the receipt of a private good. Note that this private good need not be anything like money. A person might believe that he will be highly regarded by the rest of the community and thus will be better able to get what he wants if he participates in the posse, such that a good reputation is the pay he will receive for his cooperation. This kind of pay will not have to be supplied by the sovereign. But suppose the sovereign believes she has to supply something herself to ensure their willing cooperation, meaning that she needs to offer something more, like money or land. Where will the sovereign get these sorts of goods? Assuming that she doesn't have them on hand, she can tell these six people that if they obey her punishment edicts now, she will have the power to "extort" funds from the other subjects sufficient to pay them (the extorted funds being called "taxes").

Of course, at the start of the commonwealth, the subjects would have to trust these funds would be forthcoming in the future. Could they do this? Consider that the sovereign would be putting herself in an iterated prisoner's dilemma with them; she would have to pay them if she wanted their services again, and they would have to keep rendering those services if they wanted this pay. Given that Hobbesian people are not supposed to be able to complete such iterated contracts in the state of nature, could they nonetheless be able to complete this one? I want to argue, consistent with the shortsightedness account of conflict, that they could, for two reasons. First, consider that in the state of nature the general failure of many people to understand the iterated nature of these contractual situations causes even the rational people who do understand this structure to be reluctant to trust their potentially irrational partners. But the sovereign does not need to persuade *everyone* in this state that obedience to her commands now in exchange for a future reward is only one of a series of iterated prisoner's dilemmas; she need persuade only enough of them to get a posse formed. And given that there are plenty of rational people in the state of nature who can be expected to understand the structure of this situation, she would be likely to succeed in getting enough people to create that posse. Second, recall *why* many people in the state of nature fail to understand the iterated nature of their contractual situations: As I argued in Chapter 3, such people make the easy mistake of thinking that in the state of nature, interactions are unlikely to be common enough to make future contractual interactions likely. But the nature of the relationship between a sovereign and posse members should make it clear even to those prone to taking a shortsighted perspective in the state of nature that they will be in an iterated PD situation with her and that both parties have a lot to gain if they cooperate. Hence, the chief reason for noncooperative shortsighted behavior in the state of nature (i.e., the fact that the iterated nature of the contractual situations in this state is not obvious) does not exist after the sovereign's selection. And even as the advantages of being part of the ruler's "muscle" have not been lost on the followers of Genghis Khan or Los Angeles street gang leaders, it is also unlikely they would be lost on a lot of rapacious Hobbesian people.

The sovereign can also use the prospect of future harm to accomplish the same end. Suppose you are ordered by the sovereign to capture Joe, and you refuse to obey the order because you think someone else is liable to do so. The sovereign can say to you: "If that is true, then I will order the punishment cadre to punish *you* after they capture Joe the Desperado." Suppose you said to her: "Ha! I don't believe you'll be able to get a posse!" The sovereign can reply: "Then, if you're right, you'll have to remain in the state of nature, which is *worse* for you than participating in the punishment cadre, and because everyone else is in the same position, it is likely that I will get my posse, which means it is likely you will suffer future harm. Moreover, note that even if I don't field a posse, you will be worse off than if you had participated in it." In this way, the sovereign introduces risk into the situation so as to make the action of obeying her punishment commands utility-maximizing.

So the sovereign is able to field her posse to capture Joe the Desperado either by selecting the posse members to do so and relying on them to see the rationality of participation or by offering them selective incentives in this clearly iterated PD situation. However, it does not seem plausible that rulers would be able to rule successfully with punishment posses of only minimally effective size. Ideally, the sovereign should want to increase the size of these posses to maximize their success and their power to intimidate. But she cannot do so easily. Suppose you are in a posse of six that would be minimally effective with only five people. You will rightly conclude that the other five do not really need you to catch him. "They can do it without me," you think. But, of course, if each one of them also comes to believe this, then there is a real danger that no one will do anything to catch Joe.

The free-rider situation that is now emerging turns out to be different in structure from the one we sketched previously. The perspective of this subject is that the posse in which he is involved is not a step good. *Whereas a minimally effective posse is a step good, a posse with more than the minimal number is not,* because the more people over the minimally effective number who are in the posse, the more power it has to accomplish the sovereign's command. Each person added to the posse (up to a certain point) increases the posse's power by a certain increment, so that although the posse comes into existence in one significant step, thereafter it is an example of what I call an "incremental collective good" whose production does pose a PD-like dilemma for the group.[17] Now, if each person determines that over a considerable range the increment of value from the additional security that will come to him from his joining the posse exceeds the costs of time and danger to him from participating in this force, it is straightforwardly utility-maximizing for him to join. But if (as seems more likely in Hobbes's world) each person believes that the increment of security he will receive by joining the posse and strengthening it is exceeded by the cost to him of joining, then although he would surely like the increased security, it simply is not rational for him to pay the cost of buying it.

Complicating this problem is the fact that how much deterrence a sovereign effects depends on how successful she is at capturing and convicting guilty criminals, and she

---

17 I present the exact PD-like structure in "Free Rider Problems in the Production of Collective Goods."

can surely achieve a high degree of deterrence even while stopping short of 100 percent apprehension and conviction rates. Thus, at some point, members of a minimally effective posse should refuse to obey the sovereign's orders to capture a criminal — that is, at that point at which they determine that the benefit they get from the (rather small) deterrent effect produced by the criminal's apprehension is exceeded by the cost to them of the apprehension. But this point might be very far from optimal from the group's point of view.

Clearly, the sovereign will find it desirable to overcome any cost problems involved both in increasing the posse to an optimal size and in getting the posse to find it rational to pursue every criminal she and the group wish them to apprehend. And the selective incentives just discussed, which can be useful in resolving the question of who should participate in the posse, can also be used to increase its size and guarantee its performance. In particular, the positive selective incentives (e.g., money, a fiefdom, the chance for glory) can make up the difference between the added security benefits that a person receives from joining the posse and the cost to him of doing so, such that his *total* benefits (i.e., security plus the positive selective incentive) will exceed the cost.

Indeed, eventually a sovereign would want a *permanent* enforcement community in order to wield total power effectively, and clearly she would need to pay people in some way to recruit them for this full-time job. Presumably she could use small posses to get the incentives to provide the pay she would need to hire members of this enforcement community, and thereafter this enforcement community would supply the muscle needed to maintain the state's ability to "harvest" at regular intervals the resources for that pay from the community. And the same process of offering the prospect of future harms and/or rewards I have just sketched would be used to accomplish this end. I do not wish or need to go into any more detail here about the precise steps that a sovereign could follow to build such an enforcement community. This sort of detailed study is the stuff of political theory from Machiavelli onward; one might call it the study of how to "build a power base." Los Angeles street gangs do it, Genghis Khan, Akbar, and Charlemagne did it, and, most important for our purposes, Hobbesian sovereigns could do it. Moreover, note that any disposition people might have to desire glory in Hobbes's world would actually *help* the sovereign to get the recruits she needed to build this power base, insofar as the achievement of glory can be one of the positive selective incentives inducing people to pay the costs involved in trying to inflict violence on others, although this is certainly not the only selective incentive on which the sovereign-elect need rely.

The process just sketched of using various strategies (and especially selective incentives) to procure punishment power without relying on any general "social contract of obedience" is exactly the sort of process that was implicitly used by the sovereign-entrepreneurs in the acquisition scenario. The first thing a sovereign-entrepreneur did in that scenario was to get a cadre of people to obey the sovereign's commands to inflict violence on others. And either it was straightforwardly in their interest to do so ("better to make war with him than to make it on my own," they might reason), or the confederacy leader made it in their interest to do so by offering them either a positive selective incentive (e.g., the prospect of receiving the spoils of victory) or a negative selective incentive (e.g., the infliction of harm). As the confederacy grew, positive and negative selective incentives (both of which were made possible by the initial cadre) were available to make the punishment cadre grow. And this process could snowball to the point that if this confederacy became completely dominant in the state of war, its sovereign-entrepreneur would have total power and be sovereign in fact.

Indeed, Hobbes would most likely want to ask us how we think that *our* society has been able to persuade some of its members to perform distasteful punishment chores. Do we really believe that *ethical* incentives alone (if such exist) have motivated every one of our policemen, our judges, or our lawyers to perform these tasks? Of course not. Even if moral reasons move them, people also (or mainly) do these jobs both because they know it is in their interest for *someone* to do them and because selective incentives are forthcoming to them if *they* do them (e.g., salaries or the admiration of the community).

So let us review the structure of the argument in this section. I have given two scenarios explaining how a sovereign could be empowered following his selection in a voting procedure.

> Scenario 1: (a) The sovereign is able to field minimally effective posses because participation in these posses is a battle-of-the-sexes problem for the inhabitants, and given the utilities of the situation, those who are selected by the sovereign to participate will find it rational to do so. (b) Using these minimally effective posses, the sovereign can get the power necessary to offer positive or negative selective incentives to other subjects in order to enlarge and make permanent the enforcement cadre.
>
> Scenario 2: (a) The sovereign is able to field minimally effective posses by offering them the prospect of receiving positive or negative selective incentives. (b) Same as step (b) in scenario 1.

Scenario 1 is preferable from the Hobbesian standpoint because contracts are used in this scenario only to enlarge and make permanent the sovereign's enforcement power, and *these contracts are enforceable by the sovereign.* That is, the sovereign can always field and then use minimally effective posses to punish any subject who does not perform the punishment tasks he previously agreed to perform in these contracts. Scenario 2, however, tells us what the sovereign falls back on in case the subjects are not reasoning well enough to appreciate the rationality of posse membership. In this scenario, the sovereign uses contracts offering positive selective incentives to *create* these minimally effective posses, and the sovereign must trust that the subjects making up these posses will realize that it is in their best interest to perform the agreed-on tasks in the interest of getting future positive selective incentives. However, I argued that the iterated nature of this contractual situation would be obvious enough to these Hobbesian people that they would appreciate the rationality of performance.

Hence, *there is no one-time social contract either among the subjects or between every subject and the sovereign that is necessary to empower the sovereign.* The only contracts necessary for his empowerment are the enforceable ones that he makes (only) with certain subjects (and not the whole population) as a way of enlarging or making permanent his enforcement cadre, and possibly the nonenforceable ones he might need to make with certain individuals in order to create a minimally effective enforcement cadre. The enforceable nature of the former type of contract and the clear-cut iterated structure of the latter type of contract mean that Hobbesian people in the state of nature could plausibly be said to understand and keep both types of contractual agreements. So we conclude that Hobbesian people are able to do what is required to empower the sovereign.

6.10 REVIEW OF THE ARGUMENT IN THIS CHAPTER

We have concluded our analysis and reconstruction of Hobbes's social contract theory, although, at least for the moment, that title seems rather unfortunate. To review: Hobbes's argument that the self-interested people of his state of nature would be able to select and then invest a sovereign-elect with enough power to make him sovereign goes like this:

1. It is in each person's interest to be subjugated to a sovereign rather than to remain in the state of nature.

2. A form of government (preferably absolute monarchy) and the selection of a ruler for this government can be accomplished either (a) by a voting procedure culminating in an explicit or implicit SI agreement both on the form of government and on the candidate(s) for the leadership position(s) who win the elections, or (b) by the gradual formation of and violent competition among confederacies, culminating in one confederacy becoming dominant and thus emerging as "best buy" in this state.

3. Investing the sovereign-elect with power after following procedure (2a) amounts to producing a public good, but this good can be produced by these self-interested people because it involves (a) obeying the punishment commands of *only* the sovereign-elect, which they are disposed to do insofar as the SI agreement of him as sovereign following his election makes it rational to obey only his commands as a way of resolving their coordination problem, (b) refraining from interfering with his punishment activities, which they are disposed to do, and (c) obeying his commands to punish others, which they can do because such commands either are or can be made to be (through individual contracts with the sovereign) individually rational.

We are also in a position now to understand the literal meaning of 'authorization' in Hobbes's argument. An individual authorizes another as sovereign by

1. participating with the other inhabitants of the state of nature in a process in which one of them is selected as sovereign (e.g., in a peaceful election process or in violent competition for leadership in which one confederacy emerges as dominant, followed by an explicit or tacit agreement that this individual is sovereign) and

2. obeying the punishment commands (a) of only this individual (b) to refrain from interfering in the punishment of another and (c) to actively assist in the punishment of another, insofar as these commands are (or have been made by the sovereign to be) individually rational.

When the metaphorical language is finally cashed out, we see that all of these actions involved in authorizing the sovereign can be performed by Hobbesian people. I have argued in this chapter that Hobbes has the resources to show how self-interested people can invest the sovereign with the power he needs to rule. "But," the worried reader might exclaim, "you have solved the social contract problem involved in the institution of the sovereign only by purging Hobbes's argument of a social contract made either among all the subjects or between each subject and the ruler. The only contracts that remain are certain successfully completed agreements made by the sovereign with only a few individual subjects in order to enlarge and possibly to create enforcement cadres. Is this revisionism something that Hobbes, who is supposed to be a social contract theorist, would have wanted?"

Yes. In effect, he is forced to want it. Not only is a social contract disruptive of his argument's validity, but also it is unnecessary. Indeed, even if he wanted to include a social contract into his theory, our analysis has shown that it is difficult to see where Hobbes could put it such that it would do any work for him. Still, one might worry that the justificational force of Hobbes's argument has been damaged if a social contract is removed from the theory. Of course, this worry raises the issue of what the justificational force of the social contract theory really *is,* and that issue will be explored in Chapter 9. But we can say a few things here to try to allay this worry. Although I have removed a social contract from Hobbes's argument, I have largely replaced it with either an explicit or tacit "social SI agreement" on who the sovereign will be. Creating a leader is accomplished in the first "election" story, primarily by explicit or implicit SI agreements that put the person who is elected in a position enabling him to build a power base giving him a monopoly of power in this region. In the second acquisition scenario, there is no explicit agreement on who the sovereign is, but he is finally chosen by a process that produces a "tacit" agreement or convention on one individual as leader. But both stories capture the way in which the people's "sovereign-selection problem" must be solved *interdependently* by reference to the beliefs and self-interested concerns of others. And when someone calls himself a contractarian, it would indeed seem to be because he believes that *the resolution of a moral or political problem must be achieved in an interdependent way respecting what are regarded as legitimate concerns of the individuals involved.* So Hobbes remains a contractarian in this sense of the word, despite the fact that we have purged his argument of any literal social contracts.

Indeed, our analysis of the game-theoretic structure of the problem people face when they institute the sovereign even allows us to diagnose why Hobbes thought he needed to make reference to a social contract in order to solve that problem. In order to complete a contract, one must be prepared to accept what one believes to be less than an optimal outcome in the interest of receiving some benefit; likewise, we have shown that in the interest of instituting the sovereign, many of the inhabitants of the state of nature must be willing to accept what is less than an optimal outcome (i.e., subjugation to another) in the interest of receiving some benefit (i.e., peace and security in a commonwealth). Thus, *superficially,* the PD problem facing a maker of a contract and the battle-of-the-sexes problem facing an independent in the state of nature interested in creating a sovereign appear to be the same, so that one might assume that actually creating a ruler involves being in a contractual situation in which one must perform a collectively rational but individually irrational action. We have shown, however, that the two situations do not, despite their superficial similarity, have the same game-theoretic structure. What is important from Hobbes's point of view is that the problem of selecting and empowering the sovereign is, in the main, a coordination dilemma, albeit one with considerable conflict of interest, that Hobbesian people are able to solve.

CHAPTER 7

The Failure of Hobbes's Social Contract Argument

Whilst Mr. Hobbes with one hand speciously offers up to kings and monarchs royal gifts and privileges, he with the other, treacherously plunges a dagger into their very hearts.

Richard Cumberland, *De Legibus Naturae*[1]

A good sign that Hobbes's justification of sovereignty fails is that it is rare to see someone walk away from a reading of *Leviathan* a convinced absolutist. Ever since they were first published, Hobbes's political writings, though often evoking admiration (Skinner 1972), have generally aroused intense opposition from conservative and liberal thinkers alike. As one scholar of the seventeenth century notes, Hobbes was regarded as the "Monster of Malmesbury," the "bug-bear of the nation" (Mintz 1969, vii), and another scholar of the period relates that when Clarendon decided to spend his time during his banishment in France refuting *Leviathan*, he was embarking upon a "reputable and well-thought-of task" (Bowle 1951, 33). Twentieth-century readers, although intrigued by the power of Hobbes's argument, are even more opposed to instituting any of Hobbes's ideas than his contemporaries. What these attitudes indicate is that Hobbes's argument, compelling and sophisticated though it is, fails to justify its conclusion, and in this chapter we will explore exactly where and how it fails.

The arguments I will be discussing do not attack the truth of the premises of Hobbes's argument; that is, they do not challenge the argument's soundness, only its validity. Clearly, arguments against Hobbes's psychology, or his shortsightedness account of conflict, or his regress argument, could be launched by disgruntled opponents that, if successful, would call into question the truth of Hobbes's conclusion. In the next chapter we will consider arguments against these three positions in order to see how far they succeed in casting doubt on the advisability of instituting a Hobbesian ruler. But in this chapter I want to explore what Hobbes would regard as a more serious issue, namely, whether or not his argument for absolute sovereignty is valid, given the truth of his psychology, the shortsightedness account, and the regress argument. If the argument is not valid, then *Leviathan* fails on its own terms; that is, it does not present a valid geometric deduction of Hobbes's political conclusions. In fact, we will see that it does so fail.

1 Cited by Watkins (1965a, 74).

I will be discussing two invalidity arguments in this chapter, one of which is considerably more successful than the other. And in the course of this discussion I will be making use of the interesting objections and criticisms of the little-known clerics and politicians who wrote in opposition to Hobbes's theory during the seventeenth century. None of these thinkers was philosophically adept enough to be able to launch a full-scale counterargument to Hobbes's theory in the way Locke eventually did, perhaps because they were accustomed to simple scriptural or theological justifications of political power, and hence unused to dealing with rational arguments designed to explain and legitimate a particular conception of the state. Most of them made their arguments against Hobbes by painstakingly going through the text of *Leviathan* and attempting to refute his ideas, one by one, as they came upon them. Their philosophical ineptness caused Hobbes to refer to them as "beasts" and "flies" in the epistle dedicatory to *De Homine*. But he was wrong to be so scornful of them. Because they were sincerely disturbed by the political situation in England, and fervent opponents of the solution Hobbes proposed, they put a tremendous amount of work into reading and criticizing Hobbes's writings, work that often paid off in excellent insights into where and why Hobbes's argument fails.

7.1 WOULD HOBBESIAN PEOPLE IN THE STATE OF NATURE DESIRE TO INSTITUTE A SOVEREIGN?

In this section I want to present and discuss a very natural objection to Hobbes's argument, namely, that he has failed to show convincingly that men, as *he* has described them, would find it rational to create an absolute sovereign.[2] I call this the "reason-based" counterargument against Hobbes's theory.

Consider that the people in the state of nature, faced with the choice of either creating an absolute master or remaining in this state, know that any master they create will have final and unchallengeable power to decide who will be punished, how the punishment will be carried out, and why it will be administered. This Hobbesian position on punishment led Bishop Bramhall to ask sarcastically: "Who would not desire to live in his Common-wealth, where the Soveraign may lawfully kill a thousand innocents every morning to his breakfast?" (1658, 524) This question exposes what many believe is a real problem for Hobbes: How can people who are concerned above all else to preserve themselves believe that it is rational (i.e., in their best interest) to create an absolute master who has the power to decide which of them lives or dies?

We know that Hobbes himself was disturbed by this question, because in Chapters 21 and 28 he tries to explain why the people in the state of nature, when they create a ruler with such extensive power to punish, are not doing anything contrary to their best interests. In Chapter 28, after defining punishment as "an Evill inflicted by publique Authority, on him that hath done, or omitted that which is Judged by the same Authority to be a Transgression of the Law" (*Lev*, 28, 1, 161), Hobbes says that "there is a question to be answered, of much importance; which is, by what door the

---

2   I am indebted to Israel Scheffler for illuminating conversations on the structure of the following discussion.

Right, or Authority of Punishing in any case, came in." (*Lev*, 28, 2, 161) What makes the justification of punishment difficult is the fact that "no man is supposed bound by Covenant, not to resist violence; and consequently it cannot be intended, that he gave any right to another to lay violent hands upon his person." (*Lev*, 28, 2, 161) Because a person cannot alienate his right to self-defense when he authorizes the sovereign, Hobbes concludes that the right of the sovereign to punish "is not grounded on any concession, or gift of the Subjects." (*Lev*, 28, 2, 161) However, Hobbes goes on confidently to derive that punishment power from the fact that the subjects *do* surrender to the sovereign their right to all things, including their right to determine who shall be punished:

And this is the foundation of that right of Punishing, which is exercised in every Common-wealth. For the Subjects did not give the Soveraign that right [to punish]; but onely in laying down theirs, strengthned him to use his own, as he should think fit, for the preservation of them all: so that it was not given, but left to him, and to him onely; and (excepting the limits set him by naturall Law) as entire, as in the condition of meer Nature, and of warre of every one against his neighbour. [*Lev*, 28, 2, 161–2]

The idea is that in order to give the sovereign the power to punish subjects, each person does not relinquish her right to defend herself, but only her right to all things, so that *in fact* the sovereign becomes powerful enough to inflict on any of them whatever punishments he decides are appropriate. Similarly, in a particularly striking passage on the liberty of subjects, Hobbes admits that if the subjects decide to authorize the sovereign, they will be creating an absolute power that can decide whether any given citizen lives or dies, but he maintains that this should not frighten the subjects into keeping their rights and remaining in the state of nature,

For by allowing him to *kill me*, I am not bound to kill my selfe when he commands me. 'Tis one thing to say *Kill me, or my fellow, if you please;* another thing to say, *I will kill my selfe, or my fellow.* [*Lev*, 21, 14, 112]

Once again Hobbes is contending that when people institute a sovereign, they are not alienating their right to self-defense, but only alienating their right to all things, and thus creating a sovereign *able* to inflict punishment as he chooses.

In the next section I will discuss whether or not it makes sense to maintain that the subjects create an "absolute" sovereign and yet retain a self-defense right. For now, I will assume that it does and go on to analyze whether or not, in these passages, Hobbes justifies his contention that people in the state of nature will want to create an absolute sovereign. And in fact he does not. Hobbes admits in these arguments that the authorization of the sovereign power means that every subject says to the sovereign: "Kill me or my fellow if you please." Each of them is putting himself in a position in which there is a *vastly* greater power than himself ruling over him, able to decide whether he lives or dies, and strong enough to implement that decision. So, even granted that each subject retains the right to resist that implementation, insofar as each of them knows that the sovereign will always win any fight between them, each must realize that the self-defense right does him little or no good. And so the question remains: How can it be rational for any person to risk his life and property by placing himself under the command of an unbeatable power that can inflict violence on him at will?

As we noted in Chapter 3, Hobbes believes that the risk is worth taking because remaining in the state of nature is even more dangerous, "And though of so unlimited a Power, men may fancy many evill consequences, yet the consequences of the want of it, which is perpetuall warre of every man against his neighbour, are much worse." (*Lev*, 20, 18, 107)[3] However, Hobbes's liberal critics in the seventeenth century challenged the legitimacy of this crucial step in his argument.[4] A supporter of Parliament, George Lawson, wrote that "They are very unwise, who will make a Butcher their Shepherd, or set a Woolf over their Flocks. And surely its no point of wisdom in any free-people, to trust any one man, or assembly of men, with an absolute unlimited power." (1657, 21–2) And Locke uses this same argument to attack Hobbes in the *Second Treatise*,[5] ridiculing "those thinkers" (i.e., Hobbes), who say that men would want to institute an absolute sovereign:

As if when Men quitting the State of Nature entered into Society, they agreed that all of them but one, should be under the restraint of Laws, but that he should still retain all the Liberty of the State of Nature, increased with Power, and made licentious by Impunity. This is to think that Men are foolish that they take care to avoid what Mischiefs may be done them by *Pole-cats* or *Foxes*, but are content, nay think it Safety, to be devoured by Lions. [2*T*, 93, 372]

What Lawson and Locke are challenging is Hobbes's contention that people will decide that the risks to life in the state of nature (where each of them is roughly equal in strength to the others and thus is limited in the amount of damage he can inflict on anyone else) are *greater* than the risks to life in a commonwealth, in which one person or assembly of persons has absolute power and hence can dispose of any of the subjects as desired. In the *Second Treatise*, Locke explicitly argues that men would *not* believe that the advantages of civil society would outweigh the risks to life and property in this state:

remember that *Absolute Monarchs* are but Men, and if Government is to be the Remedy of those Evils, which necessarily follow from Mens being Judges in their own Cases, and the State of Nature is therefore not to be endured, I desire to know what kind of Government that is, and how much better it is than the State of Nature, where one Man commanding a multitude, has the Liberty to be Judge in his own Case, and may do to all his Subjects whatever he pleases, without the least liberty to any one to question or controle those who Execute his Pleasure? And in whatsoever he doth, whether led by Reason, Mistake or Passion, must be submitted to? Much better it is in the State of Nature wherein Men are not bound to submit to the unjust will of another. . . . [2*T*, 13, 316–17; see also Clarendon 1676, 81–2]

And Samuel Pufendorf provides the natural extension of Locke's and Lawson's argument. According to Pufendorf, not only are the risks to life under sovereign rule much greater than Hobbes contends, but even assuming that Hobbes's shortsighted-

---

3 See also *Leviathan* (18, 20, 94), *De Cive* (*EW* ii, 1, 13), and "Six Lessons" (*EW* vii, 14 and 96).

4 Twentieth-century critics have also challenged him on this point; see, for example, Watkins (1965a, 172ff.).

5 In this regard, it is interesting to note that Locke may well have read Lawson's book. See Peter Laslett's introduction to his edition of *Two Treatises of Government* (1963), in which he includes a list of books in Locke's possession at about the time he wrote the *Treatises* (Appendix B, 146–61). One of those books was written by Lawson, and it was either his criticism of Hobbes or a larger original treatise on government entitled *Politica Sacra et Civilis* (1660).

ness account of conflict is correct, the risks to life in the state of nature are considerably less than Hobbes makes out, because the rough equality of people in this state will deter widespread violence:

equality of strength, which Hobbes proposes, is more likely to restrain the will to do harm than to urge it on. Surely no man in his senses wants to fight with a person as strong as he is, unless he is under some necessity, or in circumstances which look favorable for his success, since only fools or rash persons will unnecessarily enter a conflict where their blows are certain to be returned with equal force, and where the equal strength of both parties makes the outcome uncertain. [1934, 170]

Note that Pufendorf is arguing that the fact of their equality gives the inhabitants of the state of nature a way of solving their prisoner's dilemmas. Because any two people know that neither of them is powerful enough to decisively beat the other in war, each of them determines that the states of affairs represented by the upper right and lower left boxes in the PD matrix (Figure 2.1) are unlikely to be realized. This leads them to choose the cooperative action, which now dominates over the uncooperative action insofar as peaceful coexistence is preferable to war.

Thus, Hobbes's opponents maintain that if one contrasts the natural situation of "limited violence among equals" with life in a commonwealth in which all people are subjected to the absolute power of one man or assembly able to use them, kill them, or appropriate their goods at will, a rational individual would prefer to remain in the natural state, where the risks to life and property are less.

Hobbes's counterargument against his critics would emphasize the violence and warfare in the natural state, on the one hand, and the benefits and advantages derived from life in a commonwealth, on the other. He would use the shortsightedness and glory accounts of conflict to reply to Pufendorf that although some people in the state of nature might be deterred from attacking others in that state by the others' equal strength, there would be enough variation in human talent and ability to encourage many more people to attempt attacks against those seemingly weaker and less able inhabitants of this state. And such aggressive people would likely be spurred on by vainglory — the overinflated sense of their own abilities, talents, and power.

Hobbes would also challenge his critics' assertion that an absolute sovereign would reign like a ruthless, brutal tyrant. Indeed, he says in *Leviathan* that it would be in the sovereign's best interest to rule benevolently rather than harshly: "the good of the Soveraign and People, cannot be separated. It is a weak Soveraign, that has weak Subjects; and a weak People, whose Soveraign wanteth Power to rule them at his will." (*Lev*, 30, 21, 182) Unfortunately, Hobbes never gives a fully developed argument explaining why a self-interested sovereign's rule would be so "enlightened." Can we make this argument for him? Consider that if everyone surrendered their rights to the sovereign, he would no longer have any enemies, and he would thus be supremely confident of his ability to preserve himself. Hobbes could therefore argue that in these circumstances the sovereign would no longer find it necessary to harness the energies or appropriate vast amounts of the possessions of his subjects in order to wage war. Specifically, he would no longer have to worry about invading the territories of others to prevent them from augmenting their supply of goods with *his* possessions, nor would he need to wage war in order to meet his desires and advance his glory. And indeed Hobbes suggests (*Lev*, 19, 4, 95–6) that the sovereign would not want to appropriate large amounts of goods from his subjects in order to satisfy his desires — first, because his desires would not require such vast appropriation, and, second, because he would be able to gain *more* from his subjects if he allowed them to trade freely and acquire large numbers of possessions than if he appropriated their labor and goods. Finally, Hobbes could argue that the glory of the sovereign would be advanced when his subjects were strong and prosperous, so that a sovereign interested in advancing his reputation would rule "lightly" and benevolently so as to encourage the well-being of his people.

However, Hobbes's opponents would certainly question why this would be a likely scenario of self-interested rule. Granted that the sovereign would not need to appropriate the goods and energies of his subjects to defend himself from them, wouldn't his desire for gain and glory nonetheless dictate extensive appropriation? Hobbes says in Chapter 11 that all people, *including kings*, have an insatiable appetite for power:

> I put for a generall inclination of all mankind, a perpetuall and restlesse desire of Power after power, that ceaseth onely in Death. And the cause of this, is not alwayes that a man hopes for a more intensive delight, than he has already attained to; or that he cannot be content with a moderate power: but because he cannot assure the power and means to live well, which he hath present, without the acquisition of more. And from hence it is, that Kings, whose power is greatest, turn their endeavors to the assuring it at home by Lawes, or abroad by Wars: and when that is done, there succeedeth a new desire; in some, of Fame from new Conquest; in others, of ease and sensuall pleasure; in others, of admiration, or being flattered for excellence in some art, or other ability of the mind. [*Lev*, 11, 2, 47]

So it seems that even as a plantation owner would believe his life most happy when he had large numbers of people working only for his interest, performing only tasks that he assigned, and allowed to "own" very few possessions, so would a sovereign find it in his best interest to appropriate most of the possessions of his subjects and use their labor as he saw fit to satisfy his own desires.

But even if Hobbes could successfully counter this argument of his critics by showing decisively that a rational sovereign would best pursue his self-interest by ruling lightly and benevolently, he would still have to deal with his opponent's inevitable reminder that shortsightedness in human beings is sufficiently common that a sovereign selected by the people might well suffer from it and thus fail to appreciate this justification for moderate rule. Instead, a shortsighted sovereign likely would believe that ruthlessness and substantial domination are the ways to self-satisfaction. And this belief does not seem obviously wrong, because the supposed long-term benefits from moderate rule are not clearly greater than the benefits (in the short run and the long run) from tyrannical rule. Moreover, the desire for glory within any sovereign would encourage enslavement and impoverishment of his subjects, insofar as the sovereign's esteem would seem to be greatest when the gap between him and his subjects is large.

These considerations suggest that even if we granted Hobbes the truth of his argument that rational sovereigns would rule benevolently, the shortsightedness account of conflict would mean that when one performed any expected-utility calculation on the advisability of instituting a sovereign or remaining in the state of nature, one would have to estimate as quite high the probability that the ruler would not understand this argument and would rule tyrannically instead.

But does this really matter? Suppose we grant Hobbes's critics their claim that the sovereign would likely be, in Locke's words, a dangerous lion. Isn't danger from one lion preferable to danger from a thousand polecats? Although Hobbes does not argue convincingly that an absolute sovereign would rule benevolently, his assertion that people in the state of nature would still prefer to create an absolute sovereign (even a tyrannical one) rather than remain in the state of nature is not easy to refute in all circumstances. Given his account of human motivation and the warfare in the state of nature, it is not unreasonable to believe that, in general, even life under a cruel "plantation-owner" sovereign would be better than life in the state of nature, because at least such a shortsighted tyrannical sovereign would want to feed and clothe his slaves, and the probability that one would be killed on any given day (by the sovereign or by another subject) would be much less than in the natural state. So each person in Hobbes's story generally has a choice between a life at the mercy of every other inhabitant who is trying to destroy him or a life under one person who might well use him but who is unlikely to kill him. Hobbes seems to be right that these people's concern for self-preservation would lead them to prefer relatively secure mastery by the sovereign over a "free" life in the state of nature fraught with danger and death.

However, it is important to note that Hobbes cannot argue that people would always make this choice. Hobbes has to admit that his opponents' arguments can be right in *certain circumstances*. That is, a person or a particular faction of people might be right to decide against the advisability of submitting to a sovereign when the sovereign and/or his proponents are correctly perceived to be vicious or hateful enough to kill or severely persecute them after subjugation. (Suppose the sovereign were a Nazi and you were Jewish, or suppose he were a white supremacist and you were black.) Indeed, as we shall discuss in the next section, Hobbes himself advises rebels to continue rebelling if they believe they will be killed on surrender, "For they but defend their lives." (*Lev*, 21, 17, 112) Perhaps Hobbes might argue that such vicious behavior on the part of the sovereign would be irrational, but whether or not that is true, the fact remains that rulers have behaved and do behave this way, and whenever they do, a threatened Hobbesian person's concern for his self-preservation will clearly cause him to prefer the misery of war and the risk of death to an even more miserable subjugation and an even greater risk of death.

But whenever it is not reasonable to attribute this kind of murderous intent against one's life to a sovereign (or sovereign-entrepreneur), it looks as if the horrors of the Hobbesian state of nature are so awful that one would find life under a tyrannical sovereign to be preferable. An expected-utility calculation would dictate submission whenever life under the sovereign's rule would likely be better than life in the state of nature, and assuming Hobbes's shortsightedness account of conflict, and given the horrors of the latter state, such a calculation could be presumed to dictate submission almost always, for almost every potential inhabitant. If we find this difficult to believe, it might be because we think (as did Locke) that there is a third alternative (i.e., life under a government limited in power) that is far better than either of Hobbes's options. But Hobbes's regress argument dismisses this third alternative, and he contends that we are forced to choose between these two unsavory options: being enslaved or being dead. And if one puts it like that, Hobbes seems to be right that most of us would prefer the former.

So, given the truth of Hobbes's psychology, his shortsightedness account of conflict, and his regress argument, this reason-based counterargument put forward by his contemporary opponents fails to destroy Hobbes's argument. Although it does establish that in certain circumstances rational human beings would prefer the state of nature to submission to the sovereign (i.e., when submission would be highly likely to result in death), it does not establish that they would be irrational to submit to such a ruler in all circumstances or even most circumstances.

But from Hobbes's opponents' point of view, it would be nice to have an argument that does not merely call into question the validity of Hobbes's argument in certain unusual circumstances but that actually shows its invalidity in *all* circumstances. In the next section we will discuss such an invalidity argument, which I call the "inability counterargument," and we will see that it forces us to conclude that the Hobbesian social contract argument for absolute sovereignty ultimately fails. Once we appreciate how this argument works, we will be able to breathe new life into the contention that Hobbesian people would find it irrational to create an absolute sovereign. I shall propose in Chapter 8 that there is a sophisticated way in which the reason-based counterargument against Hobbes's theory can be redesigned so that it will work in roughly the way Hobbes's contemporary critics wished.

But before turning to the "inability counterargument," I want to discuss a disappointing but historically important theological analogue to the reason-based counterargument against Hobbes's political theory as given in this section. I mention it here because, among other reasons, it plays a central role in Locke's *Two Treatises of Government*.

It was a common assumption in the seventeenth century that because God made human beings, we are his property and, partially for that reason, subject to his commands. Filmer, Lawson, and Clarendon all used this theological fact to argue that insofar as our lives are God's property, we are not allowed to surrender ourselves up to a sovereign ruler who has absolute power to decide whether any of us lives or dies.[6] I will quote from Filmer's construction of that argument:

if no man have power to take away his own life without the guilt of being a murtherer of himself, how can any people confer such a power as they have not themselves upon any one man, without being accessories to their own deaths; and every particular man become guilty of being *felo de se?* [1648, 8; also see Lawson 1657, 66; Clarendon 1676, 40–1]

The most famous proponent of this argument was John Locke, in the *Second Treatise,* although we now see that he was hardly the originator of it. It makes its appearance in Chapter 4 on slavery in the *Second Treatise:*

a Man, not having the Power of his own Life, *cannot,* by Compact, or his own Consent, *enslave himself* to any one, nor put himself under the Absolute, Arbitrary Power of another, to take away his Life, when he pleases. No body can give more Power than he has himself; and he that cannot take away his own Life, cannot give another power over it. [*2T,* 23, 325]

---

6 This sort of argument against social contract theories goes back at least as far as Melancthon, Luther's friend, who contended that because the ruler cannot receive his power of life and death over his subjects from the subjects themselves, that power must come from God. See J. W. Allen (1928, 32ff.).

This is, in fact, the same sort of argument, in theological dress, as the secular, reason-based argument just explicated. Whereas the latter assumes a basic desire for self-preservation that makes a person in the state of nature unwilling to enslave himself to a sovereign, this argument assumes a duty to God not to enslave oneself. It is interesting to note that when drawing from the anti-Hobbes material available to him, Locke chose to emphasize the theological argument rather than the reason-backed attack. The latter makes only two brief appearances, once in the midst of Chapter 7 (Section 93) as part of Locke's attack on the idea of an absolute monarchy, and once in Chapter 2, where Locke is arguing for the idea that each man has the right to punish criminals in the state of nature; on the other hand, the former is Locke's central argument in Chapter 4 against slavery, a chapter explicitly designed to discredit a Hobbesian argument that men can "by Compact, or his own Consent, *enslave himself* to any one." (2T, 23, 325) Although the theological argument may have been persuasive to readers in Locke's day when these beliefs about God's ownership of human beings were widely held, Locke nonetheless made a mistake in emphasizing it. Whereas the reason-based argument has the potential for bringing down Hobbes's justification for absolute sovereignty from within, the theological attack is something Hobbes can quickly brush aside merely by saying that he rejects the religious "facts" and "duties" on which it is based. And if one considers the way these theological beliefs were used by royalists like Clarendon (1676, 40–1) in divine-rights justifications for strong monarchical government, Locke was ill-advised to incorporate them in a book containing his own antiroyalist social contract argument for a limited state.

But more important, this argument simply does not work as a refutation of absolute sovereignty. Hobbes can accept, if he wants, the idea that God owns us, and that we must not do anything that would damage or destroy his property, but then go on to argue that insofar as submitting to an absolute sovereign is the best way of preserving oneself, it is an action endorsed by, nay, commanded by, God, who wants his property preserved. To challenge this Hobbesian argument, Locke and Lawson would have to argue that self-preservation is not best pursued in a Hobbesian commonwealth. But we have already discussed their argument to this effect in this section, and as I pointed out, they do not have conclusive arguments to establish that this is true in all or even most circumstances.

7.2 *LEVIATHAN* SHOWN TO BE A "REBEL'S CATECHISM"

In this section, I want to discuss a problem with Hobbes's argument that has been little recognized in recent years by Hobbes scholars but that was appreciated by a number of Hobbes's important contemporary critics, including Clarendon, Bramhall, and Filmer. This problem is so serious that it renders the entire Hobbesian justification for absolute sovereignty invalid. Although, as we saw in the last section, Hobbes's argument does not fail because he cannot establish the rationality of creating an absolute sovereign, nonetheless it fails because he cannot establish, given his psychology, that men and women are *able* to do what is required to create a ruler satisfying his definition of an absolute sovereign. That is, if we assume Hobbes's shortsightedness account of conflict, his regress argument, and especially his psychological theories of human nature, we will see that the result of the only kind of "authorization" action they are able to perform will not be the institution of an absolute sovereign. Indeed, whenever Hobbes argues that people can create an absolute sovereign and that it is rational for them to do so, he has subtly but importantly changed his conception of what an absolute sovereign is and what submission to such a ruler entails. It is extremely important to appreciate that Hobbes equivocates at this crucial point in his argument in order to avoid being straightforwardly inconsistent. The purpose of this section is to expose that equivocation so as to reveal this inconsistency.

In Chapter 4 we presented Hobbes's regress argument and the conception of absolute sovereignty that his argument supports. To review: The regress argument holds that in a civil society there must be some decision and enforcement entity that limits other such entities in society but that itself has no limits, and because this entity cannot be a law or set of laws, it must be a person. (Recall also that we argued against Hobbes's claim that this entity could be a set of persons.) Hence, the result of this argument is that civil society must have a person with *unlimited* decision and enforcement powers at its helm: That person is called the sovereign, and he has the power to decide *all* questions in the commonwealth, holding power permanently insofar as he has the power to decide the most important question in the commonwealth, that is, whether or not he should remain in power.

However, can such a sovereign really be created by Hobbesian people? In Chapter 5 we explored Hobbes's contention that a sovereign is created when a person is "authorized" by his subjects, where this means that they "surrender their right to all things" to him. And in Chapter 6 we attempted to cash out this metaphorical language consistent with Hobbesian psychology; in particular, we argued that one authorizes a sovereign when one obeys his commands to punish others and, in general, when one does nothing to frustrate his enforcement powers. We found, however, that there had to be one big exception to any person's willingness to support the sovereign's punishment efforts in the commonwealth: One could never willingly obey the sovereign's command to punish oneself, insofar as doing so would endanger one's self-preservation rather than preserve it. Given a human being's inevitable commitment to self-preservation, Hobbes must grant that each human being will "surrender" her punishment powers to the sovereign only insofar as doing so will not endanger her life. Thus, according to Hobbes, each human being carries with her into the commonwealth a "self-defense" right. But if she does, is the resulting ruler a genuine sovereign? Does he still have the power to decide all questions in the commonwealth? Does he still reign permanently? In order to answer these questions, we need to know precisely what this self-defense right is and how extensive it is. It clearly precludes obeying a sovereign's commands to punish oneself, but what else does it preclude?

Hobbes does not clearly define this self-defense right. Indeed, its name suggests that it is only a negative description of the fundamental right of self-preservation. However, Hobbes has to take the position that the self-defense right is only a small part of the larger self-preservation right, distinguishable from the "right to all things" that is surrendered to the ruler so that he is made sovereign. If Hobbes does not, then obviously nothing is surrendered to the sovereign. So let us begin by defining the right very narrowly as the privilege or liberty to defend one's body if it is attacked, or to do what is necessary to procure the means (e.g., food and shelter) to assure bodily survival. On our supposition, Hobbes must expect a subject to disobey *any* command by the sovereign when obedience likely would threaten that subject's bodily survival more than would disobedience.

But if we accept this very natural interpretation of the self-defense right, then isn't this granting the subjects the right of private judgment concerning whether or not their lives have been endangered? Why doesn't it make their obedience to him conditional on his commands not threatening their lives, where *they* are the judges of this question? And because empowerment comes about only from obedience, why doesn't this make the sovereign's empowerment conditional on people's determination that such obedience is rational? Yet, insofar as it does, they do not really empower a truly absolute sovereign at all, because there is no single permanent power to decide all questions and hence ensure peace among men. Conservative readers of *Leviathan* in the seventeenth century were quick to notice these subversive implications of the self-defense right. Filmer correctly perceived that by granting that the subjects had a right to defend themselves, even when the right is very limited in scope, Hobbes makes the subjects the judges of whether or not the sovereign has endangered their survival, and hence allows the subjects to decide whether or not they will disobey certain of the sovereign's commands (1652, 4). This means that the sovereign is not the only authority in a commonwealth and that he will have to reckon with disobedience or rebellion on the part of some or all of his subjects if they decide that his laws or actions jeopardize their lives.

In fact, one of the consequences of allowing the subjects this self-defense right was Hobbes's very peculiar position on the legitimacy of rebellion in a commonwealth, a position that made all royalists who had lived through the events of the 1640s furious. Hobbes says that one is never justified in initiating a rebellion, because no man will be better off if the sovereign is deposed and the state of nature returns. However,

> in case a great many men together, have already resisted the Soveraign Power unjustly, or committed some Capitall crime, for which every one of them expecteth death, whether have they not the Liberty then to joyn together, and assist, and defend one another? Certainly they have: For they but defend their lives, which the Guilty man may as well do, as the Innocent. There was indeed injustice in the first breach of their duty; Their bearing of Arms subsequent to it, though it be to maintain what they have done, is no new unjust act. And if it be onely to defend their persons, it is not unjust at all. [*Lev,* 21, 17, 112–13]

After quoting this passage, Bishop Bramhall asks: "Why should we not change the Name of *Leviathan* into *Rebells catechism?*" (1658, 515)[7] What is upsetting Bramhall and others[8] is that in this passage Hobbes is partially condoning as right certain rebel activity in a commonwealth. He even uses the phrase 'not unjust' to describe rebellion if it is done to preserve the rebels' lives, and this usage is quite shocking, because he has defined injustice simply as disobedience to the sovereign's laws, which the

---

7 And see Clarendon (1676, 87): "[Hobbes] devest(s) his Subjects of all that liberty, which the best and most peaceable men desire to possess, yet he literally and bountifully confers upon them such a liberty as no honest man can pretend to, and which is utterly inconsistent with the security of Prince and People. . . ."

8 See also Filmer (1652, 8–9).

rebellious subject is surely committing. But probably Hobbes simply misspoke here, and really meant by "not unjust" the concept "is a prudent course of action." Indeed, it seems plausible that in this passage Hobbes is contending that although people who start a rebellion are not behaving prudently, nevertheless if they know that they will be killed by the sovereign's forces on their surrender, then their continuation of the attack and the bearing of arms becomes prudent. And clearly Hobbes makes this point, because he maintains that the rebels retain a self-defense right and hence cannot refuse to defend their lives when they are under attack. But by taking this position, Hobbes is committed to advocating the continuation of rebel activity in a commonwealth once it has begun, and hence sanctioning the internal warfare and civil strife that the creation of an absolute sovereign was supposed to end. In defense, Hobbes would, of course, stress that he argues against the legitimacy of initiating a rebellion, but his conservative critics angrily appreciate that he also condones (and must condone) as rational the continuation of rebellious activity once it has begun.[9] And not only did these critics find this condoning of rebellious activity offensive; more important, they found it inconsistent with the idea that when one subjugates oneself to a sovereign, one makes him the judge of all questions in the commonwealth and the master of every area of one's life.

However, what upset the conservatives even more was that Hobbes did not limit the scope of the self-defense right to mere bodily survival. In Chapter 21, on the liberties of the subjects, Hobbes uses a very broad notion of this right, that is, that one can rightfully resist or defend oneself against anything that *might lead* not only to death but also to mere injury of one's body, as a foundation for a number of subject liberties that would seriously undermine the supposedly limitless and absolute power of the sovereign. For example, he says that "If a man be interrogated by the Soveraign, or his Authority, concerning a crime done by himselfe, he is not bound (without assurance of Pardon) to confesse it; because no man (as I have shewn . . .) can be obliged by Covenant to accuse himselfe." (*Lev*, 21, 13, 112) Given that such interrogation is not a direct attack on the subject's bodily survival, and given that the subject is supposed to have made the sovereign his master and hence obliged himself to obey the commands of the sovereign , how can he refuse to disobey the sovereign's orders here? Is this "owning all the Actions (without exception) of the Man, or Assembly we make our Soveraign?" (*Lev*, 21, 10, 111) And what about the passage in which Hobbes says

No man is bound . . . either to kill himselfe, or any other man; and consequently . . . the Obligation a man may sometimes have, upon the Command of the Soveraign to execute any *dangerous*, or *dishonourable* Office, dependeth not on the Words of our Submission; but on the Intention; which is to be understood by the End thereof. [*Lev*, 21, 15, 112; emphasis added]

What? Is Hobbes saying that people have a right to *lie* to their sovereign, that they can refuse not only to kill other men but also to commit those actions that are dangerous or *dishonorable?* Clarendon was shocked that Hobbes would suggest that the right to defend oneself could include defending not only one's body but also one's reputation (1676, 135). In addition, Hobbes says in this paragraph that men have a

---

9   It was because of passages like this that Clarendon thought Hobbes was offering in *Leviathan* a justification of de facto power in general, and Cromwell's rule in particular. See Chapter 6, note 14.

right to choose not to obey a sovereign's command to kill another. But if all or many of the sovereign's subjects choose to exercise this "right" (believing their disobedience to be prudent), what coercive power does the sovereign have left? How can he amass an army to quell internal rebellion? How can he even create a police force that will pursue criminals, or carry out executions? The self-defense right has now been interpreted so broadly that it is essentially equivalent to the *entire* right to preserve oneself.

However, there is an important reason why Hobbes *must* broaden the self-defense right in this way. Remember that Hobbes's entire justification of the state, as we saw in Chapter 6, rests on its being conducive to a person's self-preservation. But according to Hobbesian psychology, the pursuit of this goal is central to a person's life not only outside but also inside a commonwealth. Hobbesian people do not simply forget their ultimate desire to preserve themselves when they enter the commonwealth; it remains their premier goal. But insofar as it does, each of them will determine the rationality of performing any action in the commonwealth by determining to what extent it will further this goal. So Hobbes's psychological views force him to admit that the goal of self-preservation (not merely some limited concern for "self-defense") provides the criterion for determining whether or not to obey *any* of the laws of the commonwealth. And this means that such people are incapable of letting the sovereign determine their every action; their psychology is such that they will obey a sovereign command only when, in their eyes, it will further their lives to do so.

Perhaps even more remarkably, there are two passages in *Leviathan* in which Hobbes actually admits this is so. One of them occurs in Chapter 21 in the midst of Hobbes's attempt to define the self-defense right:

When . . . our refusall to obey, frustrates the End for which the Soveraignty was ordained; then there is no Liberty to refuse: otherwise there is. [*Lev*, 21, 15, 112]

It appears from this passage that the subjects are supposed to perform some kind of expected-utility calculation about the relative benefits of obeying or disobeying the sovereign's commands, taking into consideration not only the dangers of disobedience but also the effect the action of disobedience will have on the stability and final purposes of government. But if these calculations dictate disobedience, the subject is "right" (i.e., rational) to disobey. So, by taking this position, Hobbes essentially is admitting that the self-defense right retained by each subject in the commonwealth is equivalent to the *entire* right of self-preservation and hence makes the subjects the judges of whether or not they will obey *any* of the sovereign's laws.

The second passage in *Leviathan* in which Hobbes admits that the subjects must be the ones who finally decide whether or not to obey the ruler occurs later in Chapter 21. In this passage, Hobbes contends that the ability of the sovereign to protect his subjects and make their lives secure defines the extent and limits of the subjects' rightful obedience to the sovereign:

The Obligation of Subjects to the Soveraign, is understood to last as long, and no longer, than [sic] the power lasteth, by which he is able to protect them. . . . The end of Obedience is Protection. [*Lev*, 21, 21, 114; see also DC, *EW* ii, 6, 74–5]

The interesting question one is left with on reading this passage is, *Who decides* whether or not the sovereign is adequately protecting his subjects? If a ruler is absolute sovereign, then he should have final say over what his subjects should and should not do, and hence he should be the judge of whether or not they should continue to obey his laws; but because it follows (as Filmer recognized[10]) from Hobbes's psychology that human beings will always judge any course of action on the basis of how well it furthers their self-preservation, he is committed to saying that the subjects will decide whether or not submission to the sovereign is furthering their lives. Indeed, given that psychology, we can expect them to do nothing else — whether the sovereign likes it or not. But this means Hobbes is forced to say that *an "absolute sovereign" reigns at his subjects' pleasure*, for it is they who decide whether or not obedience will secure them protection! When commenting on this passage, Bishop Bramhall appreciates not only how difficult it is for Hobbes to say anything else but also how disastrous this position is for Hobbes's political argument:

> Either it must be left to the soveraign determination, whether the subjects security be sufficiently provided for, And then in vain is any mans sentence expected against himself, or to the discretion of the subject, (as the words themselves do seem to import,) and then there need no other bellowes to kindle the fire of a civill war, and put a whole commonwealth into a combustion, but this seditious Article. [1658, 513]

Bramhall's point is that insofar as Hobbes is forced to admit that the subjects decide whether or not to continue their obedience to the sovereign, the commonwealth will inevitably degenerate into chaos and civil war.

But is Bramhall right to say this? Insofar as the self-defense right retained by the subject must be understood by Hobbes, given his psychology, as the entire right to preserve oneself, exactly why does this spell disaster for his political argument? That is, why does it mean that Hobbe's argument for absolute sovereignty is *invalid*?

Consider that an absolute sovereign is defined by Hobbes to be someone who is the *final decider* of *all* questions in a commonwealth, and whose subjects are literally enslaved to him. But if the subjects retain a right to determine whether or not to obey the sovereign's laws, then the sovereign not only fails to be the ultimate decider of every issue but also is not the decider of the most important question in the commonwealth: whether or not he will continue to receive power from his subjects. As we saw in Chapter 6, the sovereign's empowerment comes about only when the subjects obey his punishment commands. But now we see that *they decide* whether or not it is advantageous for them to obey these commands on the basis of whether or not doing so will further their self-preservation. So these "slaves" are continually deciding whether or not to let their master have the whip! Clearly this is not genuine enslavement at all, and the ruler with the whip is not someone who has absolute power to do what he wishes, but only the power to do what his subjects will *let* him do.

Indeed, as long as the subjects retain the right to preserve themselves in a commonwealth, they cannot be said to have surrendered *anything* to the sovereign. Whatever power he has been granted by the subjects for the purpose of furthering their self-preservation can and will be taken back by the subjects when they determine that doing

---

10 See Filmer (1652, 8): "[Hobbes] resolves refusal to obey, may depend upon the judging of what frustrates the end of Soveraignty and what not, of which he cannot meane any other Judge but the people."

so will further their self-preservation. And insofar as any sovereign will lose his punishment power if his subjects decide it is no longer advantageous for them to obey his punishment commands, the sovereign's power *must* be understood to be a "loan" from the people, not a permanent grant. The power he wields not only comes from them but also returns to them if *they* decide his use of it will do more to hurt them than to help them, and this is exactly the relationship that prevails between any principal and his agent. In fact, the same process of making agreements in order to institute the sovereign that we explored at length in Chapter 6 can also be used by the subjects to take back the power they lent to him, and used instead to reach agreement on lending that power to a different ruler who these subjects believe will be better able to further their self-preservation. To use Nozickean terminology: If the "protection agency" hired by the people is perceived by them to be doing a poor job of furthering their self-preservation, they may find it in their best interest to "fire" that agency and "hire" another. But this means that as long as people retain the right to preserve themselves in the commonwealth, Hobbes is also forced to admit that there is really an *agency relationship* between people and ruler, and this is exactly what he did *not* want to conclude in *Leviathan*.

But readers might question the idea that this conclusion is a disastrous one for Hobbes. Couldn't he contend that the less-than-absolute ruler-agent that Hobbesian people can create is still powerful enough to achieve peace among them? Perhaps he can — we shall explore this possibility in the next chapter — but the fact remains that in *Leviathan* he explicitly contends in his regress argument that nothing less than a ruler who reigns permanently and has the power to decide all questions in the commonwealth can end the warfare among human beings. Thus, if we accept the truth of the regress argument, we are forced to accept that the kind of ruler Hobbesian people are able to create is not good enough to secure peace. Indeed, it is useful to review components of Hobbes's regress argument that we presented earlier in Chapter 4 in order to see exactly how, given this argument, the "agency commonwealth" forced on Hobbes by his psychological views is doomed to fail. Or, to put it more crudely, it is useful to see the way in which Hobbes is skewered with his own sword.

Consider that as long as subjects retain the right to preserve themselves, and hence the right to decide whether or not to obey any of their ruler's commands, *private judgment* has not been destroyed in the commonwealth, and Hobbes himself contends, using his ethical and psychological views, that any commonwealth in which private judgment exists will be destroyed from within:

I observe the *Diseases* of a Common-wealth, that proceed from the poyson of seditious doctrines; whereof one is, *That every private man is Judge of Good and Evill actions.* . . . From this false doctrine, men are disposed to debate with themselves, and dispute the commands of the Common-wealth; and afterwards to obey, or disobey them, as in their private judgements they shall think fit. Whereby the Common-wealth is distracted and *Weakened.* [*Lev*, 29, 6, 168]

What we have discovered is that Hobbesian people are incapable of giving up their power of private judgment in a commonwealth because they will always retain the ability in a commonwealth to determine whether any action — including the action of obeying the sovereign's commands — is more conducive to their self-preservation than any available alternative. And given what Hobbes says in the foregoing passage, he would believe that the results of each subject retaining this right will be, first, debates whether or not to obey the ruler's commands that cannot be resolved in any way except by violence, followed by seditious actions by dissatisfied subjects fanning this violence, leading eventually to full-scale civil war. And as we see from their remarks cited earlier, Hobbes's contemporary critics, including Cumberland, Filmer, and Bramhall, agree with this general point. So Hobbes's regress argument in *Leviathan* (based on his psychology) against any political union in which subjects retain the right to make private judgments (and so the right to judge their ruler's performance) is also an argument against the political union Hobbes himself is forced to espouse given that same psychology.

Consider another aspect of the regress argument against agency commonwealths made in Chapter 18 of *Leviathan* involving the existence of a contract between ruler and people in these regimes. Hobbes insists (*Lev*, 18, 4, 89) that any contract-created commonwealth is doomed to fail. Because there can be no legal judge to decide any controversy about how well the ruler is living up to the agency contract, each subject will judge this question on the basis of how well the ruler is advancing her self-preservation. But such individual assessments are bound to conflict, and Hobbes believes that it will be only a short period of time before this sort of contract-created commonwealth will degenerate into a state of war as the subjects turn to violence (just as they did in England during the 1640s) to resolve their disagreements over how well the ruler is performing. But, as we have seen, in a Hobbesian commonwealth the subjects retain, by virtue of their psychological makeup, the right to decide whether or not to obey the sovereign's commands. This means that the sovereign is essentially empowered by them for as long as they believe that following his commands will be conducive to their interests, so that there is, at the very least, an *implicit agreement* between him and the subjects specifying what he must do to retain the power given to him by the subject's obedience. It follows that this "implicit agency-contract" commonwealth is doomed to fail.

The third and perhaps most significant problem introduced into Hobbes's commonwealth by the subjects' retention of the right to preserve themselves is the loss of the permanence and continuity of sovereign rule. Recall our discussion in Chapter 5 of Hobbes's official explanation of this permanence and continuity: Because the subjects "surrender their right to all things" to the sovereign, they give him a property right in them, so that if they try to take back the right they previously surrendered from either him or his successor (who has been willed that property right), "they take from him that which is his own, and so again it is injustice." (*Lev*, 18, 3, 89) There is a peculiar and intriguing moral tone to this passage that, given Hobbes's subjectivist ethical position, ought not to be there. We tried to "explain away" this moral tone in Chapter 5 by interpreting the wrongfulness of rebellion prudentially: Deposing the sovereign or refusing to obey his hand-picked successor is wrong, not because it violates some deontologically valid moral law but because it will precipitate violence and civil strife, endangering not only the lives of other members of the commonwealth but also one's own life.

But note what this prudential explanation of the wrongfulness of rebellion takes for granted! It assumes that *the subjects* can and will judge whether it is prudent for them to remain in the commonwealth or work to depose it. And we can expect that they will (rationally) choose not to obey these commands whenever doing so will threaten their self-preservation. This means that a sovereign holds power because most or all of his subjects have chosen to obey him — that is, have chosen to let him have power, which means that, in the end, he rules because *they let him rule*. But a sovereign cannot be permanently authorized when the subjects are not only able but also "prudentially obliged" to secede from his rule when their lives are, in *their* eyes, endangered. Such a ruler holds power conditionally, not permanently. And no successor of a sovereign can be assured of his property right over the subjects if these subjects are not only able but also "prudentially obliged" to rethink the advisability of their allegiance after the reins of power have been passed on. In the end, this successor receives power not when the previous sovereign bequeaths it to him, but only when the subjects decide to let him have it by obeying his punishment commands. And that decision might go against him, destroying the continuity of rule in this political society.

I believe that it is because Hobbes *cannot* permanently and absolutely bind people, as he has described them, to any ruler or ruler-successor by arguing for the prudence of their allegiance to that ruler that Hobbes's remarks on a subject's obligation to the ruler continually have a moral tone. Because his argument is critically weak at this point, he "cheats," either consciously or unconsciously, by invoking moral ideas that not only have no place in his argument but also have already been rejected in the course of making that argument. Consider his remarks in Chapter 18 on why "The subjects cannot change the forme of government." He starts out by saying that

they that have already Instituted a Commonwealth, being thereby bound by Covenant, to own the Actions, and Judgements of one, cannot lawfully make a new Covenant, amongst themselves, to be obedient to any other, in any thing whatsoever, without his permission. [*Lev*, 18, 3, 88]

Why do they need his permission? Perhaps because it is prudent for them to ask for it? But if they think another individual would make a better sovereign because he would further their preservation more effectively than the original sovereign, why doesn't prudence dictate *not* asking the original sovereign's permission and simply making the switch? But, Hobbes might contend, switching sovereigns likely will bring forth a time of bloodshed and chaos, so that it is not in one's best interest to try it. However, what if the subjects believe that the switch can be made with little loss of life, or believe that the switch is so desirable that an expected-utility calculation tells them it is worth the risk of bloodshed? Hobbes cannot rule out the possibility that situations like this could exist. And it is probably because he cannot preserve permanence of rule by appealing to prudence to block rebellion on all occasions that he suggests that the action is wrong in some objectively moral sense.

That moral tone surfaces a few sentences later when he says, as we noted earlier, that deposing the sovereign is taking from him "that which is his own," an act that is "injustice." In Chapter 5 we gave a prudential interpretation of this passage, but perhaps the more natural interpretation is a moral one, that is, that it is morally wrong to take the sovereign's power from him because that would be stealing. But where do these scruples against stealing come from? From the laws of nature, whose dictates are not even supposed to be followed if doing so will endanger one's preservation? No, these laws contain nothing that would rule out theft in *all* circumstances.

Indeed, stealing (i.e., seizing an object that another has claimed) would seem to be (prudentially) right and rational if the object is necessary for one's preservation and if taking it does not endanger one's life. Hence, far from laying a moral foundation for the *complete* condemnation of stealing, Hobbes's laws of nature and his psychology lay the groundwork for explaining when it is rational and (prudentially) correct to be a thief — even a "rebellious" thief of the sovereign's power.

So the moral tone in these passages seems to be Hobbes's attempt to circumvent deep trouble in his argument — a way to try to make the sovereign's rule permanent and his successor's rule secure, when no such permanence or continuity of rule follows from his argument. Critics such as Warrender have been rightfully sensitive to the moral tone of Hobbes's discussion of a subject's obligation to her sovereign, although missing the way in which, given Hobbes's subjectivist meta-ethics and his analysis of the validity of the laws of nature, that moral tone is completely out of place in his argument, and actually signals that argument's failure.

So, we now see that Hobbes's social contract argument is invalid: That argument cannot show that people, as he has described them, can institute what Hobbes defines as an absolute sovereign. Indeed, let us spell out this invalidity precisely:

1. In order for peace to be secured, an absolute sovereign must be created, and an absolute sovereign is defined as one who is master of all his subject-slaves; this absolute sovereign is the final decider of all questions in the commonwealth, including the question whether or not he will continue to hold power, and in virtue of deciding this last question, he holds power permanently.

2. Hobbesian people empower a ruler by obeying his punishment commands, and they do so whenever *they decide* such obedience is conducive to their best interests.

3. But from (2), it follows that the ruler created by Hobbesian people does not decide *all* questions; in particular, he does not decide for his subjects the question whether or not they will obey his commands — including his punishment commands.

4. It follows from (3) that insofar as a ruler holds power only as long as his subjects obey his punishment commands, the subjects determine (by their decision whether or not to obey these commands) whether or not he will continue to hold power.

5. Hence, from (3) and (4), Hobbesian people cannot create a ruler who meets the definition of a sovereign in (1) (i.e., a ruler who decides all questions in the commonwealth and whose reign is permanent), which, from (1), means that they cannot secure peace.

So there is no successful geometric deduction of absolute sovereignty in *Leviathan,* although Hobbes certainly tried mightily to construct one. Although most twentieth-century critics have commonly assumed that Hobbes's political conclusions can be dismissed because they rest on false premises, they have not appreciated the more important fact that the conclusions themselves do not follow from those premises. Indeed, we see that Hobbes's dilemma in *Leviathan* is identical with that of Philip Hunton. Recall the discussion in Chapter 4 of Hunton's difficulty in explaining how people who "elected" their sovereign in an original contract were not superior to their ruler even though they were his creators. Hunton ends up maintaining that the subjects *surrender* some or all of their rights to their ruler, thereby enslaving themselves to him, but Hunton also insists that they retain a "moral" power to evaluate his conduct. In the end, it turns out that Hobbes tries to hold a similar sort of contradictory position.

But we really should have appreciated that Hobbes's argument was in trouble by the end of Chapter 6. In that chapter we relied on Hobbes's psychology to specify precisely the concrete actions that Hobbesian people would take to institute a ruler. And the actions we specified *presupposed* that people always retained the right to determine if the performance of any of those actions was in their interest. Indeed, this right was at the heart of my attempt to explain how Hobbesian people could create a commonwealth, because at every state of the creation process I was concerned to show that these people would (or could) find the actions required at that stage advantageous to them. So, in setting out to define 'authorization' consistent with Hobbesian psychology, I ended up by cashing out the metaphor not of "surrendering power" but of "loaning power" to the ruler.

Indeed, the fact that I so naturally cashed out the notion of authorization consistent with Hobbes's psychology but inconsistent with his definition of absolute sovereignty suggests why so many critics have not realized that his political argument in *Leviathan* is invalid. Hobbes equivocates: He gives only a metaphoric definition of the notion of authorization, characterizing it as a surrender, such that it appears consistent with his official definition of absolute sovereignty; but when he actually uses the notion of authorization in his argument, he implicitly uses it in the way I defined in Chapter 6 — assuming that it involves obedience to the ruler *for self-interested reasons* — and linking it with a self-defense right. The fact that this use does *not* cash out the surrender metaphor and is actually inconsistent with the official definition of absolute sovereignty is therefore very difficult to see.

But can we do nothing to fix Hobbes's argument so that it can be made to succeed? That is the topic of the next chapter.

CHAPTER 8

Can Hobbes's Argument Be Salvaged?

'Tis certain, that no affection of the human mind has both a sufficient force, and a proper direction to counter-balance the love of gain, and render men fit members of society, by making men abstain from the possessions of others. . . . There is no passion, therefore, capable of controlling the interested affection, but the very affection itself, by an alteration of its direction. Now this alteration must necessarily take place upon the least reflection; since 'tis evident, that the passion is much better satisfied by its restraint, than by its liberty.

David Hume, *A Treatise of Human Nature*

Some readers may have reacted to the invalidity argument in the last chapter as follows: "Granted that Hobbesian people are unable, given their psychology, to do what is required to create an absolute sovereign, can't they still do something almost as good, namely, create a ruler who is *almost* absolute in power, even if he is dependent on his subjects' obedience for that power?" This is one of the intuitions we will explore in this chapter as we try to rehabilitate Hobbes's argument. It involves replacing Hobbes's regress argument with a new argument establishing that a less-than-absolute ruler — the kind of ruler Hobbesian people can create — is still sufficient to bring about peace. I call it Hobbes's "fallback position." But before I develop it, we need to determine if it is even necessary to do so. If the psychology of Hobbesian people is what renders them incapable of creating an absolute sovereign as defined by the regress argument, maybe there is a way for them to *transform their psychology* so that this creation is possible. I call this Hobbes's "conversion" argument, and if it works, he can save both the regress argument and its powerful political conclusion.

8.1 THE FIRST MODIFIED ARGUMENT: AUTHORIZATION AS CONVERSION

In Chapter 6 we used Hobbesian psychology to construct two scenarios of the sovereign's institution, and in both of these scenarios, when each subject authorizes the ruler, he retains his "private reason" in the commonwealth. Indeed, the sovereign-elect or confederacy leader in these accounts *relies on* the fact that the subjects will retain their ability to evaluate the rationality of actions when she attempts to find ways of getting them to join her punishment cadre. But as we saw in the last chapter, as long as the subjects do retain this private judgment, the regress argument based on Hobbes's psychology dictates that the commonwealth will inevitably dissolve. So is it possible to understand the people's authorization of their ruler differently, so that once they perform this action, they literally *lose* their private ability to judge the rationality of action?

It seems that there is. Suppose it is possible and rational for each subject to *convert* to a different standard of rationality: Whereas in the state of nature an individual would use an expected-utility calculation to evaluate the extent to which any action would be best for him, given his self-regarding desires, in the commonwealth he would convert to using the *sovereign's* expected-utility calculation to evaluate the rationality of any action — unless the sovereign permitted him to use his own, in which case, because the sovereign had endorsed his private assessment of the action, it would still be the sovereign's assessment indirectly. If this conversion were possible, creating an absolute sovereign would be accomplished by becoming *a new kind of reasoner*. The action of authorization, understood figuratively as a kind of surrender to the sovereign, would literally mean giving up one's own judgment of the rationality of an action and instead adopting the sovereign's judgment of an action's rationality as one's standard for evaluating which actions to perform. And if this conversion were rational, then it would essentially represent self-interest constraining itself for its own good, as Hume calls for in the passage quoted at the beginning of this chapter (III, ii, ii; 1978, 492).

David Gauthier has recently argued that this notion of conversion is strongly suggested in certain parts of *Leviathan* (1985, chap. 6), and he attempts to use this idea himself in his own contractarian moral theory, although he wants self-regarding utility maximizers to adopt a certain "moral" reasoning procedure, rather than adopt the sovereign's reason as a guide to action. Clearly, Hobbes would neither want nor think possible the subjects' conversion to a more moral standard of private judgment, because in Hobbes's (probably dubious) view, individual judgments using this moral standard would be bound to conflict, leading to the commonwealth's ruin. I shall not pursue this quarrel here; instead, I shall argue that Gauthier is right to say that there are passages in *Leviathan* that at least contain the hint of the idea that creating a sovereign should involve a "conversion" process in which one adopts the sovereign's reason as one's standard for evaluating actions.

For example, there is a passage on the nature of reason in Chapter 5 that might be interpreted to suggest this understanding of the sovereign's institution:

no mans Reason, nor the Reason of any one number of men, makes the certaintie; no more than an account is therefore well cast up, because a great many men have unanimously approved it. And therefore, as when there is a controversy in an account, the parties must by their own accord, set up for right Reason, the Reason of some Arbitrator, or Judge, to whose sentence they will both stand, or their controversie must either come to blowes, or be undecided, for want of a right Reason constituted by Nature; so is it also in all debates of what kind soever; And when men that think themselves wiser than all others, clamor and demand right Reason for judge; yet seek no more, but that things should be determined, by no other mens reason but their own, it is as intolerable in the society of men, as it is in play after trump is turned, to use for trump on every occasion, that suite whereof they have most in their hand. For they do nothing els, that will have every of their passions, as it comes to bear sway in them, to be taken for right Reason, and that in their own controversies: be[t]raying their want of right Reason, by the claym they lay to it. [*Lev*, 5, 3, 18–19]

In this passage, the sovereign's creation means the creation of a single reason that is a substitute for the "universal" or "objective" reason that does not exist in this world.

And although we interpreted the creation of this "single reason" in Chapter 6 as involving the bestowal of power on one person such that she alone can bring about any state of affairs she desires,[1] we can interpret this passage differently, understanding it to mean that the creation of a sovereign involves quite literally the destruction of all reason but the sovereign's own, where this destruction is to be accomplished by each subject's conversion to the use of the sovereign's expected-utility calculation to evaluate the rationality of any course of action.

Note how this idea is also suggested in the following passage describing the sovereign's role:

> it is annexed to the Soveraigntie, the whole power of prescribing the Rules, whereby every man may know, what Goods he may enjoy and what Actions he may doe, without being molested by any of his fellow Subjects. . . . These Rules of Propriety (or *Meum* and *Tuum*) and of *Good, Evil, Lawful*, and *Unlawful* in the actions of Subjects, are the Civill Lawes. . . . [*Lev*, 18, 10, 91]

Hobbes suggests here[2] that in a commonwealth, individuals are no longer supposed to define 'good' and 'bad' relative to their desires for self-preservation, but relative only to the sovereign's determination of how best to further *his* self-preservation (cf. *Lev*, 29, 6, 168). Finally, note that Hobbes also contends in Chapter 26 (and repeatedly in *A Dialogue of the Common Laws*) that only the sovereign's standard of rationality should be used by judges in a court of law:

> the doubt is, of whose Reason it is, that shall be received for Law. . . . In all Courts of Justice, the Soveraign (which is the Person of the Common-wealth,) is he that Judgeth: the subordinate Judge, ought to have regard to the reason, which moved his Soveraign to make such Law, that his Sentence may be according thereunto. . . . [*Lev*, 26, 11, 139–40]

And if a judge is supposed to use only the sovereign's reason to decide the issues before him, perhaps each subject is supposed to do the same in his determinations about how to act.

So the text of *Leviathan* suggests a literal interpretation of 'authorization' in addition to the one we gave in Chapter 6. Authorizing the sovereign on this new interpretation still involves engaging in a process that will resolve the leadership-selection problem, culminating in an explicit or tacit agreement on who the sovereign will be; but it also involves an additional action taken at the end of the process, namely, abandonment of the use of one's own expected-utility calculation to judge the advisability of performing any action, given one's own desires, and converting instead to the use of the sovereign's expected-utility calculation to judge the advisability of performing any action, given the *sovereign's* desires. No longer does a subject in a commonwealth ask: "Which action will best further my preservation?" Instead, the subject asks: "Which action will best further my sovereign's preservation?" — a question that can, however, involve determining which action will best further the subject's preservation when and if, according to the sovereign, the sovereign's own preservation sanctions it.

---

1 Elsewhere (*Lev*, 17, 13, 87), Hobbes says that to create one will from many wills is for the people to "conferre all their *power* and *strength* upon one Man, or upon one Assembly of men" (emphasis added).

2 However, note once again that the word 'power' appears in the first line, suggesting that a single reason is instituted by creating a coercive force in the ways described in Chapter 6.

Note that if Hobbesian people could actually make such a conversion, it would be remarkably easy for the sovereign to create a punishment cadre. He would merely have to say to a certain number of these people who have converted to his standard of rationality "It is best for me if you obey my punishment commands." And the converts who were using only his standard to evaluate the rationality of actions would naturally obey. Hence, there would be no need for the sovereign to dangle selective incentives in front of the converts in order to get them to follow his punishment commands, and this would mean that the sovereign would have the power he needed to accomplish any task he desired. But the situation is actually more remarkable than this, because complete conversion actually renders a punishment cadre *unnecessary* on the grounds that everyone will find it rational to do what the sovereign wants without the threat of punishment. A punishment cadre would be necessary only if converters were both able and likely to "backslide" and regain the use of their own reason, or if their conversion were only a pretense. We shall return to the possibility of "backsliding"or "dissimulating" converters in a moment.

Once this interpretation of authorization as conversion is completely stated, it becomes clear why we did not even consider it as a viable interpretation of that notion in Chapter 6. In that chapter we attempted to explain the institution of the sovereign by assuming Hobbesian psychological and physiological assumptions. But this notion of authorization appears to violate these assumptions. Imagine a Hobbesian subject being approached by a sovereign with a knife, who commands: "Stay where you are and let me put this knife into your chest!" Would not a Hobbesian person refuse to do any such thing, and run for his life? Of course, and this is what Hobbes readily admits in Chapter 21. Hobbes's physiological pronouncements are such that Hobbesian people appear to be "hard-wired" to preserve their own lives. They never "give up" this desire unless their bodily motions become wildly abnormal as a result of disease — and certainly they cannot *will* to give up this desire. But this is precisely what a conversion to the sovereign's standard of evaluating actions would require. No longer would a converted subject be pursuing the course of action that would best further his own life; instead, he would be pursuing the course of action that would best further the sovereign's life. Converting to the sovereign's standard of rationality of action would therefore mean changing one's psychology by adopting a new ultimate goal — the sovereign's preservation — and it seems at best unlikely and at worst ridiculous to think that Hobbesian people could "will" to make this their new goal. Indeed, Hobbes says in Chapter 21 of *Leviathan* that a subject is bound to a sovereign only for as long as that sovereign offers him protection, because "the right men have by Nature to protect themselves, when none else can protect them, *can by no Covenant be relinquished.*" (*Lev*, 21, 21, 114; emphasis added)

Nor does it seem possible that they could will to convert to a "mixed" goal, such as pursuing the sovereign's self-preservation unless doing so would place one's own life in imminent severe danger (say, 90 percent chance of imminent death). Doing so would seem to require Hobbesian people to perform such actions as obeying an order to testify against themselves insofar as this type of action would not result in immediate danger to their lives (although it might result in a good chance for long-term serious harm). But Hobbesian people would not seem to be able to do any such thing, as Hobbes admits in Chapter 21. Indeed, the concern each Hobbesian individual has for his life is so persistent, continuous, and inescapable that it would seem that such people would be unable to take any action that would put their lives at more risk than would other actions that were available to them. However, note that even if they could adopt this "mixed goal" and use it to judge the rationality of action, private reason still would not be destroyed in a commonwealth. It still would be up to the subject to determine whether or not the sovereign's commands had placed him in "severe imminent danger," nor does it seem obvious how that determination should go, particularly with punishment commands, which might well involve some risk to one's life. Hence, the sovereign would wield punishment power only if he could persuade his subjects that obeying his commands was not too risky, where the subjects would be the ones who defined what that meant. Such a sovereign would rule only as long as his subjects *let* him rule, so that he would be their agent rather than their master; and if we believe Hobbes's arguments in Chapter 29 of *Leviathan,* the commonwealth still would not be viable for long.

So, if Hobbes wants private judgment *destroyed* in order to ensure the commonwealth's survival, he must insist on total conversion to the sovereign's goal, and he would have to modify substantially his psychological or physiological characterizations of human beings to make this possible. Indeed, he would have to do more than this; he would also have to argue that Hobbesian people thus reinterpreted were actually *like us,* so that we real human beings would be just as able to convert to this standard of rationality as the people in Hobbes's state of nature. And it is not clear that Hobbes could pull off this project, because it is highly dubious that human beings really are able to transform themselves to the extent that this conversion story requires.

But suppose this sort of conversion were possible for both us and the people in Hobbes's state of nature; it still is not clear that they or we would find it rational, given our desires, to make that conversion, which means it still is not clear that modifying Hobbes's argument so that authorization is interpreted as conversion will make that argument valid. Indeed, I now want to argue that it would not be rational, and the reasons for the irrationality of conversion in this modified Hobbesian argument should be pondered by any contractarian philosopher tempted (as is Gauthier) to rely on some process of conversion to solve the problems generated by human rationality.

Note also that this counterargument I am about to construct is a redesigned version of the reason-based argument put forward by Locke and others in the seventeenth century and discussed in Section 7.1. Having seen that Hobbesian people are psychologically incapable of creating an absolute sovereign, I am now proposing a modification of Hobbesian psychology that would allow these people to create a sovereign by converting to his standard of reasoning. So the question becomes: Will it be *rational* for Hobbesian people, understood in this new way, to create a sovereign by converting?

Suppose a sovereign-candidate is elected by the people as described in Chapter 6, and suppose he says to his electorate: "If you obey me only when you determine that doing so is individually rational, you will be retaining your private judgment in the commonwealth, and according to the regress argument, the commonwealth will inevitably collapse. But if you abandon your private reason and convert to my standard of rationality, you will enable me to have final say on all questions in the commonwealth so that my rule will be permanent and the commonwealth secure. So convert if you want peace." Suppose further that you are part of this electorate. Would the sovereign's argument persuade you to convert?

In determining whether or not you should convert, you will realize that the sovereign's security of rule is a function of how many people in the commonwealth convert. If everybody does, he will be total master; if only you do so, his power will not be significantly different from that of a ruler whose subjects have retained their private judgment. So in considering whether or not to convert, you must determine, for any given number k of converters in the population (where k can vary from o to $n - 1$, and where n is the total number of people in the population), how much more security of power *your* conversion will bring to the sovereign and how much benefit you will receive from that increment of security created by your conversion (call this ΔV_i). Then you must compare this benefit to the cost of conversion (C_i). If $\Delta V_i > C_i$, then conversion will be individually rational for you; if $\Delta V_i < C_i$, conversion will not be individually rational for you.

Suppose k is a very low number, meaning that hardly anyone has converted. Would your conversion add to the security of the sovereign's power substantially in this situation? No. If most of the sovereign's subjects retain their private judgment, your abandonment of your own private judgment would seem to do little to make his rule more secure and the commonwealth viable, so ΔV_i would be very small. However, C_i would be large. Conversion includes giving up, first, the ability to exploit others by disobeying the sovereign's commands (e.g., the command to keep one's contract) and, second, the ability to disobey a life-threatening command. Giving up the second ability is regarded by you as particularly serious in that it means losing the capability of defending your life when it is endangered. So $C_i > \Delta V_i$ for low values of k, meaning that conversion in this situation will not be rational.

What if the value of k were in the medium range—say around 50 percent of the population? It seems reasonable to think that in this situation your conversion would do more good; in particular, it would actually help the sovereign in some measurable degree to build a permanent power base giving him considerably more power than a ruler whose subjects had not converted. Still, the contribution your conversion would make to that power base would be quite small; one individual's conversion in this situation would not add that much permanence to the power a sovereign has. Moreover, the cost of conversion for you still would be very high. So although $\Delta V_i^{k=o}$ is likely to be exceeded by $\Delta V_i^{k=(1/2)n}$, it still will be true that $\Delta V_i^{k=(1/2)n} < C_i$, meaning that, once again, conversion in this situation is not rational.

Finally, consider how you would reason if k were a very high number, at or near $n - 1$. In these circumstances, the sovereign would be, to all intents and purposes, the absolute master, because you would be the only other potential rebel (or one of a tiny minority of such rebels) in the population and hence easily subdued if you made any trouble. Because your conversion would add so little to the sovereign's permanence of power but would cost you so much, once again $\Delta V_i < C_i$ when k is at or near $n - 1$.

What we have just shown is that the subjects' attempt to produce an absolute sovereign by conversion is tantamount to attempting to produce a collective good that comes in "increments" rather than in one large "step" (the more converters, the more mastery a ruler has, that is, the closer he comes to having complete sovereign power). However, producing this good is problematic; indeed, I have just sketched what most

Figure 8.1

	k others	
	Convert	Not convert
The individual		
Convert	2	4
Not convert	1	3

Note: The numbers represent the individual's preference ordering.

people probably think of as the "classic" free-rider problem in the production of collective goods, and that sketch indicates that whereas the problem of producing step collective goods is a battle-of-the-sexes dilemma, the problem people face in the production of incremental collective goods of this sort is analogous to a one-shot prisoner's dilemma.[3] When you are in a prisoner's dilemma and you know your partner will cooperate, the cooperative action for you is never as good as the noncooperative (exploitative) action. But the same thing is true in the production of an incremental collective good: Cooperating with others by converting with them so that the sovereign is created results in a gain (life in a commonwealth is better than life in a state of war), but exploiting the others, that is, letting them convert but refraining from doing so yourself, is even better, because the cost to you of converting is always greater, no matter how many others do so, than the benefit you receive from converting. So, no matter how many others convert, it is rational for each individual not to convert.

One can therefore think of this situation as one in which each individual faces what I call an "ordered game set" of prisoner's dilemmas concerning whether or not to convert, given a certain number k of supposed converters, where k ranges from 0 to n − 1, and where n is the total number of possible converters in this state. And for every number k of supposed converters, the PD matrix (Figure 8.1) describes the individual's reasoning in this situation. Because, for each value of k, this individual faces a prisoner's dilemma, each matrix in the set dictates that the action of not converting dominates, so that every individual is rational to perform only that action, no matter whether the other individuals convert or not. But because individual preferences are symmetric, no rational individual will be disposed to convert under any circumstances, and the absolute sovereign will not be created.

But perhaps we are misrepresenting the kind of conversion that a smart sovereign, aware of this game-theoretic analysis, would require. It seems that the sovereign should issue the following order to his subjects: "Convert, or else be banned from the commonwealth and remain in the state of war."[4] By making such a threat, the

3   For a full discussion of its structure, see my "Free Rider Problems in the Production of Collective Goods."

4   Indeed, note that in his answer to the fool, Hobbes actually says that if someone shows he cannot keep a contract, he should not be allowed to enter into — or presumably remain in — the commonwealth (Lev, 15, 5, 73).

sovereign is essentially trying to treat the security and order of the commonwealth as a collective good whose benefits can be *excluded* from nonproducers. Compare a situation in which five hunters set off to kill a deer; one hunter decides to quit early, and the other four finally succeed in killing a deer. Why should these four share the benefit of the deer with the fifth indolent hunter? They need not, and they should not. His exclusion from the benefits of the hunt this time ensures that next time he will be motivated to help the other four or suffer a similar fate. The sovereign is proposing, likewise, that a subject do the work required to produce the commonwealth (i.e., convert), or else be excluded from the commonwealth.

But it is not so easy to effect that exclusion. Suppose you were threatened by a sovereign: "Convert or else be banned from the commonwealth." In this situation, you would actually have *three* options, not just two: not converting (and suffering the banishment), converting (and risking suffering the banishment), or *only pretending to convert* (and not suffering the banishment). This last option is actually a way of tricking the sovereign into thinking that you have paid the cost to produce his full sovereignty when in fact you have not; using this trick is a way of trying to avoid conversion but nonetheless enjoying the benefits provided by the commonwealth. In other words, it is a way of trying to "ride free." Let us assume that the threat to one's life in the state of nature is significant enough to make nonconversion the least desirable option. Which of the remaining two actions should you perform?

To answer this question, let us consider what benefits a genuine converter (or GC) would have as opposed to the benefits a pseudoconverter (or PC) could expect to garner:

1. Both will reap the benefits from many successfully completed contracts and many successfully produced collective goods. GCs will perform their parts of contracts and participate in producing collective goods because the sovereign commands them to do so. And PCs will generally do likewise, not because the sovereign has commanded them to do so but because his threat of expulsion provides a negative selective incentive that makes these actions individually rational for them.

2. PCs will, however, get two additional benefits: (a) They will be able to enjoy the benefits that will come from their retention of the ability either to avoid or to refuse to obey any life-threatening or harmful commands made by the sovereign. Even if this refusal is likely to be discovered and punished with expulsion by the sovereign, if the dangers posed by obeying the command are severe enough, it might still be worth it for a PC to suffer the expulsion rather than obey the command. A GC, however, can do only the latter. (b) A PC can also enjoy benefits deriving from his retention of the ability to exploit his fellows, such as not performing his part of a bargain after his partner has already performed. Of course, using this ability to exploit involves the risk of being discovered as a PC and suffering punishment. But that risk can be minimized by the PC himself; for example, he can decide to exploit someone only in situations in which the exploitation will be difficult or impossible to detect, such as reneging on an unwitnessed deathbed promise.

3. Unlike a PC, a GC cannot reap exploitative benefits, nor can he avoid obeying dangerous commands. However, a GC (a) does not risk being discovered and expelled from the commonwealth and (b) contributes to the stability of the commonwealth. That is, whereas a PC retains his private judgment in the commonwealth, and according to the regress argument thereby endangers the permanence and effectiveness of the sovereign's rule, a GC who gives up that private judgment contributes in a small way to the permanence of the sovereign's power.

So should one choose to be a GC or a PC? In order to answer this question, a rational person would perform the following calculation. First he would determine the expected utility of conversion, using his knowledge of the sovereign-elect to estimate the likelihood that he would be commanded to perform life-threatening or dangerous tasks. Call the results of this calculation EU_{gc}. Next he would calculate the expected utility associated with pretending to convert. Now what is interesting about this option is that *it can yield no less than EU_{gc} as long as he obeys all of the sovereign's commands* (assuming that the sovereign has no mind-reading device and can detect a PC only through his behavior). In fact, if he is obedient 100 percent of the time, $EU_{gc} = EU_{pc}$. But this reasoner also knows that being a PC allows him to refuse to perform dangerous commands and to refuse to obey other commands when doing so will allow him to exploit another subject with impunity. Disobedience does, however, involve the risk that it will be detected and the reasoner thrown back into the state of nature. Therefore, EU_{pc} is calculated as follows:

$$EU_{pc} = EU_{gc} + [p(EU_{sw}) + (1 - p)(u_2 + u_3)]$$

where EU_{sw} is this person's expected utility in the state of war (presumably a very high negative number), p is the probability of being detected as a PC and being expelled into that state, $(1 - p)$ is the probability that he will avoid detection when he is disobedient, u_2 is the utility he expects to get from exploiting others with impunity by being disobedient, and u_3 is the utility he expects to get by avoiding death or harm through disobedience of the sovereign's dangerous commands. So

$$EU_{pc} > EU_{gc} \quad \text{iff } p(EU_{sw}) + (1 - p)(u_2 + u_3) > 0$$

What will be the result of this last calculation? Consider the fact that you will regard EU_{sw} as a very low negative number. However, $(u_2 + u_3)$ will be a very high positive number, primarily because u_3 will be high: The utility associated with being able to disobey the sovereign's dangerous commands is significant. Admittedly, although the absolute value of EU_{sw} is likely to be greater than $(u_2 + u_3)$ insofar as surreptitiously disobeying a dangerous command might only postpone death, not avoid it (i.e., the sovereign might find out and banish you to the state of nature), it cannot be much greater. And you would believe that the chances of your disobedience being detected (p) would be very small, because detection would come about only if you were observed to be disobeying a sovereign's command, and when the punishment for disobedience (representing nonconversion) is to be returned to the dangerous state of war with the sovereign as your enemy, you would do it rarely and only in circumstances in which detection would be unlikely. In other words, as a PC, you

Authorization as Conversion

Figure 8.2

	k others	
	GC	PC
You		
GC	2	4
PC	1	3

would believe that you could *minimize* the probability of being detected as a PC, making $p(EU_{sw}) + (1 - p)(u_2 + u_3) > 0$, so that $EU_{pc} > EU_{gc}$.

Of course, a sovereign might try to convince you that the temptation to disobedience would be more than you could control and would lead you to disobey too frequently, thus making it likely that your nonconversion would be detected. Nonetheless, this argument is unconvincing, because the subject knows that by lashing himself to the sovereign's will in order not to yield to the sirens' songs of the benefits of disobedience, he not only loses the chance to exploit others but also runs the risk of indirectly committing suicide. So this subject would reason: "If I only appear to be a GC, and if the sovereign never commands me to do something so dangerous that an EU calculation tells me that disobeying it is worth the risk of detection, I shall never disobey, and he will never know the difference. But if he does make this sort of dangerous command, then because I am a PC, I at least have the capability of escaping with my life. And although I might be tempted to disobey when I shouldn't (i.e., this EU calculation might be mistaken), surely it is worth it to run this risk rather than disable myself from resisting these life-threatening commands forever. That is, surely $p(EU_{sw}) < (1 - p)(u_2 + u_3)$."

Thus, we conclude that no matter how many other subjects were to genuinely convert, if you were a subject in this commonwealth you would be rational only to *appear* to convert. Indeed, you would be facing another one-shot coordinated set of prisoner's dilemmas in which the deceitful action of pretending to convert dominates over the honest and cooperative action of genuine conversion (Figure 8.2). And because this same dilemma would be faced by every other person in the community (whose preferences are symmetric with yours), it would be rational for you and everyone else only to pretend to convert, with the result that every subject would still retain the ability to judge whether or not it was rational to obey any of the sovereign's commands. Indeed, the first time the sovereign tried (without using selective incentives) to get these so-called GCs to perform dangerous punishment tasks, they would resist, and their resistance would signal to him and to the rest of the population that he was not absolute master of the commonwealth, but only empowered to do what his subjects were willing to give him the power to do. And according to Hobbes's regress argument, such a commonwealth is unstable and will inevitably degenerate into a state of war.

Suppose that a smart sovereign who realizes that it is likely that none of the conversions by her subjects is genuine tries to secure obedience from these liars by resorting to threats of punishment enforced by punishment cadres. But this only returns us to the same relationship prevailing between sovereign and subject that the Chapter 6 scenarios established! Because it is rational *not* to genuinely convert, the sovereign is forced to assume that most or all of her subjects have not done so and thus is forced to dangle selective incentives in front of them to ensure their obedience to her commands — even her punishment commands. The necessity of such incentives means that the sovereign acknowledges that private judgment has not been destroyed in the commonwealth. And according to the regress argument, the existence of this private judgment means that the commonwealth is not viable. So we conclude that trying to coerce conversion in order to build a Hobbesian commonwealth with an absolute sovereign simply will not work.

Of course, it would work if the sovereign could prevent her subjects from dissimulating. For example, pretending to convert would be impossible for the subjects if the sovereign had a mind-reading device, and thus conversion would dominate straightforwardly over nonconversion when the selective incentives made possible by the posses were sufficient to make the benefits from the action of conversion exceed the cost of conversion. But if such a device existed, why would it be used only to ensure genuine conversions? Why wouldn't it be rational to use it in the state of nature itself, so that farsighted reasoners could ensure that their partners intended to cooperate? This device would end the distrust which produced total war in the state of nature and thus make possible enough cooperation to render the institution of the sovereign unnecessary.

So the point is this: The "degree of opacity" in human nature that makes deceit possible in the state of nature and that sows the seeds of distrust culminating in total war in that state also makes possible the mere pretense of conversion to the sovereign's reason, and any device that would render human nature transparent would not only render impossible this deceitful conversion but also render unnecessary that conversion itself. And Hobbes cannot plausibly argue that we are opaque to one another in the state of war but considerably more transparent after the creation of a sovereign.

In the end, there is only one way to render conversion to the sovereign's reason the best possible choice for each individual in Hobbes's state of nature. Imagine a device that would change people physiologically so that they could reason *only* using the sovereign's standard of rationality. Moreover, imagine that there is a procedure for using this device such that any individual would be changed by it only if *all the others* were also changed by it, *making the sovereign's institution a pure step good.* This device and procedure would make it impossible for anyone to enjoy the peace created by others' conversion without converting oneself, meaning that it would make it impossible to be a deceitful free rider. And it would solve whatever psychological or physiological impediments exist that prevent accomplishing this conversion in fact. So if such a device and procedure existed, the people in Hobbes's state of nature would be left with two choices: genuinely converting along with everyone else so as to create a commonwealth, or not doing so and remaining in the state of war. And if Hobbes's argument for the desirability of subjugating oneself to an absolute sovereign is really correct (*contra* Locke), then it should be rational for each individual to submit to this procedure and accept the device, thereby "converting" physiologically along with everyone else and instituting a completely stable commonwealth.

Indeed, science fiction writers have imagined just this sort of commonwealth. There is an episode of the television series "Star Trek" in which the hero, Captain Kirk, and his friends come across a planet in which every inhabitant has had a device surgically implanted in the neck connecting them with their sovereign—a large computer (whose institution is certainly a way to take care of the problem of sovereign shortsightedness!). The computer uses these devices to observe what actions they are performing and what words they speak, and to affect their nervous systems following any disobedient word or deed so that they suffer excruciating pain in punishment. Moreover, it is explained to Captain Kirk that this system was instituted long ago in order to secure a permanent "peace." Nonetheless, despite the fact that peace does indeed reign in the land, Kirk and his friends immediately set about trying to tear out the implants in order to restore to the planet's inhabitants their "freedom."

Hobbes's argument for absolute sovereignty is valid if conversion to the sovereign's standard of reasoning is accomplished in this sort of way. But should we take *Leviathan* to be an implicit plea for the development of such devices? The suggestion seems ridiculous. We have made Hobbes's argument valid in a way that amounts to a reductio ad absurdum of the argument. Of course, whether or not Hobbes would regard the modified argument as ridiculous is unclear. Perhaps this great lover of peace would embrace and even celebrate the idea that authorization should be understood as physiological conversion to the sovereign's reason accomplished by such devices, because, thus understood, he finally has a valid geometric deduction for absolute sovereignty and a way for human beings to achieve "lasting peace." Indeed, given modern mind-control techniques, perhaps this conversion could be accomplished without the use of surgical techniques or implants; so perhaps Hobbes would advocate mind control as the way to transform us all into permanently obedient subjects. Some might argue that this technique has already been used in totalitarian regimes in the twentieth century with some success, showing that this "ridiculous" modified Hobbesian argument has actually been taken seriously in our own time.

But providing a valid argument is not everything a philosopher wants; a good argument must also be *sound*. And the problem with the modified argument is that is seems anything but sound, in two respects. First, one of its most important premises is also one of Hobbes's most suspicious claims, that is, the claim that human beings desire *above all else* to preserve themselves. The inhabitants of the planet Captain Kirk encounters are certainly surviving, but they are surviving in a way that most of us would think was not worth the cost they were paying to do so. And bare self-preservation cannot be our highest goal if there are some prices we would simply refuse to pay to achieve it. Hence, one reason why we (and perhaps even Hobbes) would reject this modified argument as unsound is that given our real desires, such a mutilation of our nature and destruction of our autonomy would be intolerable. Here at last is one situation in which Hobbes's unqualified support for self-preservation as our premier desire makes his political argument fail.

However, there is a second, even more disturbing external attack we intuitively want to make on this admittedly valid modified argument. We are suspicious of the claim made in the argument that instituting an absolute sovereign is the *only* way to achieve peace. As we saw in Chapter 4, this claim is the conclusion of Hobbes's regress argument, which is supposed to be based on both his psychological assumptions and his meta-ethical commitments. But neither we nor Hobbes's seventeenth-century critics believe him when he says that we must decide between peace secured by a sovereign or natural war. Indeed, the "cure" for warfare proposed in the modified argument seems much too severe for the disease, maybe even worse than the disease. Hence, once again we intuitively reject the premises on which Hobbes's modified argument is based, and thus reject the argument.

8.2 HOBBES'S SECOND MODIFIED ARGUMENT: THE FALLBACK POSITION

If we do not want to make Hobbes's argument valid by appealing to hypothetical devices that change people's physiological construction, there is another modification we might make in order to render his argument both valid and at least arguably sound. Perhaps Hobbes can accept the idea that the people will always retain the right to judge whether or not to obey the ruler, but argue nonetheless that they can create a ruler who is *almost* an absolute sovereign (although not the "real thing") and who has sufficient power to end the warfare in the state of nature. If such a position were possible, Hobbes could then contend that the institution of such a ruler "counts" as the creation of government — it would be the closest thing we human beings could come to creating one (short of changing our physiological construction). I call this Hobbes's "fallback" position, and I want to present it here in order to see if it can salvage the political intuitions that motivated his failed "full sovereignty" argument.

There are three beliefs central to Hobbes's political philosophy that the fallback position attempts to save:

1. Human beings' desires are overwhelmingly self-regarding in nature, and a person's primary desire is (almost always) to further his self-preservation.
2. Because human beings' desires lead them into virtual total war with one another, peace can be achieved only if a ruler has the power to intervene in and control *every aspect* of human life (religious, scientific, economic, and social).
3. The creation of a ruler with such power is a necessary condition for the creation of a human society (i.e., there can be no human society in the state of nature; the creation of government is a precondition for its existence).

These three tenets were part of the original Hobbesian argument, but the fallback position nonetheless incorporates a fourth tenet that was not part of the original argument:

4. Because of (1), Hobbesian people are unable to surrender their right to all things to their ruler such that she can be said to "own" them; they can only lend the ruler power so that there is an agency relationship between ruler and subject.

As Hobbes himself describes them, human beings are commmitted to preserving their lives above all else, and hence they will always reserve the right to judge whether their allegiance to their ruler is furthering or endangering their preservation. And because they cannot relinquish the ability to calculate which available action will be in their best interest, they can at any time take back the control over their lives that their obedience to punishment commands had previously given their ruler if enough of them refuse (on self-interested grounds) to obey those punishment commands.

But even though, on this fallback position, people can be said only to lend their right to all things to their ruler, this loan can still be large enough to make the ruler extraordinarily powerful. Indeed, as long as *most* people are prepared not to "call in" the loan, that is, refuse to obey the ruler's punishment commands, the ruler is going to have the power necessary to interfere in every aspect of human life, and certainly enough power to deal effectively with the occasional recalcitrant who refuses to obey her. So according to this position, the Hobbesian belief that a ruler must have total power to secure peace is salvaged by the fallback position in the following way: The ruler has absolute power *as long as* most continue to maintain their loan of power to him, that is, as long as most of them continue to obey his punishment commands.

But when and how would people "call in" their loan to their ruler? Clearly they would do so whenever they determined that recalling the loan would be in their interest because it would further their self-preservation. But we should be specific about when and how they make that determination. First, it is important to note that their withdrawal can be "partial" or "complete." A partial withdrawal of power by the subjects will result if many or all of them decide not to obey a *particular* command of the ruler on the grounds that an expected-utility calculation shows the expected gains of disobedience to be greater than the expected gains of obedience. If enough subjects disobey that command as a result of these calculations (either surreptitiously) or openly — it makes no difference), the ruler will find it difficult or impossible to use his enforcement cadre (some or all of whom might themselves be disobedient) to bring about the result he desires; in other words, he will lack the political power necessary to effect this result. So the fallback position recognizes that a ruler's power is always limited to what he can use his enforcement cadre to get his subjects to do.

However, if subjects determine that they should disobey all (or almost all) of their ruler's commands, this will amount to withdrawing their power from the ruler "completely," which will mean deposing him as ruler. And they will do so whenever an expected-utility calculation tells them it is in their interest to do so. This will occur when two conditions are met: first, when the utility of withdrawal is greater than the utility of continued authorization and, second, when the risk to their lives if they withdraw is not substantial.

Let us start by looking at the first condition: When would someone believe that the utility of withdrawal was greater than the utility of continued authorization? He would do so when he believed either

1. that life in a state of nature would be better than life in the present commonwealth under his present ruler, or
2. that life in a commonwealth with a *different* ruler would be better than life in the present commonwealth under his present ruler.

Generally speaking, it is the possibility of too many of her subjects having the *second* belief that a ruler will fear most. If we accept Hobbes's or even Locke's story about the horrors of the natural state, it seems plausible that it need not be difficult for a ruler to please most of her subjects enough such that they will find life under her rule preferable to the natural state (unless, of course, her rule directly threatens their lives). However, it might not be so easy to persuade most of her subjects that life under her rule is preferable to life under *any alternative ruler.* Those subjects she does not succeed in persuading will then be disposed to withdraw their authorization completely in favor of what they perceive to be a better alternative.

However, before rebellion can be considered rational, a second condition must be satisified: The action must not be too risky. If a dissatisfied subject does not realize that any of his fellow subjects are *also* dissatisfied, then he will believe that the others will be prepared to obey the ruler's commands to punish his rebellion's efforts, and when the dangers of rebellion are factored into his calculation, he will conclude that the expected gains of rebellion are (rather dramatically) exceeded by the expected gains of continued obedience. Dissatisfaction with the ruler is therefore a necessary but not a sufficient condition for rebellion. In addition to holding either of the two foregoing beliefs, our subject would also have to believe

3. that many other people were dissatisfied and disposed to follow him in rebellion, so that the risk to his life if he should withdraw his authorization (i.e., refuse to obey the ruler's commands) would not be considerable.

That this is a factor in one's calculations is simply a function of the fact that creating a sovereign involves creating a *convention* that only this individual's punishment commands are to be obeyed. To remove this ruler, it is necessary to change that convention, and an individual subject will be successful in effecting that change only if many other individuals also desire a different convention (most likely, a different convention on who should rule). So one way a ruler can try to prevent attempts at rebellion by dissatisfied subjects is to make exchange of information among her subjects difficult, so that it will not come to be common knowledge that many of them are dissatisfied.[5] Moreover, even if it should become common knowledge that many of the citizens were dissatisfied, if there were no common agreement among them on *which* alternative ruler would be preferable to the present one, each might decide not to act on his disposition to rebel, on the grounds that doing so would only usher in a war between the rebels over who should replace the present ruler, a future that might seem far worse than continuing to be governed by that ruler.

However, if there is common knowledge of dissatisfaction among many of the subjects, and if there is general agreement on which person would be a desirable or salient replacement for the ruler, then rebellion becomes a real possibility. Of course, the fewer the rebels, the larger the support that the present ruler can receive from the populace both to thwart and to punish the rebellious efforts of the dissatisfied citizenry, and thus the more likely an expected-utility calculation will tell these dissatisfied citizens not to risk rebellion. But the larger the number of rebels, the fewer the

5 Gregory Kavka (1983c, 601–20) has explored the role that common knowledge of others' dissatisfaction plays in rebellion against tyranny. Kavka perceives his analysis as occasioned by Hobbesian reflections on government, but in a sense this is not so: If Hobbes's official argument for absolute sovereignty worked, he could argue that the institution of a sovereign would require action by the subjects that would *preclude* their rebellion in the future. Alas, the argument does not work, and the possibility of rebellion is a fact of life for any Hobbesian ruler. So Kavka's analysis implicitly assumes the Hobbesian fallback position, rather than Hobbes's official argument for full sovereignty.

number of supporters that the present ruler can use to thwart and punish the rebels, and thus the more likely an expected-utility calculation will tell any other dissatisfied citizenry to risk rebellion. And, of course, the worse the present ruler's performance, the sooner it will be that rebellion will be worth the risk, and the sooner it will be that large numbers of people will be dissatisfied enough with her performance to be disposed to rebel.

In effect, therefore, we have shown that the fallback position recognizes that a ruler must worry that the same "coordination process" that her subjects had to follow in order to institute her (as explored in Chapter 6) can also be used to depose her and to institute another ruler in her place. People are motivated in the state of nature to hire the best ruler available in the "marketplace," but because people retain the desire to preserve themselves in the commonwealth, this market motivation *remains* after the commonwealth is created. And because it remains, if people believe that the market presents them with a better potential leader, they will be able (and in certain circumstances rational) to "fire" the old leader and "hire" the new one. So when it is in their interest to do so, *people are able to change the convention about who is ruler.*

To summarize our remarks thus far: According to the fallback position, rebellion will take place in any political regime

1. when there is a widely shared belief that the state of nature would be better than life under the present ruler, such that, for a significant percentage of the population, an expected-utility calculation (taking into account the degree of support for the present ruler) will dictate rebellion and a return to the state of nature over continued obedience to the ruler, or (and this is most likely)

2. when there is a widely shared belief that life under a different (salient) ruler candidate would be better than life under the present ruler, such that, for a significant percentage of the population, an expected-utility calculation (taking into account the degree of support for the present ruler) will dictate rebellion in order to establish this rival candidate as ruler.

However, the ruler can at least try to prevent rebellion from happening by "behaving herself," that is, by instituting policies that large numbers of subjects will see as making the expected gains of continued obedience greater than the expected gains of attempting to transfer authorization to another or returning to the state of nature. Our analysis has also shown how difficult rebellion can be, so that merely lending one's "right to all things" to a ruler would seem to give her the sort of tremendous power that Hobbes believes is needed to achieve peace in a human community, and retrieving that loan can be difficult enough to make it at least *something like* a "permanent" loan.

Remarkably enough, not only is this position a possible one for Hobbes to take, but also there are passages in the text of *Leviathan* that suggest it, and we shall explore these passages in a moment. Perhaps, as a result of these passages, some readers may even have thought that this *was* Hobbes's position; after all, the power that the fallback position accords to the ruler is so substantial that it does not seem unreasonable to call her an "absolute sovereign." Still, it is important for readers to appreciate that this fallback position is inconsistent with Hobbes's main argument for and definition of absolute sovereignty in *Leviathan* and *De Cive*. According to the regress argument, an absolute sovereign is one who is "final decider" of all questions in a commonwealth, and the argument maintains that only a human being, not a set of rules, can perform this role in a commonwealth. However, the fallback position makes the *subjects* the deciders of whether or not the sovereign will continue to hold power, and this position recognizes the existence of either an implicit or explicit contract between ruler and subject that is supposed to provide the final decision criteria used by the subjects in determining whether or not the sovereign is wielding her power well. As we have noted, this means that the heart of the fallback position is an agency relationship between ruler and subject, and yet, in support of his regress argument, Hobbes insists in Chapter 18 of *Leviathan* that no commonwealth with this subject/sovereign relationship can survive, and his argument is supposed to rest on his psychological characterization of human beings.

So before we proceed any further in our evaluation of the fallback position, we must determine whether or not Hobbesian subjects and sovereigns can make and keep an agency contract of the sort required by this position.

8.3 THE "AGENCY" SOCIAL AGREEMENT IN THE FALLBACK POSITION

Our presentations of Hobbes's official argument for absolute sovereignty and his fallback position have revealed something important for our understanding of the social contract argument, namely, that there are two places for social agreements to exist in this sort of argument:

1. Agreements can take place among the people who wish to create the commonwealth, in order to resolve questions involving, first, whether or not to have a government, second, what form of government they should have and who should be their ruler, and, third, who should perform enforcement and punishment functions for the ruler.

2. Agreements can take place between the ruler and the people setting forth what conditions have to be met in order for her to receive the people's obedience (in particular, their obedience to her enforcement commands). These are standardly called "agency" agreements.

In our discussion in Chapter 6 of possible places for agreements in Hobbes's argument for absolute sovereignty, we concentrated only on trying to find agreements of the first sort. And this was because in Chapter 18 of *Leviathan*, Hobbes expressly forbade us to look for agreements of the second sort. But the fallback position does incorporate an agreement of the second sort, as does Locke's social contract argument. Indeed, even Nozick's argument for the creation of a minimal state includes an agency agreement of the second sort; after all, Nozickean people still have to hire the protection agency they prefer.

In this section, I want to consider three problems that the agency agreement seems to pose for Hobbes's argument. I will argue that all three of these problems can be overcome successfully such that the agency agreement between ruler and subject can be included in the Hobbesian political argument consistent with the psychological and ethical premises of that argument.

Agency Agreement in the Fallback Position

IS THE GAME-THEORETIC STRUCTURE OF THE AGENCY AGREEMENT A PRISONER'S DILEMMA?

Let us start with an obvious reason why it seems that an agency agreement cannot be included in any political argument with Hobbesian psychological premises: Is not an agency agreement a contract, and is it not true that Hobbesian people are incapable of keeping contracts? In Chapter 6, I was concerned to show that any (one-time) agreements among the subjects concerning which ruler to institute were not contractual in nature and were better termed SI agreements. And although I did acknowledge the existence of a few contracts between the ruler and *some* of his subjects concerning those subjects' participation in the sovereign's punishment cadre, these contracts were either enforceable by the sovereign or else *clearly* iterated in structure, so that the parties to them would find performance individually rational. However, agency agreements do seem to be agreements between the ruler and *all* of the people, of the sort that we standardly call "contractual," and they also seem to be one-time agreements. Given that we have analyzed the game-theoretic structure of one-shot contracts as prisoner's dilemmas, it would appear that this one-shot agency agreement could not be completed by Hobbesian people, and hence could not be incorporated into Hobbes's argument consistent with his psychological premises. But is this true?

It is *not*, which means, once again, that not all agreements have a PD structure. Let me make intuitively plausible the idea that agency agreements do not present prisoner's dilemmas to the participants, thereby preparing the way for the correct game-theoretic analysis of the dilemma they do pose. Consider a group of baseball players hiring a set of umpires to officiate at their games.[6] The players agree with one another to hire this particular group of people as umpires, and they agree with the umpires that they will abide by the umpires' decisions as long as these decisions are reasonable in light of the rules of baseball. It seems clear that the agreement of the players with one another to hire these umpires need not be understood as a contractual exchange of *promises*. Each of them wants to hire the umpires (consider the fact that baseball can be played only if there is an umpire behind home plate), and although there might be some difference of opinion about who should be selected, there are devices (some of which we discussed in Chapter 6) that can resolve this battle-of-the-sexes problem such that the players can coordinate on the umpires needed to resolve their problem. But there is a second agreement involved in the institution of umpires — that is, the *hiring* or *agency* agreement between players and umpires, in which the players empower the umpires to decide certain issues in the game and agree to abide by the umpires' decisions, and in which the umpires agree to make those decisions in accordance with certain rules. Does this agency agreement require an exchange of contractual promises to be kept? No. Self-interest should keep both parties true to the requirements of the bargain. The players know that the game can be played only if they are willing to submit to the umpires' decisions even when they do not want to do so, meaning that their long-term self-interest in playing the game should overcome any short-term desire to disregard or render void the (at least arguably correct) decisions of the umpires.

6 The analogy is suggested by Hart (1961, 138–42), although he actually compares political society with a cricket game.

Moreover, assuming that those people who are chosen to umpire the game *want* to perform this role, self-interest keeps the umpires "in line." Their status as hired help means they know that if they do not make decisions according to the rules, the players will be rational to fire them, because decisions that are arbitrary or not in accordance with the rules of baseball will make it impossible for the game of baseball to be played. Thus, we see that it is in the interest of *both* sides to keep their parts of the agreement: The players need not ask the umpires for a promise to abide by the rules, because the umpires' self-interest should be sufficient to secure this result; similarly, the umpires need not ask the players for a promise to abide by their decisions, because it is in the players' self-interest to do so as long as the decisions are reasonable. The completion of an agreement of this sort can be derailed only if one or both parties reason badly or if one or both parties change their minds about what they want.

We can now use this analogy to shed light on the agency agreement between ruler and people in Hobbes's fallback position. The subjects are not in a prisoner's dilemma; rather, they are in the same sort of "threat" position as the baseball players, although whereas the baseball players tell the umpires they will obey every reasonable ruling, the subjects tell their ruler they will *not* voluntarily obey any order made by the ruler to punish themselves. However, they do tell the ruler that they will obey the ruler's reasonable orders to punish others, and they tell her how they will calculate the reasonableness of her punishment orders or, for that matter, any order: They will perform an expected-utility calculation comparing the advantages of obedience against the advantages of disobedience in pursuit of what might be a better alternative (e.g., a commonwealth with a different ruler). And they know that one of the most serious drawbacks of disobedience is the undermining of the order created by having a ruler stable in power, just as the baseball players know that one of the most serious drawbacks of disobedience is the undermining of the order in the game created by that disobedience. The ruler is in the same "threatened" position as the umpire; she knows that she can wield power only if she issues orders that most of her subjects will determine to be reasonable and in their best interest to follow. Therefore, her desire to stay in power keeps her true to the terms of her hiring contract, and the people's desire to have a ruler keeps them true to their part of that contract. Note also that the agency agreement between ruler and people must be "explicit" to this extent: It must be common knowledge between both parties that the way in which she is empowered by them gives them a certain kind of threat advantage such that, in essence, she wields power on terms dictated by the subjects.

Is this agency agreement a contract? If a contract is understood as the lawyers define it (i.e., as an agreement in which there is a bilateral or unilateral *promise*), then an agency agreement is not a contract. Of course, the law recognizes something called an "agency contract," which includes one or more promises by which an agency relationship is established. Indeed, when I discussed the possibility of such a relationship existing between ruler and people in Chapter 5, I assumed for the sake of argument that creating it would require a contractual exchange of promises between the parties. However, I am now showing how the agency relationship between ruler and subject can be created by a noncontractual agreement. How is the game-theoretic structure of this noncontractual agreement different from that of a contract?

Contracts presuppose a game-theoretic situation in which one or more promises are needed to ensure that the parties to the agreement perform an action that is individually irrational but collectively rational. The following are two sorts of game-theoretic structures underlying contracts.[7]

PD Contract Games

As we discussed in Chapter 2, prisoner's dilemmas can underlie contracts, but, strictly speaking, they do so only when the participants to the contract must perform their actions independent of one another. Another way to put this point is that in a prisoner's dilemma, neither party's action is contingent on the other party's action. This independence of action holds, for example, in a situation in which the actions of the parties have to be made simultaneously, or are made out of sight of one another such that neither will know how the other acted until after they have performed their actions.

Contingent-Move "PD-like" Games

Many contracts are not independent-move games. If you and I promise to help each other harvest our crops, one of us must help harvest the crops of the other first, and then be helped with one's own harvest second. Hence, in these sorts of games,

1. the contract can be completed only in two consecutive moves, and
2. the player who moves second will choose which action to perform contingent on knowledge of how the first party performed, and
3. it is the case that either (a) one player is able through personal power or because of circumstance to force the other player to move first, or (b) no player is able through personal power or because of circumstance to force the other player to move first.

The game-theoretic structure in these situations is only *like* a prisoner's dilemma; it is *not,* strictly speaking, a prisoner's dilemma, because these games will be completed only after two successive moves, the second contingent on the first, not after two noncontingent moves. Figure 8.3 is a schema to represent the players' preferences in this sort of contingent two-move game. Player *A* can move in two possible ways (represented in the first column); player *B* can respond to either of those moves in two possible ways (represented in the second column); so there are four possible outcomes from the combinations of their moves, and the numbers in the final two columns represent their preference orderings for these possible outcomes (4 is lowest, 1 is highest).

However, it is easy to understand why these contingent-move games are readily confused with prisoner's dilemmas — the preferences for the outcomes created by the two parties' moves in this game are identical with preferences in a PD game. Standard agency *contracts* are also best understood as having this sort of game-theoretic struc-

---

7 However, I make no claim that this two-part analysis of the game-theoretic situations underlying contracts is exhaustive.

Figure 8.3

| A: move 1 | B: move 2 | Preferences for outcomes resulting after B's second move | |
		A	B
Complete	Complete	2	2
	Renege	4	1
Renege	Renege	3	3
	Complete	1	4

ture: An agent is hired and gives service to a principal in exchange for the principal's promise of eventual payment. Without the promise, it would be irrational for the agent to render service.[8]

In contrast to these two game-theoretic structures underlying contracts, in which one or more promises usually are required to achieve a cooperative outcome, there are three types of situations in which SI agreements are sufficient to effect a cooperative solution.

Coordination Dilemmas

As we discussed in Chapter 6, a cooperative solution to this type of game-theoretic problem can be effected by an implicit or explicit SI agreement, even when there is some conflict of interest (e.g., in a battle-of-the-sexes game).

---

8 However, sometimes contingent-move PD-like games *can* be completed by Hobbesian-like people precisely because of the way in which the moves of the game are contingent. Suppose two soldiers A and B are under fire from the enemy, and suppose they make a contract to remain with one another on the front line to return that fire. They know that if they both stay on the front line, they each have a 50% chance of surviving, but they also know that if one of them runs away and the other remains, the one who runs has an 80% chance of surviving, whereas the one who stays has only a 10% chance of surviving. Finally, if both defect and run, each has a 30% chance of surviving. Their preferences for the outcomes of the game match the preferences in Figure 8.3, but because either player is able to act second and make his action contingent on the first player's action, the contract can be kept. Suppose B decides to run away and throws down his gun in preparation to run. A will see this and throw down her gun also. B will then realize that if he runs, she will run also, meaning that he will have only a 30% chance of surviving. But he knows that if he stays, he has a 50% chance of surviving. So he should return to his post. But if he sees that A is tempted to run, he should make clear to her through his actions that he will run also, showing her the rationality of remaining at her post with him. So in this situation the contingency of the players' moves makes it impossible for either player to exploit the other, and the cooperative outcome is realized without any contractual exchange of promises. Thus, not all contingent-move PD-like situations require a contract for their solution.

Figure 8.4

Ruler	People	Preferences for outcomes created after the people's second move	
		Ruler	People
Govern according to terms of empowerment	Keep in power	2	1
	Depose	4	3
Ignore terms of empowerment	Depose	3	2
	Keep in power	1	4

Iterated PD Game Situations

In Chapter 2 we introduced this type of situation, distinguishing its game-theoretic features from those of a PD game and showing how a contractual exchange of promises was not required to realize a cooperative outcome. But we can now see that an iterated PD situation is in fact a "non-PD contingent-move game" — one in which the cooperative action is individually rational for both parties. Suppose, for example, that either a simple PD game or a two-move contingent PD-like situation is iterated indefinitely. Because of the iteration, each player always believes that he has the prospect of moving after the other player's move, so that his move will be made contingent on what the other player has done previously. Thus, each of them believes he always has a move in which to "punish" any uncooperative move made by the other player. This threat of punishment makes the completion of an agreement to cooperate in this situation *individually* rational, because each party knows he can be deprived of future benefits by the other party if he does not behave cooperatively on any given play.

Contingent-Move Agency Games

This is the type of game we must understand in order to appreciate the relationship between ruler and people. This kind of game also involves contingent moves, but one player is significantly more powerful than the other player, such that she can (a) move second in the game, where this move can be made contingent on how the other player has moved, and (b) secure her *most preferred outcome*. Whereas in PD or PD-like contingent-move games both players must be content with their second-favorite outcome, in this game, one player will actually be able to secure her favorite outcome.

For example, consider the agency relationship between ruler and people. The people occupy the most-powerful-player position in this sort of game, and the matrix in Figure 8.4 describes it. This set of preferences is *not* the same as the set of preferences found in a prisoner's dilemma. Whereas the ruler's preferences as a kind of "employee" are the same as the preferences of either player in a PD game, the people's preferences as a kind of "employer" are not.[9] As in a PD game, the ruler prefers most the outcome in which the people cooperate (i.e., obey) but she does not, she prefers second the outcome in which both parties cooperate, she prefers third the outcome in which neither party cooperates, and she prefers least the outcome in which she cooperates but the people do not. However, the structure of the people's preferences is importantly different. They most prefer the outcome in which both parties cooperate, they prefer second the outcome in which neither party cooperates, they prefer third the outcome in which the ruler cooperates but they do not, and (symmetrical with her least favorite preference) they prefer least the outcome in which they cooperate but she does not. So, as in a PD game, their least favorite outcome is the one in which they play the "sucker," cooperating even while the ruler does not. But unlike the situation in a PD game, their favorite outcome is universal cooperation, which is much preferred to the outcome that was their favorite in a PD game but ranks third here, namely, the outcome in which they do not cooperate but she does.

The fact that the people's preferences have this structure and the fact that they are to move second in the game give them the power to secure their favorite outcome. To see this, consider how the ruler will reason as the first player to move. She knows that if she rules against their wishes, they will fire her: Their keeping her in power when she rules badly ranks lowest for them, whereas their firing her when she rules badly ranks second highest for them. She also knows that if she rules well, they will keep her employed: Their keeping her employed when she rules well ranks highest for them; their firing her when she rules well ranks second lowest for them. So she has a choice between working hard and staying in power (ranked second) or being lazy and being deposed (ranked last). Therefore, her best move is to work hard. But this is exactly the move by her that will allow the people to secure their favorite outcome. Their preferences and power in this situation have put them in the position of being able to force her to make a first move, which will allow them to achieve their favorite outcome. However, she is not completely powerless in this situation. Because the people need her to rule, she can be assured that her least favorite outcome (i.e., her doing the job and their deposing her) is also one of their least preferred outcomes. So she has enough power over them (at least for the time being) because they need her to secure a desirable outcome for herself (although not her *most* desirable outcome). In fact, in this type of game, each party uses the other's desires to secure a favorable outcome for itself, but the employers are in a position to use the employee's needs to secure the employers' most preferred outcome. Nonetheless, how well the employee needs to work is actually a matter of degree: To stay employed, she must work just well enough to make it more advantageous to the employers to keep her rather than fire her. (So, in the end, the employers will be unlikely to be able to demand and get work from the employee exactly as they would like her to do it.)

The fact that agency agreements have this structure means that, for both players, it is *rational* to keep them! The people do not need the ruler to promise to rule well in order to expect that she will; self-interest is sufficient to motivate her to rule well in

9   In fact, I think this kind of game is standardly involved in employment contracts.

order to avoid being deposed. And the ruler does not need the people's promise not to fire her in order to expect that they will not do so, because their self-interest is sufficient to motivate them to keep a good ruler in power. So, as in any other SI agreement, self-interest alone assures the completion of an agency agreement; no exchange of promises is required for completion, because completion is individually rational for both parties.[10]

In a certain sense, the analysis I have just made of the ruler/subject relationship in this type of theory is not new. Hume was here before me, proposing in the *Treatise* that self-interest is a sufficient explanation for both political allegiance and responsible rulership. Hume disparages the idea that there is any kind of contractual exchange of promises between a ruler and her subjects, presenting the "fallacious contractual argument" as follows:

Since men enter into society, say they, and submit themselves to government, by their free and voluntary consent, they must have in view certain advantages, which they propose to reap from it, and for which they are contented to resign their native liberty. There is, therefore, something mutual engag'd on the part of the magistrate, *viz.* protection and security; and 'tis only by the hope she affords of these advantages, that he can ever persuade men to submit to him. But when instead of protection and security, they meet with tyranny and oppression, they are free'd from their *promises*, (as happens in all conditional contracts) and return to that state of liberty which preceded the institution of government. [III, ii, ix; 1978, 549–50]

This, according to Hume, is a bad argument, because a contract simply means an exchange of promises, and *it is the promissorial relationship between ruler and subject in Lockean-like social contract theories to which he objects.* Not only does he doubt that such promises were ever made historically between ruler and subject; more important, he believes that there is a superior and more natural explanation relying on *self-interest* alone for why people and ruler are right to keep their parts of any agency agreement hiring the ruler:

I shall not take such a compass, in establishing our political duties, as to assert, that men perceive the advantages of government; . . . that this institution requires a promise of obedience; which imposes a moral obligation to a certain degree, but being conditional, ceases to be binding, whenever the other contracting party performs not his part of the engagement. I perceive, that a promise itself arises entirely from human conventions, and is invented with a view to a certain interest. I seek, therefore, some such interest more immediately connected with government, and which may be at once the original motive to its institution, and the source of our obedience to it. This interest I find to consist in the security and protection, which we enjoy in political society, and which we can never attain, when perfectly free and independent. As interest, therefore, is the immediate sanction of government the one can have no longer being than the other; and whenever the civil magistrate carries his oppression so far as to render his authority perfectly intolerable, we are no longer bound to submit to it. The cause ceases; the effect must cease also. [III, ii, ix; 1978, 550–1]

Hume's remarks in this passage show that he senses the correct, non-PD game-theoretic structure of the situation following the institution of a ruler; in particular, he

---

10 Of course, the fear by both parties that the others' preferences might change can prompt them to exchange promises in an attempt to bind each other in the future to actions that they prefer to perform now but that they might not prefer then. But in this case they are essentially treating the situation as a different type of game-theoretic situation, in which the cooperative action is *not* individually rational for the other party.

understands that the conditional structure of the ruler's empowerment makes it in the interest of the ruler to rule well and in the interest of the people to maintain their allegiance to her (assuming she continues to rule well). Thus, Hume dismisses the idea that this self-interested relationship is a kind of contractual relationship, because there is no reliance on promises by either party in this relationship.

Of course, moral incentives generated by contractual promises exchanged between ruler and subject could also motivate each party to keep to the terms of the agency agreement. Hume's point is that an appeal to such promise-generated incentives is unnecessary, not that such an appeal is impossible. As he says in the preceding passage, promises are created by human convention because it is in the people's interest to create them; so if it is in people's interest to use promises to bind themselves to a government, then surely it is already (and immediately) in their interest to make the pledge, without resorting to the use of this "unnecessary shuffle."[11] Moreover, Hume believes that an appeal to moral incentives in this context is potentially harmful, because it might lead us subjects to believe that our ties of obedience are stronger than they really are, such that we obey even very irrational rulers. That is, we might believe that

our moral obligation of duty will not cease, even tho' the natural obligation of interest, which is its cause, has ceas'd; and that men may be bound by *conscience* to submit to a tyrannical government against their own and the public interest. [III, ii, ix; 1978, 551]

Some readers may question whether or not Hume is right to think that the use of contractual promises is theoretically dangerous in this way. But, as I shall discuss in the next chapter, the onus of proof will be on them to show, not only why it is not damaging to insert a contract into a sovereign/subject relationship but also why it is in any way desirable to do so. This issue is, of course, irrelevant for Hobbes, who can explain the subjects' allegiance to their ruler and the ruler's allegiance to the conditions attached to her institution only by using self-interest. And, as Hume appreciated, he can.

There is one other point to make about agency games relevant to Hobbes's argument. In Chapter 6 we discussed briefly Hobbes's contention that "coerced contracts" were no different from any other kind of contract. In that discussion we argued that he was certainly wrong to assimilate these coerced contracts to contracts with a PD structure. However, having analyzed agency agreements, we shall now see that Hobbes would be right to assimilate a coerced contract to this type of agreement. Consider a thief coming upon a traveler on the highway, pulling out a gun, and saying, "Your money or your life." In this situation, the traveler is in the first-move position; the thief has maneuvered himself into the second-move position. Their preferences over the various outcomes that could be created by their moves are shown in Figure 8.5. But note that the preferences of both players are exactly the same as the preferences of the players in the agency game. The thief is in the same position as the employer, and the traveler is in the same position as the employee—the former have both made offers that the latter cannot refuse. Hobbes's assimilation of this type of coercive situation to a

11   Rawls (1971,32) uses this term to describe Hume's attitude toward promising in the social contract.

Figure 8.5

Traveler: move 1	Thief: move 2	Preferences for outcomes following thief's second move	
		Traveler	Thief
Gives money	Doesn't kill	2	1
	Kills	4	3
Withholds money	Kills	3	2
	Doesn't kill	1	4

contractual situation is therefore right to this extent: There is *no structural difference* between such a coerced exchange and an agency agreement. Although I cannot go into this point in any detail here, this structural identity would seem to explain why those philosophers who have attempted to find a structural difference between these types of situations have failed, and it would seem to vindicate those who take a "normative" approach to defining coercion, that is, an approach that regards coercion as an act that violates certain moral norms rather than an act that takes place in a situation structurally different from all legitimate contract situations.[12]

But if there is no significant structural difference between threat situations and agency agreements, why did I argue in Chapter 6 that Hobbes was wrong to maintain that a threat agreement between sovereign and subject would legitimate a regime? My argument in that chapter was that if a sovereign secures power over a subject only by saying to her, "Obey me or be killed" (where the subject has no positive reason to obey this ruler — the *threat alone* supplies her with her incentive for doing so), his reign over that subject is not secure. The subject will obey the sovereign only as long as she fears for her life, and indeed has a motivation to kill the sovereign in order to remove the threat. But having examined the game-theoretic structure of agency and coerced-contract situations, we can now extend and deepen this argument. The central problem with an attempt to legitimate a regime via a coerced contract between sovereign and subject is that such an attempt will mistakenly *reverse* the power relationship between the people and the ruler. Although a ruler may be able to dominate each individual physically in a regime for a while (e.g., until he gets old), he can never physically dominate all of them. Hence, he has power over all of them

---

12 Frank Knight's approach to coercion is a nice example of a normative approach: "We say that the victim of a highwayman is coerced, not because the character of his choice between the alternatives presented is different from any other choice, but because we think the robber does 'wrong' in making the alternatives what they are. . . . Freedom and coercion are ethical categories." (1947, 12) And see recent articles by Cheyney C. Ryan (1980, 481–98) and Mark Fowler (1982, 329–55). Nozick (1969, 440–72) appears to endorse the rival "structural-difference" approach to coercion by presenting what appears to be a non-moral, structural analysis of coercion at the start of an article purporting to define it. But later in that article he resorts to appeals to "the morally expected" or "normally expected" course of events to distinguish between offers and threats.

only to the extent that he can enlist a significant punishment cadre that can give him the "muscle" he needs to dominate the group, and even this cadre will be effective only if it does not have to fight everyone else in society at once, but only a small minority of disobedient subjects at any given time. But this means that the sovereign gets power *from the people;* they are in the employer's position; he is not. So Hobbes simply cannot tell a coherent story that explains the sovereign's empowerment by making reference to his ability to dominate all of the subjects personally unless he makes the sovereign a superman. Of course, to an unreflective subject, it might appear as if the sovereign occupies the position of the thief or the employer, because, after all, the sovereign is the most powerful person in the political community. But such an unreflective subject has, as a Marxist would put it, a "false consciousness," not realizing that the sovereign has that position of power only because a significant percentage of the subjects empower him.

To conclude: We have shown that an agency agreement made between subject-employers and their sovereign-employee can be kept by Hobbesian people because the game-theoretic structure of this agreement is such that both players find it individually rational to keep it.

WHO MAKES THE RULER AN AGENT?

But before we conclude that we have succeeded in incorporating an agency agreement into the fallback position consistent with Hobbes's premises, we must answer a rather obvious question that arises at this point: Who is the principal making the ruler an agent? Surely not any one individual subject. I do not have the power to depose a sovereign by myself; so exactly who has the threat advantage in this agency agreement?

In fact, this question is just another way of expressing a worry that Hobbes himself has about incorporating agency agreements into his argument, that is, With whom does the sovereign make this agency agreement? Given that an individual subject cannot be an employer, the sovereign cannot make this sort of contract with each individual subject. So does this mean that the agency agreement is made with the whole subject population? Hobbes answers this question in the negative. In Chapter 18 of *Leviathan* he rejects out of hand the idea that a contract can be made "with the whole multitude, as one party to the Covenant," because "With the whole, as one party, it is impossible, because as yet they are not one Person." (*Lev*, 18, 4, 89) And, of course, he argues that they become one person only when they are subjugated to a sovereign.

So one of the reasons one might believe that the agency agreement must be excluded from the Hobbesian argument is that this sort of agreement appears to require of the subjects that they form some kind of society (perhaps a society that can be forged only contractually) prior to making the agency agreement with the ruler. Yet one of Hobbes's most powerful political intuitions is that in the state of nature, warfare would be so pervasive that no human society could exist; government, for Hobbes, is a *necessary condition* for the development of a human society. But the agency agreement appears to be inconsistent with this idea insofar as this agreement seems to be between "the people," understood as a single entity or group, and the ruler. And if the inhabitants of the state of nature have to become a society in order to create a government, Hobbes will be caught in a vicious circle, requiring government for the creation of society, but also society for the creation of government.

However, although social activity is required prior to the creation of an agency agreement with the ruler, this activity, when properly understood, is both prepolitical and possible for Hobbesian people to perform. Recall again the argument in Chapter 6 concerning how the sovereign is instituted. In both scenarios given in that chapter, her institution is accomplished when the subjects, by various means, perform (what are perceived as) individually rational actions creating a *convention* among themselves that she will rule over them. Only insofar as this convention exists does the sovereign have the power base enabling her to rule. So the people who establish and maintain this convention are the sovereign's employer. Or, to put it another way, the sovereign is hired by the sum of the individuals whose actions maintain this convention, and the sovereign is fired when these individuals no longer find it rational to act so as to maintain this convention.

This analysis confirms Hobbes's suspicion that an agency agreement requires that the people engage in social activity prior to hiring the ruler, but surely this cannot be, from Hobbes's point of view, a reason for disqualifying the agency agreement, because Hobbes believed that some social activity in the form of making and keeping a "social contract" was necessary in order to select (if not empower) a sovereign ruler from among the population in the state of nature. But our analysis also shows that it is misleading to say that "the people" give the ruler power; on the contrary, her power is the result of a lot of individuals determining, in an interdependent way, that obeying the commands of only this ruler (in particular, her punishment commands) is rational. And "the people" do not withdraw that power from the ruler if her performance is poor; rather, the loss of power is the result of a lot of individuals determining in an interdependent way that such a rebellion is possible and is in their best interest. Indeed, in our initial presentation of the fallback position, we discussed how rebellious activities are a result of calculations made by individuals concerning what is in their best interest, given information about what each other's preferences are in this situation.

Nonetheless, there is this much truth to the idea that "the people" institute and depose rulers: In order for individuals to institute a ruler, *each must coordinate (either explicitly or implicitly) with the others* on who the ruler shall be and how she shall be judged, and in order for individuals to depose a ruler, they must, once again, coordinate (explicitly or implicitly) with one another on the idea that an alternative state of affairs would be better than the present state. The process of empowering or deposing a ruler is *interdependent* because it is a process of creating or undoing a convention solving a coordination problem. Thus, although some "social" activity has to precede the institution of government, Hobbes can show that this coordinating activity does not make the individuals engaged in it *one people;* after the coordinating activities are finished, when it comes time for each to decide whether to make or to break an agency agreement with the ruler, although each individual must take into account the likely beliefs and actions of his fellows, in the end he acts alone.

Let us return to the question of who the sovereign's partner in the agency agreement is. The best way of answering this question is to determine who is in the employer's position in this situation, and the answer is those individuals whose actions maintain the convention that this person is ruler, where this set need not include all the individuals in the commonwealth and where the members of this set can change over time. The sovereign is fired when the empowerment convention dissolves, and this occurs when there are no longer enough members of the set supporting the ruler to maintain the convention. So it is wrong to say either that an individual employs the sovereign or that the group as a unified whole employs her; it is correct to say that she is employed by the set of individuals (the members of which can change over time) whose interdependent but separate actions maintain a convention that this person or institution is the ruler.

Understanding who the ruler's employer is in a commonwealth helps us to understand the surprisingly complex relationships that an individual subject has to his ruler and to his fellow subjects. Recall the structure of the fallback postion: The ruler is created after two different agreements are completed, first, the agreement among the people on who shall be ruler, where this agreement is understood as an SI agreement producing a convention in the community concerning the identity of the ruler, and, second, the agreement between the ruler and the people, where this agreement is understood as an agency agreement. But now we see that those individuals who are participating in the convention-producing SI agreement on the identity of the ruler constitute, in effect, the principal in the agency agreement with that ruler.

Now consider the position of one individual in this commonwealth. Insofar as he is part of the convention-producing SI agreement identifying the sovereign, he is "part" of the principal in the agency agreement. He is not, on his own, the principal — *he* has no power to fire the ruler. But *along with others,* he can; so in this "collective" sense he plays a principal's role. However, he also appreciates that insofar as the convention holds and the ruler is empowered, the ruler is much more powerful than he is by himself, so that he considers himself ruled by this individual (or institution). Indeed, it is important for the cause of peace that the ruler have this controlling power so that she can transform his preferences for outcomes in PD games and in other conflict games by offering him rewards or threatening him with certain negative selective incentives. So the individual can play three roles in the commonwealth:

1. He can be a member of the convention-producing set of subjects who identify the ruler.
2. Insofar as he plays role 1, he and others in this convention-producing set also play (*together*) the principal's role in the agency agreement empowering the ruler.
3. He plays the role of "subject"; that is, he is governed by the ruler, who is empowered by the convention-producing set of subjects.

And note that he need not play role 1 or 2 in order to play role 3. Even if he wants no part of the convention establishing someone as ruler, insofar as that convention exists, he is governed by the ruler as long as he remains in that political community.

The unreflective subject, possibly misled by a false ideology such as the divine-rights doctrine, knows only that he plays role 3 and does not know or believe that he plays (or can play) roles 1 or 2. The task of the contractarian political philosopher is to show him the nature of his role in the ruler's empowerment (i.e., to teach him that he is not only "governed" but also, in a particular sense, "governing" in the commonwealth).

Perhaps the deepest aspect of this analysis is the fact that it reveals subjects to be governed by a ruler only to the extent that this ruler is empowered by those who participate in the convention identifying her. And this means (as Rousseau[13] may have been the first to realize explicitly) that *the individual is actually governed by the convention-producing set of subjects* (of which he may be a member). That is, because each subject is governed by a ruler, who is in turn empowered by a group of subjects, each is governed, in the final analysis, by that group of subjects (a group of which he may well be a member). So the central point of an agency contractarian argument (of which the fallback position is one) is that *we are, in a sense, governed by ourselves,* although this phrase will sound paradoxical unless it is unpacked carefully. Indeed, the contractarian would note that it can take much theoretical work to uncover what is largely hidden from us (probably by ideology) in our daily lives, that is, the way in which we "rule" ourselves.[14]

CAN HOBBESIAN PEOPLE MAINTAIN A CONVENTION EMPOWERING A RULER?

Once we accept this analysis of who the sovereign's partner is in the agency agreement, a third worry arises about incorporating the agency agreement into Hobbes's argument. Can the contentious Hobbesian people cooperate sufficiently to maintain a convention empowering a ruler? We dealt with this question to some extent in Chapter 6, where I was concerned to show that Hobbesian people could and would find it rational to cooperate in the selection of a sovereign (either explicitly in the election story or implicitly in the acquisition story), despite their predilection to war with one another in the state of nature. But if they are to hire a ruler and keep her hired for any significant period of time, there is another way in which these people must cooperate. A person can rule only as long as there is a significant number of subjects who believe that there is large-scale support in the subject population for maintaining the convention empowering her, and this means that a sovereign rules only as long as people are prepared to cooperate with one another to maintain this convention. But do the self-interested concerns of these people make such continued cooperation impossible?

---

13 See Rousseau's *The Social Contract* (1950b), in which he distinguishes, first, the "subjects" (who play role 3), second, the ruler or government, and third, the "sovereign," that is, the "Body Politic," composed of the subjects, which can have no interest contrary to those of the subjects and whose "agent" or "minister" is the government. The sovereign might be interpreted as what I have called the convention-producing set of subjects. See especially Book I, Chapter vii, and Book III, Chapters i and iii.

14 Locke's contractarian argument also matches this analysis of the subject's three roles. Locke's argument incorporates two agreements in exactly the places at which agreements appear in the fallback position, the first of which involves creating a "political community" by the subjects, and the second of which involves creating an agency relationship between that community and the ruler. But in addition to mistaking the agency agreement for an exchange of promises, Locke appears to understand the agreement among the subjects to create the political community as a promissorial contractual exchange (2*T*, 95, 374–5, and sect. 96–9). His language therefore obscures the way in which the ruler's empowerment is best understood as arising out of a convention maintained by the subjects.

We can make this worry more precise by quoting Hobbes, who appears to have believed that this was the main problem preventing the establishment of an agency relationship in a commonwealth filled with people described by Hobbesian psychology:

That he which is made Soveraigne maketh no Covenant with his Subjects before-hand, is manifest; because either he must make it with the whole multitude, as one party to the Covenant; or he must make a severall Covenant with every man. With the whole, as one party, it is impossible; because as yet they are not one Person: and if he make so many severall Covenants as there be men . . . if any one, or more of them, pretend a breach of the Covenant made by the Soveraigne at his Institution; and others, or one other of his Subjects, or himself alone, pretend there was no such breach, there is in this case, no Judge to decide the controversie: it returns therefore to the Sword again; and every man recovereth the right of Protecting himselfe by his own strength, contrary to the designe they had in the Institution. It is therefore in vain to grant Soveraignty by way of precedent Covenant. [*Lev*, 18, 4, 89]

Hobbes is worried that because each subject wants a different ultimate goal (i.e., his *own* self-preservation), they will inevitably disagree with one another about whether or not a ruler is performing well. Each of them will be using a different criterion to make that judgment ("Is she furthering *my* self-preservation?"), and no leader can satisfy all of these criteria at once. The inevitable disagreements these subjects will have concerning how well their sovereign is performing (relative to their different standards of what a "good job" is) cannot be resolved peacefully, and those who believe they are suffering under the sovereign's rule will be motivated to rebel against her in order to replace her with a leader more to their liking.

However, our analysis of what is required to depose a ruler shows that Hobbes is wrong to think that subject dissatisfaction per se will produce revolution. Revolution will occur, of course, when each subject believes that life in a state of nature would be better than life under the sovereign, but it is not difficult for a ruler to reign well enough such that the subjects will find her reign preferable to the state of war. The situation in which revolution will most likely occur is one in which there is a common belief among a significant percentage of the population that the benefits from a change in rulership, considering the dangers involved in rebellion, will be such that an expected-utility calculation will dictate the attempt. So, assuming that the present ruler's reign is better than the state of war, the subjects will be rational to depose a ruler only if they can agree with one another that a different ruler candidate would be a "better buy" in the circumstances and that active opposition to the present ruler to establish this rival in power is rational.

So Hobbes should actually be arguing in Chapter 18 as follows: Hobbesian people's pursuit of different self-regarding goals makes the development of *factions* attempting to empower different rival ruler candidates highly likely; this means that the "turnover" among rulers in this kind of regime will be frequent, so that even if any given coup is successful and a new ruler is established, this new ruler will inevitably be faced with the same rebellious challenge to her regime as the previous ruler, with the result that the community will be plunged into frequent civil wars or else experience an endless succession of coups amounting to a return to the state of nature.

Is this corrected Hobbesian argument right? I want to let Hobbes help to supply the answer. I mentioned earlier that there are signs of the fallback position in the text of *Leviathan*. I now want to discuss passages in the text in which tenets of the position appear, and I shall argue that some of these passages even suggest how subjects can come to cooperate in maintaining a ruler in power.

8.4 THE FALLBACK POSITION IN THE TEXT

It is remarkable that in addition to constructing an argument for absolute sovereignty that we have been at great pains to present in this book, Hobbes also suggests the outlines of an argument for the very different conception of government implicit in the fallback position. In fact, we shall now see that all of those puzzling passages that we discussed in previous chapters and that we suspected should be cut from *Leviathan* actually contain tenets of the fallback position! It is no wonder that many people have been confused by the way in which the notorious Hobbes frequently sounds like Locke in *Leviathan.*[15] Moreover, a careful look at these passages will help us to see how we can show that the fallback position does not suffer from the third problem just discussed; that is, they will show us a way of arguing, consistent with Hobbesian psychology, that an agency commonwealth has a good chance of being stable and peaceful.

Tenet 4 of the fallback position explicitly maintains that a ruler cannot be made "final decider" of whether or not any of her subjects should continue to obey her, which means that she is given power only conditionally. It is an idea that Hobbes is repeatedly at pains to oppose in *Leviathan,* because a ruler who is only conditionally empowered is not an absolute sovereign; she has neither the finality of decision in all areas nor the permanence of power that Hobbes regards as hallmarks of true sovereignty. Nonetheless, I argued in Chapter 7 that tenet 4 is demanded by Hobbes's psychological characterization of human beings. Given that this is so, does Hobbes ever respond to the pressure from that psychological characterization and admit that Hobbesian people can only lend power to their ruler?

There are passages in which he does. Of course, the idea that the ruler's power is only lent to her is implicitly acknowledged in Chapter 21 on the liberty of subjects, especially when Hobbes admits that "When therefore our refusal to obey, frustrates the End for which the Soveraignty was ordained; then there is no Liberty to refuse: otherwise there is." (*Lev,* 21, 15, 112; also see 21, 21, 114) This passage confirms the idea that the subjects retain the right to disobey any sovereign command if they believe that doing so is conducive to their best interests. And as long as this is true, no sovereign can rule as master, but only as an agent of the people, empowered by them through their obedience to her commands to secure their interests, and deposed by them through their disobedience to her commands when they believe their best interests warrant it.

The idea that the sovereign is only lent power is also suggested in Chapter 16 of *Leviathan.* As we discussed earlier in Chapter 5, Hobbes's definition and use of the word 'authorization' in Chapter 16 certainly suggest that we are supposed to take this word in its legal sense, to mean the lending of power from principal to agent.

---

15 Watkins (1965a, 99) jokes that a number of critics have found Hobbes in Locke and Locke in Hobbes, thereby confusing examination candidates forced to "compare and contrast" the two political theorists. In a sense, showing that the fallback position is implicit in *Leviathan,* as well as showing why it is implicit, helps to explain the confusion.

That sense of the word fits badly with the conclusion of the regress argument that an absolute sovereign must be master of her subjects, and it is inconsistent with many passages later in Part II of *Leviathan* in which Hobbes characterizes the institution of the sovereign as involving a surrender of power by the subjects to her. But we now see that the legal sense of 'authorization' fits very nicely indeed with the fallback position, which incorporates the idea that there is an agency relationship between subject and ruler. Although Gauthier was wrong to believe that the appearance of the legal notion of authorization in *Leviathan* signals a deliberate change in Hobbes's official argument for absolute sovereignty, he might well be right to think that this word signals something else that is new in *Leviathan,* namely, the appearance of a *new* political conclusion involving a new relationship between ruler and subject that is inconsistent with the idea that the ruler is absolute sovereign!

However, there is also more subtle and, in some ways, more impressive evidence that Hobbes was forced by his psychological views to endorse this new political conclusion. As we have already discussed, Hobbes argues that "the good of the Soveraign and People, cannot be separated" (*Lev,* 30, 21, 182), and in Chapter 30 he details the kinds of policies that a smart sovereign will institute: for example, administering the same laws and rules of justice to all degrees of people (something that certainly was not occurring in the England of Hobbes's day), levying taxes on all people equally, and punishing only the guilty, for purposes of correction rather than revenge.[16] The program is quite liberal and worthy of many legitimate left-wing radicals of the day. Now why would Hobbes say that it is in the sovereign's best interest to institute these policies? One reason, as we discussed in Chapter 7, is his rather implausible belief that the more prosperous the people, the greater the ruler, and vice versa. But there is a much better reason for the prudence of these sorts of laws. Hobbes admits that the sovereign's rule lasts only as long as she provides for the preservation of the people, where "preservation" must be broadly construed. So the sovereign had better do those things that will generally be in the people's best interest, or else she will be rejected by them as their ruler. There is one passage in *Leviathan* in which Hobbes actually implies this, and it is truly jolting to the reader who has become accustomed to the philosopher's exaltations of absolute sovereignty. The passage discusses the way in which the sovereign has absolute property rights in a commonwealth, including the right to distribute land and possessions to the subjects as she sees fit, but then the philosopher concludes by saying that

seeing the Soveraign . . . is understood to do nothing but in order to the common Peace and Security, this Distribution of lands, is to be understood as done in order to the same: And consequently, whatsoever Distribution he shall make in prejudice thereof, is contrary to the will of every subject, that committed his Peace, and safety to his discretion, and conscience; and therefore by the will of every one of them, *is to be reputed voyd.* [*Lev,* 24, 7, 128; emphasis added]

Here Hobbes is actually inviting the subjects to judge whether or not the sovereign's policies bring them the security they desire, and to render those policies "void" if the decision goes against them. And surely to render a sovereign's policies void involves, at the very least, refusing to obey her commands to carry them out, and perhaps even

16 These policies are discussed in *Leviathan* (30, 15, 180; 30, 17, 181; 30, 23, 182–3).

working to depose her as sovereign. As if fearing his readers would naturally interpret this passage in either or both of these ways, Hobbes quickly follows these remarks with a disclaimer to the effect that no matter how inequitable a sovereign's distribution of land, no subject is right to rebel against or disobey her. But this disclaimer sounds unconvincing, and the passage suggests the very idea we have been looking for, namely, that the subjects should be prepared in the name of furthering their self-preservation to disobey or withdraw power from the sovereign — which means, of course, that she will wield power only as long as they let her wield it.

But in the last section, we mentioned a critical idea that the fallback position had to be able to incorporate if it was to offer a viable political solution to the Hobbesian state of war. In order for a ruler-agent to hold power for any significant length of time, the subject-principals must be able to continue to agree that she remains the "best buy in protection" in the circumstances, and the ruler must be able to know what she must do in order to continue to be perceived by them as the best buy. This means that the subjects must share a set of beliefs about how to judge her performance, such that she will know what *they* will count as acceptable legislation. To the extent that she knows what policies will likely please a great many of them, she will be able to perform as ruler so as to make enough of them believe that continued obedience to her is rational to maintain herself in power. Is there any suggestion in *Leviathan* about what the content of such beliefs will be and how they will be arrived at or developed in a community?

Remarkably enough, there is. Although throughout *Leviathan* Hobbes normally argues, consistent with his support for absolute sovereignty, that laws and policies of the sovereign are 'just' by definition, and should not be judged as either right or wrong or good or bad by the subjects, nonetheless there is a passage in Chapter 30 of *Leviathan* in which Hobbes says precisely the opposite:

By a Good Law, I mean not a Just Law: for no Law can be Unjust. The Law is made by the Soveraign Power, and all that is done by such Power, is warranted, and owned by every one of the people; and that which every man will have so, no man can say is unjust. . . . A good Law is that which is *Needfull,* for the *Good of the People,* and withall *Perspicuous.* [*Lev,* 30, 20, 181–2]

Compare that with this passage from Chapter 18:

[It] is annexed to the Soveraigntie, the whole power of prescribing the Rules, whereby every man may know, what Goods he may enjoy and what Actions he may doe. . . . These Rules of Propriety (or *Meum* and *Tuum*) and of *Good, Evill, Lawfull,* and *Unlawfull* in the actions of Subjects, are the Civill Lawes. [*Lev,* 18, 10, 91]

Whereas in the earlier chapter the sovereign was the sole judge of what was good or bad, in the later chapter Hobbes is admitting that there is a standard for evaluating law *independent of the sovereign.* Although all laws are just, not all laws are good. And because no sovereign legislator is going to say that some of her laws are bad, the judges of the goodness or badness of the laws must be the subjects, and they use, in Hobbes's words, the concept of "the Good of the People" to make that judgment.

What content does the notion of the good of the people have for Hobbes? Recall that Hobbes maintains that if there were some state of affairs that would be mutually advantageous for all people, this would be a "common good," an object that all people would cooperate in pursuing, insofar as it would further everyone's personal goals. In *Leviathan*, he regards peace as such a common good, and an economically prosperous community would seem to be another (*Lev*, 15, 40, 80). Moreover, people in the state of nature are supposed to determine that the means to a peaceful and prosperous community is the institution of an absolute ruler. However, this two-part goal is an objective that all rational people both want and *share;* so it appears to be able to serve as a common concept for evaluating the sovereign's performance.

Nonetheless, would not the subjects disagree about the means that the sovereign should use to create a peaceful and prosperous state? Indeed they could, but this is where Hobbes's laws of nature are relevant to our discussion, as the passage from Chapter 14 quoted earlier suggests. In Chapter 15, Hobbes says that these laws dictate actions that are means to the achievement of "peaceful, sociable and comfortable living" (*Lev*, 15, 40, 80). As we said in Chapter 1, they are *causal laws* — representing scientific discoveries of what actions will effect a peaceful and prosperous community. So it seems he should regard the laws of nature both as appropriate guides to the ruler's legislation and as appropriate standards for *the subjects to use* when determining how well the sovereign is pursuing the good of the people.

But not only does it seem that Hobbes *should* say this; there are passages in *Leviathan* where he very nearly does. For example, when discussing punishment, he maintains that

the Subjects did not give the Soveraign that right [to punish]; but onely in laying down theirs, strengthned him to use his own, as he should think fit, for the preservation of them all: so that it was not given, but left to him, and to him onely; and (*excepting the limits set him by naturall Law*) as entire, as in the condition of meer Nature, and of warre of every one against his neighbour. [*Lev*, 28, 2, 162; emphasis added]

Here Hobbes invokes the natural laws as if they were shared moral guidelines recognized by all human beings that *limit* and *define* the sovereign power. Similarly, he appears to use the laws of nature (and not the sovereign) to define common law when he says that "*Unwritten Customes*, (which in their own nature are an imitation of Law,) by the tacite consent of the Emperour, *in case they be not contrary to the Law of Nature, are very Lawes.*" (*Lev*, 26, 35, 147; last emphasis added)

Even more striking is how Hobbes uses laws eleven and twelve prescribing "equitable" behavior. In Chapter 15 he defines these laws quite vaguely, saying that they enjoin a ruler, first, to judge impartially, second, to ensure that those things that cannot be divided are enjoyed equally, and, third, to give objects capable of division either to the first possessor or to individuals by lot (*Lev*, 15, 23–5, 77–8). We have already quoted a passage (*Lev*, 24, 7, 128) in which Hobbes says that a sovereign's failure to deal equitably with her subjects in the distribution of lands can rightfully be "reputed voyd" by the subjects. And there is another passage in Chapter 30 in which Hobbes makes a similar point:

The safety of the People, requireth further, from him or them that have the Soveraign Power, that Justice be equally administered to all degrees of People; that is, that as well the rich, and mighty, as poor and obscure persons, may be righted of the injuries done them; so as the great, may have no greater hope of impunity when they doe violence, dishonour, or any Injury to the meaner sort, thus when one of these, does the like to one of them: For in this consisteth *Equity: to which, as being a Precept of the Law of Nature, a Soveraign is as much subject, as any of the meanest of his People.* [*Lev*, 30, 15, 180; last emphasis added]

In this remarkable passage, Hobbes actually subjects the sovereign (who is supposed to be above all law) to a "natural law" that the sovereign does not define (a strategy Locke also follows), and Hobbes assumes that the law of equity has a clear enough meaning to allow a subject such as himself to use it in determining whether or not the sovereign's behavior is truly "fair" and acceptable.

This kind of use of a natural law appears once again in a passage in Chapter 26 in which Hobbes criticizes a legal notion current in his day that a man who is charged with a crime and who flees for his life but who is subsequently found innocent must still suffer punishment for having fled. Insisting that this is tantamount to violating the seventh natural law against punishing the innocent, Hobbes declares, "This therefore is no Law of *England.*" (*Lev,* 26, 24, 145) But who is Hobbes, a mere citizen, to be telling the judiciary (which was deputed by his sovereign to use and determine law in court) what is and is not law in England? The rest of this paragraph is similarly remarkable: Attacking those who would decide what is law without allowing the admission of proof to the contrary, Hobbes argues that

For all Judges, *Soveraign and subordinate,* if they refuse to heare Proofe, refuse to do Justice: for though the Sentence be Just, yet the Judges that condemn without hearing the Proofes offered, are *Unjust Judges;* and their Presumption is but Prejudice. [*Lev,* 26, 24, 145; emphasis added]

Here Hobbes is using a law of nature to judge certain procedures as unjust, *even when those procedures are followed by the sovereign.* Yet the sovereign's word and deed are officially supposed to define justice!

So Hobbes is actually under pressure from both his psychological characterizations and his views on ethics to subordinate the ruler to "higher" and "natural" laws while crediting the subjects with the ability and even the right to evaluate the ruler's performance using these laws. According to his psychology, people are concerned to further their self-preservation both inside and outside the commonwealth. In pursuit of this goal, they create the commonwealth, instituting a ruler who can secure for them the common goods of peace and prosperity. But the laws of nature as defined in Chapters 14 and 15 are hypothetical imperatives for achieving this two-part goal. Hobbes espouses these laws because his psychology enables and even forces him to say that the cooperative forms of conduct dictated by these laws are rationally demanded in certain circumstances, given the fact that they effect peace and thus further self-preservation. Because the ruler is supposed to effect peace, her laws and policies should follow or be consistent with these laws of nature. And because people are only rational to subject themselves to a ruler if she can reasonably be said to be pursuing peace, they are rational to use the laws of nature to determine how far she is doing so. But this means that the ruler is not the ultimate source of definitions of 'good' and 'bad,' 'just' and 'unjust'; rather, these laws are! And it means that if the ruler does not act in accordance with these natural laws, it can be rational (depending on a number of other contingencies) not to obey some or all of her commands and perhaps even to depose her.

So the way in which the laws of nature must function for the subjects and the ruler in the commonwealth means that Hobbes cannot be a "moral positivist." Although he can still be a legal positivist by maintaining that something is law only if the ruler commands it, he cannot say that something is a *good* law if and only if the ruler commands it to be so, because not only do the laws of nature give independent meanings to 'good' or 'bad' laws (and maybe even to 'just' laws, given Hobbes's remarks on punishing the innocent), but also the subjects' intentions in instituting the ruler make it rational for them to use only these meanings of the terms, *not* any other meanings that the ruler might give them, in order to evaluate the ruler's performance.

It is interesting to note that in Chapter 26 Hobbes appears to back off from espousing complete moral positivism and contents himself with endorsing only legal positivism, as in the following passage:

> That which I have written in this Treatise, concerning the Morall Vertues, and of their necessity, for the procuring, and maintaining peace, though it bee evident Truth, is not therefore presently Law; but because in all Common-wealths in the world, it is part of Civill Law: For though it be naturally reasonable; yet it is by the Soveraigne Power that it is Law [*Lev*, 26, 22, 143]

In other words, something is law not because it is "reasonable" but because the sovereign commands it, and this position implies that there is a conceptual distinction between what makes something a law and what makes a law good or reasonable. Still, note the peculiar tendency in this passage to maintain that *in fact* all sovereigns have incorporated the laws of nature into their civil codes. There is a similar passage to this effect earlier in Chapter 26: "The Law of Nature, and the Civill Law, contain each other. . . ."(*Lev*, 26, 8, 138) But why should it be true that in fact all rulers have legislated according to these natural laws? Surely the laws are not so vague that *any* legislation counts as an interpretation of them; Hobbes shows what kinds of legislation can naturally be said to violate the laws of equity and the law against punishing the innocent. Moreover, Hobbes cannot say that the civil laws and the laws of nature are conceptually identified, because this would commit him to the natural-law position (i.e., the view that a command cannot be law unless it is just). So, to retain his legal positivism, he must admit that the laws of nature and the civil laws of the commonwealth are conceptually distinct. This means that it is a real possibility (although one he hates to admit) that a civil law can be in violation of a law of nature such that a subject would, prima facie, have a reason not to obey it.

So Hobbes himself provides us with the resources to defend the viability of an agency commonwealth. People's different self-regarding goals need not result in the development of factions supporting different ruler candidates; instead, it is plausible to think that their pursuit of the same common good leads them to use roughly the same criteria to evaluate the ruler's performance and thus to arrive at roughly the same conclusion.[17]

Indeed, in a deep sense, Hobbes's own methodology is forcing him to take this position. Even while claiming that an absolute sovereign must rule by defining 'good' and 'bad,' 'just' and 'unjust,' because there is no "universal reason" that provides

---

17 Note that they need not be said to use these criteria consciously. Hobbesian language consistently represents subject calculation as both conscious and deliberate; however, a modern proponent of the fallback position need not see subject evaluation in this way. It might be much more intuitive and less conscious or deliberate, such that the laws of nature are really a rational reconstruction of the evaluation process.

well-defined and common meanings of these words, Hobbes nonetheless tries to prove that this is so by relying on human reason. As John Dewey has remarked,

Hobbes is in the somewhat paradoxical opinion of holding that while all order proceeds from the unquestioned authority of the sovereign, the permanent and settled institution of sovereignty itself depends upon a recognition of the scientific truths of morals and politics as set forth by him. [1974, 23]

But what Dewey calls paradoxical now appears to be straightforward inconsistency. Hobbes cannot maintain that a sovereign is necessary to "stand in" for the absence of universal reason and moral codes even while arguing that *every person's reason* dictates performing certain cooperative actions (including the selection of a ruler, keeping contracts, being equitable, etc.) in order to achieve a desired goal. The latter argument essentially amounts to an argument for the existence of universal (or at least nearly universal) rational rules, given human beings' universal (or at least nearly universal) self-interested concern to achieve peace. And as we have discussed, these rules (or causal laws) are rules that they would naturally use to evaluate a ruler charged with pursuing this goal.

But perhaps we are being too hasty here. Perhaps, in *Leviathan,* Hobbes is not trying to say that rational rules dictating cooperative conduct do not exist, nor even that the laws have little or no umbra of certainty to receive a common interpretation, but that these laws' penumbra of uncertainty is nonetheless so large that there will be too many occasions on which people cannot agree on the interpretation or application of them, so that *in fact* disagreement and discord rather than agreement and harmony will reign among people who try to use them as common criteria for judging a ruler's performance. On this view, the sovereign is necessary not because we live in a complete moral vacuum but because the moral laws that exist are all too often too vague to receive a common interpretation from us inherently self-interested human beings. Hobbes actually says that (*Lev,* 26, 21, 143), and this is the argument I presented in Chapter 4 on behalf of Hobbes's claim that no rule-based commonwealth could survive for very long, no matter if these rules were constitutionally based or contractually based or the laws of nature themselves. So perhaps we should interpret Hobbes's argument against the viability of the agency commonwealth in this way.

But although Hobbes would be right to argue that violent disagreement among factions over the meaning of these laws certainly would be possible, he still would be wrong to think that the threat of such factional disagreement developing would render all agency commonwealths nonviable. Given that we have shown in Chapter 7 that it is impossible for Hobbesian people to institute a sovereign master, oppposing factions in a regime are left with the choice of either learning how to work with one another to maintain a ruler in power or else not learning this lesson and returning to the state of nature. And given the horrors of the latter state of affairs, wouldn't such education be possible? It might be difficult. Subjects might not want to surrender their self-interested interpretations of the nature of equity or religious truth in the interest of securing peace, but if the alternative was a return to the state of war, couldn't they do so? Although each might like to have his interpretation of the laws prevail, each would much prefer to have the laws interpreted in *some* reasonable way rather than have no agreement on the meaning of these laws whatsoever, with the result that the commonwealth would dissolve. This means that the subjects are in a battle-of-the-sexes dilemma regarding the interpretation of these laws: Although each wants his own interpretation to prevail, the dire consequences of not agreeing on some interpretation should lead rational people to accept, perhaps after much public discussion and infighting and bargaining, a nonfavorite interpretation of these laws in the interest of staying out of the state of war. In other words, arriving at a common interpretation of these laws means developing a *convention* concerning what will count as a reasonable interpretation of them (where this convention can certainly change over time), so that a ruler need not fear challenges to her rule from any of these factions if she legislates according to this interpretation. Note that this convention would develop interdependently: A kind of bargaining would take place, either explicitly or implicitly, among the factions that would, if successful, bring forth a compromise interpretation that would be acceptable to all. (If no explicit bargaining were possible, each faction might search for and accept the "salient" compromise interpretation.) Of course, Hobbesian people are not all rational, and the achievement of a common interpretation of these laws would be just difficult enough that they might not be able to pull it off. However, given its rationality and its short-term advisability, it is certainly plausible to think they *could* do so. Thus, with some help from Hobbes himself, we have solved the third problem associated with replacing the mastery relationship with the agency relationship between ruler and people in Hobbes's political argument. (Indeed, we are on the threshold of a new kind of contractarian argument concerning what the content of legislation in a political society should be. Defining the content of justice by determining what the subjects in a society can all "agree to" is an idea first proposed explicitly by Kant and developed later by such philosophers as Rawls. But it is an idea that is already implicit in the Hobbesian fallback position, because in this view, in order for the subjects to maintain a ruler in power, they must agree *in fact*, either explicitly or implicitly, on the details of a standard by which to judge the ruler's performance, where this standard will influence how a ruler — who is concerned to please her subjects so as to stay in power — will legislate.)

But it is still important to note that there is a good reason why people might fail to reach common agreement on the interpretation of these laws: If one group of people were trying to abuse or exploit one or more other groups of people in the commonwealth, the exploited or abused group would not be rational to give in and accept an interpretation of the laws permitting this exploitation or abuse. (For recent examples, consider South Africa or El Salvador, or Rhodesia before it became Zimbabwe.) *It is an important feature of an agency social contract theory that rebellion is actually justified as rational in certain circumstances.* Indeed, it follows from Hobbes's psychological premisses that no group of subjects should compromise with a faction supporting a ruler when such compromise would produce only a continuation of policies threatening their self-preservation.

In this section, I have not only concluded my argument that the fallback position is consistent with Hobbesian psychological and ethical premisses; I have done so with Hobbes's help. Many passages in *Leviathan* are hostile to Hobbes's main justification for absolute sovereignty but fit nicely into the fallback position. The appearance of these passages suggests that Hobbes was aware at some level that he had serious problems with his "deduction" of absolute sovereignty and needed to alter that argument in subtle but important ways to salvage something like the political conclusions he wanted. Appreciating the Lockean-like position that these passages outline enables us to understand why there has been such controversy over what the political argument in *Leviathan* actually is. It turns out that there are two arguments — inconsistent with one another — in the text. And this means that systematic interpreters are wrong to dismiss warnings from theorists like Warrender that there are disruptive, Lockean-sounding passages occurring frequently in *Leviathan,* although antisystematic interpreters are wrong to take these disruptive passages as evidence for the view that there is no real attempt at a geometric deduction of absolute sovereignty in *Leviathan.* What I have tried to argue in this book is that a systematic approach to Hobbes's argument reveals a sophisticated attempt at a geometric deduction of absolute sovereignty that ultimately fails. Hobbes's premises do not lead to his conclusions; instead, they generate Lockean ideas about government inconsistent with the Hobbesian political conclusion, but ideas that Hobbes naturally "slips into" because of their connections with the initial premises of his argument. In the end, the two camps of interpreters have important lessons to teach one another.

8.5 EVALUATING THE FALLBACK POSITION: HOW LOCKEAN IS IT?

So how satisfactory is the fallback position? It seems to give Hobbes everything he wants: a ruler who is (very nearly) absolute in power, an argument for how the institution of this ruler can further peace, even an argument for why it is in the ruler's best interest to further the best interests of her people. But Hobbes might worry that accepting this position would be tantamount to embracing the central tenets of the political position of his parliamentarian political opponents, whose views were later systematized and espoused by John Locke in *Two Treatises of Government.* But exactly how Lockean is the fallback position?

Consider how a social contract argument putting forward the fallback position would go:

1. Human beings are concerned to preserve themselves and do not lose that concern in a commonwealth.
2. Human self-interest dictates certain "laws of nature" that make cooperation, in principle, rational.
3. Primarily because too many of them reason badly, human beings are unable to cooperate in a state of nature, making it a state of virtual total war (but they are not so contentious that if they were in a commonwealth they would be unable to agree on how well any ruler who might be governing them was doing — see step 5).
4. A ruler with great power is necessary to end the warfare in the state of nature, and he is "lent" power by the people (i.e., they dispose themselves to obey his commands to punish others) on condition that he use this coercive power to further their good.
5. The subjects naturally use the laws of nature to provide a standard for

evaluating how well the ruler is using his power for the subjects' good, and the subjects are able to reach substantial intersubjective agreement (i.e., develop a convention) about *how* these laws are to be interpreted, so that they will be able to agree on how well the ruler is performing using this interpretation of these laws.

6. It is in the ruler's interest to abide by the conditions set by the laws in order not to lose his power; it is in the subjects' interest to continue their loan of power to the ruler as long as he has not violated those conditions, and when he does, it is in their interest to take that power from him.

7. A ruler who is judged by too many of his subjects as not having met the standard in a situation in which this widespread dissatisfaction is common knowledge will likely lose the power he has borrowed from the people.

Except for the explicit connection made between the laws of nature and self-interest, the position just outlined seems remarkably similar to Locke's social contract argument (albeit without any mention of there being a promise between ruler and people). Consider that Locke was one of the loudest advocates of tenet 4 of the fallback position, that is, the idea that the ruler is lent power on condition that he use it to further the good of the people. Repudiating over and over again the idea that there is a master/slave relationship between ruler and subject (e.g., *2T*, 2, 308; all of chap. 5; 85, 365–6), Locke calls the ruler's receipt of power from the people a "trust," which the people have a right to judge:

Here, 'tis like, the common Question will be made, *Who shall be Judge* whether the Prince or Legislative act contrary to their Trust? This, perhaps, ill affected and factious Men may spread amongst the People, when the Prince only makes use of his due Prerogative. To this I reply, *The People shall be Judge;* for who shall be *Judge* whether his Trustee or Deputy act well, and according to the Trust reposed in him, but he who deputes him, and must, by having deputed him have still a Power to discard him, when he fails in his Trust? [*2T*, 240, 476][18]

Moreover, despite his talk of social contract as an exchange of promises between ruler and people (e.g. *2T*, 122, 394), Locke also affirms the fallback position's fifth tenet that self-interest should keep the ruler true to his part of the agency agreement:

this Doctrine of a Power in the People of providing for their safety a-new by a new Legislative, when their Legislators have acted contrary to their trust, by invading their Property, is *the best fence against Rebellion,* and the probabilest means to hinder it . . . the properest way to prevent the evil, is to shew them the danger and injustice of it, who are under the greatest temptation to run into it. [*2T*, 226, 464]

And he maintains that self-interest will also make the subjects good principals, risking rebellion only when the government's performance is seriously abusive and dangerous to them (*2T*, 225, 463–4). Finally, throughout his discussion of revolution in Chapter 19, Locke assumes that the fundamental law of nature will be clear enough

18 J. W. Gough (1973, 164ff.) suggests that Locke may have had a "trust" rather than an "agency" relationship in mind to describe the ruler/subject relationship, given Locke's language in passages such as the foregoing. But Gough eventually rejects this, and I would argue that a trust relationship is not really what Locke meant, in that the subjects, for whom the trust is established, could not be said to *own* the power of their ruler-trustee, making the justification of rebellion against his rule problematic.

that people will know when their ruler has badly violated it (which is tenet 5 of the fallback position). So if Hobbes were to embrace the fallback position, he would be espousing Locke's position on the nature of the ruler/subject relationship and embracing the idea that rebellion is appropriate in certain circumstances.

Hobbes would also be embracing, whether he liked it or not, H. L. A. Hart's position on the nature of law. The agency contract between ruler and people is essentially a way for the people to set up a second-order rule empowering one or more particular individuals to wield power in particular ways. So if one adopts Hobbes's fallback position, the state does not have a human will as the source of law; instead, the state has a second-order rule, accepted by the people as they establish and maintain the government, that defines the first-order rules by reference to one or more political officials who are empowered to make these first-order rules as long as these rules have a certain content. And although Hobbes was reluctant to introduce second-order rules into an analysis of the state because he was convinced that human beings could never come to agree on what these rules meant, the fallback position presupposes that the second-order conventional rule empowering the ruler could come to be commonly interpreted by all factions of subjects such that there would be extensive intersubjective agreement on how well the ruler was adhering to that rule.

However, whereas the fallback position as I have sketched it continues to insist that political power cannot be split among branches of government or among persons, Locke argues that it can be advantageous to a community to split power among persons (2*T*, chapter x), and both he and other theorists influenced by him (e.g., Montesquieu) recognize the possibility of dividing power among branches of government.[19] Is this a real and significant difference between the two positions?

No. Lockeans could argue effectively that Hobbes was pressured by his own psychological views to move in the direction of more Lockean political conclusions. First, a Lockean would be able to argue that if Hobbes accepts the fallback position, he loses his argument against the viability of regimes in which a ruler is subjected to a constitution specifying or limiting how the ruler is to wield power. It is an important tenet of the fallback position that people are able to make and keep either an implicit or explicit agency agreement empowering the ruler, in part because they are able to reach agreement among themselves on how to evaluate the ruler's performance. But such an implicit or explicit contract essentially *limits* what a ruler can do, and if such limits are able to exist in a general way as part of his authorization contract, why can't they also exist explicitly and in detail as part of a constitution? Indeed, there might be advantages for both sovereign and subject in spelling out the kinds of actions that most subjects believe will cause them to withdraw their support; for example, it could

---

19 But Locke is not clearly supportive of this division. Although he says (2*T*, 132, 399–400) that forms of government can be "mixed," and although he gives distinctive and differing powers to the executive and legislative branches of government, he still continues to insist that the legislative branch of government is always "supreme" (e.g., 2*T*, chap. xi), implying that all power is essentially vested in the legislative branch. Montesquieu (1977), on the other hand, explicitly propounds the idea that power can be split among branches of government, in *The Spirit of Laws*, Book XI, Chapter 6, and, ironically, believes this divided system implicit in the English constitution that Locke was supposedly defending in *Two Treatises*.

help to lessen the confusion and controversies that might arise over how well the sovereign is actually doing.

But things get worse. If human beings are able to cooperate to a considerable degree in instituting and maintaining a ruler who is really their "agent" rather than their "Master," why do they need or want to institute *one* ruler with absolute power? Why can't they reach enough agreement among themselves to keep more than one ruler, or an assembly, or a "mixed monarchy" in power? And if a single ruler can be checked in his policies by the knowledge that he will be overthrown if those policies threaten too many people, why can't the same knowledge check a group of rulers or prevent branches of a divided government from invading the jurisdictions of one another — invasions that the people who created this style of government would surely oppose? Finally, if one does not buy Hobbes's claim that the self-interest of the people is more likely to be matched by the self-interest of a monarch rather than by the self-interest of an assembly or mixed group of leaders — indeed, if one thinks (as did Locke) that the *opposite* is true — then there are clear advantages, from the subjects' standpoint, in lending power to a group or to an assembly or to a government with different jurisdictional branches. And if they can cooperate well enough to maintain one person in power under an agency agreement, it would also seem that they could cooperate well enough to keep in power one or more groups who share that political power under contract.

So Lockeans would believe that accepting the fallback position essentially requires *complete* rejection of the regress argument and acceptance of a Lockean position on the variety of regimes that can be viable and effective forms of government, including the form of regime Hobbes opposed most: the "mixed monarchy." Perhaps there might be reasons for thinking that certain forms of limited governments or governments divided in power would be more difficult to sustain than simpler governments with more powerful rulers or with power invested in one man or institution (e.g., Parliament). But it would seem that Hobbes has lost the ground he would need to argue that these governments cannot succeed under any circumstances.

Nonetheless, Locke's political argument and the fallback position do appear to differ substantially on the extent of the government's power. A Lockean contends that a ruler's power should not include the ability to interfere in certain aspects of his subjects' lives (e.g., their religious affairs, certain kinds of economic transactions, certain private activities); in other words, he believes that an agency agreement *ought* to contain certain provisions about what sorts of commands people will not obey such that the ruler will not be understood to have power in those areas. The most famous Lockean exclusion of power concerns private property: "The *Supream Power cannot take from any Man any part of his Property* without his own consent. . . ." (*2T*, 138, 406–7) However, the fallback position maintains that this sort of exclusionary clause would be fatal to the project of securing peace and that *the ruler must have the power (which he may nonetheless choose not to exercise) to command his subjects in any area of their lives.*

Of course, as I suggested earlier in Section 8.2, a Lockean would argue (correctly) that this grant of power is subtly but importantly limited on the fallback position in virtue of the agency relationship between ruler and people. Remember that on this view, a ruler has power only when the people choose to obey his punishment commands. So if the ruler has trouble getting these subjects to enforce a particular command prohibiting or enjoining certain behavior, he is essentially deprived of power to legislate in that area. Thus, Locke would be right to argue that on the fallback position, the correct way of describing the extent of a ruler's power is as follows: *The ruler has the power (which he may nonetheless choose not to exercise) to command his subjects in any area of their lives, as long as enough subjects are willing to obey his punishment commands to make that interference possible.* And a Lockean would also point out that this condition on a ruler's power can make his power considerably less than total.

Nonetheless, insofar as it allows the ruler to engage in all sorts of interference in her subjects' lives, a Lockean would still believe that this grant of power is too great, because this much power is *unnecessary* to secure peace, and, in any case, this much power is *unjust*.

First, he would argue that human beings do not require extensive regulation over their lives in order for cooperation and prosperity to be achieved. Hobbes's argument that such extensive regulation is necessary follows from the shortsightedness account of conflict (supplemented by the glory account). But a Lockean would argue that these accounts cannot plausibly be understood to generate as much conflict as Hobbes requires to justify the institution of a regime with extensive regulatory powers. It is not that a Lockean would regard these accounts as wrong, so much as incomplete: He might agree that the incidence of shortsightedness could indeed be sufficient to promote widespread distrust and noncooperation, but he would also believe that Hobbes makes the mistake of thinking that this shortsightedness is *uncorrectable*. But why should farsighted reasoners despair of ever being able to educate their short-sighted partners? After all, Hobbes himself argues that people in the state of nature can come to learn the advantages of surrendering power to a sovereign in order to achieve peace. And if they can come to learn this, why cannot many, if not all of them, also come to learn that peace and the long-term benefits of cooperation can be secured through cooperative behavior in iterated PD situations? People in the state of nature need not be faced merely with a choice between continuing in a state of war or authorizing a ruler; they would seem to have a desirable third choice — avoiding a radical political solution to the state of war by behaving cooperatively themselves. This would represent a "moral" solution as opposed to a political solution to their warfare, and Hobbes provides no effective argument that people cannot decide to try the former relatively costless solution to their dilemma rather than the very costly political solution. Indeed, given the commitment of the fallback position to the possibility of people learning to cooperate on keeping a ruler in power under contract, Hobbes has good reason *not* to want to insist on the idea that shortsighted people are ineducable, and any modification of that account to allow this educability would, according to a Lockean, also make possible the achievement of peace through the institution of a limited ruler. Thus, a Lockean would believe that the requirements of the fallback position push Hobbes in the direction of the empirical positions that justify only Lockean views on the extent of a good government's power, and it is difficult to see exactly how Hobbes could resist this push.

Of course, to the extent that it seems plausible that not every shortsighted person could learn this moral lesson, a Lockean would have to admit that a mild political solution for the resulting disorder would still be necessary, but he would also have excellent grounds for arguing that this solution need not require the ruler to have the power to interfere in any area of the subjects' lives, but only quite limited power to regulate subject behavior in certain areas. This type of argument against Hobbes's theory is essentially made by Hume in the third book of the *Treatise*. Moreover, if Locke and Hume are right about the power of other-regarding motivations (e.g., those stemming from a fundamental law of nature) in human life, even the truth of the shortsightedness account of conflict as a Hobbesian would sketch it could not establish almost total warfare in that state, because a great many cooperative interactions could and would be successful in virtue of the fact that people would want to benefit their partners. And this would mean, once again, that enough cooperation among people would be possible to make Hobbes's radical political solution unnecessary to secure peace.

However, Locke would also oppose extensive political interference in subjects' lives as not only unnecessary but also unjust, a violation of subjects' *rights*. It is a hallmark of both the Lockean and the Nozickean positions on governmental power that people have a claim-right against interference in certain areas (e.g., in the area of private property) that a government may not violate, no matter what the desirable consequences of such violations. Clearly, Hobbes would and indeed *should* dismiss *this* part of the Lockean view, given his own psychological and ethical views, and maintain that a consequentialist evaluation of the extent of a state's power, given certain empirical facts, is the only moral calculation human beings can or should perform. Nor would his laws of nature preclude in all circumstances the kinds of interferences that Locke and Nozick would want precluded. As I have explicated the fallback position, a ruler can maintain power for as long as he is perceived by enough of the subjects to be furthering their self-preservation that they will maintain him as ruler by convention. This means that there might be circumstances in which he would think it not only desirable but even necessary in order to stay in power that he severely curtail the liberties of a few subjects (who will, of course, be very dissatisfied by his performance) in order to advance the interests of this convention-maintaining majority. Nor will the majority likely feel that the ruler has violated the laws of nature as long as his actions are perceived by them (rightly or wrongly) as furthering their peace and prosperity in the commonwealth. Of course, there are limits on how far that curtailment of liberty may go (if it goes too far, the majority may come to fear the government's power themselves and seek to depose it; and if the affected minority is too large, the government's power will be endangered by their dissatisfaction). But on the fallback position, the ruler is allowed to institute any policy perceived by the convention-producing set of subjects as furthering their self-preservation.

So perhaps the best way of summing up the political conclusion of the fallback position so as to reveal how it differs from the Lockean political conclusion is as follows:

The ruler has the power (which he may nonetheless choose not to exercise) to command his subjects in any area of their lives, as long as enough subjects are willing to obey his punishment commands to make that interference possible; and the subjects are rational to insist that the power of their political regime should be inversely proportional to their ability to restrain their short-term exploitative pursuits in the interest of promoting their long-term self-interest, and inversely proportional to the ability of people outside the regime to restrain their short-term exploitative pursuits against the regime in the long-term interest of maintaining peace.

The more uncooperative people are, and the more violence the subjects must endure from outside the regime, the more interference they must tolerate in their lives by the ruler to achieve peace. And the more cooperative their interactions (both with one another and with outsiders), the less the ruler is warranted in regulating their lives. To put it succinctly, the fallback position insists that *the price of liberty is rational self-restraint*, or, alternatively, *the cost of irrational unrestrained exploitation is government regulation*.

Indeed, a number of other philosophers would agree with this conclusion. Consider John Stuart Mill's contention in *On Liberty* that

> Despotism is a legitimate mode of government in dealing with barbarians, provided the end be their improvement and the means justified by actually effecting that end. Liberty, as a princi-ple, has no application to any state of things anterior to the time when mankind have become capable of being improved by free and equal discussion. Until then, there is nothing for them but implicit obedience to an Akbar or a Charlemagne, if they are so fortunate as to find one. But as soon as mankind have attained the capacity of being guided to their own improvement by conviction or persuasion (a period long since reached in all nations with whom we need here concern ourselves), compulsion, either in the direct form or in that of pains and penalties for noncompliance, is no longer admissable as a means to their own good, and justifiable only for the security of others. [1956a, 14]

The price of liberty, for Mill, is indeed self-restraint, which is made possible by people's ability to behave in a politically mature way, tolerating and participating in free and open discussion, guided by an interest in reaching the truth. Mill and Hobbes would thus agree that liberty should be allowed subjects only when the security of the community allows and/or requires it. Indeed, they might argue that the United States has remained fairly well intact (with only one civil war) for so long with the government officially shackled in these ways only because of luck and the ability of the government to figure out ways of subtly getting around these exclusions when desirable (that is, in the interest of the majority) to do so, especially in times of war (e.g., during the Civil War). So, on this view, the individual holds "trump cards" against the group only as long as it is in the group's interest to let him. We are on the threshold of a utilitarian conception of government and a utilitarian conception of "rights" here.[20]

In the end, it is primarily because of the fact that the moral foundations of the fallback position do not yield Lockean claim-rights that its political conclusion on the legitimate extent of a ruler's power differs from that of Locke. This means that the general question that Hobbes and Mill are answering in a different way from Locke and Nozick is this: What price is it rational (or morally permissible) for human beings to pay for peace? Hobbes seems to say *any* price — except perhaps physiological conversion, and even that may be acceptable. Locke and Nozick essentially say only a rather small price. And these two views represent two points on a spectrum, with physiological conversion at one end and anarchy at the other. It is not at all obvious which position on this spectrum is right, and those theorists who have lived through civil wars might agree with Hobbes that there is almost no price too great to pay to avoid this sort of hell. Nor is this question merely academic in the twentieth century;

---

20 See Mill's discussion of how individual rights are defined within utilitarian theory in Chapter 5 of *Utilitarianism* (1956b, 52–79).

many contemporary societies have had to grapple with it as they have sought to survive violent controversies among their citizens. And many have answered it in ways that Lockeans do not like, but that from the perspective of the fallback position may nonetheless be right.

From these remarks it might seem that the moral foundations of the fallback position give the view a certain "pragmatic" advantage over the Lockean view. But a Lockean would protest that these moral foundations also give it a dangerous "dark side" that should cause us to reject it. There are three aspects of this dark side.

First, as we have already noted, the fallback position not only allows but even supports the abuse of minorities in a regime by the ruler if that abuse is tolerated or approved of by the convention-producing set of citizens who either are unharmed by it or who actively benefit from it.

Second, the advocate of the fallback position would have to regard as rational a certain strategy by a ruler that a Lockean would have the moral resources to combat, namely, the strategy of "taking as much advantage as possible of the ruled people." The extent to which the ruler keeps to any terms of the agency agreement and does what the people want depends on how good they are at supervising him (e.g., how willing they are to rebel, how willing they are to be disobedient generally, and/or how effective they are when they threaten disobedience). But even as an employee who is not adequately supervised by his employer will find it easy (and indeed rational) to take advantage of his boss, so can a ruler find it both easy and rational to take advantage of a lax community of poor political supervisors. Moreover, although the people's poor supervision will not destroy the agency relationship between them and the ruler any more than it destroys this sort of relationship between the lax employer and his employee), it can result in their suffering a considerable amount of damage. Whereas the fallback position would sanction any attempt by a self-interested ruler to increase his power by taking advantage of a people who are poor supervisors, a Lockean political position would have plenty of moral resources to condemn it. The advocate of the fallback position could, of course, exhort a group of subjects not to permit this kind of strategy by the ruler to work, but this advocate would also have to admit that a ruler would be "right" to try it — not *morally* right, as Locke would understand that phrase, but right in the sense of *rational*, as that term is understood in Hobbesian ethics.

The third dark facet of the fallback position is revealed when the equality premiss of that position is realistically modified to accommodate the very real differences in power that technological advances, frequently coupled with psychological manipulation, can give certain individuals. Although Hobbes might be right that, as individuals in the state of nature, we are all roughly equal in power, he can and should acknowledge that gross inequalities in power among individuals can be artificially created through technological and psychological advances. For example, think of the technological inequality between the conquering Spanish, who had horses and guns, and the native inhabitants of Mexico and Central and South America. Or consider the technological and psychological tools that allowed white Americans to enslave blacks in the South. If the technological superiority of one group of people over another is significant enough, that opens up the possibility of *mastery*. The technologically superior group can rule over the inferior group solely through the use of coercion, such that members of the inferior group obey the superior group out of fear for their lives (although ideology and socialization can be used to make the mastered group think its subjection appropriate, or at least inescapable). In virtue of their powerlessness, a mastered people can play little or no role in the convention maintaining the regime in power. Or, to put it another way, the mastered people are disabled by their powerlessness from particpating in an agency relationship with their rulers. They do not hire their rulers; rather, they are enslaved by those who empower these rulers. A regime in which people are governed in this way represents a true "commonwealth by acquisition," but whereas such a regime cannot be expected to survive for very long if the people "acquired" are almost equal to those who conquer them (as I discussed in Chapter 6), loss of equality by virtue of technological inferiority can mean that a conquered people's chances of throwing off this kind of domination are small indeed for as long as technological superiority can be maintained by the mastering group. And note that the fallback position would actually *sanction* such mastery by the conquering group and *encourage* the development of any techniques (e.g., psychological manipulation, the development of ideology, etc.) that could be used by the mastering group to maintain its technological superiority, insofar as mastery can give its members significant economic and security advantages that allow them to further their lives. However, the Lockean position would have the moral resources to find this morally repulsive — a violation of a conquered person's right to freedom. So once again the Lockean would perceive the fallback position as missing a very important kind of moral power.

However, it is not clear that Hobbes would be troubled by the dark side of the fallback position. Instead, given his attacks on agency commonwealths in *Leviathan,* it is more likely that he would be troubled by the position's advocacy of an agency relationship between ruler and people and its legitimation of rebellion in certain circumstances. In developing the fallback position on Hobbes's behalf, I have argued that this conception of the relationship between ruler and subject — which Hobbes explicitly condemns in *Leviathan* — is actually *derived from* Hobbesian psychological and ethical premises. Thus, Hobbes, the philosopher in love with geometry, would seem to be forced to accept it as long as he remains committed to those premises. But is it really true that these premises are what make the Lockean-like conclusions of the fallback position inescapable, or does *the social contract methodology itself* essentially trap Hobbes into espousing a Lockean conception of government, so that no matter how he changes those premises, the contractarian form of argument will deny Hobbes the political conclusions he wants? In Chapter 9 we shall pursue this question, which essentially asks us to consider the nature and power of the contractarian argument itself.

How the Traditional Social Contract Argument Works

Hitherto men have constantly made up for themselves false conceptions about themselves, about what they are and what they ought to be. They have arranged their relationships according to their ideas of God, of normal man, etc. The phantoms of their brains have got out of their hands. They, the creators, have bowed down before their creations. Let us liberate them from the chimeras, the ideas, dogmas, imaginary beings under the yoke of which they have been pining away.

Karl Marx, presenting the Young Hegelians' creed

In the Introduction to this book I claimed that an analysis of Hobbes's argument is not only worthwhile for its own sake but also useful as a tool for understanding the structure and justificatory force of what I call a "traditional" social contract argument, that is, one purporting to justify the *state* (of a certain sort). In this chapter, I want to make good on that claim, first, by exploring what structure this kind of argument must have, such that it can be valid and plausible, and, second, by showing how an argument with this structure actually works as a justification of the state. I will not apply in any detailed way this analysis of the social contract's justificatory force to specific arguments given by members of this tradition, but I will at least attempt a sketch of that application for certain of its major members. Finally, although I cannot attempt here the complicated application of this analysis to twentieth-century contractarian arguments concerned to justify not only the state but also certain moral and political conceptions, nonetheless I will try to suggest how this analysis is relevant to understanding these modern arguments. Here, at last, is some of the contemporary philosophical "payoff" from our historical study of Hobbes.

9.1 CAN A CONSISTENT AND PLAUSIBLE ALIENATION SOCIAL CONTRACT THEORY BE CONSTRUCTED?

In the Introduction, I distinguished between two kinds of (traditional) social contract theories: the kind that explains the state's justification by saying that people *lend* their power to political rulers *on condition* that it be used to satisfy certain of their most important needs, and the kind that explains the state's justification by saying that people *alienate* or give up their power to political rulers in the (mere) *hope* that doing so will satisfy certain of their most important needs. Advocates of the first kind of argument are drawn to an agent/principal understanding of the ruler/subject relationship; advocates of the second kind of argument are espousing a master/slave interpretation of the ruler/subject relationship that precludes legitimate rebellion. But does

Hobbes's failure to construct a valid alienation social contract argument, unless he resorts to outlandish devices to accomplish physiological conversion, show that it is impossible for *any* theorist to construct an alienation argument that is both valid and sound?

Our analysis of Hobbes's argument appears to show that no alienation argument can be valid if it has the same structure as the official argument for absolute sovereignty propounded in *Leviathan*. That argument attempted to incorporate all four of the following propositions:

1. Human beings have a predominant reason governing their actions in the state of nature (i.e., they want above all else to preserve their lives).
2. The state's creation is justified by that reason.
3. Human beings retain the ability to judge and act from this reason in the commonwealth, and it remains unchanged in both character and predominance after the creation of civil society.
4. The state is created when its subjects alienate their power to the absolute sovereign, such that his rule is permanent, and legitimate rebellion is precluded.

The problem is that Hobbes cannot assert both tenet 3 and tenet 4. If the reason for acting that prompted people to institute the state does not go away after they begin living in civil society, which is what tenet 3 says, then the subjects should not obey a law or maintain their ruler in power if doing so would have them act contrary to this reason for acting. Indeed, if their present regime is bad enough, that reason for action may justify them in replacing their present ruler with one who can do the required job better, and this means taking back the power they previously placed in the present ruler's hands. And if there are circumstances in which it is rational for people to take back the power they have given to their ruler, then they have not alienated that power to him as long as they have not alienated the capacity to act from the reason originally justifying the creation of the state. Hence, tenet 3 is not consistent with tenet 4, but only with the conclusion of an agency social contract theory that people can only lend their power to the ruler for as long as he rules in accordance with the reason (given in tenet 3) they had for empowering him.

Therefore, we tried to determine in Chapter 8 whether or not Hobbes could replace tenet 3 with tenet 3′ such that the ruler really would own his subjects and Hobbes's alienation argument would be valid:

3′. Creating the ruler means giving up the capacity to act from this reason, and adopting instead the ruler's standard of rationality.

In this form, tenet 3′ is actually the literal meaning of tenet 4; it says exactly what subjects must do if they want to "alienate" their power to a ruler such that legitimate rebellion will be precluded and the sovereign's rule rendered permanent. Of course, it is not clear that such voluntary conversion is even possible, but aside from this, neither Hobbes nor any other social contract theorist could endorse it, because no theorist could plausibly deny that the cost would always be greater than the increment of benefit attained from conversion, given any number of fellow inhabitants of the state of nature who also convert. And for theorists such as Kant who are committed to human autonomy, it is impossible to sanction under *any* circumstances the destruction of one's freedom to reason privately.

What this analysis shows is that it is not the idiosyncratic details of Hobbes's argument that cause it to fail; it is not, for example, his psychology or even his ethical subjectivism that dooms it. Rather, *it is the structure of the social contract argument itself* that puts pressure not only on Hobbes but also on any other contractarian political theorist to abandon the idea that genuine "alienation" of one's power to the sovereign is justified. Given that they cannot incorporate conversion into their theories, they must construct their arguments by incorporating something like tenet 3, in which case they lose the very political solution for which they were trying to argue. Nonetheless, we have not exhausted every philosophical maneuver available to the clever alienation theorist. If he can establish that the reason one has for creating a state is also a reason that *always* precludes rebellion in *all* circumstances, then he has an argument in which tenets 3 and 4 can be maintained consistently. That is, subjects can be said to be bound unconditionally to the sovereign master even while retaining their ability to act from the reason that prompted them to create such mastery, because that reason simultaneously precludes them from doing anything to free themselves from subjugation.

But what would such a reason be? Kant suggests that it would be a certain kind of *moral* reason, a suggestion that appears in his sketchy but intriguing development of an alienation social contract theory in an essay (1970) designed for popular consumption entitled "On the Common Saying: 'This May Be True in Theory, But It Does Not Apply in Practice' " (originally published in 1793, and hereafter referred to as "Theory and Practice"), some of whose ideas are repeated in Kant's later political work *The Metaphysical Elements of Justice* (1965), originally published in 1797. This argument has been largely ignored by contemporary Kant scholars because of its (to our eyes) unattractive conclusions, and some may even doubt that Kant really meant it at all.[1] Such historical issues do not concern us here; whether or not Kant in his heart of hearts ever really endorsed this argument (perhaps only publicizing it to please his ruler), the argument itself interests us here because of its strategy.

In "Theory and Practice," Kant attacks what he takes to be the Hobbesian position that subjects should convert to the sovereign's standard of reason, calling the resulting regime a "paternalistic government." In such regimes,

the subjects, as immature children who cannot distinguish what is truly useful or harmful to themselves, would be obliged to behave purely passively and to rely upon the judgement of the head of state as to how they *ought* to be happy, and upon his kindness in willing their happiness at all. [1970, 74]

Insisting that such a government is "the greatest conceivable *despotism*" because it destroys individual freedom (1970, 74), Kant goes on to advocate only a "patriotic" government in which "everyone has his inalienable rights, which he cannot give up even if he wishes to, *and about which he is entitled to make his own judgements.*" (1970, 84; emphasis added)

---

1   For those interested in this historical question, Kant's complicated attitude toward the French Revolution is worth studying. See Jacques Droz (1949, 154–71), G. P. Gooch (1920, 160–82), and H. Reiss (1970).

It is important to realize that Kant takes this to be the kind of government that Hobbes advocates; otherwise it would be difficult to see how Kant's own conclusions differ from those of Hobbes, because, far from espousing the subjects' right to limit or control their ruler, Kant maintains that in a patriotic government the people have *no right* to resist or disobey him, so that he is, in effect, their absolute sovereign. Why? The answer lies in the fact that Kant believes that certain moral considerations justify the creation of the state. Although he believes that the state of nature need not be a chaotic state of total war, he still regards it as a state in which there likely would be controversies about what the moral law establishes that would be resolved only by force and violence.[2] He also argues in *The Metaphysical Elements of Justice* that moral rights, such as property rights, are merely "provisional" or "hypothetical" in the state of nature, because they will not be enforced or commonly respected, and that such rights become *real* or *genuine* only when an institution with a monopoly of power (i.e., the state) exists to enforce them (1965, 64–8).

But why can't our rights be enforced by rulers limited in power by constitutional rules or contracts with the people? Kant believes that this sort of regime opens the door to rebellion and thus to moral disorder. Using the Hobbesian regress argument, he insists that only a government with a sovereign ruler who meets Hobbes's criteria can enforce justice, that is, only a government with a ruler who is the final decider and enforcer of all questions in the commonwealth and who rules permanently:

The reason [why rebellion is always wrong] is that the people, under an existing civil constitution, has no longer any right to judge how the constitution would be administered. For if we suppose that it does have this right to judge and that it disagrees with the judgement of the actual head of state, who is to decide which side is right? Neither can act as judge of his own cause. Thus there should have to be another head above the head of state to mediate between the latter and the people, which is self-contradictory. [1970, 81]

Following Hobbes, Kant believes that if people thought they had the right to question or disregard commands of the ruler, their private judgment would clash with the ruler's judgment, creating controversy that could not be resolved by appeal to any higher mediator and that would result in the destruction of individual rights and social harmony. [However, unlike Hobbes, Kant correctly appreciates that the real danger to a contract-based regime will not be from individual disagreement but from the development of *factions* challenging the sovereign's power on the basis that he has broken the contract (1970, 83).] Thus, to prevent the destruction of *moral* order, Kant insists that although private citizens never lose their ability (or even their obligation) to evaluate their ruler's conduct using the moral law, they do not have the right to act on their negative judgments by disobeying or attempting to depose the ruler.

Noxious as this conclusion seems to contemporary readers, Kant even goes so far as to say that the conclusion follows from the *moral law* itself, because the maxim permitting rebellion generates a contradiction. In "Theory and Practice," he argues that rebellion is wrong because "if made into a maxim [it would] make all lawful

2 For example, see Kant (1965, 76–7). However, although he thinks it obvious that such controversies would occur, he seems interestingly reluctant to discuss the ways in which people in the state of nature would find the moral law vague or difficult either to follow or to understand.

constitutions insecure and produce a state of complete lawlessness (*status naturalis*) where all rights cease at least to be effectual." (1970, 82) His point, presumably, is this: Suppose we formulate the maxim

I shall oppose the state, using violence if necessary, whenever I judge, using the moral law, that it is acting unjustly.

Then we universalize it and make it into a law of nature:

It is a law of nature that every person will oppose the state, using violence if necessary, whenever they judge, using the moral law, that it is acting unjustly.

Then the maxim will fail the contradiction-in-conception test of the categorical imperative procedure. In a world defined by this universalized maxim, the state, which by definition is supposed to have a monopoly of force in order to secure justice, would in fact not have a monopoly of force in all circumstances in order to create the conditions of justice; instead, it would have to contend with the violent resistance of any of its subjects who believed they had a right to overrule its decisions whenever they judged it to be acting immorally, and this means that violence, disorder, and the lawlessness of the natural state would remain. For Kant, giving a ruler final authority to enforce justice means relinquishing all right to resist, challenge, or overrule him, in the same way that a group of baseball players' decision to give certain umpires final authority over whether or not a player is out means relinquishing any right to challenge, resist, or overrule them.

Thus, although Kant's alienation argument has the same structure as the official Hobbesian argument in *Leviathan,* the content of Kant's argument is different, because the reason Kant gives for creating the state is supposed to preclude rebellion under *all* circumstances, something that Hobbes's reason for creating the state (i.e., furthering one's self-preservation) cannot do:[3]

1. People have a predominant reason governing their actions in the state of nature. *Contra* Hobbes, this is a moral reason; it is to follow the moral law, and it is "predominant" in the sense that it is always one's authoritative reason for acting, although one does not always or even usually follow it in that state.

2. The state's creation is justified by this reason for acting (i.e., the moral law requires its institution).

---

3 However, in Part III of *Leviathan,* Hobbes does suggest (particularly in Chapter 43) that people have another reason besides self-preservation for obeying the sovereign, namely, obeying the dictates of God (although the reason Hobbes thinks one should obey God is, as I discussed in Chapter 3, because God can grant one eternal *life* if one does, and eternal damnation if one does not). This reason can function in his contract argument in something like the way Kant's reason functions. Indeed, in Chapter 43, Hobbes contends that the highest duty God sets before man is obedience to the earthly sovereign, even when that sovereign is a heretic (e.g., *Lev,* 43, 1–2, 321; 43, 22–3, 330–1). Thus obedience to God appears to be a reason not only to subjugate oneself to a sovereign but to remain subjugated under all circumstances (insofar as this is what God wishes). However, this argument is too strong, because it precludes any legitimate disobedience, even for the sake of self-defense, and perhaps for this reason Hobbes never really pursues it seriously in the course of mounting his contractarian argument in Parts I and II of *Leviathan.*

3. People retain the ability to judge and act from this reason in the common-wealth, and this reason remains unchanged in both character and predominance after the institution of the state.

4. The state is created when its subjects alienate their power to an absolute sovereign — *because the moral reasons named in tenets 1 and 2 justifying its creation also preclude them from opposing it or using force against it.*

So tenet 3 is consistent with tenet 4 because there can be no situation in which our reason for empowering the sovereign can justify disobedience or rebellion. It is not that subjects are slaves because they *cannot* oppose their master (the condition of any subject who converts to the sovereign's standard of rationality); rather, they are slaves because they believe it is their moral duty to act that way. They are not literally "sheeplike"; they only act as if they are sheep, for moral reasons.

But is Kant right that his moral law always precludes rebellion? No. Whereas it is not unreasonable to suppose that the moral law would rule out certain kinds of especially violent insurrections, it does seem unreasonable to suppose that the moral law would rule out any kind of disobedience of one's government. Indeed, Kant himself provides us with an argument to make this point, because he appears to sanction at least *nonviolent disobedience* of unjust laws in the *Critique of Practical Reason* by appealing to the moral law. In the context of a discussion of moral education in Part II ("Methodology of Pure Practical Reason") of that work, he gives as the supreme example of a moral person someone who refuses, for moral reasons, to join in accepting the ruler's execution of an innocent person, even when commanded by the ruler to do so (1956, 159–60). This person therefore judges the commands of his ruler using the same moral reasoning procedure that previously justified that ruler's institution (and that is in no way affected or changed by that institution), and this judgment leads him to oppose the command. That is, if he asked, "What if it were a law of nature that no one in this society would sanction or help to put to death an innocent person?" he would determine that this sort of world would be far preferable to a world in which they would. Indeed, the negation of this maxim would define a world in which everyone would obey the command to put an innocent person to death, and that world is surely one we could not will, so that the negated maxim would seem to fail the "contradiction-in-the-will" test of the categorical imperative procedure.

So even given the notorious vagueness of Kant's moral law, it is not plausibly construed — even by Kant — as precluding all opposition to the state. Whether or not it endorses violent disobedience of the ruler's commands, at the very least it endorses nonviolent disobedience of certain unjust commands. But this means that people do not "alienate" their power to the ruler — a nation full of Gandhis is not a nation full of slaves bound to a sovereign master. This ruler's power would not be absolute, because he would be unable to achieve any result that his subjects (through their refusal to obey his commands) did not help him to achieve, so that he would have the power to command any of his subjects only if they let him hold power by deciding (using the moral law) to obey his commands. Nor could this ruler be said to rule permanently, insofar as the people's refusal to obey his commands might be so extensive that he would essentially be deprived of all power to command, which would amount to deposing him. In the end, Kant's alienation argument fails because he cannot make plausible to us or even to himself (given what he says in the *Critique of Practical Reason*) the idea that obedience to the sovereign is *always* our *highest* moral duty. Consequently, we are left with an argument that fails in precisely the same way that Hobbes's alienation argument failed.

However, if we do consider the question whether or not the moral law can ever sanction violent rebellion, the answer will reasonably be construed to be yes, although Kant's moral test is vague enough that we cannot assert this unequivocally. For example, not trying to oust a regime committed to destroying a significant percentage of the population would seem to commit one to tolerating a moral wrong far greater than the endangerment of individual rights in a state of nature that one's rebellious efforts might create. Although the moral law might well not pass the maxim "Whenever you don't like your regime, rebel against it," because universal action on this maxim would "destroy the whole civil constitution and put an end to the only state in which men can possess rights" (1970, 81), it arguably does pass the maxim "Oppose any state that actively violates a minority's right to live, and replace it with a state that does not, using violence if necessary."[4]

So neither Kant nor Hobbes could come up with a reason for creating a state that was also a reason precluding legitimate rebellion under any circumstances. Hence, for these theorists, *the reason originally justifying that state's creation can become a reason justifying its destruction and replacement by those subjects.* The same can be said about a justification of the state's creation that invokes the desire (or obligation) to obey God. This reason was perhaps the most common one used in the various alienation social contract arguments developed during the Middle Ages. Nonetheless, no theorist who used it in his argument was able to interpret it plausibly so as to rule out legitimate rebellion in all circumstances. For example, although Suarez argues that for religious reasons the transfer of power from the subjects to the ruler in the creation of the state is in fact not a "delegation" but an "alienation," he also insists that when the life of a community of people is seriously threatened by a ruler, their resistance against their ruler is justified in the eyes of God (although if the threat is not serious, they are supposed to suffer in silence).[5] Suarez is thus trapped into trying to use the religious

---

4   Indeed, there is even a passage in *The Metaphysical Elements of Justice* in which Kant comes close to admitting this when he discusses "rebellion for necessity": "the people might have at least some excuse for forcibly bringing [the dethronement of a monarch] about by appealing to the right of necessity (casus necessitatis)." (1965, 87fn.). But note that Kant says that people are only *excused* for rebelling when their lives are endangered, and this still presumably means they can never be *justified* in this rebellious action. Does he mean that the moral law "weakly" sanctions rebellion as permissible in certain instances? Or does he mean that there are certain circumstances in which action from some inclinations (e.g., the desire to preserve one's life) is "allowable"? For Kant to mean the latter would indeed be remarkable, for if he did, then on what grounds are such actions allowable? Certainly not moral grounds. The passage provides evidence that Kant was drawn to an endorsement of rebellion, but found it difficult, in the end, to sanction it. I am indebted to Janine Jones for bringing this remark to my attention.

5   Discussed by Quentin Skinner (1978, 177–8, 183); quoted from Suarez, Volume I (1944, 171). Suarez had both political and religious purposes in mind when he said this; specifically, he wanted to be able to justify the rebellion of the English people against their heretical Protestant monarch.

reason justifying the state's creation to preclude rebellion in all circumstances and yet to justify rebellion in some circumstances. Even Thomas Aquinas falls into this trap when he suggests in *Summa Theologica* that the act of instituting a ruler involves citizens in alienating rather than delegating or lending their rights to the sovereign authority, while nonetheless insisting that subjects have the right to resist a heretical ruler who threatens the life of the community (I–II, Question XCVI, Articles IV–VI; discussed by Skinner 1978, vol. I, 62). It is as if these theorists wished to say, even as Hobbes himself may have been attempting to say, that subjects "alienate their power with a proviso"; but of course one can't "surrender" one's power to a ruler conditionally. One cannot sell oneself into slavery by saying, "I am yours as long as you do *x*." If there are conditions under which I am not yours — where I decide when those conditions are met — then you have never really owned me in the first place. You are only able to do with me what you want when I let you do so, so that I own myself all along and merely allow you (for certain reasons in certain circumstances) to have control over me.

Of course, it is at least *possible* for an alienation social contract theorist to postulate a reason justifying the state's creation that actually does preclude legitimate rebellion under all circumstances, for example, the "desire to be a slave." However, this is not a desire that is common in a human community, nor ought it to be common! So, although it is possible, by postulating this kind of outlandish reason for creating a ruler, to construct a valid alienation social contract argument using tenet 3 that also precludes rebellion, historically no one has done so, because contractarian thinkers have (naturally) wanted to explain and justify the creation of the state on plausible grounds, and the (plausible) reasons they have invoked to justify the state's creation have not been reasonably construable to preclude rebellion under all circumstances. Hence, we have yet to see a *sound* alienation argument that consistently incorporates tenets 3 and 4, and it seems unlikely that we ever shall. For what *plausible* and *legitimate* reason could one have for creating a state that also condemns one for any act of disobedience against it, no matter what the circumstances of that act?

Because we must also reject tenet 3′, the conversion tenet, a *sound* contractarian argument must endorse a plausible version of tenet 3 and hence must endorse the agency relationship between ruler and people that follows from tenet 3 whenever a plausible reason for the state's creation is postulated. It is the contractarian methodology itself, which says that government is created by people for a *reason*, that is putting overwhelming pressure on a theorist to say that a ruler is merely "hired" (not made a permanent master) for this reason. In the end, the methodology is simply trading on a very commonsense idea that even Hobbes, given his remarks in Chapter 21 of *Leviathan*, did not want to deny; namely, that a community of people cannot plausibly be understood to have a reason to sell themselves voluntarily and permanently into slavery.

However, there is perhaps an even deeper reason why this methodology forces any theorist using it to advocate an agency relationship between ruler and people. Consider the fact that tenet 3 of such an argument is naturally implied by an idea to which Hobbes and any traditional social contract theorist are deeply committed, namely, that individuals are not in any intrinsic sense defined or created by the state, but rather create the state, such that they are conceptually prior to it. Using an argument in which pre-state individuals agree to create a state for certain reasons makes sense only to those who oppose the Aristotelian view that the polis is conceptually prior to its citizens. For the traditional contractarian, the state is perceived as our creation, designed to serve us in certain ways. But if it is our creation, then it is extremely unlikely that we should, given our individualistic interests and the private reasons governing our actions, alienate our power to it. This would mean giving up our roles as its creators and maintainers, surrendering, as it were, our conceptual priority, and it does not seem that there is any reason a group of individuals could have to want to do this. Indeed, for any social contract theorist, the state's justification for each individual derives from a reason intrinsic to that human being's nature that the state has had no role in creating. Were the state to destroy somehow the individual's ability to act on that reason, it would destroy something essential to the very humanity of that person, and a destruction of something so fundamental to one's nature is not something any human being could plausibly be said to want.

This is not to say that it is impossible to offer a justification for the ruler/subject relationship as a master/slave relationship. There are anticontractarian methods of argument, three in particular, that could plausibly justify (as long as one accepts the assumptions of these methodologies) this relationship between ruler and people. First, consider Socrates' justification in the *Crito* of unconditional obedience to the state using the idea that it is conceptually prior to us, such that we are its "children" and its "slaves" [Plato 1956, 61–2 (50e–51c)]. Whereas Hobbes makes the people anterior to the state (which is explained as their creation), the Socratic argument makes the state conceptually prior to its subjects: People do not create the state's mastery; that mastery exists naturally insofar as the people are the *state's* creations. Socrates concludes, given this relationship, that these subject-slaves are not allowed to rebel against or destroy their government. Second, consider the ruler/subject relationship following from the divine-rights justification of the state. So long as the ruler is understood to hold power because he has been given it by God, the subjects are totally subordinated to him as God's representative on earth, insofar as they are totally subordinated to God. So the ruler is God's agent, not our agent; God is his principal. (However, the subjects do have the right of rebellion against their sovereign master if God withdraws power from the ruler because God perceives the ruler to be an unworthy agent.) Finally, there is the argument for mastery that Hobbes is most concerned to refute: the "Aristotelian" argument that some people (presumably, in the seventeenth century, the aristocracy) are so naturally superior to others that they have the power to rule over the inferior group. And natural slaves can no more be said to have the right to rebel against their natural masters than dogs or cows can be said to have a right to throw off the shackles of human ownership.

These forms of argument are, of course, unpalatable to twentieth-century thinkers, but that is not the point. The point is that although the relationship that Hobbes wanted to establish between ruler and people cannot be established by a contractarian methodology, it can be argued for using these noncontractarian methodologies. But note why these forms of argument work better than the contractarian approach: They *assume* the ruler's mastery over the subjects. Their arguments are designed to *reveal* us as mastered (by the community, or by God, or by other superior human beings); they are not designed to show why we should choose to be mastered.

Indeed, the futility of trying theoretically to establish mastery when it is not supposed to exist naturally was recognized by Hobbes's contemporary right-wing critics, such as Robert Filmer, who laments, of Hobbes's social contract theory,

I consent with him about the Rights of exercising government, but I cannot agree to his meanes of acquiring it . . . [I] praise his building, and yet mislike his Foundation. [1652, pref.]

Did Hobbes himself ever suspect that Filmer was right? Interestingly enough, we can find one passage in *De Homine,* a book written late in his life, that suggests dissatisfaction and even repudiation of the contractarian methodology in *Leviathan*. In the last chapter of this book, entitled "On Artificial Man," Hobbes begins by repeating the idea developed in *Leviathan* that the sovereign has been authorized to act in the name of his subjects. In this discussion it seems clear that Hobbes regards authorization to be an action establishing an agency relationship between two parties. He writes:

he is called the author, that hath declared himself responsible for the action done by another according to his will: and he that is called the *author* with regard to actions is called the *owner* with regard to possessions. Hence they are said to have authority that act by right of another. [*DH*, XV, 2, 84]

Now clearly we would expect Hobbes to go on to identify the author of the sovereign's powers as the people, just as he did in *Leviathan*. But he does not. Who is the sovereign's author? God!

all kings and supreme governors of any kind of states whatsoever bear the person of God, if they acknowledge God as ruler. [*DH*, XV, 3, 85]

Here Hobbes sets up an agency relationship between God and the sovereign; the former is the principal, and the latter is the agent. So, in this paragraph, written late in his life, we see him tentatively abandoning the contractarian methodology and appealing in an oblique and obscure way to the sovereign's "divine title" to rule, making it appear that he was aware, at some level, of what Robert Filmer knew, namely, that the social contract method fails to provide a theoretical foundation for absolute sovereignty. Hence, it is doubtful that Hobbes would accept the fallback position developed in the last chapter. If he were faced with a choice between embracing absolute sovereignty and embracing the social contract methodology — which can be used to justify the political conclusions of the fallback position but not absolute sovereignty — this passage provides evidence that, at least late in his life, Hobbes would continue to affirm absolute sovereignty, but throw out the flawed contractarian geometric deduction for it.

There are many fascinating historical questions that this analysis of the contractarian defense raises. For example: Why were people such as Hobbes attracted to the contractarian methodology, given that it made it virtually impossible for them to establish the political conclusion they wanted? Perhaps a better and deeper historical question to ask is this: Why were theorists such as Hobbes, Suarez, and Kant so afraid of the agency implications of the social contract methodology, denying those implications in a way that made their theories invalid in a fairly obvious way? I leave this for historians of political theory to answer, but I will suggest one possible reply. Perhaps these theorists regarded the regimes of their time as precarious because of the childishness and irrationality of their subjects. Perhaps they feared not only to promulgate but even to admit what the social contract methodology pressures any practitioner of it to admit: that in the end, the only "political masters" subjects have are themselves.[6]

9.2 The Justificational and Explanatory Force of Agency Social Contract Arguments

Having established in the preceding section that alienation social contract arguments cannot be soundly constructed, I want to turn now to a consideration of how agency contract arguments, when they are validly and plausibly structured, have explanatory and justificational power for those of us who are born into existing political societies.

As David Gauthier has pointed out (1979a, 11–13), there have been, in general, four ways in which social contract arguments have been interpreted, such that they can be taken to legitimate civil society,[7] but all of these interpretations are problematic. First, this form of argument might be thought to legitimate the state by providing a historical account of government's creation. On this view, social contract theorists are claiming, first, that an original contract among the people to be ruled and/or between ruler and the people (or both) took place at the start of any political regime and, second, that the contractual promises made by any subject's political ancestors at that time continue to bind the subject today. But if this is how the social contract story is supposed to work, it can be dismissed not only as a historically inaccurate account of almost every government's creation but also (even where it *might* be thought to be historically accurate) as a bad account of the source of the political allegiance owed to the state by any of the present-day descendants of the original contractors. How can our ancestors plausibly be supposed to have had the power to bind *us* to the state by *their* promises?

A second way of construing this form of argument is to say that it makes an explicit contractual promise (to the people and/or to the ruler) the source of any person's allegiance to government, where that is true not only of the original contractors but also of present-day citizens. Locke sometimes talks as though this is the point of his social contract in the *Second Treatise*. But although this interpretation explains how not only our ancestors but also we are bound to a government, it still seems false as an explanation of the past and present allegiances of countless men and women to their governments, who can remember making no such promise. As Hume wryly observes,

were you to ask the far greatest part of the nation, whether they had ever consented to the authority of their rulers, or promis'd to obey them, they wou'd be inclin'd to think very

---

6 Kant suggests that this was his reason for denying the legitimacy of rebellion under any circumstances: "If the people were to hold that they were justified in using violence against a constitution, however defective it might be, and against the supreme authority, they would be supposing that they had a right to put violence as the supreme prescriptive act of legislation in the place of *every* right and law." (1965, 140; emphasis added)

7 My understanding of these four interpretations is sometimes different from Gauthier's, and my analysis of the problems plaguing each interpretation is frequently dissimilar. This is particularly true of what he and I call the "hypothetical" interpretation, which Gauthier appears to endorse, but which I will argue is at least as problematic as the other three ways. I am also indebted to Alan Nelson for discussions of the explanatory foundation of the social contract argument.

strangely of you, and wou'd certainly reply, that the affair depended not on their consent but that they were born to such obedience. [*Treatise*, III, II, viii; 1978, 548]

Given that in recorded history few people have actually made anything like a binding promise to obey their governments, either to their rulers or to one another, this understanding of the social contract's justificational force would seem to render the argument practically worthless as a *general* justification for the source of a government's authority over its citizens.

But following up a remark made by Locke (2*T*, 119, 392–3), the social contract form of argument might be construed as establishing that one's allegiance to government can be purchased via tacit as well as explicit consent. But what is tacit consent? Philosophers have generally regarded it as the acceptance of benefits from the regime: If one takes benefits from one's political society, the assumption is that one has tacitly consented to it [Plato 1956, 61–2 (50e–51c); Locke 2*T*, 119, 392–3; Gauthier 1979a, 12; Rawls 1971, 118; Hart 1961, 85ff.]. But how well tacit consent, understood in this way, can *bind* people to their government is open to question. As Nozick has argued,

the fact that we partially are "social products" in that we benefit from current patterns and forms created by the multitudinous actions of a long string of long-forgotten people . . . does not create in us a general floating debt which the current society can collect and use as it will. [1974, 90–5]

But even if this obligation as a result of accepting benefits could be supposed to exist, it would seem to rob the social contract argument of any power to make "free consent" the source of one's allegiance to government. After all, if a general floating debt to government can be said to exist because one accepts benefits from it, then each individual would seem to have the choice between accepting the benefits conferred by the government, and thus being bound to it, or refusing the benefits and emigrating.[8] They would appear *not* to have, as a legitimate option, the possibility of accepting the benefits but nonetheless deposing the ruler should they decide his policies are oppressive. Rather than providing an interpretation of the social contract argument, this way of construing its consent talk seems to be an attack on the kind of allegiance to government which that argument aims to justify. Thus, it is no accident that Socrates uses this notion of tacit consent to argue against the legitimacy of rebellion in the *Crito* [Plato 1956, 61–2 (52)].

The failure to explain the justificatory power of social contract arguments by interpreting their contracts as historical facts (in which people consent to governments either explicitly or tacitly) has caused a number of philosophers to entertain the idea that the contract or contracts in this sort of argument are only "hypothetical" and are not meant to be historically descriptive. On this view, the point of the social contract story is not to give any dubious history lessons but to justify the state in terms of what rational people in a state of nature would agree to in a situation of relative equality. Moreover, arguments in which hypothetical contracts figure have become popular in the twentieth century, especially after the publication of John Rawls's *A Theory of Justice*. But without wishing to take any stand at this time on whether or not

8   Gauthier's discussion of tacit consent also suggests this criticism (1979a, 12–13).

it makes sense for Rawls to invoke a hypothetical agreement in his discussion of conceptions of justice, I do want to question whether or not it makes sense to say that traditional social contract theorists such as Hobbes and Locke have done so. These theorists were interested, among other things, in explaining the subjects' allegiance to government, and if their stories of states of nature and social contracting are not true, then how can these fairy tales explain the extent and nature of real people's *actual* obligations to obey their government? If I have actually made a contract with someone, then I am bound to perform what the contract requires. But if someone tells me a story in which hypothetical people make hypothetical contracts, how does that story have any effect on what I am *bound* to do? In the words of one legal theorist: "A hypothetical contract is not merely a pale form of an actual contract; it is no contract at all." (Dworkin 1976, 18)

Perhaps more seriously, even if one could explain the relevance of the hypothetical story to the real political world, the social contracts within that story render the argument at best problematic and at worst invalid. As we saw in our analysis of Hobbes's argument, one of the most important sources of chaos and violence in the state of nature is the failure of people in that state to keep contractual promises. And if government must be created because, among other things, people are unable to keep their contractual promises in the state of nature, how can they be expected to keep their promises in a social contract, either among themselves or with a ruler? Theorists such as Locke, who do not believe that people in the state of nature are completely incapable of completing contracts, do not face quite so severe a problem in explaining how a social contract can be kept, but their contract talk is still problematic. The more people who are able to complete contracts in the state of nature, the more stable and effective the government created by contract will be, but the less justification there will be for a government in the first place—and hence for the social contract creating it. And the more people there are who cannot keep their contractual promises, the greater the need for government and the social contract creating it, but the less likely there will be enough people in the community who will keep it, and hence the more likely the government created by the contract will be unstable or ineffective. So theorists such as Locke have to walk a tightrope, attempting to argue that because there are so many people who *cannot* keep contracts, government is necessary, but that there are enough people who *can* keep contracts to make the creation of government by contract possible. It is not clear that Locke or any social contract theorist can walk that tightrope successfully.

From this review of the competing interpretations of the justificational strategy of contractarianism, we can now better formulate our bafflement over its justificational force: How can it offer a real justification for any existing state if its account of how existing states are created and maintained is simply false? If states really were brought into existence and maintained by contracts, then one could understand how the social contract theorist's justification of political allegiance was built on to his contractual explanation of it. But usually states are not created by contract, and so understanding the justificational *point* of the nonexplanatory contract talk becomes difficult.

Yet what is so very odd about the social contract form of argument is that despite the confusion about how the argument works, one still seems to "feel" that it has justificational force when one is exposed to it. In this section I will try to explain and place on rational ground this "feeling" that the social contract form of argument has justificational force. But to do so, I must show that, appearances to the contrary, the argument offers a plausible *explanation* of how states are created and maintained on which its justificatory point is built. But how, the reader might wonder, can I hope to do that? Surely I cannot seriously contend that states have been created and maintained by contract! I cannot and will not. Instead, I will argue that the social contract argument should not be understood to imply that any literal contract, or even literal agreement, exists in actual political societies. Nonetheless, understood in its (nonliteral) way, its contention that a state's existence depends on the right social agreements offers a plausible explanation of what the state is and how it exists.

I will contend that the social contract argument is designed as a certain kind of *rational reconstruction* of the state *with historical import*. As Hobbes might say (*DC, EW* ii, pref., xiv), the social contract theorist figuratively takes the state apart and (rationally) puts it back together again in order to explain the structure of any *existing* state and to determine whether or not it is justified. That rational reconstruction can be presented as follows:

The social contract argument is designed

1. to explain the state as an entity whose origination and continued existence are the responsibilities of human beings (henceforth, I shall use the terms 'create' and 'maintain' to refer to the human activities resulting in the state's origination and continued existence, but, as we shall see, these terms should not be interpreted to mean that there is a *conscious intention* to make or preserve the state in the human beings who are responsible for its existence),
2. to show why human beings are justified in creating and maintaining a state,
3. to show (using 2) what kind of state they are justified in creating and maintaining,
4. to explain (using 1) what human activity brings the state into existence and what human activity maintains it,
5. to show, by giving the explanation in tenet 4, what is the actual relationship between any ruler and those subjugated to him, and
6. to show, using the relationship in tenet 5 and the reason for its creation (tenet 2), that rebellion is justified within any existing state in certain circumstances.

In the rest of this section, my task will be to show exactly how the contractarian performs this joint explanatory and justificational task.

In order to understand how the contractarian's rational reconstruction of the state works, let us start by listing the central features of the contractarian form of argument. There are three:

A state of nature. People are imagined to live in a world without government, and it is to escape the chaos of such a world that they create government.
Agreements among the people. Agreements take place among the people who wish to create a commonwealth in order to escape the state of nature. These agreements resolve the following issues: first, what form of government to have; second, who the rulers should be and how they should be chosen;

third, who should perform enforcement and punishment functions for the ruler.

An agency relationship between the people and the ruler. There is an agency relationship between the people and the ruler in which the people "hire" the ruler (by obeying him and thereby empowering him) for as long as he uses his power to further (better than any feasible alternative) their aims in accepting subjugation; this relationship is described by contractarians as effected by an "agreement" between two parties. Although alienation theorists such as Hobbes have tried to deny that this agency relationship does or should exist, I argued in Section 9.1 that such a relationship must be part of any social contract theory (including Hobbes's own) in which a plausible reason for accepting political subjugation is attributed to the people.

Understanding both the explanatory force and justificatory force of the social contract argument hinges on understanding the role each of these central components of the argument plays. First, consider talk of "states of nature." In contrast to philosophers such as Socrates and Aristotle, the social contract theorist believes it makes sense to think of individuals as conceptually prior to the political systems in which they live, and to this extent the contractarian is an individualist. To use the terminology I introduced in Chapter 1, the contractarian presupposes that none of the intrinsic features of human beings (i.e., those features that establish us as human) are *politically* created. Whether or not they are socially created is another matter; the contractarian need not take the extreme Hobbesian position that *all* intrinsic features are pre-societal as well as pre-political. Indeed, these theorists claim that the existence of any political system is the result of certain activities performed by the individuals who live in that system.

But historically the contractarians' individualism has gone deeper. Their justification of the state has depended on the idea that both our capacity to behave wrongly and our capacity to do (and know) what is right are neither socially created nor subject in any significant way to manipulation. In the traditional social contract argument, people's failure to behave cooperatively is presented as natural, rather than as socially created, and incurable through social manipulation. It is a given in the state of nature, a failure that people can hope to control and minimize (rather than cure) only through the institution of the state. But what holds true of the people in the state of nature is also supposed to hold true of us. Indeed, they are meant to be us stripped of our political clothing and much, if not all, of our social clothing (*Lev*, 13, 11, 63).[9] Hence, their remedy for war is also our remedy, because our propensity to act wrongly, like theirs, has not been created or substantially affected by our society.

Unless the contractarian takes this individualist position, his justification of the state is problematic. If, for example, our propensity to act wrongly can be remedied by our society, then why isn't the state justified only as a useful but temporary "tutor" — indeed, one we may already have outgrown? On the other hand, if our society is instrumental in making us selfish and violently competitive, whereas we

9   Pufendorf tries to make the same point (1934, 154–5, 164).

would not be so "naturally," why shouldn't we create institutions to prevent that development (rather than deal with its results), keeping the state in the meantime only if it does not encourage what we are trying to prevent? On either view, we would want the state to "wither away." Perhaps a plausible contractarian position could be developed that would see human conflict as an entirely social product, but something that no change in social interaction could prevent and no other social institution could remedy. No such theory has yet been offered.

It is in large part because Rousseau believed that our social and political life can and does profoundly affect how we behave (either for good or for ill) that it becomes problematic to say, despite the wealth of contractarian language and ideas in his works, that he used the contractarian argument to justify the state.[10] Moreover, the contractarian strategy is consciously eschewed by any Marxist, who regards human nature as in large part a social creation, powerfully influenced by life in a political regime (which is itself a function of the underlying economic structure). For a Marxist theorist, the selfish and harmful ways in which we "state-affected" people would behave outside the state are not traceable to any nature intrinsic within us, but to a "false" nature that has been created by the economic, social, and political structures in which we live, structures that the contractarian is mistakenly assuming to be intrinsic.[11] And the state is hardly an indispensable institution for the maintenance of peace and order if it is partly implicated in the fact that we would behave selfishly and violently without it.[12]

Having established a need for the state, the contractarian uses his state-of-nature story to insist that we have an authoritative reason for meeting that need; that reason is self-interested for Hobbes, and moral for Locke and Kant. But for all three, it is a reason that we are supposed to have "naturally" (i.e., in a state of nature), not one that we can have only after living in political society. The contractarian takes this position because he wants to justify the state as *freely* chosen, not chosen because our choice is essentially "rigged" by a political society that creates in us the very reason we use to choose it and that appears to justify its existence. The contractarian's concern to make our political choices "autonomous," to use Kant's word, necessitates that those choices be reflective of our real (moral or self-interested) nature, not a "false" nature created for us by a (possibly corrupt) political society. Although nothing prohibits the contractarian from basing that choice on a reason that is reflective of a "real nature" that is inherently social, traditional contractarians have located this moral (or self-interested) choice in a moral (or self-interested) nature that is in no way

---

10 See Gauthier's dicussion of this point (1977, 139). See also Rousseau's discussion of the transformative power of civil society, either for good or for ill, in *The Social Contract,* Book I, Chapter viii, and Book II, Chapter vii (1950b, 18–19, 38ff.).

11 Thus, C. B. Macpherson describes the Hobbesian state of nature as a model of "bourgeois market society" (1977, 23, 61); also see my discussion of his argument in Chapter 1, Section 1.2.

12 Marx himself wanted no part of the rhetoric of contractarianism; see his discussion of it in "On the Jewish Question," reprinted in McLellan (1977, 39–62, esp. 52ff.). Note that in this work (page 56) Marx quotes Rousseau (1950b, 38–9) on the transformative power of civil society.

defined by society nor dependent on it for its deveopment. The traditional contractarians' individualist position about the source of good human choice neatly matches their individualist position about the source of bad human choice, but it is not strictly necessary for the argument to work, because a choice reflective of a real but inherently social nature would still be a natural choice (i.e., one reflective of our nature), not one rigged by the institution to be justified, making it a "free" choice in the sense required. Only if one believes that, as Aristotle said, we are "inherently political beings" by nature must one reject the contractarian methodology, viewing it as attempting to sheer off something constitutive of what we are and making it an object of choice.

But the contractarian is expressly opposed to any theory of the state that would see it as natural rather than as a product of human choice, and this explains the nature of his commitment to human equality. As we discussed in Chapter 1, when Hobbes and Locke call people in the state of nature equal, they are trying to make the point that whatever differences in ability or strength differentiate them, these differences have no political significance (e.g., $2T$, 54, 356). No one is so superior mentally or physically as to be able to rule over everyone else without their cooperation. There are no natural masters and no natural slaves; so rulers must be chosen, because they do not arise naturally. This is a critical premiss of any social contract theory that seeks to explain political power and political subordination as something *nonnatural*, something created by human beings and maintained with their consent.

So, the first two tenets of what I earlier claimed was the justificational and explanatory structure of the social contract argument can now be fleshed out.

A traditional social contract argument for the state is designed as follows:

1. By asking us to imagine people equal to one another in a prepolitical state of nature, it presupposes that the state is a human creation that has no effect on their intrinsic nature as human beings, and it presents human beings as naturally (and inevitably) conflict-prone in that state.
2. It shows why human beings are justified in creating and maintaining the state. It relies on the conception of human nature in tenet 1 to argue that rational people (described by this conception) have a certain compelling reason (either self-interested or other-interested or a combination of both) for leaving the state of nature by creating government, where that reason is (or should be) *our* reason either for creating government if one does not exist or for maintaining it in power if it does.

Of course, these theorists have disagreed with one another concerning what this reason for creating and maintaining the state is. Hobbes argues that it is self-interested in nature, whereas Locke and Kant have argued that this reason is moral. Moreover, as we saw in Chapter 8, disagreements about what reason we have for creating the state result in disagreements about the *kind* of government we have reason to create. For Hobbes, our self-interested reason for creating the state means that we need to institute one with extraordinary power; for Locke, our moral reason for creating the state means that we need (indeed, must insist on) a state whose power is strictly limited. Hence, the third tenet of our explanation of the justificatory power of the contractarian argument goes as follows:

3. The reason given in tenet 2 for creating the state constrains the *kind* of state we should create or maintain (i.e., it tells us what kind of state is a justified political regime).

It is because contractarians' conceptions of the person differ that their descriptions of the state of nature differ, and this partially explains why the reasons they invoke to justify the state's creation differ, and why the structures of the states they advocate differ. Those states that did not serve that purpose or have that structure would still be called states by a positivist social contract theorist, albeit "unjustified" or "bad" states, whereas a natural-law theorist would most likely reserve the word 'state' to describe only power structures that do serve the purposes justifying their creation. Clearly, there is plenty of room for disagreement among practitioners of this methodology; nonetheless, despite their differences in starting points and terminology, the fundamental strategy used in their arguments for justifying political regimes (of whatever sort) is the same for all.

Those who use the hypothetical interpretation of the contractarian strategy are therefore correct that the argument is not meant as a historical account of how actual states were created; instead, it is meant, at least in part, as a rational reconstruction of the state's creation designed to expose the reasons why creating a state (of a certain sort) is justified. Nonetheless, the first three "historical" interpretations of the contractarian methodology are right that this rational reconstruction is meant to have some explanatory import regarding actual states.

One historical implication of the argument should be obvious. As we have said, when the contractarian tells us why it is rational to create government, he is assuming that any existing state was in fact created and is maintained by the people who were or are subject to it, even if it was created or is maintained by them for the wrong reasons. Social contract theorists, using their equality assumption, reject the idea that any government is "naturally" present in the world because of the natural inferiority of one group or individual to another group or individual, and they reject the idea that governments are fashioned by God. Instead, governments are explained as (to use Hume's terminology) "artificial" institutions, fashioned by those who are subject to them. Contractarians are not saying that this is the way the state *ought* to be understood; they are saying that this is a *fact* about any state that has existed or will exist on this earth.

But do people who do not even think that their governments have been created and/or maintained by them nonetheless create or maintain them unwittingly? The contractarian's explanation of how government is fashioned allows him to answer this last question with a yes. States are created and maintained, on this view, when people "consent" to a certain ruler or institution, where this consent is manifested by their obedience to his punishment commands. Of course, people might consent to and obey a ruler for the wrong reasons, reasons that might actually obscure the fact that it is their consent that empowers him; they might, for example, obey a ruler because they believe him to be a god. But it is still, according to the contractarian, their consent to his status as ruler that gives him political authority, not his so-called divine status.

But apart from its manifestation in the world as obedience to the ruler's commands, what is the nature of this consent of the people that creates and maintains the state?

This is the question that contractarians have tended to answer badly, obscuring the nature of their methodology and confusing twentieth-century philosophers attracted to it. They have tended to imply or treat this consent as promissorial contractual consent: In the story they offer of government's creation, subjects are generally described as promising, either to one another or to the ruler or both, to obey the ruler in exchange for certain advantages. This interpretation of consent quite rightly brought ridicule from Hume, and the ridiculousness of this account of how actual citizens come to be bound by their governments through consent is dangerous to the argument: How can a contractarian explain states as *in fact* created entities when the creative activity is one that it seems virtually no subject has ever performed in fact? And how does this interpretation of consent even fit within their rational reconstruction of the state, insofar as it seems difficult if not impossible to argue that because people cannot keep contracts without government, they must create government by keeping a contract?

But this promissorial interpretation of consent is neither necessary nor desirable to adopt in our understanding of how the contractarian argument works. True, people in the state of nature must resolve disagreements among themselves concerning what kind of government to have and who should rule within it, but they can resolve this two-part leadership-selection problem, as we saw in Chapter 6, by generating a convention that, once generated, is rational for them to follow given their interest in having some person or institution to rule them. Nor do they have to *intend* to generate that convention in order for it to be generated. As our Nozickean-like acquisition story of leadership selection in Chapter 6 showed, an invisible-hand process in which individuals do not have such an intention but nonetheless act rationally over a period of time can explain the generation of a leadership convention in the long term. Nozick is not any less of a contractarian because he uses in his argument a story in which the empowerment convention is not generated by an explicit agreement; indeed, his successful use of a nonagreement story simply points up the fact that creating a government involves the generation of a conventional solution to the leadership-selection problem — even as David Lewis's invisible-hand explanation of language-creation points up the fact that creating a language involves generating linguistic conventions.[13]

However, the term 'consent' means more than participating in the convention solving the leadership-selection problem; it also means empowering the leader selected. Does a contractarian need to resort to a social contract argument to explain empowerment? Again, he does not. As we saw in Chapter 6, he need only point to the fact that empowerment comes from *the people's obedience to the ruler's punishment commands,* where that means either not actively interfering in such commands or actively assisting the ruler in carrying them out. It is rational for subjects to perform the first action as a result of their participation in the leadership convention. And whereas individuals might perform the latter action only if the ruler offered incentives to them designed

---

13   This remark is made by W. V. Quine in a foreword to Lewis (1969, xi). I am disagreeing with Lewis's own view that the agreements in social contract arguments are different from conventions in that they require the ability of people to act in a collectively rational but individually irrational way.

to get them to play this role, there is no necessity that there be a *societal* contract among all the subjects, nor between the ruler and all of the subjects, to produce this empowerment, but only agreements between the ruler and certain subjects who will constitute the police force. Moreover, even these agreements need be cemented only by self-interest.

Although a variety of stories explaining the generation of the leadership convention resulting in subject obedience to the ruler might be suitable to include in the contractarian argument in order to explain the origination of any existing state, not every possible way of explaining how these conventions are produced is suited to fulfilling the contractarian's *justificatory* purposes. Given that this theorist wants to reveal, through his argument, the reasons why people *should* create a government of a certain sort (as opposed to why they have done so), he needs to invoke a story that uses within it the interests he believes justify government creation. Reasons for empowering leaders such as "wanting to make him ruler because he is God" or "obeying her because she is naturally superior to me" do not count as rational reasons for empowerment, although *in fact* they may have been people's reasons for creating or maintaining a past or present political regime. Thus, the contractarian, while explaining how any existing state is a human creation and how it is a product of human convention, must leave behind history and posit a process of state creation that will reveal what reasons make that creation *rational*.

Moreover, the particular interest that is responsible for the state's creation in these stories (an interest that might be self-regarding or other-regarding) helps us to cash out Locke's intuitive idea that a ruler can receive his power from a people who "tacitly consent" to his rule. This tacit consent is not best understood as an implied promise from the subjects following their acceptance of benefits, but as the subjects' participation in the convention empowering the ruler because of their perception that it is in their interest to do so.

However, creating a language via the convention is in one way importantly different from creating a government via convention: The latter, but not the former, results in the production of an agency relationship in which the people who empower the ruler are essentially his "hirers." The traditional contractarian standardly describes this relationship as resulting from a contractual exchange of promises. But as our analysis in Chapter 8 showed, the game-theoretic structure of the situation is such that no promise need be involved either in creating or in cementing that relationship. The interest that a people have in empowering the ruler causes them to maintain in power a ruler whose performance furthers that interest, and it is the interest that the ruler has in holding that power that causes him to wield it in a way consistent with the people's expectations of how his rule should proceed.

How is this relationship effected? It is natural for a contractarian (e.g., an advocate of the fallback position) to claim that it is effected by an (SI) *agreement* between ruler and people in which the latter give the ruler their obedience — and hence power over them — in exchange for his using that power to serve their needs. But, oddly enough, *an agreement is not necessary for the establishment of that relationship.* Even if the ruler and the people never make such an agreement, an agency relationship, perhaps unacknowledged by one or both of them, still exists simply in virtue of the *way* the ruler receives power. For example, a people who decide to regard a certain person as their queen because they believe she is divine, and thus obey her, are in fact empowering her through their obedience as a result of their interdependent acceptance of her as leader. The fact that they did not know that it was their *obedience following their participation in a leadership convention* that empowered her, not her divinity, might be greatly to her advantage; in particular, it might give her more security of reign, because her subjects would not see that they in fact have the ability (indeed, perhaps even the right) to fire her if her performance as ruler is poor. Nonetheless, in virtue of how she gets her power, the agency relationship still exists, so that if the people discover it, they will be able to play their proper role as principal. (Compare people who believe that their language came from God.) Indeed, the reason why a contractarian says that the agency relationship between ruler and people is effected by an *agreement* is to communicate the idea that actual people in actual states should be *aware* of the relationship that exists between them and the ruler and should see themselves as the ruler's employer (even if no literal agency agreement ever took place between them) so that they can control and supervise the ruler to their advantage.

Therefore, regarding the ruler/subject relationship, each of the four traditional interpretations of the social contract argument is partly right and partly wrong. The hypothetical interpretation is right that no explicit agency agreement is assumed by the contractarian to have taken place between ruler and people in any actual political regime in order to explain the nature and extent of subject allegiance to the ruler. The (noncontractual) agency agreement in this story is supposed to illuminate their relationship and need not have taken place historically in order for that relationship to exist. Once the people and the ruler come to understand the nature of that relationship, they will naturally "read into" the situation an agreement creating it, but the relationship still exists whether or not such an agreement ever took place, and whether or not the subjects and the ruler even know of it. But this analysis also shows that the three historical interpretations of the social contract argument are right to suggest that the existence of this agency relationship in any existing regime is what the argument is meant to reveal. "Even if you cannot literally be said to have made an agency agreement with your ruler," says the contractarian, "you must think of yourselves as the principal in an agency relationship with the ruler in virtue of how and why the ruler receives power from your interdependent actions of obedience." Hence, even if most of the world's population should explain why they obey their governments by saying "because I'm born to it," or "because God says I must," or "because the ruler owns me," the contractarian will nonetheless insist that his agency analysis explicates the *real* nature of their relationship with the ruler. Or, to put it another way, the contractarian argument is designed to unravel the "mystery" behind any actual ruler's power. To use the language of Marx quoted at the beginning of this chapter, it is designed to teach subjects not to "bow down before their creations." Is it any wonder that the kings and queens of Europe during the sixteenth and seventeenth centuries much preferred the divine-rights theory of the state to the contractarian view?

So tenets 4 and 5 of our account of the justificational force of the contractarian structure go as follows:

4. The state is revealed as an institution created and maintained by the people through their participation in certain conventions designating one or more of their number as leaders with certain powers, where that participation is rational if it is done for the reason given in tenet 2. The details of the creation of these conventions are not historically relevant, but instead serve justificatory interests.

5. In virtue of how government is created there is an agency relationship between ruler and people, and that relationship is spoken of as effected by an "agreement" between the two parties in order to convey to both of them that the relationship exists and thus to get them to play their roles in this relationship properly.

However, one important reason why the agency contractarian is interested in exposing the structure of the state and the nature of the ruler/subject relationship is that he has a sixth and final justificatory interest: He wants to argue for the legitimacy of rebellion in certain circumstances. It is this aspect of the argument that alienation theorists want to deny, but that I argued in the first section of this chapter they could not deny if they affirmed tenets 1 through 4 and posited a plausible reason for the state's creation. To say that a ruler is empowered by the people for a specific reason is, as we discussed, also to imply that he can be fired by them when his performance does not justify continued empowerment according to that reason. Hence, the final aspect of the justificatory strategy of the social contract argument goes as follows:

6. Insofar as the state is created by the people when they empower a ruler in the process described in tenet 4, such that there is an agency relationship between him and them, the people are justified in deposing him (or in limiting his enforcement powers) if they determine that his ruling policies are contrary to the reason (given in tenet 2) that justified his empowerment.

Together, these six tenets outline the explanatory and justificatory strategy of the social contract argument.[14]

However, there is an important reason why one might question whether or not the contractarian explanation of the structure of the state implicit in this analysis should be taken as definitive of what *all* political societies *are,* as opposed to what they *ought* to be. Contractarians such as Hobbes and Locke standardly assume that people in the state of nature are roughly equal; as I discussed, this reflects their attack on the Aristotelian idea that political subordination is somehow inherent in nature. However, even if there is no *natural* mastery of some people by others, it is true that historically people have been able to master others through superior technology (e.g., weaponry, frequently buttressed by psychological or socialization techniques). This

---

14 However, in this outline I have not given a complete analysis of the contract argument's justificatory strategy. More needs to be said about the argument's position on how the state has the moral authority to command or punish. In certain respects this is an issue that Hobbes chooses to ignore; hence, I have not explored it in this chapter (although I shall do so elsewhere). For a discussion of the issue itself, as well as a proposal for dealing with it, see G. E. M. Anscombe (1981, 136).

mastery does not fit the contractarian's picture of the structure of political subordination, but it is not the violence inherent in such mastery that is at odds with the analysis. In our reconstruction in Chapter 6 of the Hobbesian commonwealth-by-acquisition story, violence did not result in the creation of a master, but only in the selection of a ruler whose power was still dependent on his subjects' decisions to obey his punishment commands. And this means there was still an agency relationship between that ruler and his subjects. But a mastered people are disabled technologically (and perhaps psychologically) from playing any such supervisory role. In this type of regime, the power relationship between the ruler and the people is the reverse of the relationship in an agency commonwealth. To use the matrices in Figures 8.4 and 8.5, the subjugated are still players in a contingent-move agency game, but here they are not in the second-move position, but rather in the less powerful first-move position. So rather than having the power to coerce their ruler, the people are coerced by him (and his supporters).

Hence, there are really two forms of domination that our discussion has revealed: the domination of a master, and the domination of a "hired" protection agency. The contractarian story, which presupposes equality, results in the creation of only the second form of domination. But if, as seems true in the real world, equality cannot be presupposed because of technological (if not natural) superiority, then mastery can (and does) exist.

How should the contractarian describe this form of domination? Because I have presented the contractarian's "hired-protection-agency" form of domination as the contractarian's only conception of political domination, dominations of mastery would seem not to qualify as states at all. This is not to say that, in the contractarian view, a regime in which mastery exists cannot be a political regime. Consider that, given human frailty, no ruler can hope to master people by himself; he needs supporters to do so, and this means there must be an agency relationship between him and his supporters. Thus, the power relationship within the ruling clique fits the contractarian's agency analysis of a political regime. However, consider the relationship between the ruling clique and the people it masters: Should this form of domination be considered political? If it is, the contractarian's agency analysis of the state applies only to some extant political entities, although most contractarians will insist that political entities *ought* to match it.

However, it is not clear that the contractarians must make this concession. Our linguistic practices suggest that mastery is not considered by us to be a genuine political relationship: The blacks mastered by white South Africans and the West Bank Arabs conquered by the Israelis are not considered citizens of the countries in which they reside, making their subordination something that is *outside of* these political regimes. Moreover, the contractarian has available to him an argument justifying this linguistic practice. Consider Locke's description of mastery as a continuation of the state of war between the master and the enslaved people (2T, 16–17, 319–20). This domination is something into which the enslaved are coerced; they obey their master only because there are tools that force them to do so. Remove the tools and you remove the reasons they have for obedience. Hence, mastery is only as lasting as the tools that establish it. And although it is true that sometimes these tools can prevail for a considerable period, the subordination they effect is inherently unstable, because it is unwanted. Genuine peace, not only for Locke but also for Hobbes, is attained only when the reasons for warfare are destroyed. And given (as we have seen in this book) that it is irrational to destroy those reasons by destroying one's ability to deliberate freely about how to pursue one's best interest, those reasons can be destroyed only by creating a government that not only has the power to effect cooperation among people but also is tied to the people's wishes. I will have no need to fight my fellows if the conditions for cooperating with them are created by my ruler, and neither I nor my fellows will have the desire to fight this ruler if he is bringing about these conditions that I and my fellows wish.

Still, these arguments give normative reasons for denying mastery the status of a state, and if Hobbes's remarks on commonwealths by acquisitions are interpreted as remarks about mastery rather than remarks about violent methods of generating leadership conventions, then he is one contractarian who wants to avoid even this normative implication of the contractarian argument. Moreover, denying mastery the status of a state seems to make a political regime something of an ideal, for even in a society that boasts an agency relationship between people and ruler, the ruler generally tries to use certain techniques of mastery to limit the supervisory role that the people can play in these regimes. For example, because changing a ruler in a political society involves changing a convention, people can be inhibited from doing so if the exchange of information necessary for changing the convention is made difficult. It is no accident that in the Soviet Union there are restrictions on travel, on the possession of typewriters and copying equipment, and even on access to private telephone numbers. But regardless of whether or not such a regime qualifies as a state, contractarians (including the advocate of the fallback position) would insist that the people in such regimes have good reason to destroy the tools that prevent them from playing that role fully; to this extent, the agency analysis of the nature of political society has (and was meant by such theorists as Locke to have) normative power.

To conclude: If my analysis of the contractarian form of argument is correct, the name 'social contract' for this type of argument is unfortunate, given that it misleads one into thinking the user of the argument is invoking hypothetical or real contractual exchanges of promises in order to explain and justify the state. If I had my way, I would want to change the name of this argument to 'social convention theory.' But the term 'social contract' has assumed a life of its own, and I shall not be so revisionistic as to throw out the term. Suffice it to say that the term should not be allowed to mislead anyone about the real nature and role of the agreements in this type of argument.

9.3 DISSOLVING THE PARADOX OF BEING GOVERNED

There is one piece of the justificational puzzle concerning how contractarian arguments work that is still missing. As we have seen, both from my discussion in Chapters 4 and 5 of certain seventeenth-century theorists' reactions to contractarian arguments and from the discussion in Section 9.1 of Kant's reasons for endorsing the regress argument, the conception of the state implicit in the agency contractarian argument has struck many philosophers as disturbingly paradoxical, prompting them either to reject this type of argument or to attempt to mount an elaborate alienation argument to avoid it. I want to consider now what this paradox is, why it arises, and whether or not it can be dissolved.

Recall Philip Hunton's dilemma, previously discussed in Chapter 5. Hunton was a political liberal of his day, a supporter of Parliament and an opponent of Hobbes; yet he had trouble conceiving of political rulership in anything but master/slave terms. He argues that the people give their ruler power by contract. But who should judge whether or not the ruler is keeping to the terms of that contract? Hunton notes that it cannot be the people, for otherwise they would have power over their master insofar as this would give them the right to evaluate and "fire" him, leading to dissension and civil strife. But he also insists that it cannot be the ruler either, because one could never expect him to give judgment against himself using these rules, and thus any contractual restrictions on the use of his power would be meaningless. Accordingly, Hunton concludes that *no one* should judge whether or not a ruler is abusing his power! Caught between a rock and a hard place, Hunton just seems to give up.

Kant would insist that Hunton's dilemma is caused by his implicit adoption of the agency contractarian perspective on the state, that is, a perspective in which people are seen as "subjecting themselves" to a ruler via an agency contract, which they have a right to interpret and which gives them the power to fire a ruler they believe to be violating that contract. In his own statement of the regress argument, Kant rejects this idea as inconsistent. How can people create a ruler if they reserve the right to govern her themselves? A baseball umpire cannot really be said to officiate in any game in which the players reserve the right to void his decisions; so how can a ruler be expected to "officiate" in the political realm when her so-called subjects have the power (and indeed claim the right) to void her commands if they choose to do so? Moreover, there is at least one contemporary contractarian theorist, James Buchanan, who agrees with Kant that there is something paradoxical about a contractarian conception of a political regime. Buchanan believes that people empower a ruler to control them, while nonetheless claiming the right to control the ruler, and he calls this situation "the paradox of being governed":

Man's universal thirst for freedom is a fact of history, and his ubiquitous reluctance to "be governed" insures that his putative masters, who are also men, face never-ending threats of rebellion against and disobedience to any rules that attempt to direct and order individual behavior. [1975, 92]

But the paradox of living under a master whom the people believe they have both the power and right to master themselves is not a benign paradox for Kant, but involves straightforward inconsistency.

Nonetheless, Kant, Hunton, and Buchanan are mistaken; I shall now attempt to explain why there is nothing paradoxical or inconsistent about understanding governments as "hired" by the people who are subjugated to them, although I shall also try to discuss why it would be natural for someone to make the mistake of thinking that there was a paradox in this conception of government.

Let me begin by relating the history of the solution to another nasty paradox, known as the liar's paradox. Consider the sentence, "This sentence is false." The sentence cannot be true when it tells us it is false; but if it is false, then given the assertion it is making, it would seem to be true. Tarski resolved this paradox by employing what I will call a "stratification" solution. He claimed that we can distinguish two kinds of language, an *object* language and a *meta* language, where the meta language can be used to talk about the object language but is not itself part of that language. Provided that predicates such as 'is true' and 'is false' are understood to belong only to the meta language, the paradox can be avoided, because sentences that are themselves false can nonetheless be talked about and thus can be consistently described as true or false *within the meta language.* That is, the meta-language assertion that the object-language sentence is false can itself be true or false, where this leads to no inconsistency.

Tarski's stratification solution of the liar's paradox can provide a useful analogy enabling us to solve the contractarian's paradox of being governed. According to the contractarian, we should distinguish between two kinds of political realms in a state that involve two very different kinds of "governing" judgments. There is the *object realm,* in which there are *object judgments* — which we call "laws" — and which are made only by the ruler in her role as governor of the people: these judgments involve decisions concerning what those individuals subjugated to her can and cannot do, how they should be punished if they violate her prohibitions, how they can make a will, and so forth. But there is also a *meta realm* in which *meta judgments* are made by the people who are participating (or who could participate) in the convention giving the ruler power. Whereas individuals act according to object judgments but do not make object judgments (i.e., they act according to laws but do not define laws) concerning what they can and cannot do within a commonwealth, they do make meta judgments, that is, judgments about the ruler's object judgments. In particular, they determine to what degree the ruler in her legislation has adhered to the terms of her institution. Whereas the ruler makes the law by promulgating orders backed by threats or constructing power-conferring rules, the subjects make meta legal judgments about the ruler's law; in particular, they determine whether or not the laws are so bad that they should be voided, or, at the extreme, whether or not the ruler should lose power.

This stratification solution to the contractarian paradox of being governed can be clarified, once again, by using our handy baseball analogy. Suppose a group of people decide to play a baseball game on some Sunday afternoon and empower a few of their number to act as umpires. Whereas the players' role *in* the game involves adhering to the decisions of the officials *within* the game, the players also have an "extragame" role not defined by the rules of baseball, namely, the role of judging the appropriateness of the umpires' applications of the rules of baseball in the game and firing the umpires or perhaps voiding particular rulings not in accordance with the rules. Moreover, they can perform these functions not because they have this role *within* the game — no such role is defined by the baseball rules — but because they have this role "outside the game" insofar as they are the game's creators. The game they are playing is organized by them — it is *their game* — and umpires have power in the game only because the players have given them (and continue to give them) that power.

But according to the contractarian, a government should be understood as "the people's game." I do not mean to treat legal systems frivolously by calling them "games"; I intend that usage to indicate, in a broad sense, "purposive activity created for and by human beings." The crux of the social contract theorist's conception of the state is that *the state is our game.*" Although we have certain roles within the state game that are defined by the rules of that game (rules that we may have had a hand in formulating), in the end we can also play another game — a meta game — of creating, changing, or temporarily suspending the (object) game through convention-producing, convention-changing, or convention-destroying activity with our fellow subjects. In other words, as creators and maintainers of government, we are involved in a "game about a game." "Remember," says the social contract theorist, "that as a result of playing a certain kind of 'convention-producing' meta game, the state is your creation. Don't think once it is created that therefore it is an unalterable and permanent power structure to which you are subjugated. It remains your game, because the ruler can hold power only as long as enough of you play the meta game together with your fellow subjects so as to empower her, and you can change that ruler or in certain ways alter how she governs if, in the meta game, you are able to work together to dissolve or threaten the convention that gives her power." Another way to put this theorist's point is to think about what the contractarian conception of political authority is: A ruler has authority to govern only because she is granted that authority by the people she is governing, who, acting as a group, empower her via a convention. Thus, political authority, insofar as it is something created by convention, can be dissolved by convention; and the creation and dissolution of the empowerment convention is therefore activity *outside of* the legal system that this activity creates or destroys.

But how, Kant or Hobbes might want to know, can the state survive for any length of time if it has this structure? Won't the people's power to void the game that they create mean that it will be unstable or quickly collapse? Shouldn't people try to create a state that they are nonetheless incapable of voiding? The agency contractarian's answer is that they should not and need not: The commonwealth game cannot be dissolved or suspended unless the convention empowering the government in that regime collapses. And this convention will not collapse if there are only a few disgruntled citizens; rather, for the convention to collapse there must be many disgruntled citizens, among whom it is common knowledge that they are seriously disgruntled, who agree on a preferable alternative and who have the common belief that revolution is worth the risk. Moreover, they must not be so technologically or psychologically mastered that they cannot mount effective resistance to the regime's supporters. Locke was very aware of, and indeed appreciative of, these kinds of constraints on rebellion, because they allowed him to argue persuasively that the agency contract argument was not a covert appeal for anarchy (2*T*, 208–9, 452–3; see also sec. 223 and 225).

But what is perhaps most remarkable about this contractarian conception of the state is that something like the notion of sovereignty can, *in a certain sense,* be incorporated into this conception! Suppose one talks only about the object game in a political society and ignores the meta game played by the subjects in that society. In the object game there will be something akin to Austin's and Hobbes's sovereign. That is, there will be a person, or a group of persons, or a set of persons with different jurisdictions, constituting the *terminus ultimus* of the object legal system, and this ruler or group of rulers will have final power to make and enforce law in the regime and will be the power that people habitually obey. But contractarians and, for that matter, Hart will argue that one cannot end one's analysis here. Although these rulers have final lawmaking and enforcement power within the object game, this power is created and maintained by the people for reasons that the contractarian will try to specify. Because the rulers' power is created, they rule only because they have been empowered by convention to rule, or, to put it another way, they govern because there are what Hart would call rules of recognition, which the contractarian interprets as conventions created and maintained by the subjects — conventions resulting in their empowerment. And insofar as the people who create rulers' power have, in virtue of their role as creators, the ability to evaluate their rulers' performances and the ability to depose them if the evaluation is negative, the people have final say over whether or not the rulers will continue to rule, making the people the final judges in this meta political game.

Thus, in order to avoid inconsistency, one must specify when talking about the finality of decision making in a political regime whether one is referring to the object political game or the meta political game. The ruler is the final decider in the object game, but the people who can participate in the empowerment convention creating the ruler constitute the final decider in the meta game.

We are also in a position now to see why someone like Austin ignored talk of rules of recognition in his analysis of political society. If one is trying to give an analysis of only the object political game, then it is natural to take this sort of rule for granted. One specifies who or what the ruler in this object game is, where he is identified by locating whom the people obey (although one does not explain why they obey him rather than someone else), and one notes that the people obey this ruler because he has the power to threaten or reward them (one does not explain where that power comes from). One might even contend (if one believed it to be true) that the source of the ruler's legislation is some body of moral imperatives that the ruler ought to, but need not, follow in order for his commands to count as laws. But as Hart sensed and as any contractarian would immediately appreciate, this is telling only half of the story, because (outside of dominations by technological mastery) any government is empowered by a rule, where that means, from the contractarian standpoint, being empowered by a convention created and maintained by its subjects for a reason. And though the convention empowering the ruler is not part of the object political game, it is indeed part of the meta game that any political society, as a created entity, involves. Indeed, there are certain regimes in which it is difficult not to bring that meta game into an analysis of the political society, particularly those regimes in which the citizenry take their supervisory role as principal in the agency relationship with their rulers very seriously, so that the reasons they have for empowering their government operate as strict constraints on the rulers. In other regimes in which the people are much less active and concern themselves much less with what their ruler is doing, their role as principal is much easier to ignore.

Thus, we have located the source of the sovereignty theorist's mistake. States *appear* to have sovereigns only if one concentrates on analyzing the object political game while failing to appreciate the existence of the meta political game. And it appears to be inconsistent to say that "the people are subjugated to a ruler whom the people have the power to fire" only if one does not recognize that the second instance of the term 'the people' refers to the convention-producing group empowering the ruler, who must act interdependently to depose him, whereas the first use of the term refers only to the aggregate of individuals who are subjugated to the ruler because there is a convention empowering him. Finally, "agency" states appear not to be viable only if one fails to understand how substantial the "cement" of empowerment by convention is (that is, how difficult it is for disgruntled individuals to change or destroy existing empowerment conventions).

This analysis has one final and rather startling implication; if it is right, it suggests that modern democratic states have been profoundly influenced in their structure by the idea that rulers are hired by the people for reasons. Consider the fact that such regimes do no fit the classical definition of democracy; that is, they are not regimes in which *all* the people are literally members of the legislature (or, for that matter, the executive or judicial branches of government). Instead, these regimes grant people voting rights, allowing them to replace, at regular intervals, those rulers in various offices of government whom they dislike with individuals who they believe will do a better job. And in some modern democracies (e.g., the United States), people are given the legal right (via constitutional convention) to modify or change the terms of any government official's empowerment. Now, of course, the contractarian will say that the ability of the people to make such changes in who governs them, or in the terms of their governing, exist in the meta political game of *any* state. But in modern democracies this ability is incorporated into the political system such that it is subject to rules of the *object* political game. That is, in these regimes there is an attempt to define *within the object game itself* the meta political role that people inevitably have on the social contract view. For example, in these regimes, people have the legal right to change their rulers using a voting procedure at a certain time; they need not stage a rebellion to do so. Changing the rulership convention is thus made part of the very structure of the legal system. Creating such a regime is an attempt to ensure that the entire political game is less likely to disintegrate because of a violent rebellion and to enable the people to supervise their leaders closely, so that there is less chance they will be bad agents and abuse their power.

Thus, modern democratic regimes are not democratic in the *traditional* sense of that word; instead, such regimes incorporate people into government in a new way. Specifically, whereas in classical democracies the people were made direct deciders of law, in modern democracies they are explicitly granted the role of *overseer* of their rulers' performances. Clearly, the structure of these modern regimes is complicated, given the way object roles and meta roles in the political structure are mixed; thus, I cannot pursue an adequate analysis of them here. But once again we have been led to realize how an examination of the contractarian argument in general and Hobbes's argument in particular can eventually lead us to construct new philosophical views about our contemporary political life — in this case, about the very regimes in which many of us live.

Bibliography

Works by Thomas Hobbes

Leviathan, edited by C. B. Macpherson (using the 1651 "Head" edition). Harmondsworth: Penguin, 1968 (originally published 1651).

Man and Citizen: Thomas Hobbes's "De Homine" and "De Cive," edited by Bernard Gert. Atlantic Highlands, N.J.: Humanities Press, 1968 (*De Homine* originally published 1658, *De Cive* 1642).

The Elements of Law, Natural and Politic, edited by Frederick Tönnies. Cambridge University Press, 1928 (originally published 1640).

The English Works of Thomas Hobbes, edited by W. Molesworth. London: John Bohn, 1840.
  Volume i: *De Corpore* (originally published 1655).
  Volume ii: *De Cive* or *The Philosophical Rudiments Concerning Government and Society* (Latin edition originally published 1642; English edition published 1651).
  Volume iv: (a) "An Answer to Bishop Bramhall's Book Called 'The Catching of the Leviathan' " (ca. 1668); (b) "An Historical Narration Concerning Heresy, and the Punishment Thereof."
  Volume vi: (a) *A Dialogue Between a Philosopher and a Student of the Common Laws of England* (written 1666; published posthumously 1681); (b) *Behemoth: The History of the Causes of the Civil Wars of England* (written 1668; published posthumously 1682).
  Volume vii: "Six Lessons to the Professors of the Mathematics" (1656).

From the manuscript collection of the Duke of Devonshire at Chatsworth House, Derbyshire, England:

Fragment on the relation between virtue and religion (MS. D-4).

Fragment of a formal disputation between the fourth earl (first duke) of Devonshire and Hobbes, on sovereignty (MS. D-5).

"Objections to Descartes's *Meditations*." In *The Philosophical Works of Descartes,* Vol. II, translated by E. S. Haldane and G. R. T. Ross, pp. 60–78. Cambridge University Press, 1976.

Other works

Allen, J. W. 1928. *A History of Political Thought in the Sixteenth Century.* London: Methuen & Co (reprinted 1961).

American Restatement of Agency (second). 1958. St. Paul, Minn.: American Law Institute.

American Restatement of Trusts (first). 1935. St. Paul, Minn.: American Law Institute.

Anscombe, G. E. M. 1981. "The Source of the Authority of the State." In *Collected Philosophical Papers, Vol. III: Ethics, Religion and Politics,* Minneapolis: University of Minnesota Press.

Aquinas, Thomas. 1945. *Summa Theologica,* vol. II, edited by Anton C. Pegis. New York: Random House.

Aristotle. 1941a. *Politics,* translated by Benjamin Jowett. In *The Basic Works of Aristotle,* edited by Richard McKeon, pp. 113–316. New York: Random House.

BIBLIOGRAPHY

1941b. *Rhetoric*, translated by W. Rhys Roberts. In *The Basic Works of Aristotle*, edited by Richard McKeon, pp. 1317–451. New York: Random House.

Atiyah, P. S. 1979. *The Rise and Fall of Freedom of Contract*. Oxford: Clarendon Press.

Aubrey, John. 1898. *Brief Lives*, edited by Andrew Clark. Oxford: Clarendon Press.

Axelrod, Robert. 1980a. "Effective Choice in the Prisoner's Dilemma." *Journal of Conflict Resolution*, vol. 24, no. 1, pp. 3–25.

1980b. "More Effective Choice in the Prisoner's Dilemma." *Journal of Conflict Resolution*, vol. 24, no. 3, pp. 379–403.

Bacharach, Michael. 1976. *Economics and the Theory of Games*. London: Macmillan.

Barry, Brian. 1965. *Political Argument*. London: Routledge & Kegan Paul.

1972. "Warrender and his Critics." In *Hobbes and Rousseau: A Collection of Critical Essays*, edited by M. Cranston and R. Peters, pp. 37–65. New York: Anchor-Doubleday.

Barry, Brian, and Russell Hardin. 1982. *Rational Man and Irrational Society?* Beverly Hills, Calif.: Sage.

Birmingham, Robert. 1969. "Legal and Moral Duty in Game Theory." *Buffalo Law Review*, vol. 18, no. 1, pp. 99–117.

Bloch, Marc. 1962. *Feudal Society*, translated by L. A. Manyon. London: Routledge & Kegan Paul.

Bodin, Jean. 1962. *The Six Books of a Commonweale*. translated by Richard Knolles, edited by Kenneth D. McRae. Cambridge, Mass.: Harvard University Press (facsimile of 1606 edition).

Bogert, G. G. 1935. *The Law of Trusts and Trustees*. Kansas City, Mo.: Vernon Law Book Co.

Bowle, John. 1951. *Hobbes and His Critics*. London: J. Cape.

Bramhall, John (Bishop of Derry and later of Armagh). 1658. *The Catching of Leviathan or the Great Whale*, appendix to *Castigations of Mr. Hobbes . . . Concerning Liberty and Universal Necessity*. Printed by E.T. for John Crooke, at the sign of the ship in Paul's churchyard.

Broad, D. C. 1978. "Egoism as a Theory of Human Motives." In *Problems of Moral Philosophy*, third edition, edited by P. Taylor, pp. 111–18. Belmont, Calif.: Wadsworth.

Brown, Keith. 1965. *Hobbes Studies*. Oxford: Blackwell.

Buchanan, James McGill. 1975. *The Limits of Liberty: Between Anarchy and Leviathan*. University of Chicago Press.

Burke, Edmund. 1791. "An Appeal from the New to the Old Whigs." In *Works of Edmund Burke*, vol. 5, pp. 1–135. Oxford University Press.

Butler, Joseph, Bishop. 1896. *Works*, edited by W. E. Gladstone. Oxford: Clarendon Press.

Butler, Samuel. 1908. *Characters and Passages from Note Books*. Cambridge University Press.

Clarendon, Edward, Earl of (Edward Hyde). 1676. *A Brief View and Survey of the Dangerous and Pernicious Errors to Church and State in Mr. Hobbes's Book, Entitled Leviathan*. Printed at the Theatre.

1702–4. *The History of the Rebellion and Civil Wars in England*.

Clark, E. C. 1883. *Practical Jurisprudence*. Cambridge University Press.

Coke, Roger. 1660. *Justice Vindicated From the False Focus Put Upon It — By Mr. T. White Gent, Mr. T. Hobbes, and Hugo Grotius*. London.

Commons, John. 1957. *The Legal Foundations of Capitalism*. Madison, Wisc.: University of Wisconsin Press.

Cranston, Maurice, and Richard Peters, editors. 1972. *Hobbes and Rousseau: A Collection of Critical Essays*. New York: Anchor-Doubleday.

Cudworth, Ralph. 1845. *The True Intellectual System of the Universe . . . Wherein All The Reason and Philosophy of Atheism is Confuted, And its Impossibility Demonstrated*, translated by John Harrison. London: Thomas Tegg (originally published 1678).

Cumberland, Richard. 1727. *De Legibus Naturae* or *A Treatise of the Laws of Nature*, translated by J. Maxwell. London: printed by R. Philips and sold by J. Knapton (originally published 1672).

Daniels, N. editor. 1976. *Reading Rawls*. New York: Basic Books.

Dennett, Daniel. 1982. "Mechanism and Responsibility." In *Free Will*, edited by Gary Watson, pp. 150–73. Oxford University Press.

Bibliography

Dewey, John. 1974. "The Motivation of Hobbes's Political Philosophy." In *Thomas Hobbes in his Time,* edited by Ralph Ross, Herbert W. Schneider, and Theodore Waldman, pp. 8–30. Minneapolis: University of Minnesota Press.

Dowel, J. 1683. *The Leviathan Heretical.* London.

Droz, Jacques. 1949. *L'Allemagne et la Revolution Française.* Paris; Presses Universitaires de France.

Dworkin, Ronald. 1976. "The Original Position." In *Reading Rawls,* edited by Norman Daniels, pp. 16–53. New York: Basic Books.

Eachard, Rev. John. 1672. *Mr. Hobbes's State of Nature Considered, in a Dialogue Between Philautus and Timothy.*

　　1673. *Some Opinions of Mr. Hobbs Considered in A Second Dialogue Between Philautus and Timothy.*

Elster, Jon. 1979. *Ulysses and the Sirens.* Cambridge University Press.

Feinberg, Joel, and Hyman Gross, editors. 1980. *Philosophy of Law.* Belmont, Calif.: Wadsworth.

Figgis, John Neville. 1914. *Divine Right of Kings,* second edition. Cambridge University Press (reprinted 1965. New York: Harper).

　　1916. *Studies of Political Thought From Gerson to Grotius, 1414–1625.* Cambridge University Press.

Filmer, Sir Robert. 1648. *The Anarchy of A Limited or Mixed Monarchy* (reprinted 1949. In *Patriarcha and Other Political Works of Sir Robert Filmer,* edited by Peter Laslett. Oxford: Blackwell).

　　1652. *Observations Concerning the Originall of Government, Upon Mr. Hobs Leviathan; Mr. Milton Against Salmasius; H. Grotius De Juri Belli, Mr. Huntons Treatise of Monarchy.* London: printed for R. Royston at the Angel in Ivie-Lane (reprinted 1949. In *Patriarcha and Other Political Works of Sir Robert Filmer,* edited by Peter Laslett. Oxford: Blackwell). [The final discussion of Hunton is only a reprint of *The Anarchy of A Limited or Mixed Monarchy* (1648). There are editions of *Observations . . .* without the discussion of Hunton.]

　　1949. *Patriarcha.* In *Patriarcha and Other Political Works of Sir Robert Filmer,* edited by Peter Laslett, pp. 49–126. Oxford: Blackwell (written 1635–40; first published 1680).

Foot, P. 1978. "Morality as a System of Hypothetical Imperatives." In *Virtues and Vices,* pp. 157–73. Berkeley: University of California Press.

Fowler, Mark. 1982. "Coercion and Practical Reason." *Social Theory and Practice,* vol. 8, no. 3, pp. 329–55.

Frohlich, Norman, Joe Oppenheimer, and Oran Young. 1971. *Political Leadership and Collective Goods.* Princeton University Press.

Fuller, Lon, and M. Eisenberg. 1972. *Basic Contract Law.* St. Paul, Minn.: West Publishing Co.

Gauthier, David. 1969. *The Logic of Leviathan.* Oxford: Clarendon Press.

　　1977. "The Social Contract as Ideology." *Philosophy and Public Affairs,* vol. 6, no. 2, pp. 130–64.

　　1979a. "David Hume, Contractarian." *Philosophical Review,* vol. 88, no. 1, pp. 3–38.

　　1979b. "Thomas Hobbes: Moral Theorist." *Journal of Philosophy,* vol. 76, no. 10, pp. 547–59.

　　1986. *Morals By Agreement.* Oxford: Clarendon Press.

Gert, B. 1978. "Introduction." In *Man and Citizen.* Atlantic Highlands, N.J.: Humanities Press.

Gierke, Otto. 1934. *Natural Law and the Theory of Society,* translated by E. Barker. Cambridge University Press.

Goldsmith, M. M. 1980. "Hobbes's 'Mortal God': Is There a Fallacy in Hobbes's Theory of Sovereignty?" *History of Political Thought,* vol. 1, pp. 33–50.

　　1966. *Hobbes's Science of Politics.* New York: Columbia University Press.

Gooch, George Peabody. 1920. *Germany and the French Revolution.* London: Longmans.

Gough, J. W. 1936. *The Social Contract; A Critical Study of Its Development.* Oxford: Clarendon Press.

　　1973. *John Locke's Political Philosophy.* Oxford: Clarendon Press.

Greenleaf, W. H. 1972. "Hobbes: The Problem of Interpretation." In *Hobbes and Rousseau: A Collection of Essays,* edited by Maurice Cranston and Richard Peters, pp. 5–36. New York: Anchor-Doubleday.

Grotius, Hugo. 1925. *De Juri Belli ac Pacis Libri Tres,* or *The Law of War and Peace,* translated by F. W. Kelsey. Oxford: Clarendon Press (translation of 1646 text, first published 1625).

Guest, A. G., editor. 1961. *Oxford Essays in Jurisprudence.* Oxford University Press.

Hampton, Jean. "Free Rider Problems in the Production of Collective Goods." Unpublished manuscript.

Hardin, Russell. 1982. *Collective Action.* Baltimore: Johns Hopkins University Press.

   1971. "Collective Action as an Agreeable *n*-Prisoner's Dilemma." *Behavioral Science,* vol. 16, no. 5, pp. 472–81 (reprinted 1982. In *Rational Man and Irrational Society?* edited by Brian Barry and Russell Hardin. Beverly Hills, Calif.: Sage).

Harman, Gilbert. 1977. *The Nature of Morality.* Oxford University Press.

Harrison, Ross, editor. 1979. *Rational Action.* Cambridge University Press.

Hart, H. L. A. 1961. *The Concept of Law.* Oxford: Clarendon Press.

Hegel, G. W. F. 1976. *Philosophy of Right,* translated by T. M. Knox. Oxford University Press.

   1977. *The Phenomenology of Spirit,* translated by A. V. Miller. Oxford University Press.

Hill, Christopher. 1969a. *Puritanism and Revolution.* London: Panther.

   1969b. *Reformation to Industrial Revolution.* Harmondsworth: Pelican.

   1975. *The World Turned Upside Down.* Harmondsworth: Penguin.

   1977. *Milton and the English Revolution.* London: Faber & Faber.

Hohfeld, Wesley. 1919. *Fundamental Legal Conceptions.* New Haven: Yale University Press (reprinted 1978).

Hollis, Martin. 1977. *Models of Man.* Cambridge University Press.

Hume, David. 1965. "Of The Original Contract." In *Hume's Ethical Writings,* edited by Alasdair MacIntyre, pp. 255–73. London: Collier.

   1975a. *An Enquiry Concerning Human Understanding,* edited by L. A. Selby-Bigge, revised by P. H. Nidditch. Oxford: Clarendon Press.

   1975b. *An Enquiry Concerning the Principles of Morals,* edited by L. A. Selby-Bigge, revised by P. H. Nidditch. Oxford: Clarendon Press.

   1978. *A Treatise of Human Nature,* edited by L. A. Selby-Bigge, revised by P. H. Nidditch. Oxford: Clarendon Press.

Hunton, Philip. 1643. *A Treatise of Monarchy.* London: printed for John Bellamy and Ralph Smith, and are to be found at the three Golden-Lyons in Corn-hill.

   1644. *A Vindication of the Treatise of Monarchy.* London: printed for John Bellamy, at the sign of the three Golden Lyons in Cornehill neare the Royal-Exchange.

Kant, Immanuel. 1956. *Critique of Practical Reason,* translated by Lewis White Beck. Indianapolis: Bobbs-Merrill.

   1965. *The Metaphysical Elements of Justice,* translated by John Ladd. Indianapolis: Bobbs-Merrill (originally published 1797).

   1970. "On the Common Saying: 'This May Be True in Theory, But It Does Not Apply in Practice.' " In *Kant's Political Writings,* edited by Hans Reiss. Cambridge University Press (originally published 1793).

Kavka, Gregory. 1983a. "Hobbes's War of All Against All." *Ethics,* vol. 93, no. 2, pp. 291–310.

   1983b. "Right Reason and Natural Law in Hobbes's Ethics." *The Monist,* vol. 66, no. 1, pp. 120–33.

   1983c. "Rule By Fear." *Nous,* vol. 17, no. 4, pp. 601–20.

Kelsen, Hans. 1945. *The General Theory of Law and the State,* translated by Anders Wedberg. Cambridge, Mass.: Harvard University Press.

Knight, Frank. 1947. *Freedom and Reform.* New York: Harper & Row.

de La Mothe Le Vayer, François. 1669. "Discours pour Montrer que les Doutes. . . ." In *Ouvres de François de La Mothe Le Vayer.* Paris: L. Billaine.

Laslett, Peter. 1960. "Introduction." In *Two Treatises of Government* (by John Locke), edited by Peter Laslett, pp. 15–161. Cambridge University Press (reprinted 1965. New York: Mentor).

Lawson, George. 1657. *An Examination of the Political Part of Mr. Hobbs his Leviathan.* London: printed by R. White for Francis Tyton at the three daggers in Fleet Street, near the Inner Temple Gate.

1660. *Politica Sacra et Civilis.* London.

Lewis, David. 1969. *Convention: A Philosophical Study.* Cambridge, Mass.: Harvard University Press.

Locke, John. 1954. *Essays On the Laws of Nature.* Oxford: Clarendon Press.

1964. *An Essay Concerning Human Understanding,* edited by John Yolton. London: Dent.

1965. *Two Treatises of Government,* edited by Peter Laslett. New York: Mentor (originally published 1960. Cambridge University Press).

1972. "Of Ethics in General" and "Thus I Think." In *The Life and Letters of John Locke,* edited by Peter King, pp. 306–16. New York: B. Franklin.

Luce, R., and H. Raiffa. 1957. *Games and Decisions.* New York: Wiley.

Lucy, William (Bishop of St. David's). 1663. *Observations, Censures and Confutations of Notorious Errours in Mr. Hobbes his Leviathan and other {of} his books.* London.

Mackie, John. 1977. *Ethics: Inventing Right and Wrong.* New York: Penguin.

McLellan, David. 1977. *Karl Marx, Selected Writings.* Oxford University Press.

McNeilly, F. 1969. *The Anatomy of Leviathan.* New York: St. Martin's Press.

Macpherson, C. B. 1968. "Introduction." In *Leviathan,* edited by C. B. Macpherson, pp. 9–63. Harmondsworth: Pelican.

1977. *The Political Theory of Possessive Individualism: Hobbes to Locke.* Oxford: Clarendon Press.

Mill, John Stuart. 1956a. *On Liberty,* edited by Currin V. Shields. Indianapolis: Bobbs-Merrill.

1956b. *Utilitarianism,* edited by Oskar Priest. Indianapolis: Bobbs-Merrill.

Mintz, S. I. 1969. *The Hunting of Leviathan.* Cambridge University Press.

Mohan, Matthen, and Edwin Levy. 1984. "Teleology, Error and the Human Immune System." *Journal of Philosophy,* vol. 81, no. 7, pp. 351–72.

Montaigne, Michel de la. 1922. "Apologie de Raimond Sebond." In *Les Essais de Michel de Montaigne,* edited by Pierre Villey. Paris: F. Alcan.

Montesquieu, Baron de la Brede et de (Charles Louis de Secondat). 1977. *The Spirit of Laws,* edited by David Wallace Carrithers. Berkeley: University of California Press.

Morgenbesser, Sidney, Patrick Suppes, and Morton White, editors. 1969. *Philosophy, Science and Method: Essays in Honor of Ernest Nagel.* New York: St. Martin's Press.

Morrall, John B. 1971. *Political Thought in Medieval Times.* London: Hutchinson.

Nagel, Thomas. 1959. "Hobbes's Concept of Obligation." *Philosophical Review,* vol. 68, pp. 68–83.

Nash, J. F. 1950. "The Bargaining Problem." *Econometrica,* vol. 18, no. 2, pp. 155–62.

1953. "Two Person Cooperative Games." *Econometrica,* vol. 22, no. 1, pp. 128–40.

Nozick, Robert. 1969. "Coercion." In *Philosophy, Science and Method: Essays in Honor of Ernest Nagel,* edited by S. Morgenbesser, P. Suppes, and M. White, pp. 440–72. New York: St. Martin's Press.

1974. *Anarchy, State and Utopia.* New York: Basic Books.

Oakeshott, Michael. 1947. "Introduction." In *Leviathan* (by Thomas Hobbes), edited by M. Oakeshott, pp. vii–lxvi. Oxford: Blackwell.

Olson, Mancur. 1965. *The Logic of Collective Action.* Cambridge: Harvard University Press (reprinted 1971).

Parfit, Derek. 1984. *Reasons and Persons.* Oxford: Clarendon Press.

Passmore, J. 1951. *Ralph Cudworth.* Cambridge, Mass.: Harvard University Press.

Pears, David. 1984. *Motivated Irrationality.* Oxford: Clarendon Press.

Pennock, J. R., and J. W. Chapman, editors. 1972. *Coercion.* Chicago: Aldine.

Peters, R. S. 1956. *Hobbes.* Harmondsworth: Penguin.

Plamenatz, John. 1965. "Mr. Warrender's Hobbes." In *Hobbes Studies,* edited by K. Brown, pp. 73–87. Oxford: Blackwell.

BIBLIOGRAPHY

Plato. 1956. *Euthyphro, Apology, Crito,* translated by F. J. Church. Indianapolis: Bobbs-Merrill.

Popkin, Richard. 1979. *The History of Scepticism from Erasmus to Spinoza.* Berkeley: University of California Press.

———. 1982. "Hobbes and Scepticism." In *History and Philosophy in the Making,* edited by R. Popkin. Washington University Press.

Pufendorf, Samuel. 1934. *De Jure Naturae et Gentium* or *The Law of Nature and Nations,* translated by C. H. and W. A. Oldfather. Oxford: Clarendon Press (originally published 1688).

Quine, W. V. 1977. "Facts of the Matter." In *American Philosophy from Edwards to Quine,* edited by R. W. Shahan and A. R. Merrill. Norman: University of Oklahoma Press.

Randall, J. H. 1961. *The School of Padua and the Emergence of Modern Science.* Padova: Editrice An Tenore.

———. 1940. "Scientific Method in the School of Padua." *Journal of the History of Ideas,* vol. 1, no. 2, pp. 177–206.

Rawls, John. 1971. *A Theory of Justice.* Cambridge, Mass.: Harvard University Press.

Reiss, Hans. 1970. "Introduction." In *Kant's Political Writings,* edited by H. Reiss, pp. 1–40. Cambridge University Press.

Ritchie, D. G. 1893. *Darwin and Hegel.* London: Sonnenschein & Co.

Rousseau, J. J. 1950a. "A Discourse on the Origin of Inequality." In *The Social Contract and Discourses,* translated by G. D. H. Cole, pp. 175–282. New York: Dutton.

———. 1950b. *The Social Contract.* In *The Social Contract and Discourses,* translated by G. D. H. Cole, pp. 1–141. New York: Dutton.

Ryan, Cheyney C. 1980. "The Normative Concept of Coercion." *Mind,* vol. 89, pp. 481–98.

Scanlon, T. M. 1982. "Contractualism and Utilitarianism." In *Utilitarianism and Beyond,* edited by A. Sen and B. Williams, pp. 103–28. Cambridge University Press.

Schelling, Thomas. 1960. *The Strategy of Conflict.* Cambridge, Mass.: Harvard University Press.

Sen, Amartya. 1967. "Isolation, Assurance and the Social Rate of Discount." *Quarterly Journal of Economics,* vol. 80, pp. 112–24.

———. 1973. *On Economic Inequality.* Oxford: Clarendon Press.

———. 1974. "Choice, Orderings and Morality." In *Practical Reason,* edited by S. Körner, pp. 54–62. Oxford: Blackwell.

Skinner, Quentin. 1972. "The Context of Hobbes's Theory of Political Obligation." In *Hobbes and Rousseau: A Collection of Critical Essays,* edited by M. Cranston and R. Peters, pp. 109–42. New York: Anchor-Doubleday (a previous version was printed in 1966 as "The Ideological Context of Hobbes's Political Thought." *Historical Journal,* vol. 9, pp. 286–317).

———. 1978. *The Foundations of Modern Political Thought.* Cambridge University Press.

Spinoza, Benedict. 1951. *The Chief Works of Benedict Spinoza: Political Treatise; Theologico-Political Treatise,* translated by R. H. M. Elwes. New York: Dover.

Strauss, Leo. 1952. *The Political Philosophy of Hobbes.* University of Chicago Press.

Suarez, Francisco. 1944. *Selections From Three Works,* translated by G. Williams, A. Brown, and J. Waldron. Oxford: Clarendon Press.

Tawney, R. H. 1972. *Religion and the Rise of Capitalism.* Harmondsworth: Penguin.

Taylor, A. E. 1965. "The Ethical Doctrine of Hobbes." In *Hobbes Studies,* edited by Keith Brown, pp. 35–55. Oxford: Blackwell.

Taylor, Michael. 1976. *Anarchy and Cooperation.* London: Wiley.

Tenison, Thomas. 1670. *The Creed of Mr. Hobbes examined; in a feigned Conference between him and a Student of Divinity.* London.

Torretti, Roberto. 1978. *Philosophy of Geometry from Riemann to Poincaré.* Dordrecht: Reidel.

Tyrrell, James. 1692. *A Brief Disquisition of the Law of Nature.* London: printed and are to be sold by Richard Baldwin, near the Oxford Arms in Warwick Lane (a paraphrase of Cumberland's *De Legibus Naturae* "with the Right Reverend Author's Approbation," supplemented by Tyrrell's own criticisms of Hobbes at the end).

Ullmann-Margalit, Edna. 1977. *The Emergence of Norms.* Oxford: Clarendon Press.

von Leyden, W. 1954. "Introduction." In *Essays on the Law of Nature* (by John Locke), edited by W. von Leyden. Oxford: Clarendon Press.

Wallis, John. 1656. *Due Correction for Mr. Hobbes: Or school discipline, for not saying his lessons right. In answer to his Six Lessons. . . .* Oxford.

Warrender, Howard. 1957. *The Political Philosophy of Hobbes.* Oxford: Clarendon Press.

1965. "A Reply to Mr. Plamenatz." In *Hobbes Studies,* edited by K. Brown, pp. 89–100. Oxford: Blackwell.

Watkins, J. W. N. 1965a. *Hobbes's System of Ideas.* London: Hutchinson.

1965b. "Philosophy and Politics in Hobbes." In *Hobbes Studies,* edited by K. Brown, pp. 237–62. Oxford: Blackwell.

Wilkins, David. 1737. *Conciliae Magnae.* London: Sumptibus R. Gosling.

Wilks, Ivor. 1969. "A Note on Sovereignty." In *In Defense of Sovereignty,* edited by W. J. Stankiewicz, pp. 197–205. Oxford University Press.

Winstanley, Gerrard. 1941. *The True Levellers Standard Advanced.* In *The Works of Gerrard Winstanley,* edited by G. H. Sabine, pp. 247–66. Ithaca: Cornell University Press.

Woodhouse, A. S. P. 1966. *Puritanism and Liberty.* London: Dent.

Index

DATE DUE

MR 16 '88			
DEC 1 0 90			
MAY 1 7 2000			
JAN 1 7 2000			
APR 3 0 2001			
MAY 05			
MAY 3 1 2007			
MAY 2 2007			
JAN 0 7 2011			
MAY 2 1 2008			
NOV 2 0 2008			
NOV 3 0 2008			

DEMCO 38-297